REMAINS
Historical and Literary
CONNECTED WITH
THE PALATINE COUNTIES OF
Lancaster and Chester

Volume XL – Third Series

MANCHESTER
Printed for the Chetham Society
1995

Reform and Respectability

The Making of a Middle-Class
Liberalism in early nineteenth-century
Manchester

Michael J. Turner, B.A., M.A., D.Phil

General Editors: J. K. Walton, P. H. W. Booth

MANCHESTER
1995

SUPPORTED BY
·A·G·M·A·
ASSOCIATION OF
GREATER MANCHESTER
AUTHORITIES.

The publication of this book has been assisted by a grant from
the Scouloudi Foundation in association with the Institute of
Historical Research, by a publication subvention awarded by the
Humanities Research Board of the British Academy, and by a
grant from the Association of Greater Manchester Authorities,
for all of which the society is most grateful.

Reform and Respectability
The Making of a Middle-Class Liberalism
in Early Nineteenth-Century Manchester

by Michael J. Turner

ISSN 0080–0880

Published for the Society by Carnegie Publishing Ltd,
18 Maynard Street, Preston
Typeset in Linotype Stempel Garamond by Carnegie Publishing
Printed and bound in the UK by Cambridge University Press

British Library Cataloguing-in-Publication Data
Turner, Michael J.
 Reform and Respectability: Making of a Middle-class
 Liberalism in early 19th-century Manchester.—
 (Chetham Society Series, ISSN 0080-0880; Vol. 40)
 I. Title II. Series
 942.733081

 ISBN 1-85936-024-6

Contents

Acknowledgements

M ost of the research for this book was completed in Manchester, Oxford and London, and I would particularly like to thank those who staff the Bodleian Library, the archives room at the London School of Economics, Chetham's Library in Manchester, Salford Local History Library, the John Rylands Library in Manchester and the archives and local history rooms at the Manchester Central Library.

For encouragement and advice at various times I am grateful to Harry Pitt, James Campbell, Bill Jenkinson, David Hargreaves, Felicity Heal, Ian Kershaw, Bob Shoemaker, Richard Carwardine, Linda Kirk, Philip Richardson, Ralph Griffiths, Peter Spence and David Howell. My thanks are also due to Paul Booth, John Walton and the council of the Chetham Society.

The interest and good wishes of my wife Catherine, my parents and our family on both sides of the Atlantic have greatly facilitated my research and writing, and without their moral support this whole exercise would have been far less agreeable than it was. I am happy to have the chance to thank them and to say that here, at last, is something to show for all the times they have wondered about what I was doing. Catherine has also shaped this book in many small ways, not least by reading drafts, asking questions and helping me to compile an index.

Finally I would like to acknowledge an enormous debt of thanks to Angus Macintyre, formerly of Magdalen College, Oxford, who tragically died in December 1994. He expertly guided the work that went into my doctoral thesis (on which this book is based), and indeed went above and beyond the call of duty. He was unstinting in his kindness to me, and I always found his advice to be excellent and unfailingly helpful. He is very sadly missed.

Some of the material in chapters III, V and VI has previously appeared in *Historical Research* 67 (October 1994), *History* 79 (June 1994), and *Northern History* 30 (October 1994). During the final stages of research and writing before the publication of this book I was assisted by a small grant from the Scouloudi Foundation. In

1987–90 I was the holder of a British Academy studentship and in 1991 I received a much appreciated financial award from Worcester College, Oxford.

Any errors and shortcomings in this book are entirely my own responsibility.

M.J.T.

List of Abbreviations

Biographical References	Pamphlets, letters, cuttings, obituaries in the Local History Department, Manchester Central Library, card-indexed.
B.J.R.L.	*Bulletin of the John Rylands Library*
C.H.J.	*Cambridge Historical Journal*
C.L.M.	Chetham's Library, Manchester
D.N.B.	*Dictionary of National Biography*
Ec.H.R.	*Economic History Review*
E.H.R.	*English Historical Review*
H.J.	*Historical Journal*
H.S.A.N.Z.	*Historical Studies of Australia and New Zealand*
I.R.S.H.	*International Review of Social History*
J.R.L.	John Rylands University Library of Manchester
L.S.E.	London School of Economics
M.C.L.	Manchester Central Library
M.R.	*Manchester Review*
M.R.H.R.	*Manchester Region History Review*
N.H.	*Northern History*
P.&P.	*Past and Present*
P.L.P.L.S.	*Proceedings of the Leeds Philosophical and Literary Society*
P.P.	Parliamentary Papers
S.H.	*Social History*
S.L.H.L.	Salford Local History Library
T.H.S.L.C.	*Transactions of the Historic Society of Lancashire and Cheshire*
T.L.C.A.S.	*Transactions of the Lancashire and Cheshire Antiquarian Society*
T.M.S.S.	*Transactions of the Manchester Statistical Society*
T.R.H.S.	*Transactions of the Royal Historical Society*
T.U.H.S.	*Transactions of the Unitarian History Society*

Introduction

I

This study aims to contribute to our understanding of the development of early nineteenth-century provincial liberalism in England. It will concentrate on the ideas and activities of a small group of respectable reformers who rose to have a decisive influence on the affairs of early nineteenth-century Manchester, perhaps the most socially, politically and commercially vibrant provincial town of the period. The book will fill a gap in our picture of Manchester liberalism and show how and why such post-1832 events and movements as incorporation (1838), the Anti-Corn Law League (established in 1839) and 'Manchester School' (a description thought to have first been used in the House of Commons in February 1846) could materialise and, indeed, even be viable.

This investigation of a less-known period in Manchester's history, before the League and the mid-Victorian era, will elucidate the opinions of identifiable liberal reformers (a 'small but determined band' as one of their number called them) on subjects such as local government, the role and influence of the press and public opinion, social reform, economic policy and parliamentary representation. One of the premises of the book is the need to question the often-accepted view of Manchester as a completely liberal town, commercially and politically, by the 1820s. Local politics, society, business and religion will be examined and related to wider trends in early nineteenth-century England in order to provide a detailed account of one important component of respectable provincial reformism. This study will emphasise the local dominance of a Tory-Anglican elite and the campaigns against local rulers staged by ambitious, public-spirited townsmen. The social, political and economic roots of these campaigns must be investigated and due credit given to the role of the band, a group of eleven likeminded friends who helped to create the environment within which the incorporation movement and the Anti-Corn Law League could flourish.

Members of the band were predominantly non-Mancunian in

origins, Unitarian in religion (though their most active member, Archibald Prentice, was a Scottish Presbyterian), young (aged under 32 in 1815) and engaged in the manufacturing and trading of cotton goods. They have not previously been given the attention they deserve. Nor has the tension within developing Manchester liberalism been clarified adequately. Disagreements within the band reflected divisions among Manchester reformers generally (and indeed also reveal much about the wider uncertainties within northern reform circles in this period). Most of the band can be taken to represent a paternalistic, humanitarian, conscience-driven wing of provincial liberalism, and they were not comfortable with the dogmatism and *laissez-faire* preferences of many of their fellow reformers.

It is hoped that this work will make valuable contributions to our understanding of early nineteenth-century politics and society in at least three ways. It is a corrective, forcing a revision of older and more recent writing which has exaggerated the political and economic liberalism of Manchester in the period before incorporation and the establishment of the League. In books and essays by G. B. Hertz (1912), L. S. Marshall (1946), V. A. C. Gatrell (1976, 1982), and to a lesser extent Donald Read (1959, 1961) and John Seed (1982, 1985), there are claims and assumptions which, on closer inspection, prove to be ill-founded. This book is also meant to save the band from undue neglect, examining and explaining its contribution to Manchester affairs and northern provincial reformism. Quite simply, there would have been no incorporation, no League, no Cobden and Bright and no Manchester School if not for the band. Hence the book will reject the theses of Norman McCord (1958, and subsequent reviews and articles) and especially N. C. Edsall (1986). It is unfair and inaccurate to view members of the band as marginal, unimportant figures. They did the essential preparatory work for later movements and campaigns, and in their own time they had considerable influence over the course of events in Manchester. Thirdly, the book will expand and supplement the historiography by providing a convincing account of Manchester history in the late eighteenth and early nineteenth centuries (the crucial formative years about which far less has been written than the post-1832 period), and by adding to our understanding of contemporary provincial reform campaigns and liberal ideas. Some historians have made highly questionable statements about the dominance of liberal politics, free trade and *laissez-faire* political economy in pre-Victorian Manchester. Perhaps these mistakes have been compounded by a tendency to look at the League and at mid-Victorian Mancunians and project their ideas and practices back into a period when conditions were quite different. To do this is to lose an appreciation of the struggle faced by members of the 'small but determined band' and to underestimate the band's importance and achievements.

II

Active in Manchester politics from about 1812, and especially after Peterloo in 1819, members of the band led an attempt to break the hold on local affairs that had been enjoyed by a select Tory-Anglican circle for several decades. This control was exercised in an increasingly partisan fashion after the late 1780s. The respectable reformers also interested themselves in a wide range of economic and social matters: free trade and the extension of local commerce, education, moral improvement, public health, welfare reforms, poverty and labour issues. They pioneered a new kind of political journalism in the provinces, vital for the formation and direction of liberal opinion and for the organisation of reform campaigns. The band helped to establish the *Manchester Guardian* in 1821 and, when this proved lukewarm under its editor John Edward Taylor, the more progressive members turned the *Manchester Gazette* into a political weapon and the tireless promoter of the public good. Prentice was its editor and was later owner-editor of the new *Manchester Times* (1828–47). A self-styled 'rational radical', his leading articles were truly tracts for the times, challenging, insistent and imbued with honesty and conviction. His colleagues, notably John Shuttleworth, also engaged in newspaper writing, and most were prominent platform speakers in these years. A rising level of influence during the 1820s laid the foundations for electoral victory in newly-enfranchised Manchester in 1832 and incorporation as a municipal borough in 1838. The band led the incorporators, provided Manchester with its first mayor in Thomas Potter, and helped to found and lead the Anti-Corn Law League.

Members of the band represented important aspects of Manchester liberalism in this era. Theirs was a reformist, humanitarian, public-spirited creed, solidly based on a belief in progress. Yet the band was not an entirely cohesive unit. Some members wanted greater and quicker reforms than others, and some were more enthusiastic about fashionable social and economic doctrines. There was internal

friction within Manchester liberalism. The acceptability and applicability of *laissez-faire* were important causes of disagreement, as was
the whole tangled issue of political rights and participation. These
differences were perhaps most apparent in the arguments over the
Guardian's editorial line after about 1824.

What follows is a thematic study of the principles and public
efforts of the 'small but determined band', a group that provides
extremely useful avenues of inquiry into one variety of early
nineteenth-century provincial liberalism. Perhaps historians know
less than they implicitly claim about reform movements in the period
from 1815 to 1832. Certainly our understanding of them can only be
improved by detailed local studies of the kind now offered. As was
suggested above, for all that has been written about Victorian Manchester, northern Chartism, the League and the Manchester School,
less has been said about the period before the late 1830s during which
these movements and ideologies were gestating. It is hoped that the
present study will help to rectify this problem by focusing on the
progressive, assertive, insistent and at times fragmented phenomenon
that was liberalism in the leading provincial town of England before
the passing of the Great Reform Act.

III

What *was* respectable middle-class liberalism in the Manchester
context? Though it is difficult to be exact about the meaning of such
terms as 'respectable', 'middle class' and 'liberal', they were central
to the reformers' self-perception. The terms seem to have denoted
independence, property (usually commercial), education, cultural
interests, breadth of view and personal talent (especially in business).
The terms were not meant to be precise social descriptions but
suggested individual, group and even local pride, as well as sound
moral character. Indeed, these words probably did have more of a
moral than an economic meaning. They also involved a particular
political viewpoint, one that upheld the values of efficiency, self-reliance, merit, commerce, the free church and free state, as opposed
to dependence, privilege, the rural south, exclusivity, hierarchy and
aristocracy. Members of the band called themselves and were referred to as 'liberal', 'rational radicals', 'reformers' and 'friends of
progress'. In the Manchester of the 1820s and 1830s liberalism was
neither a carefully formulated political programme nor a hard and

fast ideology set in tablets of stone. It was still evolving. But it was distinctive, and the appellation 'liberal' was increasingly in use. For some it indicated rectitude, assertiveness, integrity and progressivism in the public sphere, while for opponents of reform it was a pejorative term to be used in describing harmful, novel or disruptive opinions. To be a respectable liberal in early nineteenth-century Manchester was to be a friend of reform, local and national, and to be actively engaged in activity which promoted such change. The 'small but determined band' and its circle included men who were highly dissatisfied with their present, with Manchester public affairs, with the polity, social relationships and economic system of Britain, and with the restricted status, rights and expectations to which they themselves would be condemned if they did not protest and struggle for change. Nevertheless, as suggested above, Manchester liberalism in these years was itself internally divided, not just on the extent or speed of desired changes but occasionally on the fundamentals of social policy, commercial improvements and political participation.

Definition also presents difficulties in connection with the lower social stratum to which Manchester's respectable reformers often made appeals for support. The term 'middling sort' was and is used, indicating a marginal, uneasy group lacking a firm social identity. No clearer terminology seems to have been used even by its own members. In Manchester the middling sort consisted of small property-holders and lesser ratepayers: petty traders, publicans, small producers, clerks, shopkeepers and some craftsmen. These men could be non-deferential, assertive and aware of their insecure social position (seen in such characteristics as the fear of falling back into the ranks of common labour). They may have been conscious of their position between unskilled inferiors and propertied superiors. They could be literate and articulate, and often possessed special skills (in retailing, for instance). Their political outlook was shaped in part by nonconformity, individualism, urban experience and a direct personal involvement in trade. One important proviso, however: it is clear that urban social structures could remain fluid and vague, and that neither the middle class nor the middling sort in Manchester were inevitably reformist in political attitudes. It is unwise to assume too close a correlation between economic and social status and political allegiance. The members of the band, indeed, had to strive long and hard to build up a support base in Manchester, and even in the 1830s the Manchester reform movement was largely opportunistic, issue-related and intermittent in character, not continuous or irresistible.

1 The 'Small But Determined Band' and Its Predecessors

1. THE 'SMALL BUT DETERMINED BAND'

The 'small but determined band' (a phrase coined by one of its number, Richard Potter) provided a permanent nucleus for the activities of Manchester's respectable reformers from the 1810s to the 1840s. The band could be a loose and informal arrangement at times, with members drifting in and out and working with other political allies from the business community or middling sort according to the issues and exigencies of the time. But there were eleven individuals in these years who, though not always in complete agreement with each other, normally worked as an identifiable team and shared a similar approach to the public questions of the day.

Among the most active and radical members of the band was Archibald Prentice (1792–1857), propagandist-in-chief in his newspapers the *Manchester Gazette* (1824–28) and *Manchester Times* (1828–47).[1] Most members of the band were Unitarians, but Prentice was a Presbyterian originally from Covington Mains in Lanarkshire. His father had been a well-respected tenant farmer, and Prentice could proudly trace his ancestry back to prominent local Covenanters who had fought and died in the cause of religious liberty, one of the many causes he himself was to advocate ceaselessly in his newspapers. Among the combatants at Bothwell Brig in June 1674 were

[1] On Prentice's life and career, see his *Historical Sketches and Personal Recollections of Manchester* (1851) and *History of the Anti-Corn Law League* (2 vols, 1853); D. Read, introduction to third edition of Prentice's *Sketches* (1970); P. Ziegler, 'Archibald Prentice', in *Biographical Dictionary of Modern British Radicals*, eds. J. O. Baylen and N. J. Gossman (2 vols, 1979 and 1984), ii, p. 422; J. Evans, *Lancashire Authors and Orators* (1850), pp. 204–8; R. Dunlop, 'Archibald Prentice. A Page in the History of Journalism', *Macmillan's Magazine*, lx (October 1889), pp. 435–43; A. Somerville, 'Archibald Prentice of Manchester', in his *Free Trade and the League* (2 vols, 1853), ii, pp. 380–99; *D.N.B.*, xlvi, ed. S. Lee (1896), pp. 301–3.

his forebears the laird of Staine (also named Archibald Prentice) and Alexander Reid, the Linlithgow farmer whose autobiography was first edited by Prentice in 1822. The theme running through Prentice's historical and biographical notes in the volume, not surprisingly, is the rank injustice of persecuting individuals for their opinions.[2] He never lost his love for Scotland nor his pride in his ancestry, and both sentiments were gratified by his membership of the Manchester St Andrew's Society. This body brought together Scotsmen living in the local area. Prentice was a prominent member, participating in the society's educational, political and recreational activities, and presiding over such functions as the St Andrew's Day dinner of 1830.[3]

Born in November 1792, Prentice moved to Glasgow in 1809 as apprentice to the manufacturer Thomas Grahame. He developed his interests in literature and politics, and began to receive a political education in the liberal circles of the town. His future friend and political associate, Alexander Somerville, recorded that Prentice 'had the privilege of being a listener to the conversation of well-informed and liberal men at the tables of his cousin (David Prentice) of the Glasgow Chronicle, and of Mr Charles Tennant, the great manufacturing chemist who had procured him his station.'[4] Prentice's cousin David founded the reformist *Glasgow Chronicle* in 1811 and was its part-owner and editor until his death in 1837.[5] Some of Prentice's earliest political writings appeared in his cousin's paper. His activities in Glasgow greatly influenced his future endeavours in Manchester. He moved in a distinctive political and social milieu. Prentice's employer Thomas Grahame belonged to an old family of Glasgow solicitors, and the Grahames were closely tied to the eighteenth-century mercantile elite of the town. Thomas's elder brother, Robert, was active in the local Whig cause from the 1790s and was one of the 'clique', the dominant party in local politics during the 1830s. The leading proprietor of the *Glasgow Chronicle* was John Douglas, a veteran Whig who stood as a candidate in the 1832 Glasgow parliamentary election. In 1833 Robert Grahame was the first Lord Provost of the reformed Glasgow town council. Another brother of

---

[2] *The Life of Alexander Reid, a Scottish Covenanter, written by himself and edited by Archibald Prentice, his great grandson* (1822).
[3] *Times*, 13 Nov., 4 Dec. 1830, 28 May, 25 June, 19 Nov. 1831.
[4] Somerville, *Free Trade and the League*, ii, p. 383.
[5] A. Andrews, *The History of British Journalism* (2 vols, 1859), ii, pp. 291–2.

Thomas was the poet James Grahame, and the connection with literary men is further established by the fact that David Prentice was a godson of the poet James Thomson. The *Glasgow Chronicle* and the Manchester *Gazette* and *Times* all reflected in some degree their editors' interest in literature.[6] Archibald Prentice married into the Thomson family in June 1819. His brother-in-law, Philip Thomson, helped out with the *Gazette* in the 1820s.[7]

In 1811 Prentice became the travelling agent or 'bagman' of Thomas Grahame's firm, with a salary of £100 a year. He enjoyed his job immensely: 'Our house has a good name, and its friends are hospitable to its representative'. In 1815 Grahame took him into partnership. That year also saw the movement of the firm from Glasgow to Manchester. Prentice had visited Manchester on his commercial travels, and convinced Grahame that the business opportunities in the capital of the cotton trade were too good to ignore. The two men established a fustian warehouse in Peel Street.[8] It was not long before Prentice had associated with other members of the band, and his skill and persistence as an agitator made him increasingly prominent. Eventually the Manchester Tories tried to chastise him with a libel accusation after he had ridiculed the men behind a petition against the Reform Bill. The matter came to trial in summer 1831 and the prosecution failed.[9] Prentice began writing articles for Cowdroy's *Gazette*, the organ of Manchester liberals, soon after he settled in the town. He purchased the paper in 1824 with the backing of his wealthier friends. Under him the *Gazette*, and from 1828 the *Times*, became persistent exponents of advanced opinions. Prentice was a talented writer and speaker – clear, forceful and persistent.[10] Norman McCord has called his history of the League, written in 1853, neither well-planned nor well-written, but this may be

[6] Information about the Glasgow background was very kindly supplied by Dr John McCaffrey of Glasgow University.
[7] L. H. Grindon, *Manchester Banks and Bankers* (1877), pp. 202, 259, 261–4; L.S.E., Richard Potter Collection (i-v, xi-xiiiA), diaries, correspondence, press cuttings, xii, pp. 195–6, a letter of 5 May 1828 in which Prentice refers to Thomson as his sub-editor.
[8] Prentice, *Letters from Scotland, by an English Commercial Traveller* (1817), p. 43, and *Sketches*, p. 66.
[9] *Times*, 16 April, 2, 16, 23, 30 July 1831; *Report of the Trial of Archibald Prentice for an alleged libel on Captain Grimshaw, at the Salford Quarter Sessions, 14 July 1831*, ed. A. Prentice (1831).
[10] e.g. Evans, *Lancashire Authors*, pp. 204–5.

balanced by Donald Read's view that, in his day, Prentice's editorials contained probably the best writing in all the newspapers of Manchester, Leeds and Sheffield.[11] It is also true that in his own day Prentice's writings were often well-received, and highly recommended in several contemporary journals.[12] Some commentators, notably N. C. Edsall,[13] have been dismissive of Prentice's role and contribution, but it is clear that in Manchester Prentice did play a central role in the formation and rise of the reformist vanguard. The success of this party, and then of the League, owed much to men like Prentice who did most of the groundwork and preparation. He wholeheartedly devoted his newspapers to political debate, suffering financially because of this, and was always ready to stand up and make his opinions heard.

Like others in the band Prentice involved himself in a wide variety of public activities. He donated money to various institutions and causes, but his main assistance was given in his newspapers and on the platform. He was not as wealthy as his friends and his pecuniary contributions were normally on a more modest scale. He gave constant attention and publicity to educational, moral, charitable, political and social issues, was interested in the needs and concerns of the lower ranks, believed that fundamental reforms were necessary to improve the workings of state and society, and constantly attempted to produce 'right opinion' and to prompt others into useful public endeavours. He lectured on such matters as infant schools, temperance, emigration and wages, as well as on political subjects.[14] In much of what he wrote and said Prentice displayed great admiration for the philosopher Jeremy Bentham. It was one of the high points of his life when he met and dined with the aged Bentham in April 1831. He called Bentham's writings 'my political text books', and was glad that he had opportunities to disseminate Benthamite ideas during his own public

---

[11] McCord review, *Ec.H.R.*, 22 (1969), pp. 146–7; D. Read, *Press and People 1790–1850* (1961), p. 89.

[12] e.g. *New Methodist Magazine*, *World*, *New Monthly Magazine* and *Edinburgh Theological Magazine*. See advertisements in *Times*, 3 Dec. 1831.

[13] N. C. Edsall, *Richard Cobden. Independent Radical* (1986), p. 34.

[14] e.g. Prentice, *Remarks on Instruction in Schools for Infants* (1830), *A Tour in the United States, with two lectures on Emigration* (1849), *Sanitary and Political Improvement promoted by Temperance* (1849), *Lecture on the Wages of Labour as affected by Temperance* (1851), *One Day's Rest in Seven. The Right of the Working Classes* (1855).

career.[15] Prentice was the first of four members of the band to be elected to the famous Manchester Literary and Philosophical Society, the keystone of local culture and enlightenment, which he joined on 22 January 1819.[16] Although a sober and serious-minded person, Prentice was sociable and a great raconteur and conversationalist. He was known as a well-read, humorous, intelligent and cultured individual. His days as a commercial traveller provided him with many of his favourite stories, and his *Letters from Scotland* (1817) and *Tour in the United States* (1849) display his wit, his enjoyment of the camaraderie and experiences of travel, and his penchant for observation and description of people and places. Like his friends he enjoyed important social occasions, as in September 1828 when a fancy dress ball was one of the events making up the Manchester Music Festival in aid of charity. Prentice attended in Highland dress, predictably, and of other members of the band William Harvey dressed as Robin Hood, John Shuttleworth as a German baron, J. E. Taylor a barrister and F. R. Atkinson a courtier.[17] Prentice was fond of poetry and music, especially that from his native land, which he found impressive and moving. He also enjoyed art exhibitions.[18]

Prentice had great personal courage, displayed not only in his public career but by such events as his beating-off of three highwaymen who attacked him late one night as he was travelling home from the *Times* office. A strong-willed and fiery individual, he almost came to blows with local Tories at an election meeting in August 1832, and in 1836 he challenged one of them to a duel during a ball when he overheard some insulting remarks about his Highland costume. Prentice was remembered as 'a hard-headed Scotchman', 'a Saul in stature', of 'heroic and commanding presence' and an earnest politician: 'the advocacy of political justice rose to the rank of a religion'. His life was not without personal tragedies, as when he had

---

[15] Prentice, *Sketches*, ch. 24, and *Some Recollections of Jeremy Bentham* (1837).

[16] *Complete List of the Members and Officers of the Manchester Literary and Philosophical Society* (1896).

[17] See Evans, *Lancashire Authors*, p. 208, and Dunlop, 'Archibald Prentice', p. 443 for portraits of Prentice as the socially-accomplished provincial gentleman, the welcome dinner guest and relater of witty anecdotes. On the ball, C.L.M., Hay Scrapbooks (edited and compiled by Revd W. R. Hay), uncatalogued and only partly paginated, xvA.

[18] e.g. Prentice, *Letters from Scotland*, pp. 80, 115–16.

to give up the *Gazette* in 1828 because of financial problems, and when he lost his children. His infant son died in 1821, and his fifteen-year-old daughter in 1835.[19] But he was proud of his journalistic achievements, and Grahame, Prentice and Co. did well before he entered journalism full-time. The firm had moved by 1821 from Peel Street to a more desirable location in Cannon Street, the centre of the warehouse district. Prentice originally resided in Salford, but by 1832 lived in the comfortable surroundings of All Saints' Place, Chorlton Row. He later moved out to Higher Broughton and then to Plymouth Grove, away from the business centre towards the suburb of Ardwick. He attended the Presbyterian church in Greenhays.[20] Prentice was a police commissioner before 1828 and a town councillor after 1838. He never made much money from his newspapers, and when he left journalism he worked in the municipal gas office and benefited from an annuity purchased for him by his friends. In view of his long and active public career, it is a fitting end to Derek Fraser's study of Victorian urban politics that there should be a brief account of Prentice's activity,[21] for Prentice is a symbolic figure, representative of the assertive and public-spirited local politician of the age. Politics gave identity, dignity and opportunity to Prentice and others in the band.

It was in the warehouse of Thomas and Richard Potter that meetings of the band first took place. The Potters were originally from Tadcaster in Yorkshire, where their father John had been a shopkeeper and farmer. He was evidently successful, for when he died in 1802 he left a £12,000 fortune. Thomas (1773–1845) and Richard (1778–1842) were the third and fourth of four sons. They gained an early business training at the family farm and shop, and then moved into textiles. The Manchester warehouse was established in 1801 by Thomas and an elder brother, William, with capital supplied by their father. Richard joined them almost immediately, after serving as a draper's assistant in Birmingham. William left the firm in 1806.[22]

[19] 'Some Epitaphs of Editors', obituaries and press cuttings in Local History Dept. M.C.L., *Biographical References* (card-indexed); J. T. Slugg, *Reminiscences of Manchester Fifty Years Ago* (1881), pp. 288–9; *Times*, 4 Aug. 1832.
[20] 'Archibald Prentice', *Biographical References*; *Pigot and Dean's Manchester and Salford Directories*, 1813, 1815, 1817, 1821, 1824, 1832.
[21] D. Fraser, *Urban Politics in Victorian England* (1976), p. 285.
[22] Potter Collection, especially i, pp. 1–2, 116–21, iii, pp. 56–105, 110, 213; G. Meinertzhagen, *From Ploughshare to Parliament. A short memoir of the Potters of Tadcaster* (1908), pp. viii, xix, 2–3, 13–17, chs. 5, 7, 8.

Thomas and Richard steadily accumulated great wealth and became prominent in Manchester affairs. Their warehouse and office were moved from 43–4 Cannon Street to more commodious premises at 90 Cannon Street in the 1820s. They took a partner, S. H. Norris, in 1830. When Norris retired in 1836 he was replaced by F. Taylor. Soon after this Thomas's son John, also to be active in local politics, was made a partner. The Potter residences reflected their affluence and standing. By 1824 Thomas was living at Broomhill in Pendlebury, and by 1832 at Buile Hill, Pendleton. At Buile Hill, well away from the central commercial district, Thomas built a large mansion for his family set in modest but impressive grounds. Richard was living in Chorlton Row by the mid-1820s, and by 1832 he had moved to Stony Knolls, on Bury New Road. This was after he had considered buying a rural estate, an idea he abandoned because of the expense.[23]

In the early years of the Potter firm, Richard did much of the travelling while Thomas concentrated on expanding its business and increasing its profits. They were active in commercial as well as political campaigns. Thomas was a prominent member of the Chamber of Commerce and a director during the 1820s. He was also on the special committee of four members appointed in December 1820 to make a report on the state of the cotton trade, a good indication of his high reputation for business knowledge and talent.[24] Richard was a member of the chamber and, with Prentice and others, could be outspoken in his advocacy of liberal commercial ideas at its meetings. The Potters participated in many charitable, cultural and improving ventures. Like others in the band they were aware of the responsibilities that went with wealth and status. Members of this group were also proud and assertive, jealously protecting their good name and reputation. When the radical William Cobbett made some disparaging remarks about the Potters' humble origins in 1832, at the time of Richard's campaign to be elected as M.P. for Wigan, Richard responded immediately with a piece on the Potters' social advancement since they had left Tadcaster. Their careers showed what could be achieved by the wholehearted adoption of a creed of self-reliance, improvement, regular habits and personal progress.[25]

---

[23] *Pigot and Dean Directories*, 1824, 1832; T. Swindells, *The Rise and End of a City 'House'* (undated); 'Sir Thomas Potter, first mayor of Manchester', *Biographical References*; Potter Collection, xiiA, pp. 181–3.
[24] *Manchester Chamber of Commerce Monthly Record*, 33 (1922), pp. 105–6.
[25] Meinertzhagen, *Potters of Tadcaster*, preface, p. xv.

Though the Potters' mother was a Methodist, in Manchester the brothers were committed Unitarians. They joined the Cross Street congregation and became closely involved with the liberal-Dissenting body's advance into the public arena. Thomas was a trustee of the Cross Street chapel from the 1820s.[26] Of the two Richard was probably the more active politician, at least before 1830. From his youth, as his diaries show, he was extremely interested in contemporary political issues. He was always ready to express an opinion and to act upon it, and apparently so single-minded that he had little time for anything except political and religious debate. John Shuttleworth of the band joked about this in a friendly letter to Richard Potter of March 1829. He enclosed a religious tract for Potter to read, and added: 'I have no news that you have any interest in, for I imagine unless it was connected with Radicalism or Unitarianism you would set no value upon it'.[27] As Richard increasingly involved himself in local politics the Potters' business was left largely to Thomas, who became known for his application and devotion to trade. The firm continued to prosper. It was already a flourishing concern in 1815. In that year the Potters' warehouse was rated at £140, ranking twentieth in rateable value among the 110 warehouse firms participating in the opposition to the government's proposed export duty on cotton manufactures. The new Potter warehouse at 90 Cannon Street was a special purpose-built, five-storey edifice constructed in the early 1820s. Most of the wealthier firms built such premises in the 1820s and 1830s, finding the older warehouses (often converted cellars or houses used because of their central location) wholly inadequate to deal with Manchester's expanding trade. As the business district expanded southwards to take advantage of lower rents and more space, the Potters were among the first to move their premises, from Cannon Street to George Street in 1836.[28]

The arrangement whereby Richard devoted himself to politics and Thomas concentrated more on the Potters' business was one that

[26] Potter Collection, iii. 205–6, iv. 32, 39; Slugg, *Reminiscences*, pp. 173–4; T. Baker, *Memorials of a Dissenting Chapel* (1884), pp. 117–18.

[27] Meinertzhagen, *Potters of Tadcaster*, p. 251.

[28] Slugg, *Reminiscences*, p. 20; R. Lloyd-Jones and M. J. Lewis, *Manchester and the Age of the Factory* (1988), pp. 219–21; R. Smith, 'Manchester as a centre for the Manufacture and Merchanting of Cotton Goods 1820–30', *University of Birmingham Historical Journal*, 4 (1953), p. 64; D. A. Farnie, 'The Commercial Development of Manchester in the later nineteenth century', *M.R.*, 7 (1954–6), p. 329.

suited the brothers well. Richard was remembered for his 'keen enthusiasm for philanthropy and reform', while Thomas was 'quite as keen but not as hot as Richard, a practical man of few words and less writing, and not so apt to be run away with his feelings'.[29] If Richard was the archetypal agitator, a man who would ceaselessly express his advanced opinions and would be willing to do so even if it meant standing almost alone, which it sometimes did, Thomas tended to be less impatient and insistent. He would join a campaign once it had started, but was not necessarily among its most active initiators. He was painfully aware of the ease with which political agitation could get out of hand, and as a man of property, wealth and business he disliked excessive radical plebeian involvement in politics. When he chaired a huge open-air reform meeting on Camp Field in October 1831, he was disgusted and inconvenienced by the swamping of the assembly by rowdy supporters of the local plebeian radical leadership.[30] Prentice remembered Thomas as 'benevolent, strong of purpose and energetic, always willing to aid the cause of reform but taking little or no part in public questions'.[31] This moderation in his conduct probably helped to pave the way for his rise to the office of mayor after Manchester was incorporated in 1838. Members of the band were leaders of the incorporation campaign. Both Potters had previously been police commissioners. Contemporaries respected them for their charity, their commitment to political and religious liberty, their simple and unequivocal oratory, their sense of duty, industry, perseverance, wealth and influence.[32] Thomas Potter's open-handedness, for example, was such that he paid the whole of John Bright's expenses incurred at the 1843 Durham by-election.[33] This was a family that rose, through the creation of wealth and participation in public affairs, to join the governing and privileged

[29] Meinertzhagen, *Potters of Tadcaster*, preface, p. x. Georgina Meinertzhagen was Richard Potter's grand-daughter.
[30] Absalom Watkin, *Extracts from his Journal 1814–56*, ed. A. E. Watkin (1920), pp. 153–6; Prentice, *Sketches*, pp. 398–40; *Times*, 15 Oct. 1831; *Guardian*, 22 Oct. 1831.
[31] Prentice, *Sketches*, pp. 73–4.
[32] e.g. *Sir Thomas Potter, Knight, Magistrate and first Mayor for the Borough of Manchester* (1840); *A Prayer and Sermon in Cross Street Chapel Manchester, on the Sunday after the interment of Sir Thomas Potter* (1845).
[33] K. Robbins, 'John Bright and the Middle Class in Politics', in *The Middle Class in Politics*, eds J. Garrard, D. Jarry, M. Goldsmith, A. Oldfield (1978), p. 23.

classes of provincial society. As well as being mayor, Thomas became a magistrate and was knighted when Queen Victoria visited Manchester in 1840. Richard was M.P. for Wigan from 1832–39, and in parliament showed particular interest in political, economic and educational reforms. When he left the Commons he retired to Cornwall, and died in Penzance in July 1842. Thomas died in his Buile Hill mansion three years later. One of Richard's daughters married the brother of Lord Macaulay, and another married Captain (later Admiral) Anson. Richard's son, named after him, was a lawyer and later the chairman of the Great Western Railway. Thomas's first son John was also mayor of Manchester, and was knighted in 1851. When he stood as a candidate at the 1857 Manchester parliamentary election it was stressed that Sir John Potter 'follows his father's principles'. Thomas's second son, Thomas, was M.P. for Rochdale and spent over 30 years in the Commons.[34]

John Edward Taylor (1791–1844) began contributing articles to Cowdroy's *Gazette* in 1812, having been in Manchester since 1805.[35] He was born in Ilminster, Sussex, the son of a Unitarian schoolmaster and minister. The family had Manchester origins, and moved to the town when the father secured a post at the Hulme boys' academy. By now Taylor's father was a Quaker, but he himself remained a firm Unitarian. He attended the Cross Street chapel and by 1840 was a trustee.[36] In 1824 he married his cousin Sophia Scott, daughter of a Unitarian minister in Portsmouth. When his father died in July 1817, Taylor wrote some memorial verses which reveal much about his own character. Their emphasis was on independence, on thinking and acting for oneself according to the dictates of conscience, and on the importance of basing one's conduct on reason and altruism.[37]

---

[34] 'Thomas Potter' and 'Richard Potter', *Biographical References*; Meinertzhagen, *Potters of Tadcaster*, pp. 260–61.

[35] On his life and career, *D.N.B.*, lv, ed. S. Lee (1898), pp. 448–50; Prentice, *Sketches*, p. 73 onwards; D. Ayerst, *Guardian: Biography of a Newspaper* (1971), pp. 15–91; W. H. Mills, *The Manchester Guardian. A Century of History* (1921), pp. 5–84; I. & C. Scott, *A Family Biography* (1908), 75 copies printed for private circulation, pp. 135–340; H. McLachlan, 'The Taylors and Scotts of the Manchester Guardian', in his *Essays and Addresses* (1950), pp. 70–93; 'John Edward Taylor', obituaries and cuttings, *Biographical References*; *Guardian*, 10 Jan. 1844.

[36] Slugg, *Reminiscences*, p. 173; Baker, *Memorials*, pp. 117–18.

[37] 'On Viewing the Dead Body of My Father', in Scott, *Family Biography*, p. 150.

Such sentiments were common to others in the band. In 1806 Taylor had been apprenticed to the manufacturer Benjamin Oakden, who later made him a partner. But Taylor preferred the merchanting to the production side of the cotton trade, and soon formed a partnership with John Shuttleworth. They were dealers in cotton, twist and weft, and had premises in the Toll Lane Buildings.[38] Taylor involved himself in local affairs at an early age. He became the secretary of the Manchester Lancasterian School, for example, while still in his apprenticeship. He was interested in political journalism, and active in local liberal circles by the time of the Exchange Riot of April 1812. This disturbance was partly caused by the Prince Regent's decision to retain the Tories in office when constitutional checks on his powers lapsed. The local establishment blamed some of Manchester's respectable reformers for agitating the lower ranks, and it was rumoured that Taylor and Shuttleworth were especially culpable as authors of a placard entitled 'Now or Never'. This accusation against him prompted Taylor to make the comments which resulted in his trial for libel in March 1819, a time when Manchester Tories were eager to strike a blow at their opponents. Taylor was acquitted, and the affair gained some notoriety because it was the first time a defendant was allowed to call evidence in justification for an alleged libel.[39]

Taylor made a telling contribution to the Peterloo controversy with his *Notes and Observations* of 1820, which served as a clarion call for the local liberals.[40] When some of the band helped to establish a new reformist newspaper in 1821, the *Guardian*, Taylor was selected as editor. As Prentice recalled, Taylor had evinced 'a youthful ardour for liberty which promised fair to continue under any circumstances'.[41] Taylor continued his business partnership with Shuttleworth until March 1823, and then devoted himself full-time to the *Guardian*. By the mid-1820s he had moderated the tone of the paper, which caused a rift between him and some of the others in the

---

[38] *Pigot and Dean Directories*, 1813, 1815, 1817, 1821.

[39] *Gazette*, 3 April 1819; Prentice, *Sketches*, ch. 9; *A full and accurate Report of the Trial of Mr J. E. Taylor, of Manchester, for an alleged libel on Mr John Greenwood of the same place, at Lancaster, on Monday March 29th, 1819*, ed. J. E. Taylor (1819).

[40] Taylor, *Notes and Observations, Critical and Explanatory, on the Papers Relative to the Internal State of the Country recently presented to Parliament: To which is appended a Reply to Mr Francis Philips's 'Exposure'* (1820).

[41] Prentice, *Sketches*, pp. 73–4.

band. This was exacerbated as he increasingly sided with the 'high' party in local affairs, but there was still some common ground between Taylor and others in the band on political questions and matters of social, cultural and economic improvement. Taylor was a leading member of the Chamber of Commerce, and his *Guardian* was to be renowned for its business coverage. He made the newspaper an extremely profitable venture. Taylor was to be remembered for his literary abilities, strict morality and staunch Unitarianism.[42] He was also culturally active and was elected a member of the Literary and Philosophical Society in April 1828.[43] He was a police commissioner before and a town councillor after incorporation. He lived in Islington Street, Salford, until about 1829 (next door to Prentice for a time), and then with growing wealth he moved to more comfortable locations, the Crescent in Salford, Woodland Terrace in Broughton, and finally Beech Hill in Cheetham.[44] He died at home in this pleasant suburb in January 1844. He had suffered from a bronchial complaint of increasing severity since 1829.

John Shuttleworth (1786–1864) was Taylor's business partner for a number of years.[45] In 1815 he was living in Oldfield Road, Salford. He soon moved out to Ardwick, then still a semi-rural suburb, and from the mid-1820s he lived in Chorlton Row. When his partnership with Taylor ended he took commercial premises alone in the New Market Buildings.[46] Unlike the rest of the band Shuttleworth was a native Mancunian, born in Strangeways. He was a Cross Street Unitarian, and his brother was a Unitarian minister.[47] Shuttleworth took a lively interest in contemporary political and social issues. Prentice described him as 'intellectual, eloquent and bold'.[48] As well as being allegedly involved in the agitation which caused the Exchange Riot of April 1812, Shuttleworth participated in the

[42] 'John Edward Taylor', *Biographical References*; 'A Brief Memoir of Mr J. E. Taylor', *Christian Reformer*, xi (1844), pp. 9–17 (possibly written by John Shuttleworth); *A Sermon preached in the Cross Street Chapel Manchester, January 14th 1844, on the occasion of the death of Mr J. E. Taylor* (1844).
[43] *Members and Officers of the Literary and Philosophical Society*.
[44] *Pigot and Dean Directories*, 1815, 1817, 1821, 1824, 1832.
[45] On Shuttleworth see Archives Dept. M.C.L., Shuttleworth Scrapbook; 'John Shuttleworth', *Biographical References*; *Guardian*, 28 April, 3 May 1864 (obituaries).
[46] *Pigot and Dean Directories*, 1821, 1824, 1832.
[47] Slugg, *Reminiscences*, p. 174.
[48] Prentice, *Sketches*, pp. 73–4.

petitioning campaigns of the veteran reformer Major John Cartwright in 1812–13, and in organising the defence of the Manchester Thirty-eight, a group of mainly plebeian reformers charged with administering an illegal oath in August 1812. Richard Potter also took part in these activities, as did Thomas Walker, the ageing Unitarian reformer and merchant who had been president of the Manchester Constitutional Society in the early 1790s.[49] Shuttleworth was beginning to write for Cowdroy's *Gazette* at this time, and in later years wrote many articles for local newspapers. These pieces did not deal exclusively with politics. His survey of education in Manchester appeared in the first issue of the *Guardian* (5 May 1821), and his articles on concerts, exhibitions and other social events were used by the *Gazette* and *Chronicle*, among others. He did not write much for the *Guardian* after 1825, which reflects the rupture between Taylor and others in the band. Shuttleworth was also able to gratify some of his literary and cultural interests through membership of the Literary and Philosophical Society, which he joined in October 1835. He later wrote papers for the Manchester Statistical Society, of which he was a member, and in 1861 he composed a history of the Manchester gas establishment. He was appointed auditor of the gas accounts after the passing of the 1824 Manchester gas act. Shuttleworth's commercial expertise is reflected in the many pieces he wrote on the cotton trade.[50]

Along with others in the band Shuttleworth was active in improving ventures, charitable work and political campaigning. He was a member of the Chamber of Commerce and, like his friends, a convinced free trader. He took part in many of the campaigns and meetings staged in Manchester which concerned local economic interests, and had a reputation for good oratory. He was tall, with a loud and distinctive voice, and would prepare his speeches on trade, reform and other questions beforehand and learn them by heart. In 1831, though, one critic did say that his speeches contained too much

---

[49] Shuttleworth Scrapbook, loose leaves, letters from Walker (21 Aug. 1812) and Cartwright (24 Feb. 1813); *A Correct Report of the Proceedings on the Trial of Thirty Eight Men . . . At Lancaster, on Thursday 27 August 1812. With introductory narrative by John Knight, one of the Defendants* (1812); Potter Collection, xiiiA, pp. 176, 181–3.

[50] Shuttleworth Scrapbook, for a selection of his articles; *Members and Officers of the Literary and Philosophical Society*; Shuttleworth, *Some Account of the Manchester Gas Works* (1861).

reason and not enough imagination or emotion.[51] Shuttleworth retired from business in 1857. He was a police commissioner before
incorporation and one of the first aldermen elected in 1838. He
retired from this position in 1860. He also became a magistrate in the
later 1830s. He was the local distributor of stamps for 25 years,
originally appointed in 1834. Some said he was given this office for
political services to the Whig government, others that this was a
Whig tactic to make him tone down his radicalism. After Peterloo
and during the 1820s and 1830s he was an active and valued correspondent of several M.P.s, and of prominent reformers in other
regions. He was remembered for his 'liberality and public spirit'. He
died at the age of 78, having outlived most of his old friends and
political comrades.[52]

Fenton Robinson Atkinson (1784–1859) was a Manchester attorney. He was a Unitarian, born in Leeds. His father was a manufacturer, and the family moved from Leeds to Westhoughton near
Manchester in the mid-1790s. Atkinson had no interest in trade and
from his youth displayed strong literary tastes and artistic talents. If
not for poor eyesight he might well have followed a career in the
arts. Instead he entered the legal profession, and qualified in 1810.
He was to gain a high reputation as a lawyer and literary man. He
proved an avid book collector and put his first library up for sale in
1817, intending to give up this activity, but in the following years his
intense bibliophilism resulted in the collection of a massive library
covering many subjects. He was said to be familiar with every single
item. From 1817 he had his own law firm. He later took on three
partners, including his own son, who became head of the firm when
Atkinson died. By the late 1820s the firm was known as one of the
best in the district. (It still survived under the name of Atkinson,
Saunders and Co. in the 1930s.) F. R. Atkinson was known as a
particularly good bankruptcy lawyer. In 1832 his talents and legal
knowledge were held by his friends to qualify him for the vacant
post of coroner for the Manchester division, but as usual the post
went to the nominee of the local Tory establishment.[53] Atkinson's

[51] *The Falcon, or Journal of Literature*, i (5 Nov. 1831), pp. 2–3.
[52] *Guardian*, 28 April, 3 May 1864; Slugg, *Reminiscences*, p. 174; much of his
correspondence survives in Shuttleworth Scrapbook.
[53] *Examiner and Times*, 12 July 1859 (obituary); 'F. R. Atkinson', *Biographical References*; S.L.H.L., Brotherton Scrapbooks, xi, pp. 67–8; *Guardian*, 14
July 1832; Slugg, *Reminiscences*, p. 3.

attempt to become coroner can be seen as one aspect of the liberal-Dissenting body's challenge to local Tory dominance, but on this occasion it was not successful. Still, Atkinson certainly made a success of his chosen profession, demonstrated not only by his reputation but also his affluence. By 1832 he was living in St James's Square. He later moved out to Oak House, Pendleton, and the Grove in Withington. He was less active professionally during the 1840s and wanted to move further into the country. He had a rural retreat in Alderley Edge, Cheshire, and another sign of wealth is his ownership of railway shares.[54]

Atkinson was a charitable, sociable individual, a keen researcher and collector of books, and a member of several learned and cultural societies. He was interested in public affairs and collected many political tracts.[55] When Prentice first met him he was 'an able lawyer and thorough hater of oppression, whose legal knowledge and earnest love of liberty were soon to be effectively used on behalf of the illegally oppressed'.[56] He helped the Manchester Thirty-eight in 1812, and was Taylor's solicitor at the latter's libel trial in 1819. He provided legal advice and representation for some of the Peterloo wounded.[57] Atkinson was mentioned in Cartwright's letter to Shuttleworth of 24 February 1813 concerning reform petitions, and his early interest in radical politics is also indicated in a letter sent to Shuttleworth in May 1810 from London, where Atkinson was completing his legal training. He asked his friend to send him a copy of Cowdroy's *Gazette* every week, told of his recent purchase of a collection of Paine's letters, and complained that he had not yet been able to procure any of Bentham's writings.[58] Atkinson involved himself regularly in the band's public endeavours, and had a special interest in education and in commercial reforms. He often wrote articles for various journals, though normally on non-political subjects. He wrote some literary pieces for the Manchester *Exchange Herald* in 1809, and was a contributor to the series 'Bibliographiana'

---

[54] *Pigot and Dean Directory*, 1832, and *Biographical References* for residences; for the rural retreat ('Woodleigh') and railway shares, Archives Dept. M.C.L., Atkinson Papers (family and personal), M 177/7/7–8.

[55] See Atkinson Papers, M 177/7/9/1–17.

[56] Prentice, *Sketches*, pp. 73–4.

[57] *Trial of Thirty Eight Men*, introduction; *Trial of J. E. Taylor*, p. 11; *Gazette*, 9 Oct. 1819.

[58] Atkinson to Shuttleworth, 19 May 1810, Shuttleworth Scrapbook, loose leaves.

which appeared in that newspaper in 1815–16. Some of his pieces on bibliography also appeared in the *Gentleman's Magazine* and *Notes and Queries*.[59] One of his friends was James Crossley, a lawyer, local antiquarian and sometime president of the Chetham Society. Atkinson's letters to him highlight their mutual interest in literary matters.[60] A renowned authority on books and literature, Atkinson was on good terms with local writers, antiquarians and booksellers. Throughout his life he remained a keen collector. He put his large second library up for auction in May 1858. The sale lasted over ten days, and the 13,000 volumes in the collection were sold for over £2,000.[61]

Another of the men mentioned in Cartwright's letter to Shuttleworth of February 1813 was Edward Baxter (1779–1856), a Unitarian cotton merchant. His partner was named William Croft. By 1820 he was living in the fashionable Mosley Street, then full of large town houses (later part of the warehouse district), and the Baxter and Croft warehouse was at 35 Cannon Street. It was rated at £120 in 1815, ranking thirtieth in rateable value among the 110 warehouse firms participating in the opposition to the proposed export duty on cotton goods.[62] Baxter attended the Mosley Street Unitarian chapel. This congregation was smaller but only a little less wealthy and influential than the Cross Street body. In fact the two congregations were closely linked by intermarriage, familial migration, and by association in public activity.[63] Baxter achieved the same kind of wealth and status as the Potters, and his respectability ensured that he gained a hearing at most important public meetings in Manchester and made him a suitable chairman at such meetings. Prentice described him as 'a man of rough energy, whose prosperity in business had not yet abated his earnestness for

[59] Archives Dept. M.C.L., F. Leary, The History of the Manchester Periodical Press ms., 1889, p. 119; *Exchange Herald*, March–August 1815, April, June 1816.

[60] C.L.M., James Crossley Papers, Mun. E. 36. Six of Atkinson's letters remain, spanning the years 1829–56.

[61] *Guardian*, 10 May 1858; *Examiner and Times*, 5, 17 May 1858; sale catalogue is in Atkinson Papers, M 177/7.

[62] *Pigot and Dean Directories*, 1815, 1817, 1821; Lloyd-Jones and Lewis, *Manchester and the Age of the Factory*, pp. 219–21.

[63] Slugg, *Reminiscences*, p. 175; V. A. C. Gatrell, 'Incorporation and the pursuit of Liberal Hegemony in Manchester 1790–1839', in *Municipal Reform and the Industrial City*, ed. D. Fraser (1982), p. 25.

reform'.[64] Baxter involved himself in many local commercial campaigns and was a member of the Chamber of Commerce; along with his friends he was persistent in his efforts to make the body more advanced in its principles and more assertive in its public advocacy of liberal economic policies. He was a generous subscriber to relief funds and other worthy causes, improving ventures and institutions, as well as an active politician on the side of reform and progress. He was a police commissioner and active with his friends in the campaign for incorporation. Like them he was also a man of some culture and refinement. If Prentice and Atkinson were lovers of literature, Baxter's fondness was for painting and music. He built up a large collection of artwork which he offered for sale by public auction in 1829 because he was planning to take a long trip abroad (possibly to do the 'grand tour', long regarded by the wealthy as an essential part of the cultural enlightenment of the individual). There were 156 paintings, drawings and engravings listed in the sale catalogue, which stated that many of the items 'would do honour to the best collections in this country'.[65] Baxter sometimes helped in the selection of pieces for local art exhibitions.[66] He indulged his musical interests through membership of such groups as the Friends of Apollo, a society of respectable townspeople which arranged concerts and often staged them in members' houses.[67]

Joseph Brotherton (1783–1857) was one of those who, like Prentice, gave evidence on behalf of Taylor in the latter's libel trial in 1819. His evidence 'seemed to tell on the jury'.[68] He was born in Whittington, near Chesterfield. His father John was an excise officer who was promoted to a post in Manchester in 1789. By the later 1790s John Brotherton had established himself as a cotton manufacturer in Oldfield Road, Salford, in partnership with Messrs Harvey and Booth. John Brotherton had married a Harvey and both families had roots in the same part of Derbyshire. Joseph Brotherton became a partner in the firm in 1802. In 1809 his father

---

[64] Prentice, *Sketches*, pp. 73–4.
[65] Arts Dept. M.C.L., *A Catalogue of the extensive and valuable collection of Pictures, the genuine property of Edward Baxter Esq. of Manchester* (1829); Potter Collection, xiiiA, pp. 181–3.
[66] e.g. Archives Dept. M.C.L., Royal Manchester Institution, Letter Book, Baxter to J. W. Winstanley (secretary of the Institution), 25 March 1834.
[67] e.g. Archives Dept. M.C.L., Bury Papers, Baxter to Charles Bury (Salford calico printer), 14 Nov. 1823.
[68] *Trial of J. E. Taylor*, pp. 24–6; Slugg, *Reminiscences*, p. 284.

died and he made a new partnership with his cousin William Harvey. Joseph had married William Harvey's sister in 1806, so the two families were indeed very close. By 1819 Brotherton had made a modest fortune. He decided to retire and devote himself to public service and religious pursuits. As with others in the band, his sense of duty and belief in the need for action were considerably strengthened by Peterloo. He had been a member of the Bible Christian church in King Street, Salford, since 1805, and was greatly influenced by its minister, William Cowherd, a convinced Swedenborgian who preached the necessity of abandoning all meat and alcohol. Brotherton and his wife became vegetarian and teetotal in 1809. Brotherton wrote and spoke on vegetarianism and teetotalism in subsequent years, stressing their usefulness in promoting spiritual and physical health.[69] When Cowherd died in 1816 the church was in debt. Brotherton became its minister and helped to improve its financial situation, and in 1837 he, William Harvey and Harvey's partner, Charles Tysoe, became the trustees of the church and its assets after a legal suit initiated by Cowherd's heirs. Brotherton's whole approach to public affairs was based on an omnipotent morality, a conviction that his purpose was to do all he could for others. In his scrapbooks he noted that 'the self-interested man is the enemy of all other men', and 'the material man does not know God'. In common with his Unitarian friends Brotherton favoured a rational approach to religion and morality, asserting that it was impossible to believe what could not be understood.[70] His scrapbooks also demonstrate his great interest in public affairs and local issues. Prentice remembered him for his 'firmness of principle' and

---

[69] *D.N.B.*, vi, ed. L. Stephen (1886), p. 466; E. O'Brien, 'Joseph Brotherton', *Eminent Salfordians*, 1 (1982), pp. 17–35; Brotherton, *On Abstinence from Intoxicating Liquor* (1821), biographical introduction by W. E. A. Axon (1890); W. Cowherd, *Facts Authentic in Religion and Science*, ed. J. Brotherton (1816); S.L.H.L., Brotherton, Commonplace Book 1809–16 (unpaginated); *Mr Brotherton's Religious Opinions*, undated pamphlet, based on his preface to Cowherd's *Facts Authentic*; Brotherton Scrapbooks, e.g. iv, p. 39, 'Reasons for Abstaining from Eating the Flesh of Animals'; A. Smith, *Salford Sketches* (1976), pp. 27–30; *Guardian*, 13 Jan. 1857 (obituary); 'Speech of Joseph Brotherton, M.P., at the Vegetarian Banquet held at Hayward's Hotel Manchester, 28 July 1848', *Vegetarian Tracts*, 8 (1848); T. Costley, *Lancashire Poets and Other Literary Sketches* (1897), pp. 64–5; 'Joseph Brotherton', *Biographical References*.
[70] Brotherton Scrapbooks, ii, p. 17; *Brotherton's Religious Opinions*.

'amenity of manner'.[71] Brotherton became known locally as a 'friend of the people', a man of philanthropic kindness, honesty and great application. He was a benevolent employer and always eager to promote the better health and welfare of the cotton workers. This explains his prominence and consistency in the movement for factory reform. He was also a strong advocate of free trade and religious toleration.[72] Under Brotherton's administration the King Street church was fully involved in improving causes. Brotherton himself had a lifelong interest in education and the provision of libraries and other such facilities for the people. He promoted friendly societies and gave money to relief funds.

Unlike others in the band Brotherton had held local office before the 1820s. He was one of the overseers of the Salford poor in 1812–13. His experiences at this time prompted one of his most successful public crusades, that to reform the Salford Charities.[73] Brotherton was often a member of deputations sent to parliament to represent local needs and desires. He was Salford's M.P. from 1832 to 1857, having been instrumental in securing the town's inclusion in the Great Reform Act. His sense of duty prompted him to give his constituents annual accounts of his conduct as their representative.[74] He was a magistrate from the mid-1830s. In parliament he distinguished himself for his quiet but effective work on behalf of liberal causes and, always an idiosyncratic person, was to be remembered for his habit of invoking the midnight rule for the ending of the day's business.[75] Brotherton resided in fairly humble dwellings. Though he had retired with a fortune, he was not hugely wealthy and in any case made a merit of 'simplicity in living and the strictest integrity in all things'. He lived in Hampson Street, Salford, and then from about 1824 in Oldfield Road, Salford. By the time of his death he was living at Rose Hill on the Bolton

[71] Prentice, *Sketches*, pp. 73–4.

[72] Brotherton Scrapbooks, vols ii-xii; *Mr Brotherton's Speech on the Corn Laws, at the Town Hall Salford, 23 June 1841* (1841); *Brotherton's Religious Opinions*.

[73] O'Brien, 'Joseph Brotherton', pp. 22–4; Brotherton, Commonplace Book for the history of the Salford Charities; *Gazette*, March–April 1828; Brotherton Scrapbooks, ix, p. 80, xi, pp. 19, 34–5.

[74] S.L.H.L., Brotherton, *To the Electors of the Borough of Salford*, annual addresses 1832–57, incomplete.

[75] Archives Dept. M.C.L., F. R. Atkinson, Scrapbook, 'Mrs Brotherton putting the House of Commons to bed' (cartoon).

Road.[76] A modest man who was generally and genuinely respected, when Brotherton died a subscription was opened to pay for a statue in his honour. This was erected in 1858 and the inscription on the base was similar to a reply Brotherton had made in the House of Commons in February 1842, when he was accused of acting against the factory system to which he owed his wealth: 'My riches consist not in the extent of my possessions but in the fewness of my wants'. The money left over from the statue was used to purchase books for local libraries and other establishments for workers' education.[77]

William Harvey (1787–1870) joined Brotherton in many of the latter's activities.[78] He too was born in Whittington, the son of a retired Nottinghamshire yeoman. He came to Manchester in 1804 and was apprenticed to a cotton manufacturer named Railton. He later joined the firm of his relatives, the Brothertons, and then entered into partnership with his brother-in-law Joseph. When the latter retired in 1819 Harvey formed a partnership with his friend and fellow Bible Christian Charles Tysoe. Harvey was of advanced political views and 'wore the Radical white hat when it required some moral courage to do so'. He was teetotal, a vegetarian and pacifist, and a campaigner for the anti-tobacco movement. He entered public affairs with the same benevolent, moralistic approach as Brotherton displayed; both men based their conduct on a practical and rational Christianity. Harvey was known as a charitable and philanthropic employer. Harvey, Tysoe and Co. had an office and warehouse in New Cannon Street and a spinning factory in Canal Street, off Oldfield Road, Salford. The London *Morning Chronicle* reporter A. B. Reach visited the mill in 1849 and found the proprietors to be 'gentlemen who exert themselves to the utmost to promote the social comfort and improvement of their workpeople. In the admirably-ordered establishment which they possess are workmen who have toiled for the same masters for more than forty years'.[79] Harvey lived in Regent Road and then in Trafalgar Square, Salford. After 1832 he moved to Acton

[76] *Biographical References*; *Pigot and Dean Directories*, 1817, 1821, 1824, 1832.
[77] O'Brien, 'Joseph Brotherton', pp. 33–5.
[78] The main sources for Harvey are obituaries in *Salford Weekly News*, 31 Dec. 1870; *Guardian*, 31 Dec. 1870; *Courier*, 29 Dec. 1870.
[79] A. B. Reach, *Manchester and the Textile Districts in 1849*, ed. C. Aspin (1972), pp. 13–14.

Square.[80] He retired from business in 1864 and his sons took charge of the firm. Harvey joined the others in the band in most of their political and social activities. He spoke at public meetings dealing with important reforms, and supported many charitable and improving ventures. Like several of his associates he had risen to prominence in local society and affairs by the mid-1830s. He was a constable of Salford in 1834 and later a police commissioner. After Salford's incorporation in 1844 he was one of the first aldermen elected, and he remained one until his death. He was twice elected mayor, in 1857 and 1858, was boroughreeve in 1852–53, and became a magistrate in 1858. Along with most of the band Harvey was one of the earliest members of the Anti-Corn Law League.

Another man who was as active in Salford as in Manchester affairs was John Benjamin Smith (1794–1879). Smith was a Cross Street Unitarian.[81] He was born in Coventry; his father Benjamin was a silk throwster. In 1808 Smith entered the office of his uncle Joseph, a Manchester cotton merchant, and by 1814 he was managing the whole correspondence of the firm and regularly attending sales in London (much to the firm's profit). Benjamin Smith left Coventry and became the partner of his brother Joseph, but this arrangement ended in 1826 and there were then two separate firms. When his father died in 1830 J. B. Smith became the head of Benjamin Smith and Sons, later known as J. B. Smith and Co. The firm had a warehouse and office in Cotton Court. Smith made a large fortune and retired in 1836. He had been interested in public affairs for many years, and kept records of his thoughts on the most pressing issues of his era. He was a particularly avid free trader. The copy of Adam Smith's *Wealth of Nations* in his father's library had been the object of much veneration: 'I used when a boy to pore over this book with more pleasure than any other. I was captivated with its simplicity, sound sense and convincing arguments'.[82] Though he had been

[80] *Pigot and Dean Directories*, 1817, 1821, 1824, 1832.
[81] Slugg, *Reminiscences*, p. 173. For what follows see Archives Dept. M.C.L., J. B. Smith Papers, especially J. E. Cornish's biography (1887) in Memoranda and Letters (on certain public and private affairs, with biographical sketches of J. B. Smith), Smith's Reminiscences, and Newspaper Cuttings of Speeches and Letters by J. B. Smith and articles referring to him; also 'J. B. Smith', *Biographical References*; biographical introduction to Smith's account of Peterloo, in *Three Accounts of Peterloo by Eyewitnesses*, ed. F. A. Bruton (1921), pp. 59–61.
[82] Smith, Reminiscences, pp. 1–2.

politically-interested during the war, and though his liberal views were confirmed by the 1815 corn law, he does not appear to have been active in local politics until after Peterloo. He mixed socially with others in the band and joined them in the local political and commercial controversies of the 1820s and 1830s. He devoted himself fully to this activity after his retirement from business. Smith became a magistrate in 1835. He was a leading member of the League, became president of the Chamber of Commerce in 1839, and was M.P. for Stirling 1847–52 and Stockport 1852–74. (He had already stood unsuccessfully for Blackburn in 1837 and Walsall and Dundee in 1841.) His prominence made him the target of heated attacks, as in March 1852 when the Tory *Stockport Advertiser* condemned his political principles, Unitarian religion, oratory, and involvement with the failed joint stock bank established in Manchester by local reformers in 1829.[83]

With reference to the era of Cobden and the League, N. C. Edsall has applied the same dismissive epithets to Smith as to Prentice.[84] The fact is that Smith, Prentice and their fellows had been locally active in the reform interest for years before Cobden appeared, and they played an essential role in the formation of the support base which Cobden later used in his personal rise to local and national significance. Back in the 1820s and early 1830s Smith joined others in the band in their reform campaigns, and was often a speaker at important public meetings. A man of literary talent, he also helped in the drawing up of petitions, resolutions and other public statements of the respectable reformers. He was an extremely active propagandist during the 1832 parliamentary elections in Manchester and Salford.[85] In 1835 he was asked to assist a local Unitarian minister who wanted to organise a body of talented writers who would use their skills to spread religious truth.[86] Smith also wrote on the cotton trade and the plight of the handloom weavers in the 1830s.[87] His wealth and status are indicated by his residences. Like some of the others in the band he was able to move away from the

---

[83] Smith, Newspaper Cuttings, p. 29.

[84] Edsall, *Richard Cobden*, p. 42.

[85] Archives Dept. M.C.L., J. B. Smith, Papers and Letters relating to the Parliamentary Elections in Manchester and Salford 1832.

[86] Revd J. R. Beard to Smith, 9 March 1835, in Smith, Memoranda and Letters, p. 6.

[87] See essays and papers in Smith, Memoranda and Letters, pp. 29–57.

commercial centre of Manchester towards the suburbs and country-side. He lived in Islington Street, Salford, and later in Pendleton. By the time of his death he had gone to King's Ride, Ascot.[88]

Absalom Watkin (1787–1861) was born in London, the descendant of a long line of Flintshire landowners and farmers.[89] His father had been a soldier, wheelwright and vintner, but died during Absalom's youth. This prompted the latter to go to Manchester for a business training with his uncle John, a cotton merchant. In 1807 Watkin became the master of the firm. Its premises moved several times, but were mostly in Cannon Street,[90] and the firm was still doing business in the 1920s. Watkin was registered as a calico, twist and weft dealer. His greatest loves did not include business, however, but gardening, literature, study and debate. He seems to have been a pious man who rejected materialism and believed that merchants should concern themselves with higher things. He had some oratorical talent, and J. T. Slugg was to name him and Shuttleworth as 'perhaps the most effective speakers in Manchester' during the 1820s and 1830s, 'Watkin being the more refined and Shuttleworth being possessed of more power and energy' (though in 1920 the *Guardian* was to state that Watkin had spoken with 'a sepulchral voice and an awkward manner').[91] Watkin had literary and propagandist skills which were recognised by his friends and put to use in the reformers' campaigns. It was Watkin who drew up the public remonstrance after Peterloo, many of the pro-reform addresses and resolutions of 1831–32, and some of the declarations of the anti-corn law movement in the later 1830s. Watkin was a member of the Literary and Philosophical Society, elected in January 1823,[92] and among his other intellectual and cultural interests were education, poetry, country walks and travel in general, as displayed by the books he read and lectures he attended. He was sociable and an accomplished conversationalist. In October 1807 he helped to form the Sciolous Society for mutual improvement, and in 1810 he joined the Literary and Scientific Club. He later became its historian. He liked to recall his

[88] Smith, Memoranda and Letters; obituary in *Biographical References*.
[89] On Watkin see his *Journal, Fragment No. 1* ed. E. W. Watkin (1874), and *Fragment No. 2* ed. E. W. Watkin (1878).
[90] *Pigot and Dean Directories*, 1815, 1817, 1821, 1824, 1832.
[91] Slugg, *Reminiscences*, p. 174; *Guardian*, 24 April 1920 (a review of Watkin's *Journal*).
[92] *Members and Officers of the Literary and Philosophical Society*.

meetings and conversations with such radical celebrities as John Thelwall, William Cobbett and Richard Carlile. Watkin became a magistrate in the mid-1830s. His third son Alfred was also a magistrate, and a town councillor for over 20 years before becoming mayor of Manchester in 1873–74. Another son, Edward, was a writer and M.P., was knighted, and married into a wealthy publishing family.[93]

Watkin differed from the rest of the band in that he was an Anglican, but like his friends he sympathised with a rational approach to religion and believed that the world had a coherent plan to it. He was not anti-Dissent, and favoured religious liberty as strongly as political and commercial liberty. Though not a staunch reformer early on, Peterloo convinced him of the need to question the conduct of the established authorities, and he already had strong social and business links with others in the band. He joined them increasingly in their political, charitable, commercial and improving campaigns, but remained reluctant to become too involved in public life. He was remembered as a modest and unobtrusive man. Certainly he was of a very serious frame of mind. At the age of only 23 he made out a full and detailed plan for his future life. He wanted to train himself to renounce unnecessary conversation and trifling pursuits, and every day to set aside a period for study. He calculated that when he was 35 he would have money and knowledge enough for extensive travel, to which he would devote seven years. He would return and write an account of his experiences in order to show the effects of Christianity in promoting the happiness of mankind, and then he would engage in work to spread Christianity and contentment.[94] Watkin was not able to do all that he had hoped, but his strongly moralistic approach to public questions meant that he supported many activities designed to extend philanthropy and progress. As he recorded in June 1831, 'to take an interest in the affairs of our fellow men is one great source of comfortable feeling'.[95] He was well-known locally as a man of wealth and respectability. Like some of his friends he was able to move out to the suburbs, to Broughton in the 1820s, to Stony Knolls on Bury New Road by 1832, and later to the pleasant rural village of Northenden. His

[93] Watkin, *Journal*, p. 107; T. Swindells, *Manchester Streets and Manchester Men* (1907), pp. 37–9.
[94] 'A Plan for the Proper Employment of my Time from this Day, May 18 1810, to the Day of my Death', in Watkin, *Fragment No. 1*, pp. 9–19.
[95] Watkin, *Journal*, p. 151.

business success also made him a natural candidate for a place on the board of such institutions as the Manchester Fire Assurance Company, established in 1824.[96]

The participation of these men in public affairs, and the direction their activity took, were in some measure an outcome of the theological and social imperatives operating within the band. Their approach was characterised by reasonableness, by a spirit of toleration and by an assertiveness which came naturally to men rising in social and economic importance, but which could also be a response to prejudice or criticism from outside their group. Shared political and economic principles bound members of the band together, but so did a serious, moralistic way of looking at the world. The two Cowherdites, Brotherton and Harvey, gained from their Bible Christianity a readiness and a motivation to engage in activity that could benefit others. Their sect was imbued with a sense of 'religious brotherhood' with all other Christians, which disposed them to charity, understanding, fellowship and loving their neighbours. There were elements of mysticism in their creed, but there was also a dominant role for reason, seen in the taste for science, Bible criticism and in a wider setting the attempt to spread and strengthen reason through educational and philanthropic work. The zeal for reforms was related to the view that many features of the Church–state system could not stand up to the test of reason. The desire for reforms could also be Bible-based and shaped by a particular interpretation of scripture, though it is true that the Bible Christians were often assailed for their alleged eccentricity and dangerous tenets.[97] William Cowherd himself was a temperamental and unstable character who broke with the Established Church and then with the main body of Swedenborgians,[98] and his followers seemed to many to be the agents of schism, confusion and error. The future Manchester

[96] *Pigot and Dean Directories*, 1821, 1824, 1832.
[97] W. R. Ward, 'Swedenborgianism: heresy, schism or religious protest?', *Studies in Church History*, 9 (1972), pp. 303–9; V. Tomlinson, 'Postscript to Peterloo', *M.R.H.R.*, 3 (1989), pp. 51–9.
[98] *Monthly Observer*, Feb. 1859; *D.N.B.*, xii, ed. L. Stephen (1887), pp. 378–9.

boroughreeve Benjamin Braidley, an Anglican merchant, keen educator and home visitor, was horrified when one of his friends became a Cowherdite, and tried in vain to talk him out of this conversion. Braidley regarded the 'fall' of this individual as an instructive lesson for others.[99] There was controversy in 1820 when a 'True Nonconformist' wrote to the liberal *Gazette* and asserted that religious unity was an unrealistic, harmful distraction. A 'Swedenborgian' (possibly Brotherton) replied with a defence of fellowship and toleration,[100] but this did not prevent the sect of Brotherton and Harvey from being disliked and distrusted. Perhaps these attacks and the comparatively small size of the Bible Christian group helped to make it more cohesive and assertive. In any case the Bible Christians had a high public profile, involving themselves in many of the good works of the period.

Much of this holds true for the Manchester Unitarians, who had seven of the band among their number. The Manchester Unitarians were also of a tolerant and rational character. They were not strongly sectarian, though often had to close ranks when attacked. In 1820, one 'very respectable' correspondent of the radical Manchester *Observer* rejected the charge that he and other Unitarians were blasphemers and non-Christians. He argued that Jesus was a Unitarian, and that the Bible did not support the doctrine of the Trinity.[101] The Unitarians tended to hold relaxed attitudes to doctrine, believing that one's conduct and lifestyle were more important than any rigid adherence to particular theological tenets. At Cross Street there was no doctrinal test on ministers or members of the congregation. The atmosphere was liberal, tolerant and informal. Some dissatisfaction with this had prompted a group to break away and establish the Mosley Street chapel in 1788–89. This smaller but

---

[99] Archives Dept. M.C.L., B. Braidley, Diary (2 vols), i, pp. 148, 152, 157.
[100] *Gazette*, 28 Oct. 1820.
[101] *Observer*, 26 Feb. 1820. For what follows see F. Kenworthy, *Cross Street Chapel in the Life of Manchester* (undated); R. Wade, *The Rise of Nonconformity in Manchester, with a brief sketch of the History of Cross Street Chapel* (1880); Baker, *Memorials*; E. Wright, *Mrs Gaskell. The Basis for Reassessment* (1965), pp. 25–36; H. McLachlan, 'Cross Street Chapel' and 'Our Aims and Ideas', in his *Essays and Addresses*, pp. 94–111, 337–50; F. Kenworthy, 'The Unitarian Tradition in Liberal Christianity', and F. Micklewright, 'A New Approach to Unitarian History', both in *T.U.H.S.*, 8 (1943–6), pp. 58–67, 122–9; R. V. Holt, *The Unitarian Contribution to Social Progress in England* (1952).

similarly respectable congregation preferred to use a regular printed form of prayer,[102] and argued that the preaching in Cross Street had been insufficiently Unitarian. But the two congregations remained close despite this difference, and cooperated in educational, political and other efforts. The dominant Cross Street body never became strongly sectarian, and its relaxed approach probably helped to foster good relations between the Unitarians in the band and men of other Dissenting sects who were involved in reform movements, because the differences in theology were not allowed to be obstacles to public cooperation. The Unitarians in the band evinced a public-spirited concern both for individuals and for society. They were tolerant and reasonable, outward-looking but not evangelical, un-dogmatic, more concerned about ethics and conduct than doctrines. The movement away from doctrine can be linked with their belief in the freedom of each person to interpret the Bible as he or she liked, and with the individualistic and libertarian ideas of the moderate Cross Street majority. The Manchester Unitarians were noted for their wealth and respectability. They were social and cultural leaders. Perhaps a narrow sectarianism would have damaged their prospects and ability to rise. They wanted to remove obstacles, not to perpetuate them. Forward-looking and progressive, but with a keen sense of tradition and their intellectual heritage, the Unitarians' liberalism in theology complemented and confirmed (and was confirmed by) a liberalism in politics. Their desire was to impose their own image of what society should be, to whatever extent possible.[103]

The Unitarians in the band were socially and politically assertive. They were impatient with their present, with civil disabilities, a static and exclusive political system, unadventurous and restrictive commercial policies, and difficulties in the way of personal advancement. The desire for reform meant a predilection for radicalism of a rational and constructive kind. Benthamism was attractive because it seemed

[102] J. Aston, *A Picture of Manchester* (1816), pp. 96–7.
[103] Some of these points are covered in three essays by John Seed: 'Unitarianism, political economy and the antinomies of liberal culture in Manchester 1830–60', *S.H.*, 7 (1982), pp. 1–25; 'Gentlemen Dissenters: the social and political meanings of Rational Dissent in the 1770s and 80s', *H.J.*, 28 (1985), pp. 299–325; 'Theologies of Power: Unitarianism and the social relations of religious discourse 1800–50', in *Class, Power and Social Structure in British Nineteenth-Century Towns*, ed. R. J. Morris (1986), pp. 108–56.

to offer avenues which could lead to progress, reform and efficiency.[104] But the theology was always present in the background, no
matter how preoccupied with politics and secular power relationships
the Unitarians in the band became. The Arian roots of Unitarian
theology were of key importance here. Arius (c.250–336, born in
Libya) was probably the first important theologian to make a clear
distinction between God and Jesus. He did this because he believed
that there was no necessary connection between the existence of an
ordered world and the 'Logos', the divine capacity to create an ordered world. Arianism sought to reconcile God's utter freedom with
His rationality. Jesus Christ was a knowable likeness of God but not
part of the life of God. God was knowable only in His world-oriented
aspect; apart from this He was unknowable and free. These ideas were
taken further by Socinus (1539–1604, born in Siena), who unmistakably denied the divinity of Jesus. But dogma was to be less important
than its implications for real situations, at least as far as the Manchester Unitarians were concerned in the early nineteenth century. The
Arian emphasis on the utter independence and separateness of God
undermined the notion of 'God's Will', and this could lead to a potent
and energetic voluntarism. Nothing was settled, so there could and
should be opportunities for reforms in the public sphere and advancement in the personal sphere. It was not wrong for individuals to seek
and take up such opportunities. Perhaps members of the band adapted
their theology to suit their own circumstances and ambitions. It was
not clear that God had decided that some men should be rich and
others poor, some have authority and others none, for God was
absolutely free and was not tied to such a formula. There was, therefore, nothing to stop a person from rising in the world or engaging
in movements to reform and improve state and society. What was
needed was effort, faith, self-dependence and good works. What this
entailed was a concern about conduct rather than strict dogma.[105]

---

[104] I. Sellers, 'Unitarians and Social Change', *Hibbert Journal*, 61 (1962–3),
pp. 16–22 (Varieties of Radicalism), 76–80 (Benthamism and Liberty); I. Sellers,
'Prelude to Peterloo: Warrington Radicalism 1775–1819', *M.R.H.R.*, 3 (1989),
pp. 15–20. The connections between (non-Trinitarian) heterodoxy and political radicalism have also been investigated in J. C. D. Clark, *English Society
1688–1832* (1985), though see critique in J. Innes, 'Jonathan Clark, Social
History and England's Ancien Regime', *P.&P.*, 115 (1987), pp. 165–200.
[105] On Socinus and Arius, *Oxford Dictionary of the Christian Church*, ed.
F. L. Cross (1974), pp. 80–81, 84–5, 1266–7; R. Williams, *Arius. Heresy and
Tradition* (1987), pp. 175–7, 230–33.

The Unitarians were the dominant group within Manchester's liberal-Dissenting body. As they became more and more prominent in local affairs, indeed, they were often singled out for attack by the local Tory establishment because of both their politics and their theology. The Tory *Mercury* condemned a Unitarian dinner in April 1823 for drinking to the 'sovereignty of the people' while refusing to toast the king's health, and this after the organisers had declared that politics would be avoided. In the mid-1820s the *Guardian* used parliamentary debates on the marriage laws to stress that Unitarians deserved the right to profess and promulgate their principles, and to demand that Unitarianism should cease to be an offence at common law. In 1827 the Tory *Courier* hoped that the latest measure to relieve Unitarians from the Anglican marriage ceremony would be soundly defeated, because even if limited relief to tender consciences was partly bearable, this bill was offensive to 'the soundest principles of religion and morality'.[106] In 1832, when Unitarians were leading movers in the election campaigns to secure the return of liberal, free trade candidates for Manchester and Salford, one writer condemned this 'seditious junto' and described Unitarianism as an amalgam of 'confidence and obstinacy, deceit and hypocrisy, interest and design, and every wicked principle which needs a forgery to give suspicious falsehood the appearance of truth'. Unitarians were said to have promoted discord, faction and mischief for decades. They had been ceaselessly active in opposition to authority, it was asserted, and were hated by every other sect. The *Courier* stated that Unitarian involvement in the parliamentary reform campaign and 1832 elections proved that the Church was in serious danger.[107] Earlier controversies in Manchester, mostly carried on in articles and correspondence in local journals, had involved disagreements about the divinity of Christ, relations between Unitarians and 'Orthodox Dissent', religious truth, the movement from moderate Arianism to Socinianism and 'error', and the Unitarians' claims to their chapels and endowments.[108] These attacks on the Manchester Unitarians increased their

[106] *Mercury*, 29 April 1823; *Guardian*, 10 April 1824, 11 June 1825; *Courier*, 7 July 1827.
[107] 'To the Free and Independent Electors of England', handbill dated July 1832, Brotherton Scrapbooks, xi, p. 14; *Courier*, 16 June 1832.
[108] See Braidley, Diary, ii, pp. 102, 122–3; Archives Dept. M.C.L., G. Hadfield, The Personal Narrative of George Hadfield MP (1882), pp. 87–92; *The Manchester Socinian Controversy* (1825).

self-assertiveness, as did their belief in reform and consciousness of social and economic importance. Cross Street provided a political and religious base for Manchester's respectable reformers. The congregation was cohesive, exclusive and dominated by men of wealth and status who were ready and eager to enter provincial public life. Their conduct was shaped by their minority position, their resentment against constitutional barriers to full citizenship, the long 'open trust' dispute over the Cross Street body's right to occupy and administer property originally entrusted to its Trinitarian predecessors (a dispute in which members of the band became involved and which was settled in 1844), the close family ties within the congregation and its liberal doctrine and selective membership (in contrast with newer Unitarian chapels which were more sectarian and more popular).[109] Cross Street provided a headquarters and a forum, a launching-pad for a public career, and a base not only for political activity but for educational and philanthropic work and full involvement in Manchester's cultural advancement. Membership of this congregation reflected a range of preferences and aspirations, theological, social, intellectual, political, economic and moral.[110]

Though he was not a Unitarian or a Bible Christian, Prentice differed little from his allies in the way he approached the salient questions of the age. He was equally committed to tolerance, improvement, justice and liberty. As did others in the band, he opposed disabilities imposed by the state on account of religious opinions. When writing in 1830 of the restrictions on Jews, he denounced disabilities as 'equally adverse to sound policy and the tolerant spirit of Christianity'. He later recalled Viscount Sidmouth's 1811 bill to control Dissenting preachers, stating that the Dissenters' submission and loyalty during the war years was 'rewarded by a kick . . . which taught them that to retain even the share of liberty they possessed

---

[109] Gatrell, 'Incorporation and liberal hegemony', pp. 25–8; R. M. Montgomery and F. Hankinson, 'The Dissenters Chapels Act 1844', *T.U.H.S.*, 8 (1943–6), pp. 45–55; Holt, *Unitarian Contribution*, pp. 338–9. On the respectability of the Cross Street body, J. Aston, *The Manchester Guide* (1804), p. 121; Slugg, *Reminiscences*, pp. 173–4; Baker, *Memorials*, for the trustees.
[110] Though important, theology was one among many reasons for attendance at Cross Street. For some of the congregation it might not even have been the main one. As John Seed has suggested, 'affiliation to a Unitarian congregation in the early nineteenth century was never merely a theological predilection. It was much more a matter of what essential social and ideological functions such a congregation served'. Seed, 'Theologies of Power', p. 142.

they must energetically demand those which were denied to them'.[111] As he favoured the use of reason in politics, so also did Prentice accept some application of rationality in religion. He believed that the 'truths' of science came from God, and in 1825 called religion 'the great master science'.[112]

The years between 1815 and 1832 saw members of the band react against many disadvantages and problems. In view of what has been discussed above, they may have seen themselves as outsiders. In some ways they were regarded as such. The early gatherings in the Potter warehouse surprised some contemporaries because it was not usual (or wise) for commercial men to ally themselves with political movements unless these were in support of the local and central authorities.[113] The desire for change and an impulse for commitment and action characterised the band's involvement in many social, political and economic spheres, and behind it all was a belief in personal merit and effort, voluntarism and self-reliance. There was a desire to change the Church-state system and to create alternatives to it, to give attention to matters not covered by the local or central authorities, to find new ways of dealing with the dominance of a Church that was unacceptable and an exclusive and corrupt political system to which the band could not yet fully belong. There was an animus against privilege, monopoly and perceived injustices, rooted both in theology and in liberal political principles. It was expected that parliamentary, ecclesiastical and commercial reform would provide openings and opportunities for members of the band and their children. Their religious nonconformity and political liberalism formed essential parts of their self-understanding and identity,[114] and they may also have been influenced by, and participated in, the rise of a middle-class consciousness. Theirs was the peculiarly middle-class political creed which K. Robbins has identified, based on efficiency not indolence, merit not privilege, the commercial and industrial north not the effete south, and free churchmen and a free state in place of the established order.[115] Members of the band must also have been influenced by a

[111] *Times*, 10 April 1830; Prentice, *Sketches*, p. 21.
[112] *Gazette*, 19 March 1825.
[113] e.g. Swindells, *City 'House'*.
[114] See useful comments in R. E. Richey, 'The Origins of English Radicalism: the changing rationale for Dissent', *Eighteenth-Century Studies*, 7 (1973–4), pp. 179–92.
[115] K. Robbins, 'Bright and the Middle Class', p. 21.

sense of urban pride, identity and responsibilities, which prompted their participation in local government disputes and in educational, cultural and philanthropic activity. The gentrification which A. J. Kidd has seen as one characteristic of the Manchester middle class in the nineteenth century [116] was only partly achieved by some of these respectable reformers. There was a clear desire for social and political influence, acceptance and property, and there was a movement towards the suburbs and country (and even Cornwall or Ascot), but these took a long time to materialise and did not sever all connections with Manchester. In the first half of the nineteenth century no member of the band failed to act on a sense of duty to improve the town and the lives of its inhabitants in one form or another.

2. REFORMERS IN MANCHESTER, 1780–1815

Among the other influences affecting the band was the example set by their predecessors in Manchester reform movements before the end of the war. An identifiable reforming party was active in Manchester from the late 1780s to the late 1790s, led by well-to-do Dissenters from the local business community. These were educated, public-spirited men who were successful in commerce and manufacturing, and who displayed a wide range of philosophical, scientific and political interests. Several belonged to the renowned Literary and Philosophical Society. Among the most prominent of these reformers were George Philips, from a wealthy Unitarian cotton family, James Watt junior, son of the inventor, Thomas Cooper, chemist, lawyer and Paineite, and Thomas Walker, a wealthy Unitarian cotton merchant and manufacturer.[117] Walker (1751–1818)

---

[116] A. J. Kidd, 'The Middle Class in nineteenth-century Manchester', in *City, Class and Culture*, eds A. J. Kidd and K. W. Roberts (1985), pp. 1–25.
[117] *Biographical Memoir of Thomas Walker Esq., of Manchester* (1820); F. Knight, *The Strange Case of Thomas Walker* (1957); D. Malone, *The Public Life of Thomas Cooper* (1926); E. Robinson, 'An English Jacobin: James Watt jun. 1769–1848', *C.H.J.*, 11 (1953–5), pp. 349–55; T. Walker, *A Review of some of the Political Events in Manchester during the last five years* (1794); P. Handforth, 'Manchester Radical Politics 1789–94', *T.L.C.A.S.*, 66 (1956), pp. 87–106; L. S. Marshall, *The Development of Public Opinion in Manchester 1780–1820* (1946), ch. 6; Prentice, Sketches, chs. 1, 2; J. Bohstedt, *Riots and Community Politics in England and Wales 1790–1810* (1983), pp. 103–12, 120 (though Bohstedt mistakenly states that Walker was an Anglican).

was the leader of the group. The first important political campaign in which these men engaged was the anti-slave trade agitation, which was most forceful in the years 1787–92. This agitation involved men of differing political and religious opinions and was only clearly the work of the respectable liberals after 1790.[118] By this time party divisions in Manchester were more clearly defined. The 1787–90 campaigns for the repeal of the test and corporation acts solidified these distinctions and, as a local historian James Wheeler was to say, signalled the beginnings of 'a constant ferment in the town, which after the commencement of the war never subsided'.[119] The locally-dominant Anglican-Tory oligarchy and its supporters celebrated the Dissenters' defeat on the test and corporation acts by establishing the Church and King Club in March 1790. This gave the conservatives and loyalists a central, public and prominent organisation that served as a focus for their political activities in the town. Before long the group collecting around Walker had founded a rival liberal association. Their enthusiasm for the activities of the French revolutionaries, and their desire to provide local reformers with a forum for discussion and mutual encouragement, a counterweight to the Church and King Club, and an impulse for perseverance despite the disappointment on the matter of the test and corporation acts, led them to establish the Manchester Constitutional Society in October 1790.[120] Walker was president and Cooper chief propagandist. The printer Matthew Faulkner helped with the publication and distribution of the society's enlightening handbills and pamphlets.

The liberals could get no coverage from the established local newspapers and it was eventually decided to set up a new paper, an alternative organ of communication and information that would enable the reformers to present their case more effectively. Finance came from the wealthier reformers, and Faulkner and his partner Birch acted as printers and publishers of the new journal. Cooper was the main editor and most influential contributor. The first issue of the

[118] E. M. Hunt, 'The Anti-Slave Trade Agitation in Manchester', *T.L.C.A.S.*, 79 (1977), pp. 46–72.
[119] G. M. Ditchfield, 'The Campaign in Lancashire and Cheshire for the repeal of the Test and Corporation Acts 1787–90', *T.H.S.L.C.*, 126 (1977), pp. 109–38; J. Wheeler, *Manchester: its political, social and commercial history, ancient and modern* (1836), p. 92. On the general social antagonisms of the period, Bohstedt, *Riots and Community Politics*, ch. 3.
[120] *Rules and Orders of the Manchester Constitutional Society, instituted October 1790* (1791).

Manchester Herald appeared on 31 March 1792. As the prospectus declared, 'no fear nor favour shall prevent us from making our publication decidedly the PAPER OF THE PEOPLE'.[121] The newspaper was quickly known for its extensive reportage and comment on public affairs. As Donald Clare has said, it was 'probably the first provincial newspaper to be established for purely political reasons'.[122] The notion of the provincial newspaper as a political organ capable of creating and directing opinion really begins with the *Manchester Herald*, and this notion was to animate the band in later decades. The Tories soon recognised the importance of a newspaper to the success of the radical cause, and the effectiveness of the *Manchester Herald* can be judged by the bitterness of the campaign against it. Eventually, in the spring of 1793, five ex-officio informations and six indictments were laid against Faulkner and Birch. They fled to the U.S.A. and the last issue of the newspaper appeared on 23 March 1793.[123]

The notoriety of the Constitutional Society had increased dramatically in April 1792 when Cooper and Watt presented its address of congratulation to the Jacobin Club in Paris. Edmund Burke drew attention to the matter in the House of Commons, accusing Cooper, Watt and the Constitutional Society of dangerous and disloyal designs. Cooper responded with a pamphlet attacking Burke's 'gross blunders and obvious misrepresentations'.[124] The Manchester conservatives began to look for ways to combat the rise of advanced views, but reformist zeal in the district would not die down. May and June 1792 saw the formation of two largely plebeian radical clubs, the Patriotic and Reformation Societies, committed to peaceful reforms and operating under the patronage of Walker's group. Their members were mostly weavers, labourers and journeymen. Concern was expressed because they had respectable backing.[125] From early

---

[121] Prospectus is in Leary, Periodical Press, p. 70; also Archives Dept. M.C.L., J. Harland, Manchester and Lancashire Collection (scrapbook), p. 256.

[122] D. Clare, 'The Local Newspaper Press and Local Politics in Manchester and Liverpool 1780–1800', *T.L.C.A.S.*, 73–4 (1963–4), pp. 107, 112.

[123] Leary, Periodical Press, pp. 73–6; Handforth, 'Manchester Radical Politics', pp. 95–6; Walker, *Review*, p. 25; A. Goodwin, *The Friends of Liberty. The English Democratic Movement in the Age of the French Revolution* (1979), pp. 228–30.

[124] T. Cooper, *A Reply to Mr Burke's Invective against Mr Cooper and Mr Watt in the House of Commons on 30 April 1792* (1792).

[125] Knight, *Strange Case of Thomas Walker*, p. 79; Goodwin, *Friends of Liberty*, p. 235.

summer 1792 Manchester Tories prepared themselves for a trial of strength. On 4 June 1792, after a loyalist meeting and an illumination to mark the king's birthday, a large and unruly section of the assembled crowd attacked two Dissenting chapels (one of them the Mosley Street Unitarian chapel). The authorities did not intervene.[126] The propaganda campaign against Walker and the Constitutional Society was stepped up, and in September 1792 a total of 186 Manchester innkeepers and publicans signed a declaration of loyalty and banned reformers' clubs from their premises. Some had probably had their licences threatened.[127] Henceforth the Constitutional Society met at Walker's house in South Parade, and the plebeian Patriotic Society was given the use of Walker's warehouse to the rear of the living quarters.[128] Controversy and argument continued unabated, and the public mind was continually agitated as the French Revolution began to take a more extreme and violent path. Meanwhile George Philips had written his influential *The Necessity of a Speedy and Effectual Reform in Parliament*. This advocated the granting of the vote to every citizen, men and women alike, only excluding children and the insane. Philips also argued for electoral districts containing equal numbers of voters, voting by ballot and the closing of the poll in one day, and regulations to prevent disorders and undue influence at elections. He advocated the payment of M.P.s and the abolition of qualifications so that any citizen could stand as a parliamentary candidate. He also wanted annual parliaments, a system of rotation so that no M.P. could sit for more than three years and no more than two-thirds of the members of one parliament could sit in the next, the separation of ministers from the legislative assembly, and the authorising of constituents so that they could discharge unsatisfactory representatives.[129] The resilience of local radicalism brought forth another spate of loyalist-inspired mob

---

[126] Prentice, *Sketches*, pp. 6–7; Walker, *Review*, pp. 33–40; Knight, *Strange Case of Thomas Walker*, pp. 76–8; Malone, *Public Life of Thomas Cooper*, p. 57.

[127] Prentice, *Sketches*, pp. 7–8, in which he condemns the sordid alliance of parsons and publicans; Handforth, 'Manchester Radical Politics', p. 99; copy of declaration in Hay Scrapbooks, xiv (unpaginated). One Manchester public house still had its 'No Jacobins Admitted' sign up in 1825: J. Reilly, *The People's History of Manchester* (1859), p. 281.

[128] Walker, *Review*, pp. 41–3.

[129] G. Philips, *The Necessity of a Speedy and Effectual Reform in Parliament* (1792), p. 54.

activity in December 1792. The *Manchester Herald* offices were attacked, as was Walker's house and that of the spinner William Gorse, where the Reformation Society had been meeting. As before the authorities did not stop the disturbances. Walker's protests were upheld by C. J. Fox and Charles Grey in the Commons on 17 December 1792.[130]

From 12 December 1792 the Manchester conservatives had an active and powerful organ designed to put paid to Walker's party, the Association for Preserving Constitutional Order and Liberty as well as Property against the various efforts of Levellers and Republicans (A.P.C.O.).[131] The name resembles that of the government-sponsored association founded by John Reeves in London in November 1792, but Manchester loyalism had a dynamic of its own and did not have to depend on promptings from elsewhere. There is no evidence in the A.P.C.O.'s records of any close collusion with the Reeves body. The A.P.C.O. worked hand in hand with the local authorities, and indeed the magistrates and town officers were among its leading members. The body undertook to discover and bring to justice all authors, publishers and distributors of seditious and treasonable writings, 'and especially all persons who shall be engaged in any societies or combinations for the dispersion and promotion of such doctrines'.[132] The A.P.C.O. subjected all suspect persons to surveillance and aimed to better the reformers in every department, publicity, propaganda, influence over public opinion, control of Manchester affairs. The A.P.C.O. was behind the persecution which forced Faulkner and Birch of the *Manchester Herald* into exile, and then brought on the trial of Walker for conspiracy in April

---

[130] Walker, *Review*, pp. 54–68, 70–85; Knight, *Strange Case of Thomas Walker*, ch. 9; Prentice, *Sketches*, pp. 9–11; A. Booth, 'Popular Loyalism and Public Violence in the Northwest of England 1790–1800', *S.H.*, 8 (1983), pp. 299, 301; handbills in Hay Scrapbooks, xiv; *Hansard's Parliamentary History*, x (1817), Dec. 1792–March 1794, 128–37, Debate on Mr Grey's Complaint of a Libel entitled 'One Pennyworth of Truth from Thomas Bull to his Brother John'.

[131] C.L.M., Association for Preserving Constitutional Order (A.P.C.O.), constitution and minutes of committee; Prentice, *Sketches*, ch. 27 (supplementary chapter); Hay Scrapbooks, xiv (unpaginated); Knight, *Strange Case of Thomas Walker*, chs. 10, 11; Handforth, 'Manchester Radical Politics', pp. 99–100; A. Mitchell, 'The Association Movement of 1792–3', *H.J.*, 4 (1961), pp. 56–77.

[132] A.P.C.O., minutes of inaugural meeting, 12 Dec. 1792.

1794.[133] Walker was acquitted, but his personal wealth was seriously depleted by the trial and his health suffered. This trial frightened many reformers into inactivity.

Walker would probably not have been the victim of such persecution, and the *Manchester Herald* and Constitutional Society would not have come to such ignominious ends, had the local reform party not been so isolated. Isolation exacerbated the problems likely to be faced by any group in a minority position, and it is not only to be explained by reference to the seemingly irrepressible wave of loyalist sentiment which was spreading over the country in the early 1790s. The years 1789–93 were good ones for the Manchester cotton trade, but many workers felt insecure because of rising mechanisation, while masters remembered the bad years of the 1780s and were anxious to retain their newly comfortable status. Loyalist propaganda could appeal to both classes by emphasising the links between security, prosperity and the established order in society and politics, with the implication that reforms would mean uncertainty and disruption. Alan Booth has suggested that the reformers could not secure a wide basis of support because they failed to direct their appeal to the economic self-interest of the working man.[134] This is a sound view. The Walker party did concentrate on public affairs and political principles. Less attention was paid to the everyday concerns of the workers and to economic issues in general, although the economic consequences of government policies were increasingly discussed in the reformers' propaganda as the war progressed. If the Constitutional Society had made a mistake in neglecting to offer something to the lower ranks, it was one that was not repeated by the band after the war. The band engaged wholeheartedly in discussion of economic theory and policies. After 1815 Manchester's business system was becoming far more developed, of course, and the cotton trade's dynamic role in the nation's overall economic expansion was also far more in evidence. Circumstances therefore dictated

[133] A.P.C.O., minutes of committee meeting, 24 Dec. 1792; Prentice, *Sketches*, pp. 5–6, 11–15; *The Whole Proceedings on the Trial of an indictment against Thomas Walker of Manchester and others . . . for a conspiracy to overthrow the Constitution and Government, and to aid and assist the French (being the King's enemies) in case they should invade this kingdom*, ed. T. Walker (1794); Handforth, 'Manchester Radical Politics', pp. 102–4; Walker, *Review*, pp. 96–122.
[134] Booth, 'Popular Loyalism', pp. 303–5.

that reformers *had* to address social and economic issues in order to make their public activity relevant, to gain backing from lower social ranks, to indicate more effectively those changes needed in society and government, and (often) to serve their own commercial interests.

Whatever the reasons for the downfall of the Constitutional Society, its efforts were not forgotten. Walker and his allies provided an example and a stimulus to younger men who began to be active in Manchester reform circles towards the end of the war. Members of the band were aware of what had happened in the 1790s and were inspired by the struggles of Walker's group. This is obvious from the early chapters of Prentice's *Sketches*. Walker's fame as a reformer lived on, and his son was also to be a prominent Manchester liberal. C. J. S. Walker (1788–1875) sometimes joined members of the band in their activities from the end of the 1820s, and was later a town councillor and local magistrate.[135] When he spoke at the meeting of 22 September 1831, held to urge the House of Lords to pass the Reform Bill without delay, he was followed by Richard Potter. Potter climbed on to a table,

> and with a voice struggling with emotion, but with the greatest energy, exclaimed: 'This is the son of the late venerable Thomas Walker, the great patriot, who was mobbed in his house and tried at Lancaster for being an advocate of that reform which is now sanctioned by the king and his ministers. (Tremendous applause.) I rejoice to see the day when his principles are cherished by a whole people. I especially rejoice to see the son thus nobly advocating the cause in which the father suffered so much'. The applause which followed this emphatic address was deafening, and was repeatedly renewed after Mr Potter had taken his seat.[136]

Two points made by Thomas Walker in the conclusion of his *Review* of 1794 were to have a special influence on the activity of the band.[137] The first was Walker's recognition that it would take a long time to correct embedded injustices and anomalies. Walker stressed that reformers should not be put off by the obstacles facing them,

---

[135] 'C. J. S. Walker', *Biographical References*. His Christian names were chosen in honour of his two godfathers, Fox and the earl of Derby: Charles James Stanley.

[136] *Times*, 24 Sept. 1831.

[137] Walker, *Review*, pp. 126–7.

but should persist in their efforts even if they saw no immediate results. These results might only be evident in future generations. Members of the band shared such sentiments, and their perseverance was one of their greatest attributes. Without it the Tory hold on local affairs would not have been shaken off for decades. Prentice echoed Walker's view, and in his *Sketches* and newspapers often expressed a determination to engage in good works even if the intended beneficiaries failed to see that in Prentice and the band they had friends and defenders. The second point made by Walker was that the progress of reform was often retarded by ignorance. He was convinced that a political campaign required the assistance of information, and what was most needed was a universal system of education. Again the band agreed. The band's enthusiasm for all kinds of formal and informal education stemmed from the belief that more education would mean more support for reform, because the people would be better able to see what was wrong with the established order. There was also the conviction (influenced by Benthamite writings) that education should be and would be the basis of political rights. Members of the band were keen to educate those sections of society they deemed worthy of enfranchisement, and devoted much time, money and attention to libraries, mechanics' institutes, lectures, infants' schools and similar organs of improvement.

Reform activity in Manchester died down after Walker's trial, not least because the war brought with it an increased pressure to conform. There was a peace movement in the town, led at first by respectable Unitarian textile masters like Walker, George and Robert Philips, Samuel Greg and John and Arthur Clegg, but the anti-war meetings of the 1790s were not as effective as they might have been because they were denied official civic sanction (the town officers refused to preside), and because they were nearly always countered by loyal meetings and addresses.[138] Nevertheless, the events and arguments of the war years became a central part of developing radical folklore. Many of the grievances of the postwar era were traced back to the war. Blame was assigned to those responsible for domestic policy and the conduct of the war and to men who, in the local arena, had supported those responsible. Members of the band were fully imbued with the sentiments of Manchester's wartime

---

[138] On meetings of 1791 and 1795, reports and handbills in Hay Scrapbooks, xiv (unpaginated), xvii, pp. 55–7, 148–52; A.P.C.O., minutes, Nov.–Dec. 1795; Wheeler, *History*, p. 93; Prentice, *Sketches*, p. 29.

liberals, recording their own opposition to the war and sense of outrage at its effects.[139] The crucial connection between 'rational Christianity' and the ebullience of liberalism and protest during the war has been highlighted by J. E. Cookson.[140] The opponents of the war tended to collect around religious congregations. In part the protests were a natural progression from the test and corporation acts repeal campaigns of 1787–90. It is significant that many Unitarians provided local leadership and direction for the provincial protests. This was the case in Manchester. The salient characteristics of the wartime friends of peace were also those of Manchester's liberal-Dissenting leaders during and after the war: group consciousness, provincialism, rational Christianity and nonconformity (and so religious grievances), a desire to respond to the impact of loyalism, concern about the effects of the war and of government commercial policy, cohesion caused by the sense of being outsiders, and the 'animus against oligarchy' (Cookson's phrase) which could not fail to draw in disciples from a provincial, industrial, non-Anglican middle class.

Manchester was not free in these years from a more threatening brand of radicalism and protest than that articulated by the respectable friends of peace. A Manchester Corresponding Society was operating from early 1796, and there was also some United Irish and United English activity, but this does not seem to have had much respectable involvement and the surveillance and repression of the authorities prevented any serious risings.[141] Local officers were among the most committed of participants in the politics of alarm in the war years, and the Manchester district saw the establishment of

[139] e.g. Watkin, *Fragment No. 1*, pp. 59–64, *Fragment No. 2*, p. 47; Prentice, *Letters from Scotland*, pp. 79–80, *Sketches*, p. 18, chs. 1–5; Potter Collection, i, pp. 50–54, 59–65, 88, 179, 189–90, iii, p. 27; Meinertzhagen, *Potters of Tadcaster*, pp. 63–4, 71, 73, 112–13; Smith, Reminiscences, p. 2.

[140] J. E. Cookson, *The Friends of Peace. Anti-War Liberalism in England 1793–1815* (1982), pp. 5, 23, 191.

[141] Goodwin, *Friends of Liberty*, pp. 399, 433, 439; J. Ann Hone, *For the Cause of Truth. Radicalism in London 1796–1821* (1982), pp. 89, 103; A. W. Smith, 'Irish Rebels and English Radicals 1798–1820', *P.&P.*, 7 (1954–5), pp. 78–85; M. Elliott, 'The Despard Conspiracy Reconsidered', *P.&P.*, 75 (1977), pp. 46–61; A. D. Harvey, *Britain in the Early Nineteenth Century* (1978), pp. 85–7; Marshall, *Public Opinion*, pp. 121–5; A. Booth, 'The United Englishmen and radical politics in the industrial northwest of England 1795–1803', *I.R.S.H.*, 31 (1986), pp. 271–97; on fears about a possible French invasion of Ireland, Hay Scrapbooks, xiv.

several loyalist associations and volunteer units. There were close links between the loyal associations and the volunteers.[142] Protest movements in Manchester were muzzled or rendered relatively impuissant in the 1790s. In 1808 the protest against the Orders in Council was matched by a loyalist pro-war address.[143]

Yet reformist sentiment in Manchester of the moderate, respectable and constitutional kind survived even though the liberals remained relatively weak. Petitions for peace in 1807 and 1808 gained over 41,000 signatures between them,[144] some tribute to the efforts of reformist leaders during the preceding fifteen years. The determination and strong convictions of these men had been displayed by such activity as the foundation of the Manchester Thinking Club, which began meeting in the mid-1790s. The meetings were avowedly political demonstrations, for members would sit in complete silence from beginning to end as a protest against coercive legislation. Members took the Foxite position that the government was subverting English liberties, and showed the authorities that they would never stop a man from thinking, however draconian the law became. The *Gazette* praised the club and its escape from 'constitutional muzzles' through silent contemplation, and welcomed this demonstration that Manchester men could and would think for themselves.[145]

It was the establishment of the *Gazette* in 1795 that was probably of greatest importance in ensuring the survival of a respectable liberalism in Manchester during the war. William Cowdroy was its editor and printer, and sole proprietor from 1799. He had an established liberal reputation and appears to have been a friend and

---

[142] R. Dozier, *For King, Constitution and Country* (1983), pp. 140–54; A.P.C.O., minutes, Oct. 1794, Jan.–Feb. 1797; Wheeler, *History*, p. 97; Prentice, *Sketches*, pp. 27–9; J. R. Western, 'The Volunteer Movement as an anti-revolutionary force', *E.H.R.*, 71 (1956), pp. 603–14; J. E. Cookson, 'The English Volunteer Movement of the French Wars 1793–1815: Some Contexts', *H.J.*, 32 (1989), pp. 867–91; Bohstedt, *Riots and Community Politics*, p. 82.

[143] Cookson, *Friends of Peace*, p. 222.

[144] *Gazette*, 22 Aug., 28 Dec. 1807, 3, 12 March, 25 May 1808.

[145] J. W. Hunter, 'The Clubs of Old Manchester', *Papers of the Manchester Literary Club*, ii (1876), p. 24. The Thinking Club seems to have been part of the national protest which began late in 1795 after the passing of the 'Two Acts', designed to combat radical societies, large assemblies and 'seditious' opinions. E. Royle and M. Walvin, *English Radicals and Reformers 1760–1848* (1982), pp. 76–9.

correspondent of such prominent London radicals as Thomas Hardy and John Thelwall.[146] The *Gazette* did well, circulating widely in Lancashire, Cheshire, Derbyshire and Yorkshire. Sales reached a wartime high of 1,700 a week in the summer of 1796, and never fell below 1,000. The *Gazette* followed the *Manchester Herald* in the large amount of space given to politics and the regular insertion of editorial comment. As Donald Clare suggests, the success of the *Gazette* indicated that many in the region were still sympathetic to the cause of reform, and revealed that a provincial paper could realistically hope to exert influence.[147] Certainly the *Gazette*'s progress alarmed local anti-reformers. Manchester Tories tried to interfere with the *Gazette*'s circulation and distribution in the later 1790s, and in the spring of 1798 Cowdroy's sons (Thomas and William junior) were arrested on a charge of printing treasonable matter. They were released after 12 weeks.[148]

A residue of committed liberalism survived in Manchester despite the pressures to conform. There was, in addition, an extremist quasi-revolutionary wing among Manchester's plebeian reformers, though this was short-lived and fragmentary and never seems to have posed so much of a threat as the local authorities believed. But economic hardship[149] did at times provide a wider support for radical nostrums, both moderate and extreme, swelling the number of townsmen who were willing to sign a peace petition or attend a reform meeting.

In the first decade of the nineteenth century the challenge to the establishment, local as well as national, became closely associated with the activities of Joseph Hanson of Strangeways Hall, a radical manufacturer who advocated manhood suffrage and allied himself with the labouring ranks on such matters as wages and working conditions. Hanson was born in 1774, the son of a wealthy Manchester check manufacturer. The family were Unitarians and attended Stand chapel in Pilkington, just outside Manchester.[150] Hanson first

[146] Leary, Periodical Press, pp. 81, 87; Hone, *Cause of Truth*, pp. 103, 106, 110, 137, 150.
[147] Clare, 'Local newspaper press', pp. 107–8, 113–14.
[148] *Gazette*, 6 Feb., 16 April 1796; Leary, Periodical Press, pp. 84–5.
[149] G. W. Daniels, *The Cotton Trade during the Revolutionary and Napoleonic Wars* (1916), useful on the Manchester economy.
[150] 'Joseph Hanson', *Biographical References*; R. T. Herford, 'Joseph Hanson, the Weavers' Friend', *T.U.H.S.*, 8 (1943–6), pp. 17–26; *A Short Sketch or Memoir of the late Joseph Hanson Esq, of Strangeways Hall* (1811).

rose to public notice in November 1798 when he became involved in a dispute about the salaries and conduct of local officials. He urged Manchester leypayers to keep a clear check on what was done with public funds.[151] In 1803 Manchester was gripped by another wave of volunteer enthusiasm and Hanson raised his own unit, but by December 1805 he had become disillusioned with the movement. Units had originally been formed for good patriotic purposes, he said, but these had been lost sight of as men pursued personal and party ambitions. Hanson issued a shilling pamphlet (printed by William Cowdroy junior), in which he condemned such developments and advocated a reform of the volunteer establishment, new training methods and better allowances for clothing and attendance. A bitter pamphlet war ensued, with Hanson being accused of misrepresentation and disloyalty. Some of Hanson's supporters wrote in his defence.[152] His controversial career continued as he involved himself in the peace movement. In December 1807 he tried unsuccessfully to get the town officers to call a public meeting to petition for peace. He had prepared a petition of his own, dealing with the effects of the war on commerce and complaining about low wages, poverty and unemployment, a sign of Hanson's growing concern for the plight of the labouring ranks. Yet another phase of print warfare ensued after Hanson published a pamphlet in which he defended the peace movement. This work recited political and economic grievances, stressed the injustice and impolicy of continuing the war, and attacked the opponents of the peace and reform movements. The pamphlet gave a clear and forceful exposition of the views of Hanson and the rising number of Mancunians who were beginning to look upon him as their spokesman. It was a measure of Hanson's effectiveness that his work sold well and that the response to it by local Tories was so vitriolic. One reply came from Alfred Mallalieu, member of a prominent Tory cotton and literary family, who accused Hanson of espousing 'a doctrine which, if not absolutely

---

[151] Hanson's address to the leypayers (Nov. 1798) is in Hay Scrapbooks, xvi, pp. 317–18. A ley is a local tax.

[152] J. Hanson, *Brief Remarks on the Present Volunteer Establishment* (1805); 'A Volunteer', *Letter to Lieutenant Colonel Joseph Hanson, containing concise observations on his Brief Remarks* (1805); 'An Englishman', *A Letter to Lieutenant Colonel Joseph Hanson* (1806); 'An Advocate for Truth', *Cursory Strictures on the Concise Observations of a Volunteer* (1806).

French, is of French extraction, rendered more palatable by an English dress'.[153]

Meanwhile Hanson had been attempting to win a seat in the House of Commons. His opponents put this down to vanity and personal ambition, while supporters pointed to his desire to serve the people and look after their interests in parliament. He had previously presented himself as an independent candidate in Chester and Stafford, but failed in both boroughs after entering the field too late. He may have believed he had a better chance at Preston in the summer of 1807, but again he entered the field late. The wide potwalloper franchise nevertheless gave some cause for confidence. Hanson's involvement in the weavers' campaign for minimum wage legislation, and his independent, populist stance on other political and economic questions, assured him of a strong support base among the labouring ranks, but he was unable to extend his appeal to other groups of voters. The limited nature of his programme and the lateness of his arrival combined with the influence of the entrenched Stanley and corporation interests to deny Hanson the victory he sought, but he was gratified by the extent of his support among the common folk, his 'true constituents', and by the winning of over a thousand plumper votes.[154]

Hanson's greatest claim to fame rests on his championship of the handloom weavers' call for protective legislation. The weavers were probably suffering more than any other body of textile workers during the war. A labour surplus, falling wages and the disruptive social and psychological effects of developing industrialism left them vulnerable and discontented. Hanson had close personal contact with many weavers engaged in outwork around the Manchester district, and his family's firm was a substantial employer in the locality.

---

[153] *Gazette*, Dec. 1807–Jan. 1808; J. Hanson, *A Defence of the Petitions for Peace* (1807); A. Mallalieu, *Remarks on Joseph Hanson's Defence of the Petitions for Peace* (1808); *A Reply to the Real Writer of the Defence of the Petitions for Peace, comprehending a review of the Assumed Author's proceedings for some time past* (1808).

[154] *Short Memoir of Hanson*, pp. 12, 24–5; also addresses in the collection *Address of Joseph Hanson to his Friends and Country, with many particulars from the contested Election in Preston, till his return from the King's Bench* (1809): 'To the Cotton Weavers of Preston', 'To the Independent Electors of the Borough of Preston'. The potwalloper suffrage in Preston gave the vote to adult males who could prove six months' residence, were not a charge on the poor rate, and who 'had a family and boiled a pot' in the borough.

A bond of sentimental attachment seems to have grown up on both sides.[155] Hanson was certainly concerned about the plight of the workers. In his pamphlet on the volunteer movement he had urged that lower class recruits should be paid a fair rate for their time and involvement, and one of the basic motivations for his interest in peace petitioning was his desire to protect the dignity, independence and economic prospects of working people. When the possibility of a minimum wage bill for weavers was first seriously mooted early in 1807 Hanson was sympathetic, and he approved of the idea at the time of the Preston election that summer. By the winter of 1807–8 the weavers' leaders were beginning to consider wide scale and prolonged industrial action in an attempt to force the authorities to listen to their pleas. There was a solid strike throughout the Manchester area from May to June 1808. A minimum wage bill was drawn up and submitted for the consideration of the legislature, but was rejected.[156] Large protest meetings occurred in Manchester on 24 and 25 May 1808. Moved by the spectacle of poor and frustrated weavers walking to their meeting place on St George's Fields, Hanson ordered £40 worth of bread and refreshment to be distributed among them. He also decided to attend the meeting of 25 May and address those present. When disturbances followed this meeting the local authorities singled Hanson out for blame. It was suggested that his words had encouraged sedition and riot. He was indicted for a conspiracy, and tried in March 1809. Despite a weak case the prosecution was successful and Hanson was sentenced to six months' imprisonment and a £100 fine. Richard Potter was present at the trial and was struck by Hanson's impressive show of integrity, typified by his declaration: 'the consciousness of my innocence will enable me to support myself under this or any other punishment this honourable court might have thought proper to inflict'.[157]

By now Hanson had become a popular hero, and nearly 40,000 people subscribed to a fund to purchase the gold cup that was

[155] *Short Memoir of Hanson*, pp. 22–3.

[156] *Mercury*, 31 May 1808, for a copy. See also Bohstedt, *Riots and Community Politics*, ch. 6.

[157] *Short Memoir of Hanson*, p. 14; Herford, 'Joseph Hanson', pp. 19–20; *Address of Hanson to his Friends and Country*, pp. 34–52; *The Whole Proceedings on the Trial of Joseph Hanson . . . for conspiring to aid the weavers of Manchester in raising their wages* (1809); Potter Collection, xi. 3; Wheeler, *History*, pp. 103–4; Prentice, *Sketches*, pp. 31–3.

presented to him on his release.[158] Prison ruined his health, though, and he retired to a villa in Pendlebury. Before his death he did cooperate with the weavers' leaders once more, in 1811 when a petitioning movement for relief spread across the northern counties. He also went to London to give evidence to the parliamentary committee appointed to consider the weavers' distress. Hanson died in September 1811, aged only 37. Thousands turned out for his funeral.[159] His fame outlived him and his local reputation as 'the weavers' friend' lasted into this century. His activities, like those of Thomas Walker, provided later Manchester reformers with examples and encouragement. Members of the band admired Hanson greatly. Prentice called him 'impulsively benevolent',[160] and by including Hanson's career in the early chapters of his *Sketches* Prentice showed how Hanson's activity helped to further the 'progress of public opinion' in Manchester. It is surprising that Hanson has been neglected by historians of this period. John Bohstedt recognises his importance as a 'gentleman maverick' but gives Hanson only superficial attention in an account of Manchester affairs between 1790 and 1810. J. E. Cookson deems Hanson 'perhaps the archetypal popular leader' and 'the first in a long line of notable radical demagogues in early nineteenth-century Lancashire', and yet only really mentions him in passing.[161]

The final years of the war were years of economic hardship in Manchester, punctuated only by modest and temporary recoveries.[162] The Napoleonic decrees were still having some effect, as was the deterioration in Anglo-American relations. The liberal-Dissenting leaders were prominent in the petitioning campaigns against the Orders in Council in 1808 and 1812, and when these were withdrawn it was claimed as a great victory by many provincial reformers. In Manchester a further impulse for reformist activity came in 1812 and

---

[158] Hay Scrapbooks, ix, p. 176; Herford, 'Joseph Hanson', p. 24; *Short Memoir of Hanson*, pp. 15, 28; *Address of Hanson to his Friends and Country*, includes account of Hanson's return from prison, the presentation of the cup, and his reply to the 39,600 subscribers.
[159] Herford, 'Joseph Hanson', pp. 24–5; *Short Memoir of Hanson*, pp. 16–18, 20–21; Hay Scrapbooks, xiii. 7.
[160] Prentice, *Sketches*, p. 23.
[161] Cookson, *Friends of Peace*, pp. 187, 210; Bohstedt, *Riots and Community Politics*, pp. 82, 148, 150–52.
[162] Daniels, *Cotton Trade*, pp. 76, 78–81; C. Emsley, *British Society and the French Wars* (1979), pp. 130–32, 137–8, 153–7.

1813 from the political missionary tours of the veteran radical Major Cartwright. Cartwright visited Manchester and the nearby towns, and one of his most important contacts in the district was John Shuttleworth. The two men corresponded about reform petitions. Cartwright, Shuttleworth, Atkinson, Richard Potter and Thomas Walker were also involved in the affair of the Manchester Thirty-eight, helping to raise funds and organise legal defence. All thirty-eight defendants were acquitted of the charge of administering an illegal oath. The most prominent reformer among them was John Knight, a schoolmaster and former manufacturer who had been an active radical in the district for some time.[163] Continuing political controversy was a cause and a result of the Exchange Riot of 8 April 1812. In a period of social and economic hardship, the rulers of Manchester organised a loyal meeting in support of the Regent's decision to retain the Tory government in office. Constitutional restrictions on his power had lapsed and the respectable reformers had hoped for a new set of ministers, but their placarding of the town and their calls for a decisive expression of protest led to the disturbances of 8 April and, of course, to the accusation against J. E. Taylor that he had been the author of one of the offending handbills.[164]

Party feeling in Manchester was solidified by the formation of the Manchester Pitt Club in December 1812. This succeeded the A.P.C.O., which had ceased its activities in 1799, and provided the Tories with another large, active, central organising body to co-ordinate the local political activities of conservatives and anti-reformers.[165] The appearance of the club added to the party and sectarian enmity in Manchester which had recently been exacerbated by disputes over such matters as the education of the poor. During the winter of 1811–12 there was heated argument over the Tory-Anglican leaders' decision to establish two National Schools in Manchester and Salford. Some Lancasterians objected, and the correspondence pages of the local papers were full of comment.[166]

---

[163] Shuttleworth Scrapbook, loose leaves; Potter Collection, xiiiA, pp. 176, 181–3; *Trial of Thirty Eight Men*, especially Knight's introduction, pp. i–viii.
[164] Shuttleworth Scrapbook, loose leaves; Prentice, *Sketches*, pp. 48–52; Wheeler, *History*, p. 105; Smith, Reminiscences, p. 6; S. Bamford, *Autobiography*, ed. W. H. Chaloner (2 vols, 1967), i, *Early Days* (1849), pp. 295–7; Bohstedt, *Riots and Community Politics*, ch. 7.
[165] C.L.M., Manchester Pitt Club Papers, 1812–31 (3 vols); Prentice, *Sketches*, ch. 26 (supplementary chapter).
[166] e.g. *Exchange Herald*, 24 Dec. 1811, 7, 21, 28 Jan. 1812.

(Shuttleworth, Atkinson and Taylor participated in the administration of the Lancasterian School, established in 1809.) Tension increased as the region saw outbreaks of luddism. In south Lancashire the disturbances of these times involved not only machine breakers but criminals, food rioters, radicals and trade unionists as well as spies and *agents-provocateurs*. Lancashire luddism was a general protest movement. Its aims were not very clearly defined, and this made it possible for the authorities to believe that some political purpose lay behind the disturbances. Many informants were (or claimed to be) sure that industrial aims were a cover for something else, and some magistrates repeated this in their reports to the Home Office.[167]

Manchester's respectable reformers shared an equivocal attitude to the events of these years. It was pleasing that the Dissenters as a body had been taught a lesson by Sidmouth's bill to control the licensing of their preachers, for they now saw that quiet submission to the established authorities could do them more harm than good. It was also encouraging that many working people had been taught a lesson by what Prentice called a 'truthful teacher', want. They were abandoning their old unthinking allegiance to the established order.[168] But the release posed problems, and Manchester merchants and manufacturers could hardly express anything but disapproval for luddite excesses. This was true of reformers as well as conservatives. 'A starving people are seldom a reasoning people', Prentice later remarked. 'Ordinary suffering leads to inquiry as to its real cause, but destitution directs attention only to the nearest seeming cause'.[169] This led to the masters being identified as oppressors, when many of them were genuinely concerned about the problems of their employees. The band wanted to make this clear, and wanted

---

[167] On Lancashire luddism, M. Thomis, *The Luddites. Machine Breaking in Regency England* (1970), chs. 1, 2, 3, 6; F. O. Darvell, *Popular Disturbances and Public Order in Regency England* (1969), chs. 3, 5, 7–11, 14–16; J. R. Dinwiddy, 'Luddism and Politics in the Northern Counties', *S.H.*, 4 (1979), pp. 33–63; V. Tomlinson, 'Letters of a Lancashire Luddite transported to Australia, 1812–16', *T.L.C.A.S.*, 77 (1967), pp. 97–125; C. Calhoun, *The Question of Class Struggle: Social Foundations of Popular Radicalism during the Industrial Revolution* (1982), ch. 3; Emsley, *British Society*, ch. 8; J. R. Dinwiddy, *From Luddism to the First Reform Bill* (1986), pp. 19–27; R. Glen, *Urban Workers in the Early Industrial Revolution* (1984), chs. 7, 8.

[168] Prentice, *Sketches*, pp. 25, 34, 37–47.

[169] Prentice, *Sketches*, p. 47.

to highlight the *real* causes of and remedies for contemporary social, political and economic ills. This was why it was so important to educate and inform. The Exchange Riot is significant because this was one occasion when the respectable reformers did mobilise the lower ranks. Alarmed by the size and character of the crowd gathering on 8 April 1812, however, they dissociated themselves from the protest movement. Characteristic fear of plebeian involvement in politics prompted those who had fostered the opposition to the pro- government meeting at the Exchange to think twice about stepping forward as the leaders of this opposition. Yet, as Prentice recalled, the veteran reformer Thomas Kershaw (a calico printer who had acted with Walker in the 1790s) said that one good thing had come out of the Exchange Riot: 'we had no Church and King mobs after that'. Another of Prentice's acquaintances reflected that after this event 'the old dominant party appeared to feel that they had an opposition to contend with, and they became less arrogant in their conduct'.[170]

Predictably, the greatest blame for the problems of the war years and the immediate postwar period was reserved for the Tory government. 'No greater crime can be committed by rulers than to lunge into unnecessary wars, and to waste the blood and treasure of the community in avoidable and useless contests', declared Watkin in 1814.[171] In this and other statements and activities of band members here discussed, we can discern those features of their thought and approach to public questions that were most prominent in their postwar campaigns in Manchester. There was a readiness and desire to create and direct public opinion, to teach the distressed and discontented about the best ways of improving their condition, and

---

[170] Prentice, *Sketches*, pp. 48–52. John Bohstedt has suggested that the Exchange Riot was significant because it was the first time the reformers appeared to 'license' public political violence, whereas previous Manchester mobs had been at the beck and call of the local authorities and were anti-reform in temperament. Bohstedt, *Riots and Community Politics*, p. 161. This interpretation is questionable. Far from approving of the Exchange Riot, the respectable reformers wanted nothing to do with it and in fact did all they could to distance themselves from what occurred. Nor did 1812 mark the end of possible collective action against reformers. The years 1817 and 1819, for example, were to see an anti-reform belligerency that was every bit as strong as pro-reform, anti-authority sentiment.

[171] Watkin, 'The Wars against Napoleon' (a paper read to the Literary and Scientific Club), *Fragment No. 1*, p. 59.

to elucidate political anomalies and social injustices that needed to be removed. There was the identification of the Tory ministers and their local adherents as the villains of the piece. There was the recognition of the need to mobilise numbers, and the willingness to do so, but the suspicion that those mobilised might be uncontrollable once set in motion. The band aimed to recruit followers from lower social strata, but wanted to make sure that these followers would not go beyond the programmes formulated on their behalf.

The political conflicts and controversies which raged in Manchester from 1815 to 1832 took place in a town undergoing enormous social and economic change. The population was rising rapidly, as was Manchester's industrial and commercial importance. The local business community spearheaded this expansion and seized on the advantages it made available, growing in wealth, pride and assertiveness, and looking forward to the time when commercial men could shape national affairs as well as those of Manchester itself. This was particularly true of the liberal-Dissenting body within the respectable business community. For years this body had resented its almost total exclusion from the local power structure, and during the decades after the end of the war it channelled this resentment into positive action and launched a determined assault on local Tory dominance. It was members of the band, 'missionaries of a new enlightenment' in Donald Read's phrase,[172] who stimulated and led most of the protest and assertive activities of Manchester's respectable middle-class and middling sort reformers after the war. They were a distinctive group. They were young, mostly non-Mancunians, and with the exception of the attorney Atkinson they were all initially cotton merchants or manufacturers. Socially they were upwardly mobile. In religion they were Protestant Dissenters, particularly Unitarians. Only Watkin was an Anglican. They were a serious-minded and public-spirited set of rational, Christian, liberal reformers, conscious of prevalent injustice, and strongly moved by the moral impulses which they believed should be behind the drive for political and social improvement. David Prentice, cousin of Archibald, could have been speaking for the band when he wrote in 1832: 'As every case of morals is included in the Divine injunction, to do to others as we would have others do to us, so every difficulty

---

[172] D. Read, *Peterloo: The Massacre and its Background* (1973), p. 62.

in politics is obviated by the maxim that what is morally wrong can never be politically right.' [173] The band tended towards political liberalism in response to several factors, especially the existence of local and national structures of influence which excluded any groups subscribing to political or religious heterodoxies. The band's non-conformity, provincial and class pride, economic and social prominence, intellectual and cultural pursuits, individual and collective assertiveness, and belief in the Benthamite principle that what was participated in by all would be to the benefit of all, gave this progressive vanguard the power, cohesion, permanence and will to succeed that was to be indispensable to Manchester reformers as a party when they challenged the local rulers after 1815. External and internal circumstances combined to make members of the band the disturbers of the accepted, the challengers of established authorities and ideas. They denied that institutions were sacrosanct in themselves, and asserted that what really mattered was the way institutions were used and the character of those who did the using. Peterloo confirmed these beliefs and strengthened the respectable reformers' readiness to act. The massacre also enlarged the number of people willing to join them.

Following S. G. Checkland, we might identify two ways of looking at radicalism. We might concentrate on the 'heroic' aspects, and regard the radical as a spontaneous phenomenon, a person who can see how society must be changed and who can impose himself on events and carry them in a chosen direction. Or we might concentrate on the 'social' aspects, and decide that it is the trends within society that produce both a radical point of view and its skilled and powerful spokesmen, men who are not prime movers (as they might think) but 'simply the most susceptible and effective among the moved'.[174] Both sets of influences helped in the making of the band. Baylen and Gossman have pointed out that radicalism cannot be defined by looking at issues alone. Much was illogical and much depended on personality and temperament. Radicalism was 'less a programme than a state of mind, a sense of moral outrage against privilege, waste and abuse of power'. There had to be a desire for change, a rejection of arguments based on custom and tradition. Radicals tended to belong to self-conscious and aggressive

---

[173] D. Prentice, *Letter to the Electors of the West of Scotland* (1832), pp. 2–3.
[174] S. G. Checkland's review of D. Read, *Cobden and Bright. A Victorian Political Partnership* (1967), in *Ec.H.R.*, 22 (1969), pp. 149–50.

groups 'who saw themselves as outsiders and drew spiritual nourishment from a Christian concept of mankind's duty to act on the command of conscience'.[175] Again, these remarks clearly apply to the 'small but determined band'.

---

[175] Baylen and Gossman, *Modern British Radicals*, introduction, especially i, p. 5.

11 *The Band and the Manchester Newspaper Press*

1. THE DEVELOPING PROVINCIAL PRESS

Much has been written about the influence achieved by provincial newspapers before the early Victorian age. One contemporary wrote in 1836 that provincial papers 'have now a sway and importance far greater than is commonly assigned to them',[1] and more recent commentators have painted a picture of a politicised and politically influential provincial press at work well before the end of the eighteenth century.[2] Though the press did not achieve the status and dignity of a 'Fourth Estate' until after the middle of the nineteenth century,[3] newspaper influence and an expanding readership were increasingly perceptible from the 1790s. It is difficult to determine exactly when provincial newspapers began to devote attention and space to public affairs, both local and national. The change from a mere advertising sheet, from pages filled with trivia and items of ephemeral interest, with no editorial comment, limited local intelligence and only out-of-date news taken from London papers, to the well-organised paper giving more coverage to events of local and national importance, and informed comment on those events, with clarity and good literary style, was a change that took decades to be accomplished. Perhaps the decisive period,

---

[1] 'The Journals of the Provinces', *Colburn's New Monthly Magazine and Literary Journal*, xlviii (1836), pp. 137–8; see also J. Grant, *The Newspaper Press. Its origins, progress and present position* (3 vols, 1871–2), iii, ch. 9.
[2] e.g. G. A. Cranfield, *The Development of the Provincial Newspaper* (1962), pp. 117–21, 271. See also J. Brewer, 'The Press in the 1760s' and 'The politicians, the press and the public', in his *Party Ideology and Popular Politics at the accession of George III* (1976), pp. 139–60, 219–39; I. R. Christie, 'British Newspapers in the Later Georgian Age', in his *Myth and Reality in Late Eighteenth Century British Politics* (1970), pp. 311–33.
[3] G. Boyce, 'The Fourth Estate: the reappraisal of a concept', in *Newspaper History*, eds G. Boyce, J. Curran, P. Wingate (1978), pp. 17–38.

when change occurred quickest for the provincial newspaper (as for many other aspects of social thought and practice), came in the years 1790–1820. The events of these years created an unprecedented level of interest in public affairs and a rising demand for information. The *Manchester Herald* in 1792–93 and Cowdroy's *Gazette* from 1795 were both distinguished for their coverage of and comment upon important public issues. They appealed to and represented Manchester's reformers. To some extent they were preaching to the converted, reflecting a body of liberal opinion that already existed in the neighbourhood. But they also helped to enlarge the number of people who were at least partly receptive to the reformers' doctrines and arguments. By popularising opinions, identifying abuses and injustices, and appealing for the exercise of reason rather than bias and intolerance on the part of the reader, the *Herald* and *Gazette* made people think and for this they incurred the wrath of Manchester's ruling party. In most cases, of course, newspapers and public opinion had a symbiotic relationship. Most newspapers were as much led by public opinion as they were leaders of that opinion. The important point about members of the band, and especially Prentice, is that they were determined to be leaders not followers.

It was many years before journalism was accorded the dignity and reputation of a respectable profession. Only in the 1820s and 1830s did editors and proprietors come to be regarded as 'gentlemen', and their rise from an inferior social status had been a slow one. Too many had gone in for scurrility, blasphemy and falsehood in their attempts to satisfy the baser appetites of a reading public which, if it was interested in public affairs, was no less interested in being entertained by prurient and sensationalist matter. Respectable society regarded newspapermen as unscrupulous adventurers who lacked business acumen, integrity and good family connections. They seemed to be irresponsible, dishonest and immoral, and were especially unpopular amongst politicians.[4] But in time the situation changed. The early nineteenth century saw more men of education and literary talent engaging in newspaper work. Their conduct came

[4] A. Aspinall, 'The Social Status of Journalists at the beginning of the Nineteenth Century', *Review of English Studies*, 21 (1945), 216–32; Grant, *Newspaper Press*, i, pp. 229–30, ii, p. 452; A. J. Lee, *The Origins of the Popular Press 1855–1914* (1976), pp. 104–17; L. Brown, *Victorian News and Newspapers* (1985), pp. 75–8.

The character of the profession was raised both

to be regarded as more acceptable and they themselves became more respected socially. The character of the profession was raised both in London and the provinces. The *Westminster Review* stated in 1829 that 'the general character of the Newspaper Press is high and honourable'.[5] Provincial editors began to be known for their deep knowledge of public affairs, devoted many hours to political reading, and familiarised themselves with all relevant statistics, issues and arguments. By the 1830s, suggests G. A. Cranfield, provincial newspapers had taken their place among the most prominent agents influencing the course of local and national affairs. They were nearly all devoting considerable space to such affairs, and 'had now completely abandoned any pretence to neutrality'.[6] This was certainly true of Manchester. It is noteworthy that newspapermen were increasingly regarded as respectable at the same time as their papers (and they) were becoming more politically partisan.

Along with developments in editorial techniques and the art of presentation came developments in production, organisation and printing methods. The Stanhope iron hand press (the first model used by the *Guardian*) was invented in 1798, and improved versions (the Columbian, Albion and Imperial) were made available in the early decades of the nineteenth century, though these did not greatly increase the rate of output. The iron hand press was not capable of more than 250 impressions an hour. The Koenig steam press, capable of 1,000 impressions an hour, was patented in 1811. Provincial proprietors did not have the money of their London counterparts and were slower to introduce new technology. In any case the lower circulations of their papers did not necessitate a conversion to steam for decades to come.[7] The first two provincial papers to have steam presses were both Manchester papers, Sowler's Tory *Courier* from 1825, and the *Guardian* from 1828. Another feature of the advancing newspaper press was the growth of trade unionism among the

[5] 'The Newspaper Press', *Westminster Review*, xix, 10 (Jan. 1829), pp. 233–4.
[6] 'Journals of the Provinces', pp. 139–41; E. Porritt, 'Newspaper Work when the Century was young', *Sell's Dictionary of the World's Press*, (1896), pp. 17–29; G. A. Cranfield, *The Press and Society from Caxton to Northcliffe* (1978), pp. 198, 201.
[7] E. Howe, *Newspaper Printing in the Nineteenth Century* (1943), pp. 1–8; A. E. Musson, 'Newspaper Printing in the Industrial Revolution', *Ec.H.R.*, 10 (1957–8), pp. 411–26; I. Asquith, 'The structure, ownership and control of the press 1780–1855', in Boyce et al., *Newspaper History*, pp. 98–115.

workforce. Manchester had a small but active printers' association from the 1790s.[8]

A provincial newspaper could be very expensive to run, and advertising income was therefore essential. Charles Knight, of the Society for the Diffusion of Useful Knowledge, estimated in 1836 that a provincial newspaper without advertisements would have to sell 3,500 copies just to break even.[9] The vast majority of provincials sold less than a thousand copies a week. This helps to explain why many provincial proprietors were also printers. A small circulation paper could not normally generate enough income to exist as an independent enterprise, but it could supply useful additional revenue to a printer. Costs could be covered by the printing business as a whole rather than by the newspaper alone. Newspapermen valued advertisements as a source of income and also because they helped to increase a paper's circulation. Certain kinds of notice attracted certain kinds of reader, and increasing circulation in turn attracted advertising customers.[10]

It is clear that newspaper reading was becoming one of the prevalent habits of the age, and it was not confined to one particular social rank. Anyone who wanted access to newspapers could find it. Sales figures were not readership figures, and the stamp meant that newspapers could have free use of the postal service. Asa Briggs has pointed out that taxation 'was sometimes less burdensome than a first glance might suggest'.[11] One commentator in 1836 thought that a single newspaper was read by ten to twenty different people. In 1830 the *Westminster Review* stated that 'each copy of a liberal newspaper printed in Manchester has from fifty to eighty readers'. Though this figure was high, it was supported by 'persons likely to be well-acquainted with the fact'.[12]

---

[8] A. E. Musson, *The Typographical Association. Origins and History up to 1949* (1954), pp. 3–15, 27–33; *Manchester Typographical Society 1797–1897. Centenary Record* (1897), which praised 'the energy, the foresight, the determination to combine' of early Manchester letterpress printers (pp. 6–7).
[9] C. Knight, *The Newspaper Stamp and the Duty on Paper* (1836), p. 41, cited in T. R. Nevett, *Advertising in Britain. A History* (1982), p. 48.
[10] Nevett, *Advertising in Britain*, p. 48; Cranfield, *Press and Society*, pp. 184–6; Brown, *Victorian News*, p. 23.
[11] A. Briggs, 'Press and Public in early nineteenth-century Birmingham', *Occasional Papers of the Dugdale Society*, 8 (1949), p. 115.
[12] 'Journals of the Provinces', p. 142; 'The Provincial, Scotch and Irish Newspaper Press', *Westminster Review*, III, 12 (Jan. 1830), p. 74.

2. THE FOUNDATION OF THE
MANCHESTER GUARDIAN

When members of the band began to participate in Manchester affairs during the last years of the war, they were in no doubt as to the importance of the press in the task of forming and directing local opinion. The examples set by the *Herald* and *Gazette* suggested that a well-conducted newspaper with a vigorous, explicitly reformist editorial line could be the most powerful weapon in the Manchester liberals' arsenal. If the *Herald* and *Gazette* had been forerunners, however, it was left to the band to establish the genuine article, a newspaper that would enjoy a long life and a wide readership, and give far more space to political news and comment than any provincial weekly had ever done before. The band wanted a newspaper that would gain the backing of much respectable opinion in Manchester, and at the same time exercise a directing influence over men of lower social strata (sometimes encouraging, sometimes restraining, according to prevalent circumstances). Such a paper would use the force of opinion in campaigns for reform, and help to overthrow the forces of reaction and intolerance that were locally and nationally dominant. The *Guardian* was originally conceived in these terms. Unfortunately it failed to live up to such expectations, and this led to disagreements within the band about the way it was being conducted. The more advanced reformers in the band decided to abandon the *Guardian* and look elsewhere for an effective newspaper organ, and this gave yet another stimulus to the development of political journalism in Manchester.

For many years it was to Cowdroy's *Gazette* that Manchester reformers looked for information and guidance. By 1812 Shuttleworth and Taylor were writing articles for the elder William Cowdroy, who died in November 1814 and was succeeded as proprietor and editor by William Cowdroy junior. Prentice began to write for the *Gazette* after settling in Manchester in January 1815. On one occasion he asked Cowdroy junior if he ever felt he should refuse to insert some of the less restrained items submitted by his young and enthusiastic contributors. Did he not fear indictments? 'Not I', Cowdroy replied, 'write away'. Despite Cowdroy's courage, though, the authorities' attitude towards the liberal press in the years after 1815 did sometimes prompt his contributors to tone down their articles for his sake.[13] Political tension in Manchester increased as the band, this new crop of young, energetic, respectable and affluent liberal-Dissenting leaders, emerged to articulate grievances and to campaign for change. The ruling party was always keen to strike a blow against its challengers, and one opportunity came in July 1818 when Taylor was passed over for the minor office of assessor at a meeting of Salford police commissioners. He was considered to be unsuitable because he was a reformer and, allegedly, the author of the handbill which had caused the Exchange Riot six years earlier. This latter accusation was made by a prominent Tory manufacturer, John Greenwood. Taylor denied all connection with the handbill, but his demands for an apology came to nothing. Determined to uphold his good name, he made the matter public and condemned Greenwood as 'a liar, slanderer and scoundrel'. He was indicted for libel and the case was heard at Lancaster in March 1819. Taylor conducted his own defence, advised by the lawyer Atkinson. Prentice and Brotherton gave evidence on his behalf, and others of the band were in court to give moral support. The verdict of 'not guilty' was a victory for the band and for Taylor.[14] He had shown courage and had emerged with credit from the affair, and he and his friends could carry on their political campaigns with the assurance that their opponents were not unassailable. Importantly, Taylor's performance led his friends to think that he might have the talents and principles that would make him a fine newspaper editor.

By now Taylor had been writing for the *Gazette* for about seven years. His interest in political journalism had no doubt been encouraged back in 1813, when he visited Leigh Hunt of the radical London *Examiner* during the latter's two-year prison sentence for a libel on the Prince Regent.[15] The agitations of 1817 and 1819 were also influential, and Taylor made an important contribution to the post-Peterloo protest with his *Notes and Observations*. By this time the *Gazette* was heavily reliant on Taylor and Prentice for its best

[13] Prentice, *Sketches*, p. 109; Mills, *Guardian History*, pp. 20–1.
[14] Prentice, *Sketches*, pp. 132–45; Mills, *Guardian History*, pp. 30–33; F. S. Stancliffe, *John Shaw's 1738–1938* (1938), p. 161; Gazette, 25 July 1818, 3 April 1819; *Chronicle*, 31 Oct. 1818, 10 April 1819; *Mercury*, 4 Aug. 1818; Ayerst, *Guardian Biography*, pp. 15–16; *Trial of J. E. Taylor*, pp. 3–10 for Taylor's introduction, pp. 24–5 for Brotherton's evidence, p. 27 for Prentice's evidence.
[15] Ayerst, *Guardian Biography*, p. 17; Mills, *Guardian History*, pp. 8–9.

political pieces, and both men seem to have sent accounts of Peterloo to the London papers immediately after the event. These helped to establish the 'radical version' of Peterloo long before any official version was presented. (Taylor later modified his view of Peterloo, and this may have contributed to his estrangement from Prentice.)[16] Peterloo gave members of the band an opportunity and a motive to step up their activities, and the number of people who were prepared to act with them rose considerably, such was the outrage created by this event. The band entered the 1820s with enlarged prospects for the exercising of influence. In order to exploit these opportunities it was important to have the right equipment, and a vigorous reform newspaper was the top priority. It is also possible that these liberals, as propertied and well-to-do cotton businessmen, wanted to give reform campaigns a more respectable character and, importantly, a more respectable leadership. The excesses of popular radicalism in the preceding years had convinced many that calm discussion was better than mass meetings and wild speeches. Such calm and rational discussion could be led by a newspaper in which the band would express its opinions accurately and effectively.

Prentice and the more advanced reformers in the band decided that the *Gazette* could and should be converted into a more efficient organ of liberal principles. The advice of John Smith of the *Liverpool Mercury* and Edward Baines of the *Leeds Mercury* was sought, and Prentice also consulted the proprietors of the *Scotsman* and his own cousin David Prentice, editor of the *Glasgow Chronicle* between 1811–37. The first plan was to buy the *Gazette* and keep Cowdroy on as printer and publisher. The wealthier members of the band and some of their prosperous friends and business partners, mostly Unitarians, agreed to advance the sums that would be needed, and Taylor was spoken of as prospective editor. According to Prentice, Taylor was chosen because he was the only member of the band not fully occupied with business concerns, and because he seemed to have the qualities required in a spirited advocate of reform.[17] For some reason Prentice makes no mention of Taylor's undoubted talent as a writer and the role this must have played in prompting

---

[16] Taylor's changing position on Peterloo has been investigated in R. Walmsley, *Peterloo. The Case Reopened* (1969), especially chs. 19, 30; see also Local History Dept. M.C.L., unpublished ms. copies of Walmsley's 'Peterloo Magistrate' (1967) and 'The Peterloo Reopener and his Critics' (1969).

[17] Prentice, *Sketches*, pp. 202–3.

others to see him as a newspaper editor. Perhaps Prentice was jealous
that he himself was not selected. To be fair, however, there is no
evidence that he sought the editorship or had any desire at this time
to leave his muslin warehouse in Peel Street. In any case, negotiations
with Cowdroy failed and this made it necessary to establish a completely new paper.[18] The risk fell on the creditors who agreed that
their money should be repaid only if the new paper was a success.
This arrangement was helpful, since the reformers knew that their
paper would be in advance of public opinion and would need time
to establish itself. Ten men put up £100 each and an eleventh put up
£50. Baxter and the Potters were among those contributing to the
loan. The more advanced members of the band never expected the
new paper to be cautious, or Taylor to need spurring on. Yet the
prospectus of the new *Guardian*, which appeared in the spring of
1821, was disappointingly vague and moderate. Some in the band
argued that care and patience were needed, that potential advertisers
should not be alienated and that it was best to wait for the right
opportunities to spread reformist ideas. But Prentice was surprised
that even before the first issue of the *Guardian* had appeared, business considerations were held to be almost as important as the
paper's political content.[19]

The first issue appeared on 5 May 1821. At first the newspaper
made slow progress. Cowdroy's regular readers preferred to stay
with the *Gazette*, and Wheeler's *Chronicle* remained the most
popular paper with advertisers, as it had been for many years. Some
of those connected with the *Guardian* were initially discouraged.
This may have made them more willing to conciliate readers and
advertisers, though obviously they hoped they could avoid any
sacrifice of principle. But as Taylor looked for ways to make the
paper more acceptable to the influential, so the road down which he
took it became more objectionable to other members of the band.
Prentice was certain that the slow progress of the *Guardian* made

---

[18] Cowdroy was still only 46 but died within a year of his refusal to sell the
Gazette, in March 1822. W. E. A. Axon, *The Annals of Manchester* (1886),
p. 165; C. H. Timperley, *Manchester Historical Recorder* (1874), p. 87. Had
Cowdroy died earlier the *Guardian* might never have been started, because
his widow would probably have sold up as she did in 1824 when an offer was
made by Prentice.
[19] Read, *Press and People*, pp. 79–82; Ayerst, *Guardian Biography*, pp. 22–3;
Prospectus of the Manchester Guardian (1821); Prentice, *Sketches*, pp. 202–7.

Taylor more cautious in his liberalism.[20] The paper only prospered after the Dicas trial of March 1823, which confirmed that the *Guardian* was going to be a commercial undertaking as well as, or even instead of, a political one. John Dicas was a former Manchester attorney who had been imprisoned for fraud and who, by 1823, had set up as a banker in Flintshire. Some of his banknotes found their way to Manchester and Taylor warned about his past, suggesting that these notes could not be trusted. This was an important warning at a time when the local business community was concerned about the unsound currency and banking system of the country. Dicas took Taylor to court for libel but gained only derisory damages, and grateful Manchester businessmen helped Taylor to pay his legal costs.[21] After the trial the direction in which the *Guardian* was going seemed abundantly clear. As Prentice recalled: 'The paper had the advantage, from that time, of being considered the guardian of the commercial interests of the town and neighbourhood – a reputation much more valuable, in a pecuniary point-of-view, than the fame of being the advocate of popular rights'.[22] The *Guardian* began to make money and Taylor was soon able to pay back the £1,050 advanced for the paper's establishment. He returned the last part of the loan in May 1824.[23] Now he was sole and independent proprietor as well as editor. He could do what he wanted with the *Guardian*.

Taylor had a clear and fixed approach to journalism. He liked to have a dialogue with his readers, and did not want to appeal only to men of one political grouping. His cousin and fiancée, Sophia Scott, wrote only days after the appearance of the first *Guardian* that Taylor had received 'encouragement from all parties', very gratifying in view of 'all the party feeling which has existed'. Taylor himself stated in the first *Guardian* that political comments would be made in such a way 'that even our political opponents shall admit the propriety of the spirit in which they are written, however fundamentally they may differ from their own principles and views'.[24] Prentice

[20] Prentice, *Sketches*, pp. 208, 228–9.
[21] *Guardian*, 7 Sept. 1822, 1 Feb., 29 March, 12 April, 7 June 1823; *Mercury*, 25 March 1823; Read, *Press and People*, pp. 83–4.
[22] Prentice, *Sketches*, pp. 239–40.
[23] Ayerst, *Guardian Biography*, p. 53.
[24] S. Scott to R. Scott, 8 May 1821, in Scott, *Family Biography*, p. 184; *Guardian*, 5 May 1821.

was not the only one in the band to be dissatisfied with Taylor's management of the *Guardian*, but he was probably the first to express his misgivings with any force. Prentice's criticism of Taylor was made all the more heated by other quarrels between them. They argued in May 1821 over Taylor's Malthusian stance on poor law reform, for example, and soon afterwards over his eagerness to appear reasonable and respectable to Tories who sat on the Market Street Commission, the street improvement body of which Taylor was also a member.[25] Taylor and Prentice had originally been fairly close friends. They had lived next door to each other for a time in Islington Street, Salford, and Taylor was one of those who had first introduced Prentice to the rest of the band. But Prentice was touchy on the matter of allegiance to principles. He believed that to abandon sound aims and opinions and to turn one's back on the cause of the people was to give up all claims to the trust, confidence and admiration of others. Prentice stayed true to the reform cause and attacked Taylor because he thought Taylor had strayed from it,[26] and the criticism became more insistent after July 1824 when Prentice became a newspaper editor in direct competition with the *Guardian*.

Though Prentice and others were disappointed by the *Guardian*'s politics, as a provincial newspaper it set high standards from its first issue. Printed and published from offices at 29 Market Street (and then 64 Market Street from February 1831), it was a well-organised, neatly laid-out newspaper containing a balanced mixture of news and comment. There is no doubt that it was a trend-setter in provincial journalism and that other papers to some extent followed and tried to emulate its techniques and presentation. But not everything the *Guardian* did was new. Donald Read has said that in its use of editorial articles the *Guardian* 'was breaking virtually new ground in Manchester journalism'.[27] This is questionable, for the *Herald* and *Gazette* had both given regular and detailed editorial comment. The *Guardian* did not really innovate in this field, but did confirm that the editorial would be a regular and recognised feature of the provincial weekly. Taylor's assistant was Jeremiah Garnett, a production manager who had practical experience of printing and newspaper

---

[25] Prentice, *Sketches*, pp. 209–10, 212–15.
[26] Taylor's obituary in *Guardian*, 10 Jan. 1844 (probably written by his partner Jeremiah Garnett), denied that he had retreated from an advanced reforming liberalism.
[27] Read, introduction to Prentice's *Sketches*, p. viii.

work. He had formerly worked for the Manchester *Chronicle*. Garnett was to become a full partner and for forty years took on much of the reporting and production work at the paper. He was the son of an Otley paper manufacturer, a Unitarian like Taylor, a moderate reformer and the originator of an effective shorthand style which enhanced the *Guardian*'s reputation for good reporting. Taylor's literary skills also contributed to the *Guardian*'s progress. As his fiancée said in 1821, 'he writes and composes with greater facility than any person I ever saw', and the writer of one obituary notice after Taylor's death pointed out that although some disliked the editorial line he had followed, nobody could deny that his writing was of the highest standard.[28]

As did other provincial weeklies the *Guardian* laboured under duties on paper and advertisements as well as the 4d. stamp duty, which necessitated a charge of 7d. for each issue. Early income from sales was not high, which made advertising revenue important and also forced Taylor to offer printing services, as his competitors did. The workforce was small to begin with, but grew as the *Guardian* prospered. Late in 1825 Taylor purchased a Columbian press, a slight improvement on the Stanhope model, and in 1828 he installed a steam press. By now the *Guardian* was selling 3,000 copies a week, and a steam press was essential if Taylor was to keep up with demand.[29] The appointment in 1830 of the *Guardian*'s first full-time reporter, John Harland, another Unitarian and formerly a printer with the *Hull Packet*,[30] was the first stage in a greater specialisation of functions at the *Guardian* (and soon at other provincial weeklies). To some extent staff remained interchangeable, which led to problems with the Manchester Typographical Society on matters such as wages and functions, but no serious disputes occurred.[31] Taylor recognised that if the *Guardian* was going to be a success it would have to give readers what they wanted. This was why there could be no total devotion to politics. Politics would be featured, but not to

[28] Scott, *Family Biography*, p. 184; Mills, *Guardian History*, p. 55; 'Brief Memoir of Taylor', (possibly written by Shuttleworth), pp. 14–15.
[29] Ayerst, *Guardian Biography*, pp. 23, 25–30; Slugg, *Reminiscences*, pp. 283–7; Brown, *Victorian News*, p. 38; Mills, *Guardian History*, pp. 44–8, 64.
[30] Read, *Press and People*, pp. 86–7, and 'John Harland: the father of provincial reporting', *M.R.*, 8 (1957–9), pp. 205–12; Local History Dept. M.C.L., John Harland, Harland Annals 1806–68 (microfiche), pp. 8–9 and entries for 1820–32.
[31] *Manchester Typographical Society Centenary Record*, pp. 8–12.

the exclusion of other material. Above all it was to be journalistic excellence that was to make the *Guardian*'s reputation, and in some ways the other Manchester papers followed the lead of their newest competitor in improving their style and presentation. This was necessary to retain readers. By the time of Taylor's death in 1844, says W. H. Mills, 'the Guardian was respected for fulness and accuracy of news, but was not read for ideas'.[32]

In its early years the two outside pages of the *Guardian* were made up and printed by Thursday night or midday on Friday, ready for publication on the Saturday. The first page was normally devoted to advertisements. If there were not enough to fill it the page would be left open until the last minute in the hope that more would be sent in. Wheeler of the *Chronicle* would not accept any notices after 1 p.m. on a Friday, but the *Guardian* would often accept advertisements up to the very moment of going to press. The back page would be given to miscellaneous items of news and trivia, letters to the editor, and such regular features as a weekly list of bankruptcies. Apart from regular features and any important news stories, much of the matter appearing on the back page was of a kind that could be held over if there was unexpected pressure on space. Friday was a busy day because of the arrival of the London mail. The two inside pages would be kept open until late in the evening so that the latest foreign news, parliamentary reports and commercial information could be inserted. The inside pages might carry accounts of the stock exchange, the Liverpool cotton market and various other commodity markets. Leading articles appeared on the inside pages. They normally dealt with national or international politics, local issues and important commercial questions. Their position on the inside pages made it possible for them to be written on Friday night, or brought up to date if they had been written earlier.[33]

Perhaps it was inevitable that the *Guardian* should have been closely identified with the local business community. That community would have to provide Taylor with most of his readers and advertising customers, and he was bound to try and give it the kind of newspaper it wanted. It is also significant that the proprietors of all the other Manchester papers were primarily printers or book-

---

[32] Mills, *Guardian History*, p. 38; see also his 'Manchester and its Press', in *The Soul of Manchester*, ed. W. H. Brindley (1974), p. 158.
[33] See *Guardian* from May 1821 onwards; Ayerst, *Guardian Biography*, pp. 30–8; Mills, *Guardian History*, p. 37.

sellers, while Taylor and his circle had long been involved in various branches of the textile trade. Taylor himself had started out as a manufacturer's apprentice and was later in partnership with Shuttleworth as a cotton and twist dealer, Watkin and Smith were cotton merchants, the Potters traded in fustians, linens and cotton goods, Baxter in ginghams and shirtings, Brotherton and Harvey were master spinners and Prentice a muslin merchant. Taylor soon set himself up as an expert on commercial affairs, printing lengthy articles in the *Guardian* on labour relations, the currency, market trends, and the causes of and remedies for business depressions. Occasionally the paper also carried articles on trade by some of Taylor's circle (Shuttleworth, for example, though his contributions dwindled from the mid-1820s, supporting the idea of a rift between Taylor and others in the band). From its earliest issues the *Guardian* seemed determined to serve the business community. Taylor and Garnett both subscribed to the Exchange and Garnett was often to be found there, gathering information and assessing opinion. *Dicas v. Taylor* signified and confirmed the bond between the *Guardian* and the Manchester business community. So did Taylor's coverage of the activities, meetings and campaigns of the Manchester Chamber of Commerce.[34] In 1921, the centenary year of the *Guardian*'s establishment, president of the chamber, Sir Edwin Stockton, sent the best wishes of that body to the paper's editor C. P. Scott, Taylor's nephew, and assured him of the great service the *Guardian* was still doing to local commerce. If not for the *Guardian* Manchester businessmen would have been 'as a rudderless ship on an uncharted ocean'.[35] Such remarks demonstrate that Taylor's ambitions and hopes for his paper had been completely fulfilled.

[34] L. S. Marshall thinks that the establishment of the chamber in 1820 and of the *Guardian* in 1821 were to have a controlling influence on the social, political and economic development of Manchester in the nineteenth century. They demonstrated that 'liberalism' was to dominate. See Marshall, *Public Opinion*, chs. 7, 9, 10. Such a thesis is open to question, not least because liberalism was only one of many creeds influencing social, political and economic thought and activity in nineteenth-century Manchester, and it could be argued that liberalism never achieved ascendancy. Marshall's timescale is defective in any case. There were relatively few liberals in Manchester in the 1820s.

[35] Stockton's remarks were reported in *Manchester Chamber of Commerce Monthly Record*, 32 (1921).

Sales of the *Guardian* were initially about 1,000 a week. They reached 2,000 by the end of 1823, and 3,000 in 1825.[36] The first issue of the *Guardian* contained 47 advertisements, but the weekly average for 1821 as a whole was 31.[37] The average for 1822 was 39 advertisements per issue and for 1823 (the year of the Dicas trial) 65. Late in December 1823 the *Guardian* carried 100 notices in a single issue, the target Taylor had long been setting himself. On 28 December he told his fiancée that he had been 'astonished' at the number of advertisements. He also said he had decided to purchase some small type 'to enable me to compress the advertisements into less compass. This will be an expense of £150 or £170, which I did not intend incurring at present; however, I really cannot say that I regret being obliged to do so'. Certainly the *Guardian* was doing well. All expenses were being covered by newspaper profits and by job printing, and Taylor expected a net profit of £550 for the second half of 1823.[38] In 1824 the *Guardian*'s number of advertisements per issue hardly fell below 80 and was sometimes over 100, the yearly average being 85. The average for 1825 was 104, for 1826 it was 125, and 136 for 1827 and 1828. The average for 1829 and 1830 was 143 and for 1831 was 158. In May 1832 the paper contained over 200 advertisements for the first time. The average for 1832 was 184. Most advertisements were for medicines, new publications, lotteries, such services as shipping and coaches, property for sale, private schools, entertainments, missing persons, situations vacant, and there were also official announcements from the Manchester police office or in the form of resolutions passed at important town meetings. Sometimes local politicians would address the public on important matters, and their statements took the form of advertisements and were carried on the front page. It is clear that the *Guardian*'s reputation and circulation made it attractive to advertisers. The lawyer George Hadfield, a Congregationalist and an ally of the band from the early 1820s, was disappointed by the *Guardian*'s politics and yet 'I was an ardent supporter by Adverts'.[39] Even though Taylor's services had

---

[36] Read, *Press and People*, appendix p. 211; Ayerst, *Guardian Biography*, p. 38; A. P. Wadsworth, 'Newspaper Circulations 1800–1954', *T.M.S.S.*, (1954–5), pp. 1–15.
[37] These averages are based on figures collected for every fourth issue of the *Guardian*.
[38] Taylor to Sophia Scott, 28 Dec. 1823, in Scott, *Family Biography*, p. 189.
[39] Hadfield, Personal Narrative, pp. 67, 81.

been lost to the advanced reformers, Hadfield recognised that Taylor's paper was a good one in which to advertise.

3. ARCHIBALD PRENTICE
AND HIS NEWSPAPERS

There is no doubt that Prentice's ceaseless agitation for reforms, on the platform as well as in print, helped to create an environment in which the band and its allies could realistically hope to exercise some influence on the course of local events. Although we should be wary of the self-praise exhibited occasionally in his own writings, it does seem that Prentice played a significant role in the informing and directing of local opinion, and in view of this his relative neglect by historians is puzzling. It is difficult to determine precisely how important his role was, though Prentice himself was pleased and satisfied in 1850 that he could look back on his career and see that many of the principles he had consistently advocated were now widely shared, and many of the reforms he had anticipated were now realised. His whole attitude and behaviour had been governed by his principles, those of the 'rational radical', which he never abandoned (unlike his erstwhile colleague Taylor). He always believed that they would one day be successful, and he was convinced that he himself had a role to play in this success.[40] But Prentice was not the only one campaigning for reform and trying to influence local opinion, nor was the agitation of the band the only factor shaping local affairs. Prentice's newspapers, moreover, were not the best sellers in Manchester because his advanced ideas and his style of newspaper management were found by many to be unpalatable. Hence his advocacy of reform and liberal principles was only one of many reasons for their advancement and successes, though in Manchester at least it was a crucial one.

Prentice was among those who were convinced that the Manchester reformers should have their own newspaper. He realised that an efficient, independent organ was needed if they were going to expound their views with clarity and effect. An example had been set by the *Herald* and *Gazette*, of course, and in postwar Manchester many liberal-minded men recognised the value of an outlet for

[40] e.g. Prentice, *Sketches*, pp. 246, 332.

advanced views and a means of exerting influence. Prentice was the heir of this type of journalism, and it was largely due to his work that Manchester should have been the place in which the idea of a reform press as an influence on local (and through local on national) affairs received its fullest expression in the early nineteenth century.[41] Prentice played a prominent part in the negotiations which eventually led to the establishment of the *Guardian* in 1821, though he did not himself put up any money, never achieving the same high affluence of his friends the Potters and Baxter. Disappointed and angered by Taylor's 'apostasy' from liberal principles as editor of the *Guardian*, Prentice, the Potters, Baxter and some of their colleagues decided that a second newspaper would have to be secured to give the advanced reformers the outlet they required. In the summer of 1824, encouraged and financially backed by his friends, Prentice purchased the *Gazette* from Cowdroy's widow and set out to make it what the *Guardian* should have been, the active organ of respectable middle-class radical opinion.[42]

Prentice had probably been shaping the *Gazette*'s editorial policy for years anyway, from the time of his early contributions and particularly after Taylor had gone to the *Guardian* in 1821 and William Cowdroy junior had died in March 1822. It is unlikely that Cowdroy's widow, proprietor after her husband's death, wrote the *Gazette* editorials herself. Prentice paid her £800 for copyright and materials, with a further £100 to be paid annually for the following eight years. He also spent £300 on a new press and type.[43] The prospectus for the new series of the *Gazette* emphasised its 'hatred to misrule' and 'a wish to promote, and a disposition to rejoice in, all that tends to ameliorate and improve the condition of mankind'. The conductors would not be partisans but nor would they make the paper 'a mere chronicle of news without any decided political character. They claim as journalists the right they would exercise as individuals, not unnecessarily to obtrude on others their religion,

---

[41] Ziegler, 'Archibald Prentice', p. 422: not altogether sympathetic towards Prentice, but at least prepared to admit that he 'shared in the pioneer growth of the provincial weekly as a medium of opinion'.

[42] Years later even the *Guardian* was forced to acknowledge that its sternest critic had never abandoned a principle and had been unswerving and uncompromising in his adherence to the good causes in which he believed. See obituary in 'Archibald Prentice', *Biographical References*.

[43] Prentice, *Sketches*, p. 246; Leary, *Periodical Press*, p. 160.

their politics or their literature, but firmly and independently to advocate and defend the principles on which they act'.[44] Members of the band, notably Shuttleworth, helped with the running of the *Gazette*, and Prentice was also assisted by his brother-in-law Philip Thomson (another Scot of some literary merit). Prentice's main financial backers appear to have been Richard Potter and Edward Baxter, and he was keen to open the venture up to other 'shareholders' so as to relieve his friends from too heavy a financial commitment.[45] The immediate outlay of £1,100, with a further £800 to be paid in instalments, was a large sum and considerably more than the £1,050 donated for the establishment of the *Guardian* three years previously.

The first *Gazette* edited by Prentice appeared on 10 July 1824. It was issued from offices he had taken in Police Street. The office was moved in June 1825 to Market Street, a more central location, 'for the greater convenience of our readers and advertising friends'.[46] Prentice had decided on his new venture for two reasons: his belief that an economic depression was on the way and that his cotton business would not survive, and his desire to 'contribute something to the formation of a right public opinion'.[47] It has been stated that he had great faith in his principles and a firm belief that they would one day prevail. It was in this spirit that he ran his newspaper. He wanted to instruct and to guide, and the emphasis was on political comment. Indeed, comment was given at the expense of items normally expected from a newspaper, even though the prospectus had promised an eclectic content. The *Gazette* reached a circulation of about 1,700 a week in September 1826, a considerable advance on the 1,000 when Prentice took over, but by this time the *Guardian* was averaging over 3,000 sales a week.[48] If respectable Manchester readers wanted a reformist newspaper, they wanted the moderate *Guardian* rather than the more advanced *Gazette*.

It was not due to poor sales, however, that Prentice had to relinquish his newspaper in August 1828. By January of that year he was in serious financial difficulties, something he explained at length in an address 'To the Readers of the Gazette' dated 12 January 1828.

---

[44] Prospectus is in Brotherton Scrapbooks, ii, p. 31.
[45] e.g. Prentice to R. Potter, 5 May 1828, Potter Collection, xii, pp. 195–6.
[46] *Gazette*, 11 June 1825.
[47] Prentice, *Sketches*, p. 246.
[48] Read, *Press and People*, appendix pp. 211, 213.

As was characteristic of his style the address took the form of a direct and personal communication between Prentice, the teacher, and his flock, the *Gazette* readers. He explained that his newspaper was beginning to do very well. Its circulation was improving, as were its journalistic standards, profitability and reputation for influence and honest opinions. 'But having accomplished this much I find myself, for a time at least, overwhelmed with engagements resulting in a great measure from my efforts to improve my paper, and to make it that which was capable of being made'. Prentice's financial resources had been exhausted and he now faced bankruptcy. The commercial depression of 1826 had harmed one of his creditors, and stamp payments were proving a heavy burden. Prentice accepted that he had not been as watchful over his accounts as he should have been. His attention had been taken by editorials, circulation and advertising matters, and he had also been distracted by a serious family illness. He concluded the address by hoping for the continued patronage of his readers, 'for everything which improves the condition of my paper will improve the situation of my creditors, and facilitate my arrangements with them. Of those who owe me money, I earnestly solicit an early payment'.[49] Prentice continued with the *Gazette* in his straitened circumstances for a further six and a half months until he had no option but to sell. He appears to have paid his creditors back at a rate of only 1od. in the pound.[50] Unlike Taylor, Prentice never reaped large financial rewards from his newspapers and when he left the business in the late 1840s he could not afford not to work. (He took employment in the municipal gas office.) His concern to save money while a newspaperman led to the one main incident in his career when he fell foul of the Manchester Typographical Society. In 1825 his desire to cut costs led him to adopt a piecework system at the *Gazette*. The Typographical Society opposed this, but Prentice enjoyed the respect and affection of his printers and they stood by him rather than take action against him. They were expelled from the society as a result. In spite of the society's opposition, moreover, piecework was soon being used in the production of other Manchester newspapers.[51]

---

[49] *Gazette*, 12 Jan. 1828; Prentice, *Sketches*, p. 328.
[50] Read, *Press and People*, p. 88.
[51] Musson, *Typographical Association*, p. 32; *Manchester Typographical Society Centenary Record*, pp. 8–9.

As a business venture the *Gazette* was a failure, but Prentice was never interested in a newspaper primarily as a business venture. To him a newspaper was a political organ. Even so, his claims about the extent to which he had improved the *Gazette* were far from empty. He had increased its sales considerably, by roughly 70 per cent in fact, and he had also attracted more advertisements. The average number of advertisements per issue from January 1815 to July 1824 (when Prentice took over) was 33. In Prentice's first five months as proprietor and editor (August to December 1824) the average was 40. In 1825 the average was 43 per issue, and 44 in 1826 and 1827. From January to August 1828 the average was down to 38, possibly a reflection of the paper's growing financial difficulties and the declining confidence in it of advertising customers.[52] Prentice had improved the *Gazette*'s presentation and layout, and had supplied a good deal of useful news and information as well as entertaining miscellanea, correspondence, poems and extracts from literary classics. He had also included commercial news, though not as much as was supplied in the *Guardian*. But the *Gazette* did not attract many general readers because it tended to concentrate on local and national politics. Prentice was not too concerned about giving his readers variety, and this probably held his sales down. The *Gazette* never became the paper of a particular class or type of reader in the way that the *Guardian* became the favourite paper of the Manchester cotton businessmen. Prentice's appeal was directed more to the middling sort and to the literate or 'thinking' portion of the labouring ranks, and there was only a limited number of newspaper buyers among these groups.

Prentice had to sell the *Gazette* in August 1828, but this did not mark the end of his newspaper career. Despite the 'disastrous and almost heartbreaking' failure of the *Gazette*, Prentice was determined not to give up. 'There were duties to be done, and I resolved with the help of God that they should be done'.[53] His creditors assured him that he had suffered because he was in advance of public opinion and because of circumstances over which he had no control. Several helped to form the joint stock company which established the new *Manchester Times* in the autumn of 1828. The Potters and Baxter again put up much of the money that was needed. Members

[52] These averages are based on figures taken for every fourth issue of the *Gazette*.
[53] Prentice, *Sketches*, p. 332.

of the band obviously valued Prentice's public services enormously; he had the talent and determination and they had the means to help him use his abilities on behalf of good causes. He began as editor of the *Times* and then purchased full control in May 1832 in partnership with William Cathrall. Cathrall, a Wesleyan who had some experience of the newspaper business, previously worked for the Manchester *Chronicle* and for some years had acted as the Manchester reporter for *The Times* of London. Prentice and Cathrall were joint managers, printers and publishers of the paper, and also carried on a general printing business. The first issue of the Manchester *Times* appeared on 18 October 1828, published from offices in Angel Court just off Market Place. (The premises moved in March 1829 to Market Street.) Prentice promised to be tireless in his advocacy of reforms, especially parliamentary reform, the repeal of the corn laws and the separation of Church and state. In 1850 he could look back and say that this pledge had been kept. Other newspapers might have called for reforms, but not as persistently or continuously as his *Times*, 'which waited not for the favourable tide of public opinion, but strove to create it'. The prospectus of the *Times* solicited the support of all who wanted Manchester to have a paper devoted to the welfare of the people, and attacked the *Guardian* 'of which the apostasy is so notorious'.[54]

Under Prentice the *Times* did well and quickly established a sure footing in the provincial newspaper market. By December 1828 it had agents in many large towns and cities, including London, Edinburgh, Glasgow and Dublin.[55] Weekly sales began at about 1,400 and passed the 2,000 mark within a year. After a slow start the number of advertisements per issue picked up too. The average for October to December 1828 was 29. In April 1829 the number of notices in a single issue passed 50 and the average for the whole year was 43. There were 77 advertisements in the issue of 1 May 1830, and the average for 1830 was 48. The average for 1831 was down to 39, and that for 1832 was 40.[56] (As will be seen, circulation figures never matched the peak of 1830; not for nothing was 1830 also the best year for advertisements

---

[54] Prentice, *Sketches*, p. 33; *Times*, 14 March 1829, 28 April, 19 May, 4 Aug. 1832; Swindells, *Manchester Streets*, pp. 53–4; Slugg, *Reminiscences*, pp. 288–90; Leary, Periodical Press, p. 181 (and pp. 174–5 for prospectus).
[55] *Times*, 19 Dec. 1828.
[56] These averages are based on the number of notices in every fourth issue of the *Times*.

in this period.) Clearly Prentice was losing out to the *Guardian* in advertising customers and revenue, but he was at least getting sufficient income from advertisements to help keep his newspaper in operation. The quality of the *Times* as a newspaper was higher than that of the *Gazette*. The *Times* was better organised. There were bolder headings and similar material was grouped together, such as market prices and commercial information. The print was larger and easier to read, and there were clear titles for important news items. Prentice probably began with a Stanhope or Columbian iron hand press, but by the mid-1830s the *Times* office had a steam press partly operated by hand.[57] Prentice was more concerned than he had previously been about making his newspaper attractive as well as informative. In November 1828 he told readers that he would endeavour to stick to an 'arrangement': foreign news and political discussion on page two, domestic news and correspondence on page three, local intelligence on four and five, 'literature and miscellaneous intelligence forming light table talk' on six and seven, and 'markets, bankruptcies etc.' on page eight. He was also keen to deal with potential administrative problems. Correspondence containing news was welcome at any time, but Prentice stated that other letters should be received by Thursday of each week, and should be signed since 'we cannot state facts on anonymous authority'. Advertisements should be sent as early in the week as possible, he added, and arrive no later than 2 p.m. on Fridays.[58] For all his concern about making the *Times* a newspaper with a wide appeal, though, Prentice's main interest remained political news and comment, and he still faced complaints from readers who wanted a proper newspaper rather than a weekly political tract.

Was Prentice as successful a journalist, commentator and instructor as he liked to think? It would be going too far to call him conceited. He honestly thought he had achieved something, and was pleased and proud to recall his endeavours, as anyone would be. He said he was regarded as a 'political teacher' by men who had read his newspapers from their youth to adulthood.[59] His calls for reason and restraint during the economic distress of 1825, he believed, had helped to prevent an accumulation of bitterness between workers and employers.[60] His advocacy of Benthamite ideas through his

[57] Slugg, *Reminiscences*, pp. 288–90.
[58] *Times*, 21 Nov. 1828.
[59] Prentice, *Sketches*, preface (Dec. 1850) to first edition.
[60] e.g. *Gazette*, 10, 17, 24, 31 Dec. 1825; Prentice, *Sketches*, p. 270.

career helped to make them 'the guiding principles of many ardent friends of liberty'.[61] His June 1826 list of one hundred boroughs which returned two hundred MPs, while they had a combined population lower than that of unrepresented Manchester, aided the cause of parliamentary reform because 'men committed it to memory and taught from it as from a text'.[62] His July 1826 leading articles 'On the Causes and Cure of the Present Distress' were reprinted as cheap pamphlets and 'carried instruction to tens of thousands who seldom had the chance of seeing a seven penny newspaper'.[63] His constant exposure of 'landlord fallacies' helped to make Manchester the headquarters of the anti-corn law movement. 'Certain it is that during that memorable contest I was often cheered by the assurance of young, able and energetic men, throwing their life and soul into the agitation for free trade . . . that their first lessons in a generous political economy were derived from me'.[64] Such self-congratulation may seem excessive, but Prentice was in the position and did have the ability to wield influence. Nor was he just out to sing his own praises. What he wanted was to set an example, to show what could be done if an individual had the energy and determination to do it. Prentice wanted to encourage and stimulate others, and this was the motivation behind his political and newspaper career.[65]

Obviously it is difficult to measure influence, but Prentice did have an audience, and a constant one at that. His newspapers, admittedly, were not the best sellers in Manchester. As we have seen, sales of the *Gazette* reached over 1,700 per week in September 1826. Sales of the *Times* began at about 1,400 a week in October 1828, cleared 2,000 in October 1829, reached a high of over 4,000 in July 1830 (overtaking the *Guardian* and becoming one of the best-selling provincials in the

---

[61] *Gazette*, 25 Dec. 1824, for an early editorial advocating the greatest happiness of the greatest number; Prentice, *Recollections of Bentham*, p. 3, and *Sketches*, ch. 24.

[62] *Gazette*, 3, 24 June, 1 July 1826; Prentice, *Sketches*, p. 283, and *Organic Changes necessary to complete the System of Representation partially amended by the Reform Bill* (1839), p. 18.

[63] *Gazette*, 15, 22 July 1826; Prentice, *Sketches*, p. 284.

[64] Prentice, *Sketches*, p. 334.

[65] Prentice, *Sketches*, p. 332. Donald Read has written that the self-congratulatory reminiscences of provincial newspapermen, and their belief in their own influence, were 'undoubtedly justified'. Read, 'North of England Newspapers and their Value to Historians', *P.L.P.L.S.*, viii, part 3 (Nov. 1957), p. 208.

country), then fell to about 2,400 in the mid-1830s. Circulation figures then fluctuated, though never went below 2,400 and were frequently above 3,200. The *Guardian* never fell below 3,000 copies a week after 1825, and by the mid-1830s sold well over 4,000. When it became a bi-weekly in 1836 the weekly sale was over 4,900. The Tory *Courier*, established in January 1825, was selling about 1,800 copies a week in 1828 and reached 2,400 in May 1829. Its sales stood at 4,000 in 1839.[66] But even if Prentice's newspapers were not the best sellers, it should be stressed again that circulation figures were not readership figures. A correspondent of the *Times* in 1836 reckoned it had 25 readers per copy.[67] Prentice did have a sizeable audience for his views. He was well-known locally (though not always liked), and many were affected by what he thought and wrote. He was, for example, instrumental in the adoption of the Whig vice-president of the Board of Trade, Charles Poulett Thomson, as a second reformist, free trade parliamentary candidate in Manchester in 1832: 'having the direction of such influence as a popular newspaper possessed, some importance was attached to the course I might pursue'. Prentice exposed another candidate, S. J. Loyd, as lukewarm on reform, and helped to prevent his return. Richard Cobden admitted to Watkin in September 1837 that Prentice had played the key role in Loyd's defeat.[68]

Yet Prentice's style of writing and editorial policy present problems, and he was possibly not as influential as he could have been or as he thought he was. Accepting no half-measures, ceaseless and single-minded in his advocacy of reforms, he led by example and lived his public life according to the adage that 'the only way to move men is to show that you yourself are moved'. But this very single-mindedness damaged the appeal of his newspapers: they were too political. Prentice was to lose his *Times* in the late 1840s partly because of this over-concentration on political comment. He devoted his columns to the anti-corn law campaign, but the League's leaders saw that such a paper could only have a limited appeal and readership. They wanted a true newspaper, one that was commercially

[66] Read, *Press and People*, appendix pp. 211–13, 217.
[67] *Times*, 1 Oct. 1836.
[68] Prentice, *League*, i, pp. 20–21; Watkin, *Journal*, pp. 191–2. Prentice commented on the unsuitability of Loyd in virtually every issue of the *Times* between July and December 1832. In addition, he almost single-handedly destroyed Loyd's credibility as a reform candidate by his insistent questioning at an election meeting in Chorlton on 2 August 1832.

successful as well as politically useful, and John Bright helped to establish the *Manchester Examiner* in 1846. So strong was this competitor that Prentice retired from the *Times* in 1847, and his paper was subsequently absorbed by its new rival.[69] Prentice was never interested in providing a general newspaper, and even 'A Constant Reader' felt he had to tell Prentice in 1831 that 'the most hearty reformers have WIVES and SISTERS and DAUGHTERS, who have not all their ardency in political affairs, and to whom a little more LIGHT READING than you have given us would be most acceptable'.[70]

Prentice's editorials, like his books and pamphlets, were clear, concise and well-written, but his frequently pedagogic tone might also have put people off. He thought of himself as a teacher. He seemed always to be claiming, for instance, that he knew what the workers' best interests were even if they themselves sometimes did not. He often had trouble getting his message across because, not surprisingly, the intended beneficiaries of his advice and guidance resented being spoken down to. Prentice would also associate himself with causes that were not particularly popular with working people, such as Sabbath observance and temperance. Such causes, and the manner in which they were advocated, may have distanced Prentice from the lower classes. Certainly he came in for censure from popular politicians and journalists. William Cobbett condemned him for his 'worse than animal ignorance' in 1828, and in 1833 one local radical paper called him 'the most noisy in self-applause of all reformers'.[71] At the first public meeting of the Manchester Political Union in November 1830 one worker denounced him as a 'saucy Scotsman', and a large operative contingent at an Exchange meeting early in the Anti-Corn Law League's campaign gave 'three groans for Archibald Prentice'.[72] Perhaps he was misunderstood. Although genuinely concerned for the well-being of the operatives he was only fleetingly successful in communicating this concern, and when people refused to listen he carried

---

[69] One of Prentice's closest friends, John Childs (a Suffolk printer, free trader and campaigner against monopoly restrictions on the printing of the Bible), was outraged by the way he had been treated by the League leaders. See Dunlop, 'Archibald Prentice', pp. 441–2.

[70] *Times*, 5 Feb. 1831.

[71] Prentice, *League*, i, pp. 3–6; *Manchester and Salford Advertiser*, 31 Aug. 1833.

[72] *Times*, 27 Nov. 1830; Prentice, *League*, i, p. 116.

on regardless. 'Though it is a thankless task to serve the public', he told Richard Potter in 1827, 'my temperament would lead me to serve them even in spite of their abuse'.[73] In later years, the former Lancashire radical leader, Samuel Bamford, described Prentice as 'a shrewd and clever man, worthy of more substantial respect from the public than he receives'.[74] This comment indicates that working men and others could indeed find Prentice unconvincing, even though he believed he was acting in their own best interests. Yet he was not always unpopular among local operatives. In July 1825 he was toasted by the spinners' union for his help in the agitation for Hobhouse's factory bill of that year, and when he became a town councillor in 1838 it was as an elected representative of New Cross ward, in the working-class Ancoats district.[75] But he probably did talk over the heads of some workers, and indeed most respectable reformers must have had this problem of communication. In Manchester it seems that the operatives never completely trusted the middle-class reformers. A cleavage between classes was one of the main features of the structure of the cotton industry, and the 'them and us' mentality gave psychological support to the already wide economic and social gap.

Prentice was more effective in communicating with the ambitious and assertive reformers of the middling sort, the publicans, shopkeepers, clerks, small traders and craftsmen to whom his instruction and guidance might have been most palatable. They picked up on his messages of encouragement and self-reliance, his belief in progress, reform and personal merit. Prentice had less appeal for those with different preferences and concerns. If some in the labouring classes found him objectionable, despite his devotion of so much time and energy to their causes, so too did many of the larger merchants and manufacturers in the local business community. Prentice's papers, vehicles for his own opinions and principles, had only limited appeal for the well-off men of property and commerce. On most political and economic questions they preferred the *Guardian* which, incidentally, was far less interested in the workers' hopes, claims and aspirations than were Prentice's *Gazette* and *Times*. Prentice was very much in favour of some paternalist protection for workers, for example, whereas Taylor took the employers' side

[73] Prentice to R. Potter, 3 Oct. 1827, Potter Collection, xii, pp. 119–21.
[74] See interview with Bamford in Evans, *Lancashire Authors*, pp. 18–19.
[75] *Gazette*, 16 July 1825; Brotherton Scrapbooks, x, p. 31.

against such interference.[76] By 1842 the Exchange newsroom, frequented by the merchants and manufacturers, was taking twelve copies of the *Guardian* twice a week, a total of 24, and only four copies of the *Times* per week.[77] The *Guardian* seems to have told its readers what they wanted to hear, gradually inserting its own principles until it could be said both to form and reflect local opinion. Prentice was not so discreet, and his ideas failed to attract a wide following from the affluent while his tone and language limited his appeal to the labouring ranks. In 1836 one commentator stated that the art of good editorial writing consisted in finding a middle way: an editor had to write with force and authority, but ensure that his articles were not pitched too highly. He should give instruction without seeming to give instruction.[78] This happy medium seems often to have eluded Prentice. But he was certainly sincere. Perhaps he thought that this was enough and that readers would appreciate honesty and straightforwardness. This was the basis of his appeal. He tried to sell integrity. It is debatable whether, once sold, integrity remains integrity.

Prentice would not have changed even if he could. The way in which he conducted his newspapers stemmed from his powerful sense of duty and mission, an adjunct of his strict morality and Presbyterian creed. A newspaper was not just a commercial venture. Nor was it meant merely to entertain. The journalist should be an instructor. Prentice had clear notions on the relationship between the press and public opinion:

> Although in the first instance, a newspaper may be established in consequence of the demand for the expression of particular opinions, and may be continued mainly to reflect the political feeling of a portion of the community, it begins to act upon the public mind and, in its turn, assumes to dictate or insinuate the views of its conductors, and from being an organ becomes an instructor - for evil or good, as the case may be.[79]

[76] The *Westminster Review*'s idea ('Provincial, Scotch and Irish Press', p. 73), that the *Guardian* was the 'temperate medium of reconciliation between the extravagant commands of the masters and the unjust demands of the workmen', is quite untenable. It was always patently clear whose side the *Guardian* was on.
[77] Read, *Press and People*, p. 202.
[78] 'Journals of the Provinces', p. 147.
[79] Prentice, *Sketches*, p. 211.

A newspaper editor could and should use the influence of his position, Prentice insisted. To him, his was the only style to adopt. He was no J. E. Taylor. His purpose was to make opinion, not money. He told his readers in 1834 that 'the desire to promulgate sound opinions is quite as strong a motive with us as any mere business temptation'.[80] This is why he had no hesitation in devoting his newspaper to the League's anti-corn law agitation, to the almost total exclusion of other subjects,

> an occupation of space for eight years, more probably than any weekly newspaper ever devoted to a single object . . . I was often told that it would be more to my interest if I made the Manchester Times more of a newspaper. It mattered not. If journalism was not to effect public good it was not the employment for me.[81]

An avid reader of Bentham, Prentice shared the Benthamite view of public opinion as an essential safeguard against misrule and as something that could best operate through the medium of the newspaper press.

Was Prentice truly independent as a newspaper editor, or was he the tool of others? In attempting to laud and defend Taylor, David Ayerst has cast doubts on Prentice's independence and seems to regard him as the creature of those who financially backed his newspapers, particularly the Potters and Baxter.[82] This is an unacceptable interpretation. Ayerst fails fully to appreciate why the *Guardian* was established in the first place. He defends Taylor, but Taylor was the one at fault. It was because of Taylor's departure from the original plan behind the *Guardian* that the Potters and Baxter decided to put money into another newspaper. According to Ayerst, Prentice was selected by them and then used by them. In fact, it is clear that Prentice acted as he wanted to act. He was not used, for such a thing would have been repugnant to him. Ayerst makes much of the fact that Taylor paid off his backers and became a free man. So did Prentice. But even before May 1832 he was not unfree, and he was probably more independent than Taylor in the sense that

---

[80] *Times*, 4 Jan. 1834.
[81] Prentice, *League*, i, p. 89. On his approach to journalism see also Somerville, *Free Trade and the League*, ii, p. 397; Grant, *Newspaper Press*, iii, p. 362; 'Provincial, Scotch and Irish Press', p. 74.
[82] Ayerst, *Guardian Biography*, pp. 52–4, 87–8.

Taylor was far more concerned about such things as the good opinion of advertisers. Ayerst misunderstands the true nature of the relationship between the Potters and Baxter on one side and Prentice on the other. They were extremely close friends. They trusted each other and thought alike on most important questions of the day. It is clear that Baxter and the Potters preferred Prentice's strongly political style of journalism. They believed in the propriety and usefulness of his long, detailed and unequivocal weekly editorials. Prentice had the talent, they had the money to enable him to use it. This was a partnership. Prentice was not their servant at all, and neither side would have regarded this as tolerable anyway. Prentice was not told what to write by his financial backers. They were his friends and political allies, and there was already agreement between all of them on what a reformist newspaper should be saying.

There are plenty of signs that Prentice was independent. He often adopted opinions and courses which even his friends regarded as too radical. They remained aloof, for example, from the political union Prentice helped to establish in 1830, partly because they considered its character to be more 'popular' than was prudent. Prentice gave the union extensive coverage in the *Times*.[83] In May and June 1828 Baxter expressed anger at Prentice's policy on the Manchester police bill, particularly his agreement with some outspoken leaders of the middling sort radicals,[84] and at a police meeting in June 1828 Prentice publicly disagreed with Richard Potter when Potter asked him, in the interest of conciliation, to withdraw his motion for the dismissal of the law clerks to the police commission. Prentice's argument was that they were the tools of the ruling party rather than the advisers of the whole police body.[85] A few weeks after this Prentice was again at variance with Baxter, on the propriety of paying the expenses of the Manchester deputation sent to parliament to present the town's case for the parliamentary representation of Penryn, a corrupt Cornish borough. Baxter thought it fair to allow the expenses but Prentice opposed, claiming that the deputation had bargained for a £20 franchise which had not been approved by the town.[86] Another

[83] For the union's council, *Times*, 4 Dec. 1830. None of the band served on it except Prentice.
[84] Baxter to R. Potter, 30 May and 25 June 1828, Potter Collection, xii, pp. 235–6, 241–3.
[85] *Gazette*, 24 May, 7 June 1828.
[86] *Gazette*, 26 July 1828.

example of Prentice's independence is his coverage of a Unitarian dinner in August 1824. Unlike most of the band Prentice was not a Unitarian but a Presbyterian. In his remarks on the dinner he paid tribute to the benevolent and liberal spirit of the Manchester Unitarians, but added:

> For ourselves we must honestly declare that, highly as we respect many of the individuals of that sect, and readily as we acknowledge the goodness of their intentions, we should regret exceedingly the progress of opinions which we consider as founded on superficial and partial views of that written word to which we all appeal as the standard of religious truth.[87]

Prentice would never have made such comments had he been in the Potters' pockets. He was free to praise or condemn whenever he wanted to. His newspapers were, and were meant to be, the organ of a particular party, the band, but took this stance through choice and not compulsion. Prentice was a valued ally rather than a hired political hack. The Potters and others gave their money and did not expect or receive slavish adherence in return. All they wanted was for Prentice to write what he himself wished to write.

It is true that Prentice's financial problems during the winter of 1827–28 did lead to some talk about Watkin succeeding him as editor of the *Gazette*. Watkin later wrote that this plan fell through because of his own desire for editorial freedom.[88] But Watkin obviously misunderstood what was happening. There was still no doubt about Prentice's talents, and Prentice continued editing the *Gazette* until August 1828. Then he was set up with the *Times* in October. The wealthier members of the band did not think of Watkin because they wanted a tool. They were looking for someone they knew and in whom they had confidence, someone who could be expected to conduct the *Gazette* in the same forthright and uncompromising manner that Prentice had employed. They quickly realised that nobody fitted the bill better than Prentice himself. Although they might have been disappointed that the *Gazette* under Prentice had lost money, they were in no doubt that it was worthwhile to continue backing him and enabling him to do the public service for which he was suited. The offer to Watkin does not appear to have

---

[87] *Gazette*, 14 Aug. 1824.
[88] Watkin, *Journal*, p. 122.

been too serious anyway, and he was not passed over because he wanted independence. Prentice was never anything but independent. The simple fact was that the band preferred Prentice's brand of radical journalism to the more moderate alternatives (including Watkin's) that were possible.

Prentice's consistent and outspoken advocacy of reforms made him unpopular with Manchester's Tories and dominant 'high' party. He and his papers were often attacked at Tory meetings and in local Tory papers. It seems that Prentice also suffered from the discrimination exercised by the ruling party in the patronage of, and placing of advertisements and notices in, the local newspapers. The discrimination described by Arthur Aspinall in his study of the central government's dealings with the press could certainly have its local counterpart: 'local authorities . . . must have followed the government's example in discriminating against newspapers politically hostile to themselves'. In May 1829 Prentice was certain that his *Times* was being passed over by the police commissioners when they sent out their official advertisements.[89] Prentice frequently railed against the Manchester Tories in his editorials, and it was not long before they were stung into some decisive action to try and silence him. An opportunity arose in March 1831 when Prentice wrote an article ridiculing the men behind a petition opposing the Whigs' Reform Bill. One of them had Prentice indicted for libel. This was the ruddy-complexioned John Grimshaw, a retired infantry officer, a member of the Tory John Shaw's Club and former vice-president of the Manchester Pitt Club, 'commonly called Captain Grimshaw', Prentice wrote, 'principally remarkable for giving bawdy toasts and for a countenance which seems to blush at his own lewdness'. The case was heard in July 1831, and Prentice conducted his own defence as Taylor had done in 1819. He reiterated the point that Taylor had then made, that the jury could not convict unless presented with proof that the statements in question were false. Prentice was also fortified by communications with Bentham, whom he had visited while in London in April 1831. The jury failed to agree on a verdict and the prosecution failed, which to Prentice was as good as a full acquittal. Bentham sent his congratulations and Prentice and the band celebrated a victory over the local Tories, who were clearly

---

[89] A. Aspinall, *Politics and the Press 1780–1850* (1949), p. 133; *Times*, 16 May 1829.

alarmed at the growing strength of the Manchester liberals. As Prentice said during the trial, 'a labourer I have long been in the field of parliamentary reform, and for my labour in that field rather than for any injury to Captain Grimshaw, I suspect I owe my appearance before you today'. Prentice had in reality been on trial for his political opinions, and he emerged from the contest unscathed.[90]

4. NEWSPAPER WARFARE IN MANCHESTER

By the time the *Guardian* was established in May 1821 there were already six weekly papers in Manchester, four of which appeared on Saturdays. These were the *Chronicle, British Volunteer, Observer* and *Gazette*, while the *Exchange Herald* and *Mercury* appeared on Tuesdays. From January 1825 there was a new Saturday paper, the *Courier*. The *Chronicle* was owned by the Wheeler family and was a Tory paper, established in 1781. The *Courier* was owned by the Sowlers. It was ultra-Protestant and more obviously Tory than Wheeler's paper. The *Exchange Herald* was established by Joseph Aston in 1809 and was Tory, though more moderate than the papers of Wheeler and Sowler. Its publication day changed from Tuesday to Thursday in 1825, and then in October 1826 Aston sold his paper to Sowler. There was thus a change in editorial policy, and from the end of 1831 the *Exchange Herald* appeared on Wednesdays. The *Mercury*, established in 1752, and *British Volunteer*, established in 1804, belonged to the Harrop family and were Tory papers. Both were sold to Taylor in December 1825. The radical *Observer* led a stormy existence from January 1818 to September 1822, and the plebeian radicals did not have another newspaper organ of their own until the end of the 1820s. The licensed victuallers of the district established the *Manchester and Salford Advertiser* in November 1828 on non-political lines. Then it was briefly under the control of two Tory editors, before being taken over in September 1830 by the Irish-born radical pamphleteer and politician James Whittle. The *United Trades Co-operative Journal* lasted from March to

---

[90] *Times*, 26 March, 16 April, 23, 30 July 1830; Prentice, *Sketches*, ch. 24, and *Recollections of Bentham*, pp. 12–14; Dunlop, 'Archibald Prentice', pp. 440–41; *Trial of Archibald Prentice*, pp. 12–16 for the relevant part of Prentice's address; Leary, *Periodical Press*, p. 189; Stancliffe, *John Shaw's*, pp. 133, 179; Pitt Club, ii, p. 40.

September 1830 and was the organ of radical trade unionist John Doherty. It was succeeded by the *Voice of the People*, edited by Doherty, which first appeared in January 1831. This paper only lasted for nine months.[91]

Journalistic competition in Manchester was fierce. To survive and to prosper a newspaper had to try and increase its share of the market by any means possible, for the number of people who could afford newspapers at 7d. a copy was limited. It has been estimated that Manchester's Saturday papers sold at a rate of about one copy for every nineteen or twenty inhabitants, which made saturation a dangerous possibility. It is true that Manchester was a rapidly expanding town, that the demand for newspapers was noticeably rising, and that many Manchester papers were sold outside the immediate neighbourhood. These factors were to the advantage of proprietors and editors, but the market was still limited and the ability to compete was still an essential requirement. Nor were business considerations the only factor making for intense rivalry. This period saw the local newspapers adopt editorial policies that were more and more closely related to partisan political lines. As Tories, liberals and radicals collided in local and national affairs, so did the Manchester papers attack and argue with each other on all the main public issues of the time. This development was strongly influenced by the aims with which the band entered newspaper activity. The idea that a newspaper could and should be an effective political organ, capable of forming and directing opinion, lay behind the early contributions to Cowdroy's *Gazette*, the establishment of the *Guardian*, the purchase of the *Gazette* and the establishment of the *Times*. As members of the band began to speak up for Manchester's respectable reformers, so their newspaper opponents began to devote more space to political information and comment, presenting alternative views of contemporary events. Political animosities combined with business rivalry and made Manchester a veritable cockpit of newspaper warfare.[92]

In such an atmosphere of fierce competition it was necessary for a newspaper continually to extend the services it offered and improve

[91] Leary, Periodical Press, is a useful general account, but detailed information about the Manchester press is best gained from the newspapers themselves.
[92] Some of these points are discussed in Ayerst, *Guardian Biography*, p. 41; Mills, *Guardian History*, pp. 42–4; D. Read, 'Reform newspapers and Northern opinion c.1800–48', *P.L.P.L.S.*, viii, part 4 (Jan. 1959), pp. 301–12.

content, advertising, news, presentation and delivery. All these and related matters had to be gradually perfected in order to attract and hold on to a portion of the reading public. The *Guardian* was a trend-setter in many of these fields and, keen to impress, always took care to announce all new improvements it made in newspaper techniques, presentation and organisation. The introduction of smaller type, the enlargement of columns, the changes in format to provide more space and the use of new presses were all referred to by Taylor as proof that his newspaper was worthy of attention and support. He did occasionally have to apologise, though, for late deliveries and poor legibility.[93] The improvement of the *Gazette* was rather slower, although by the time Prentice took over in July 1824 it was a more organised, attractive and useful newspaper than it had been ten years earlier. In August 1824 Prentice altered the arrangement and format of the *Gazette*, putting advertisements on the inside pages and opting for five wider columns per page rather than the previous six. A few months later Prentice gave notice that he was going to install improved printing devices. He explained that the smallest types were no good unless used on paper of very fine quality, and he hoped that his new machines would give a clear and distinct script that was well-suited to the paper the *Gazette* was obliged to use.[94] Lacking the kind of revenue from sales and especially from advertising that the *Guardian* enjoyed, Prentice's improvements were on a more modest scale than Taylor's (and by his own admission he was far more concerned with political content). But the need to compete for readers remained important, and Prentice continued to try and improve format and presentation and create more space as his newspaper rivals were doing. The *Times* was more polished and attractive than the *Gazette* had been, with larger print, clearer titles and the grouping of similar material. By 1831 Prentice apparently had the time, will, money and confidence to make major changes. The *Times* was published in folio form rather than quarto from the end of 1831, with smaller print and the use of other space-saving devices.[95]

As well as competing for readers the Manchester papers had to compete for advertising customers. Frequent appeals would be made to prospective customers as newspaper proprietors and editors

[93] *Guardian*, 1 May 1824, 17 June 1826, 6 Jan. 1827, 8, 15 March 1828, 24 Dec. 1831.
[94] *Gazette*, 7, 14 Aug., 25 Dec. 1824.
[95] *Times*, 24 Dec. 1831, 7 Jan. 1832.

pointed to the advantages to be gained by placing notices in their particular papers. Naturally the main advantage was publicity. Those papers selling most copies each week would be of greater use to advertisers than those with poor sales. Advertisers might also be interested in reaching readers of a certain profession, class or locality, and this too could come into consideration. In the main, though, newspapers emphasised their circulation figures when soliciting advertisements.[96] This was one reason why they disputed each other's circulation claims. Once a customer had been attracted to a particular paper he had to be regularly assured of the value of his choice as a medium for his notices. Another important requirement was that advertisements should reach their destination well before the time of going to press. Prentice, Taylor and their fellow newspapermen often made this point to customers. In August 1830 Prentice said that notices should reach the *Times* office by 7 p.m. on Friday nights. He was unwilling to insert late advertisements if this meant leaving out important items he had planned to include.[97] Taylor had fewer qualms, and in December 1829 referred to a recent occasion when he had excluded news because of the late arrival of advertisements.[98] If forced to make the choice, it seems, Taylor would put in advertisements instead of news and articles. Prentice no doubt disapproved but it was Taylor who made money, and this was largely because the *Guardian* was so popular with advertisers. For decades the Manchester paper carrying the most notices had been the *Chronicle*, but the *Guardian* surpassed it during the course of 1829.

Taylor also came out the victor when he and Prentice established rival Tuesday commercial papers in August 1825, and this affair must have added to the rising personal animosity between the two men. The battle commenced when it became known that Joseph Aston was to change the publication day of his *Exchange Herald* from Tuesday to Thursday. This left an opening and Prentice was the first to act. On 2 August 1825 he issued a prospectus for a new Tuesday commercial paper, the *Manchester Commercial Journal*, to be devoted to mercantile news and miscellaneous items of general interest. Taylor followed two days later with the prospectus of his *Manchester Advertiser*. Prentice was furious. He had, after all, first mentioned a scheme for a Tuesday paper in his *Gazette* of 16 July 1825. Taylor

[96] e.g. *Gazette*, 13 Nov. 1824.
[97] *Times*, 28 Aug. 1830.
[98] *Guardian*, 12 Dec. 1829.

claimed that his plan for a Tuesday paper had been 'frequently avowed in conversation with his friends'. Prentice was unimpressed. Why had Taylor not announced his plan openly 'till our preparations were commenced, and the public were appraised of our intentions?'[99] Taylor did not reply, but it does seem that Prentice's announcement about a new paper was the spur. On 8 August 1825 Taylor's wife wrote to her brother:

> Edward is intending to commence a new Tuesday's paper. He has long been thinking of it, and repeatedly urged to do it, but he felt reluctant to injure the others published on that day. When, however, Mr Prentice announced his intention, Edward thought there was no further occasion for delicacy on his part, and felt it would not do to give him the start.[100]

Taylor had already established a close relationship with the local business community via the columns of his *Guardian*, and his *Advertiser* was to further this development. The Tuesday *Advertiser* seems to have left Prentice's *Journal* far behind, and the latter venture cost Prentice a lot of time and money with only limited returns. The *Journal* does not appear to have lasted beyond the summer of 1826, though this was not through lack of trying. Prentice repeatedly attempted to drum up support for his Tuesday paper, advertising it in the *Gazette* and emphasising its value. He even transferred regular *Gazette* features into the *Journal*, such as the series 'Men and Books', and was keen to point out that his two papers complemented each other and were equally deserving of patronage: the *Gazette* was suitable for the head of the family and the *Journal* for the whole family.[101] But these appeals failed to have much effect. Taylor had already found the formula that attracted the local merchants and manufacturers, and the early lead gained by the *Advertiser* over the *Journal* proved irreversible. With the *Advertiser* to supplement the *Guardian*, Prentice's *Journal* was surplus to requirements.

Taylor soon decided to expand his journalistic activities even further. In November 1825 he purchased the copyrights of the *Mercury* and *British Volunteer*, previously owned by the Tory Harrop family. James Harrop junior explained that 'family arrangements' had made it 'imperative upon him that these journals should

[99] *Gazette*, 6 Aug. 1825.
[100] Sophia Taylor to R. Scott, 8 Aug. 1825, in Scott, *Family Biography*, p. 458.
[101] *Gazette*, 10 Oct. 1825.

be disposed of'. Taylor was eager to acquire them, realising that they would give him a commanding position in both the Tuesday and the Saturday markets. He estimated that the purchase would add up to £800 a year to the income of his newspaper business. He purchased the copyrights for £1,100.[102] The *Mercury* was amalgamated with the *Advertiser*, and the *Volunteer* with the *Guardian*. Prentice and other critics of Taylor were to argue that the purchase of Harrop's papers marked a further stage in his retreat from liberalism, which was already obvious before December 1825. To them it was clear that he modified his editorial line in the *Guardian* so as to retain the patronage of former readers of the Tory *Volunteer*. Whether or not Taylor was guilty of this, the *Guardian*'s circulation did rise immediately after the amalgamation. In the five weeks before the event the *Guardian* sold about 2,322 copies a week. In the five weeks after, its sales went up to 3,012 a week.[103] Many previous readers of the *Volunteer* must have stayed with the combined paper.[104] The rising sales of the *Guardian* must also have contributed to the continuing increase in its advertising business.

Taylor was not the only one interested in newspaper amalgamations. On one occasion Prentice himself effected such a coup. He had been forced to give up the *Gazette* in August 1828, and that paper had passed into the hands of the Cobbettite writer and politician James Whittle. But under Whittle the *Gazette* rapidly declined, and by May 1829 it was again up for sale. Now at the *Times*, Prentice quickly came forward as a buyer (the copyright cost him only £50) and issued a long and enthusiastic address to the readers of the combined paper. He expressed his 'heartfelt gratification' at being able to renew his communication with *Gazette* readers, and pointed out that the amalgamation would have no effect at all on the radical stance of either paper (unlike the situation with the *Guardian* and

[102] *Mercury*, 29 Nov. 1825; Scott, *Family Biography*, p. 459.

[103] *Guardian*, 7 Jan. 1826. A few months later Prentice was to lament that his own circulation had been approaching the largest number any Manchester paper had ever had, until 'the incorporation of the Volunteer with the Guardian placed the latter decidedly first'. *Gazette*, 17 June 1826.

[104] Ayerst estimates that 500 of the *Volunteer*'s 800 subscribers remained with the combined Saturday paper. Ayerst, *Guardian Biography*, p. 60. Prentice claimed that the deal with Harrop added a thousand Tory readers to Taylor's subscription list. Prentice, *Sketches*, p. 286. On Taylor's alleged attempts to trim between liberal and Tory positions, see 'The Radical Tailor turning his Coat' ('A most excellent new song'), Brotherton Scrapbooks, v, p. 24.

Volunteer). He was sure that the combined paper would do well and expected a circulation of 3,000 copies a week in the near future.[105] His confidence was justified. His incorporation of the *Gazette* and *Times* seems to have had a most beneficial effect on his sales and advertising business. Both were increasing before the amalgamation, but that event confirmed and perpetuated the development and may also have speeded it up. By January 1829 the *Times* was selling 1,200 copies a week, and 2,000 by April 1829. After amalgamation in May the circulation went up to 2,200 in June 1829, 2,500 in January 1830, and reached 3,000 in the summer of 1830. The number of advertisements per issue also went up. In the six months before amalgamation the *Times* averaged 37 notices in each issue, and 47 in the six months after amalgamation.[106]

Unlike Taylor, though, Prentice never made large profits from his newspapers. His technological and organisational improvements were slower, and like most provincial newspapermen he had to exploit other possible sources of income. From early in 1826 he was running a letter-press printing service in the *Gazette* office in Market Street, and by July 1830 he had established a printing shop in Great Ormond Street, Chorlton Row. In 1832, now in partnership with William Cathrall, he extended his printing service with the purchase of new equipment. He became a bookseller, and regularly used his newspapers to advertise the items he had for sale. He also advertised his own books and pamphlets. Some of this material was based on his lectures or on editorials and articles he had originally written for his papers.[107]

Manchester newspapermen could go in for printing and bookselling to increase their incomes, but they still had to find ways of making their papers more appealing. One tactic was to run special features and articles in the hope of holding readers or attracting new ones. The *Guardian* always gave a lot of space to commercial news and comment, but also began to offer special features such as the series 'The State and Prospects of the Cotton Trade', lengthy and detailed articles appearing periodically from September 1823. The early pieces were written by Shuttleworth and the later ones by

---

[105] *Times*, 30 May 1829.
[106] Circulation figures are in *Times*, 20 Feb., 23 Oct. 1830. Advertisement averages are based on figures taken for every fourth issue of the *Times*.
[107] *Gazette*, 17 June 1826, 26 April 1828; *Times*, 30 Jan., 10 July, 4 Dec. 1830, 24 Sept. 1831, 4 Aug. 1832.

Taylor himself. Among the special features offered by Prentice was extensive parliamentary coverage at times of high political excitement. He also offered free supplements on occasion, as in April 1831 when the House of Commons voted on the Reform Bill. In December 1830 he gave away a free copy of the *Westminster Review* article on the ballot with each *Times* sold. In November 1831 his readers had a choice between the ballot article and Colonel T. Perronet Thompson's *Catechism of the Corn Laws.*[108] All this was costly, but Prentice always wanted to help create 'right opinion' and he must also have hoped to attract more readers by offering such extra services. As well as using these inducements, newspapers might regularly devote considerable space to items calculated to generate the most interest among sections of the local reading public. A newspaper might become renowned for its weekly attention to certain subjects or types of news, and readers might buy it primarily because they were attracted by such contents. Prentice was known for such things as his attention to politics and to workers' issues, and the *Guardian* for its commercial coverage. Prentice would also write on commercial questions but not as often as Taylor. Taylor gave much space to foreign news too, of value to Manchester businessmen whose trading interests were spread all over the globe. One-upmanship was rife among Manchester newspapers. To get a scoop was a major achievement and worthy of lengthy self-congratulation. In July and August 1827, during the long dispute in Manchester over the erection and furnishing of new Anglican churches, Prentice made much of the fact that his *Gazette* was the only local paper to give space to a recent Leeds vestry meeting which had refused to allow a rate to be levied for these purposes.[109]

The competition amongst Manchester's newspapers meant that editors would make claims and boasts not only about scoops, general progress and usefulness, but also about the influence they were having. Nobody did this more than Prentice. Often the claims about influence were related to those about circulation figures. The latter were a subject of much argument. Prentice clashed with the *Courier* in 1825 and with the *Manchester and Salford Advertiser* in 1829 about circulation figures. In March 1830 it was the *Guardian's* turn to argue with Prentice, but when he challenged Taylor and Garnett

[108] *Times*, 18 Dec. 1830, 19 March, 2 April, 26 Nov. 1831.
[109] *Gazette*, 28 July, 4, 11 Aug. 1827.

to allow an independent investigation into the comparative sales of the *Times* and *Guardian* they declined.[110] A particularly heated argument over profitability and circulation was that between the *Times* and the *Voice of the People*, the workers' paper commenced by John Doherty and the National Association for the Protection of Labour (N.A.P.L.) in January 1831. Prentice considered his own *Times* the most suitable paper for 'thinking' operatives, and declared that those behind the *Voice* had no idea of the costs and effort involved in establishing a newspaper. He continued his warnings and was attacked for 'labouring under the insidious character of a friend to the workman' and wanting 'the exclusive right of being the worker's teacher and counsellor'. Prentice may have been worried about competition from the *Voice* and the loss of some of his own plebeian readers. Perhaps he did not like the idea of someone else setting themselves up as the journalistic champion of the labouring poor. He assumed that the operatives needed to be informed and instructed, but insisted that they needed the right instruction, the kind that could only come from the *Times*. To some extent, though, Prentice was motivated by a real concern for the workers. He truly believed that Doherty was fooling them, using their money for a project that was not in their best interests and was bound to fail. All that he said about the problems facing the *Voice* was vindicated in September 1831 when that paper ceased publication. Prentice looked back on the whole affair and declared that it had been his duty to warn the workers of the costs involved in establishing and running a newspaper. He had been denied the credit of disinterestedly cautioning the workers of their certain loss, but Doherty's faction had known he was right and had kept the truth from them. The *Voice* had only lasted for nine months. It had cost the workers £1,500 and in return they had received nothing, no rise in wages or social improvements (as advocated by the *Voice* in conjunction with the N.A.P.L.), and no increase in political knowledge.[111]

Manchester newspapers criticised each other for a variety of reasons. Comments might be made, for example, about inferior

---

[110] *Gazette*, 4 June 1825; *Times*, 14, 21 Feb., 5, 19 Sept. 1829, 22 Feb., 27 March 1830; *Guardian*, 13, 20, 27 March 1830.
[111] *Times*, 20, 27 Nov. 1830, 19, 26 Feb., 1 Oct. 1831; *Voice*, 12, 19, 26 Feb., 5 March 1831; R. Kirby and A. E. Musson, *The Voice of the People: John Doherty 1798–1854, trade unionist, radical and factory reformer* (1975), p. 248.

journalistic style, as when the *Courier* ridiculed the 'ponderous prose' of the *Guardian* in February 1830.[112] Accusations about inaccurate or biased reporting were legion, particularly in relation to such local events as meetings of the police commission.[113] Editors attacked each other on the grounds of truthfulness and also of usefulness. The *Guardian*'s claim to pre-eminence as a commentator on commercial affairs was often disputed. The *Courier* rejected most of what 'new political economy' had to offer, and repeatedly argued with Taylor on economic matters.[114] Prentice also attacked Taylor for claiming expertise and writing in the fashion of one who believed himself to be alone in fully understanding commercial issues. In 1829–30 the two men argued about the approach, character and gravity of the latest cyclical depression in the cotton trade.[115] Shuttleworth also joined in the criticism of Taylor. He had earlier written some commercial pieces for the *Guardian* which had been greatly admired in local business circles, but when Taylor began to print a new series of articles under the same title ('The State and Prospects of the Cotton Trade') Shuttleworth was keen to dissociate himself from the erroneous opinions which he thought they contained. He wrote Taylor an open letter on this matter in January 1830.[116] Soon there was an argument over Taylor's treatment of a town meeting on 25 February 1830, which had discussed taxation, the currency and prevalent economic distress. Shuttleworth and Richard Potter both took exception to Taylor's stance and used the correspondence pages of the *Times* to publicise their views. One of the points at issue was Shuttleworth's opinion that 'the average rate of profits is perhaps the most unerring criterion and the most certain standard of national prosperity', and another was Taylor's verdict on the size and respectability of the attendance at the meeting.[117]

---

[112] *Guardian*, 27 Feb. 1830. Taylor replied that yes, his prose was ponderous in the sense that it fell heavily upon those against whom it was directed.

[113] e.g. *Gazette*, 15 March, 12, 19 April 1823, 17 Nov., 1 Dec. 1827; *Guardian*, 29 March, 12, 19 April, 22 Nov. 1823, 24 Nov., 8 Dec. 1827.

[114] e.g. *Courier*, 22 Aug., 5, 12, 19 Sept. 1829; *Guardian*, 29 Aug., 5 Sept. 1829.

[115] *Times*, 14, 28 Feb., 8 Aug. 1829, 30 Jan., 20, 27 Feb. 1830; *Guardian*, 7, 28 Feb., 7 March, 1 Aug. 1829, 9, 16, 23 Jan. 1830.

[116] *Guardian*, 30 Jan. 1830; *Courier*, 6 Feb. 1830. See also Shuttleworth's piece on Taylor's commercial articles (dated Jan. 1831) in Shuttleworth Scrapbook, p. 37.

[117] *Times*, 13 March, 13 April 1830; *Guardian*, 27 Feb., 6, 13, 20 March, 10 April 1830; Shuttleworth Scrapbook, pp. 75–7; *Chronicle*, 20 Feb. 1830.

A prominent feature of newspaper rivalry in Manchester were the remarks that editors made against each other concerning alleged violations of respectable and appropriate journalistic conduct. The *Guardian* condemned Prentice in August 1830, for example, because he had restricted the access of reporters to a dinner in the Salford town hall attended by the celebrated radical Henry 'Orator' Hunt. Prentice was on the organising committee of this event, and had suggested that no reporter should be admitted unless he purchased a dinner ticket. The *Guardian* seems to have believed that Prentice was trying to give his own *Times* an unfair advantage in the coverage of an event of great local interest.[118] An editor would sometimes deem it necessary to devote space to vigorous self-defence if ever his good character as a newspaperman was brought into question. Prentice defended himself against character slurs in the *Manchester and Salford Advertiser* in September 1829 and November 1831, after being accused of dishonesty and impropriety,[119] and he was also quick to respond whenever another paper touched on a subject he still felt strongly about, the bankruptcy which had forced him to give up the *Gazette* in 1828.[120] In December 1822 the Tory *Chronicle* was so vitriolic in its condemnation of Taylor's recent remarks about the conduct of local magistrates that he was prompted to defend his personal integrity against such abuse. He stated that he had only criticised magistrates for specific acts in court, that he had been discriminatory in his remarks, and that if an official was guilty of improper conduct in his public capacity then a newspaperman was perfectly free to comment on this conduct. Taylor then turned the tables on the *Chronicle* and accused it of a range of journalistic misdemeanours such as inaccurate reporting and mercenary tendencies.[121] In May 1823 it was Aston's *Exchange Herald* that incurred Taylor's wrath. Aston had accused Taylor of claiming personal exemption from all criticism.[122]

Perhaps the bitterest critics of Taylor, though, were members of the band. As well as charges of apostasy there were allegations that he was guilty of impropriety as the editor of a public journal. He

---

[118] *Guardian*, 21 Aug. 1830.
[119] *Times*, 5, 19 Sept. 1829, 12 Nov. 1831.
[120] e.g. *Guardian*, 27 Feb. 1830; Shuttleworth Scrapbook, p. 77; *Times*, 13 March 1830, 12 Nov. 1831.
[121] *Guardian*, 21, 28 Dec. 1822, 4 Jan., 8 March 1823.
[122] *Exchange Herald*, 15 May 1823; *Guardian*, 17 May 1823.

seemed to be eager to cast aspersions on his former friends whenever he had cause to notice them in his columns. Arguments with Prentice were numerous, and some of Taylor's differences with Shuttleworth and Richard Potter have already been noticed above. In the summer of 1828 it was Baxter who engaged in disputation with Taylor. Baxter and the others had been angered by the alliance of the *Guardian* with the 'high' party in local affairs, and particularly by that paper's advocacy of an unpopular Manchester police bill. At a meeting on 16 July 1828 Baxter pointed to inaccuracies in the *Guardian's* reports relative to the bill. There followed a much publicised correspondence between Baxter and Taylor on the matter, with Baxter also claiming to have been personally insulted. He strongly objected, for instance, to Taylor's coupling of his name with that of William Whitworth, the volatile corn dealer and spokesman of the 'low' party, the smaller ratepayers who opposed the bill. The *Guardian* concluded that 'it is not we who have sought, in the difference of our opinion on a public measure, pretexts for the total disruption of a private friendship'. Prentice pointed to the irony that it had been he and Baxter 'who, in a mistaken estimate of (Taylor's) principles, originated the scheme of putting him into the station he now fills as proprietor of the *Guardian* . . . This unfortunate step is, in their estimation, the heaviest of their political sins'.[123] Taylor provoked another of the band, Thomas Potter, in March 1830 when he ran an article on the activities of the Society for the Preservation of Ancient Footpaths. This body had been formed by the band and its allies to protect the public's right of way whenever local paths and roads were illegally closed up. Taylor's article seemed to accuse Thomas Potter of hypocrisy, for it emphasised that Potter himself had recently diverted a path which ran across his property in Pendleton. Potter was incredulous. His had been a legally sanctioned act and was done with the knowledge and approval of his neighbours. How could Taylor group him together with offending landowners, farmers and others who illegally blocked footways? He wrote to the *Times* rejecting Taylor's comments and stating that this insult

> only adds to the disgust with which I had previously regarded Mr Taylor's public career, and to the exceeding regret I had for several years felt that I and my brother, by our pecuniary aid and by our personal exertions and influence, were instrumental

[123] *Guardian*, 26 July, 2, 9, 16 August 1828; *Gazette*, 9 Aug. 1828.

in establishing a paper which instead of being the honest defender has been the inveterate foe of popular rights.[124]

The charges of apostasy came so often from his former friends that Taylor must have quickly tired of replying to them. Every few months, though, he would feel obliged to write a piece in self-defence to illustrate his honesty and consistency. He often repeated the point he had made in letters to Richard Potter in October 1826: it was not his views that had changed but prevalent political circumstances. Toryism was not as rampant and unreasonable as in the past, Taylor claimed, and public men had a duty to adapt their conduct and statements according to changing conditions.[125]

At times it seemed as if the newspapers of Taylor and Prentice hardly agreed on anything. On certain public issues, of course, they did agree, perhaps differing on the speed and extent of the reforms required, but reasonably united on the need for reforms and the general direction these reforms should take. The disputation was normally due as much to a clash of personalities as to disagreement on issues. Another important feature common to both was their criticism of Tory newspaper opponents. Criticism came not only on political grounds, but could also be related to alleged violations of correct journalistic conduct. The target of comment was often the *Courier*. The *Courier* was established in January 1825 because some local Tories thought that they needed a more vigorous and accomplished organ than they could then rely on to combat the papers of Prentice and Taylor. These two editors were quick to attack its improprieties, and did so with almost as much force as they employed to condemn its politics. In October 1825, for example, Prentice accused the *Courier* of printing literary extracts which had been 'surreptitiously obtained' and inserted without permission. During the subsequent controversy he questioned the *Courier*'s honesty and sources of information.[126] The most important non-political quarrel between the *Guardian* and the *Courier* in these years related to the latter's inclusion of unstamped supplements with its main issues during the summer of 1827. Taylor and Garnett wanted to do the

---

[124] *Mercury*, 9 March 1830; *Times*, 13 March 1830; Shuttleworth Scrapbook, p. 77. Such was the bitterness created by this affair that Shuttleworth threatened to give Taylor a flogging. Potter Collection, xi, p. 141.
[125] Potter Collection, xii, pp. 107–8, 111–16; Meinertzhagen, *Potters of Tadcaster*, pp. 226–34.
[126] *Courier* and *Gazette*, 1, 8, 15, 22 Oct. 1825.

same thing, such was the pressure on available space, and pointed to the *Courier*'s conduct when informed by the stamp office that the issuing of such supplements could not be permitted. Thomas Sowler was outraged and dubbed them 'The Informers'. The *Guardian* immediately rejected his charge about 'discreditable feelings of uneasiness at the success of rival publications'.[127]

'The Manchester Newspapers of the present day are polished and urbane in their conduct towards each other, compared with what they were about the time of the calamitous event called the Manchester Massacre.' So said the *Westminster Review* in 1830.[128] It is a view that cannot be accepted. The same goes for what was stated by a writer on the press in 1836. He thought that the personal responsibility under which a provincial editor was placed 'renders him careful to guard himself against personal violence or invectives; and there is scarcely an instance in which any attacks on private character appear, or that the war of words between journalists, which makes up so large and so vulgar a portion of the daily prints, rages in county papers'.[129] None of this applies to the Manchester papers in the period under review. The heated criticisms and persistent attacks made by editors against each other on a wide range of issues relating to political stance, truthfulness, usefulness, journalistic conduct, popularity and influence among readers demonstrate that moderation, urbanity and courtesy had no place in the Manchester newspaper arena. The examples given above represent only the tip of the iceberg. Every single week brought forth some kind of unfavourable comment from one newspaper about another. Rivalry was intense because the newspapers were competing for readers and advertisers. The market was limited and it was impossible that an editor could have any choice but to enter into newspaper warfare. The strong political divides in the town likewise meant that there would be no peaceful coexistence among Manchester's editors. The local papers were all political organs, some more persistently and more clearly

[127] *Courier* and *Guardian*, 18, 25 Aug., 1, 8 Sept. 1827.
[128] 'Provincial, Scotch and Irish Press', p. 73.
[129] 'Journals of the Provinces', pp. 139, 148.

than others, but all of them commenting on the major public issues of the day according to particular political creeds. Due largely to the exertions of the band, exertions to create and direct opinion which necessitated a firm response from conservatives and anti-reformers, the office of a Manchester newspaper in these years was no place for the timorous and non-committed. The essence of Manchester journalism in the pre-Victorian era was commercial competition, political rivalry and personal rancour.

III The Band, Local Affairs and Local Government

In 1815 Manchester's local government institutions were archaic, insufficient and largely under the control of a dominant Tory oligarchy. Gradually this 'high' party admitted a number of wealthy moderates and Whigs, and together these allies attempted to protect the established order and the influence of large property-holders against assaults from Manchester's reformers and marginal groups. Local government conflicts polarised Mancunians along political and social lines. Large property confronted small property, respectable reformers faced conservatives of a similar social and economic status, and men of the middling sort aided or abetted the respectable politicians while sometimes speaking and acting for themselves.[1] The liberal and Dissenting anti-establishment body within the respectable business community sought a greater share of local influence, and members of the band shaped and spearheaded the challenges to the ruling party. They often provided leadership and spokesmen for the large number of reform-minded smaller ratepayers and men of the middling sort who were interested in the causes of economy and administrative improvement, and who began to take a far more active role in local political disputes during the 1820s.

I. THE HEGEMONY OF THE 'HIGH'

In 1788 the manorial steward, William Roberts, stated that all political and religious disputation should be kept out of local government. The views of an officer were unimportant, he said, and all that

[1] Manchester's local government in this period comprised of four overlapping units, the respective rights and jurisdictions of which were a source of much confusion. There was the old manorial (township) administration of the court leet, the parish (which had six divisions), the police commission established in 1792, and the Salford Hundred (the province of Quarter Sessions).

mattered was the proper performance of an officer's duties.[2] But as factional struggles gripped Manchester it was natural for local Tories to defend themselves and strengthen their control over local affairs. Among other steps there was a new ruling that the court leet and its officers had to be 'men who testify an affectionate loyalty to the King, a veneration for the Constitution, and a proper sense of the blessings which flow from them, without which no man ought to be invested with any public trust whatsoever'.[3] The manorial court leet was the main unit of local government until the 1792 Manchester police act, and even after the act it continued to appoint the borough-reeve and constables, Manchester's chief civic officers.[4] The fact that the 1792 act could be sought and obtained was partly a mark of the Tories' confidence. It is also true that Manchester urgently needed administrative improvement, that the act may have been seen by some as a defensive measure (in view of the assertiveness of Manchester Dissenters, who had played a prominent role in the recent test and corporation acts repeal campaigns), and that police matters were current at this time (the 1792 parliamentary session also saw debates over the Middlesex justices bill, for example). Manchester's rulers probably saw that they had a good chance of getting an act and, more importantly, of getting the kind of act they wanted. The outcome was the establishment of the new police commission. Its promoters had reason to think that control would fall to them, not least because the £30 qualification for commissioners ensured some selectivity. Early financial and organisational problems hindered any remarkable improvement in the standard of local government, but the police commission quickly superseded the court leet and by about 1810 the Tories had monopolised all the main posts in the commission just as in the manorial and parochial bodies and on the exclusive local magistrates' bench. Any scandal affecting one branch of local administration inevitably affected the others too, since it was common knowledge that the magistrates, the jurors of the court leet, the boroughreeve, constables and manorial officers, the officers of

[2] W. Roberts, 'A Charge to the Grand Jury of the Court Leet for the Manor of Manchester' (1788), in *Records of the Manchester Court Leet*, ed. J. P. Earwaker (12 vols, 1884–90), ix, p. 233.
[3] Earwaker, *Manchester Court Leet*, ix, p. 252.
[4] The first volume of A. Redford, *The History of Local Government in Manchester* (3 vols, 1939), is the indispensable source for Manchester's local government in this period.

the parish and the leaders of the police commission all belonged to the same closely-knit oligarchy.[5]

This oligarchy drew in members of such Tory bodies as the Association for Preserving Constitutional Order (1792–99), John Shaw's Club (originally founded in 1738) and the Pitt Club (established in 1812). John Shaw himself, an innkeeper, was a market looker in the 1780s, and James Billinge, a fustian manufacturer, member of the A.P.C.O.'s executive and a president of John Shaw's in the 1780s, was a churchwarden, a constable and the boroughreeve of Manchester for 1788–89. Billinge was also on the jury of the court leet, as were other John Shaw men at various times. The dye manufacturer Thomas Fleming was a member of John Shaw's and the Pitt Club, treasurer of the police commission from 1810 to 1819, a highway surveyor for nearly twenty years and a member of several executive police committees. He was accused of corruption by the local reform party in the later 1810s. Other John Shaw and Pitt Club men included manufacturer John Greenwood, a sidesman at the collegiate church in 1805, a juror of the court leet in 1813, boroughreeve of Salford for 1818–19 and the man who brought libel charges against Taylor. Of the eighteen boroughreeves and constables who served Manchester from 1792 to 1797, sixteen were members of the executive committee of the A.P.C.O.[6] Of the 511 men listed in the

[5] Redford, *Local Government*, i, pp. 195–200, 240–43, 258; Gatrell, 'Incorporation and liberal hegemony', pp. 34–5, 60; D. Foster, 'Class and County Government in early nineteenth-century Lancashire', *N.H.*, 9 (1974), pp. 48–60. Before the band's time, accusations about corruption and inefficiency in local government were made most forcefully by the public accountant and bail officer, Thomas Battye, who wrote several pamphlets on local issues of which the most important was *A Disclosure of Parochial Abuse in the Town of Manchester* (1796). See also F. R. Atkinson, Scrapbook, cartoon 'An Enemy to Parochial Peculators' (1807). In view of Manchester's institutional weakness and inefficiency, and the exclusive, oligarchic nature of local government, it is difficult to accept John Bohstedt's claims that Manchester was relatively well-governed, that there was no enduring patronage network in local government, and that the local magistrates' bench was opened up before 1810 to allow an influx of men from mercantile backgrounds. Bohstedt, *Riots and Community Politics*, pp. 75–6, 79–80, 102.
[6] Stancliffe, *John Shaw's*, pp. 45–6, 97, 105, 133, 161, 179; Pitt Club, iii (membership and accounts book); A.P.C.O., minutes and proceedings (attendance lists); A. Mitchell, 'The Association Movement of 1792–3', *H.J.*, 4 (1961), p. 65 n. 57; boroughreeves and constables are listed in Harland, Manchester and Lancashire Collection, p. 136.

Pitt Club membership book, at least 111 (22 per cent) served as churchwardens, overseers, sidesmen or other parish officers in the period from 1790 to 1832.[7] The continual presence of committed Tories within the parochial administration was assured when individual members of the Pitt Club could hold parish offices for several years at a time. Three or four years was common, but one man held offices for as many as eleven years and another was in office for nine years. The parish was split into six divisions (Manchester, Salford, Blackley, Newton, Withington and Stretford), with several offices belonging to each. It was not difficult for the ruling party in Manchester to colonise particular divisions, and retain authority by having supporters switch to different divisions every so often. The same names recur again and again in the lists of officials.[8]

The group holding sway in Manchester was very much a closed circle, and though there was no professed 'test' local officers had to have the right political opinions and credentials. This meant that the same men held several offices at once, or else changed from post to post within the local government structure. From 1814 to 1833 nine men served as constable and then as boroughreeve, and five men served as constable or boroughreeve for two successive terms.[9] Control over the appointment of boroughreeves and constables was important for many reasons, not least because they had the power to veto town meetings on particular subjects. They would simply refuse to call them when requisitioned. Sometimes the reformers would go ahead and hold a public meeting anyway, but if they did this their deliberations lacked official civic sanction, and if they did not they acknowledged the ruling party's ability to prevent the expression of opinions it found unpalatable. The jurors of the court leet normally included the local oligarchy's most prominent members, men who gave life to such organs as the Pitt Club and who for years selected themselves and their friends for the most important local offices. In 1823 the jurors included Joseph Green, a merchant,

---

[7] These calculations were reached by comparing lists in the Pitt Club membership book with Local History Dept. M.C.L. (f. MSC 331. 86), List of parish officers and J.P.s (1720–1912), compiled by P. Stephen from apprenticeship indentures.

[8] Parochial appointments were advertised every April in the *Mercury*. The offices were filled at a parish meeting each Easter Tuesday.

[9] See lists in Harland, Manchester and Lancashire Collection, p. 136. These and other manorial appointments were made each Michaelmas.

constable 1814–15, boroughreeve 1816–17 and a churchwarden; Gilbert Winter, a merchant, boroughreeve 1823–24 and also a churchwarden; J. B. Wanklyn, merchant, constable of Manchester 1825–26 and Salford 1826–27, boroughreeve of Salford 1829–30 and a senior churchwarden of Manchester in the mid-1830s; James Brierley, a future magistrate, a churchwarden and the boroughreeve of Manchester 1820–21 and 1821–22. Other 1823 jurors, the calico printer Jeremiah Fielding, drysalter Thomas Hardman and cotton merchant William Garnett, were all at some time the holders of parochial, manorial or police offices. In 1830 the jurors included former and future parish officers such as the merchant John Bradshaw, merchant and manufacturer Aspinall Philips, master spinner John Barlow and calico printer John Chippendale, as well as banker Samuel Brooks, constable 1827–28, master spinner Robert Ogden, constable 1828–29, iron and timber merchant Thomas Sharp, constable 1819–20, and Benjamin Braidley, a merchant and manufacturer who had been a churchwarden and was to be constable 1830–31 and boroughreeve of Manchester 1831–32 and 1832–33.[10]

The control of the ruling group was self-perpetuating. Not only was the selection of officers in the hands of the same individuals for long periods of time, but outgoing officers could themselves nominate their successors, as was the case with churchwardens and overseers. There was controversy in March 1823 when the Revd W. R. Hay resigned as chairman of the Salford Quarter Sessions and was succeeded by Thomas Starkie. The *Guardian* suspected that there had been a plot to make sure Starkie was appointed. By parliamentary act the Salford magistrates had the power collectively to select their own chairman, but this procedure had apparently been bypassed. It was no accident that Starkie was a man with the 'right' political outlook, asserted the *Guardian*, and one favoured by Hay and those chosen few to whom Hay had first intimated his desire to step down.[11] The oligarchy also controlled appointments to the police committees. In November 1830 when the membership of the finance committee was being discussed, Richard Potter protested that it consisted solely of wealthy men. He pressed for the inclusion of a few shopkeepers to give it some 'mixed blood', but his proposal

---

[10] Lists in *Guardian*, 18 Oct. 1823, 16 Oct. 1830; Harland, Manchester and Lancashire Collection, p. 136; occupations in *Pigot and Dean Directories*, 1821, 1824, 1832.
[11] Hay Scrapbooks, xi, p. 175; *Guardian*, 1 March 1823.

was rejected. Members of the band could see that the reconstitution of the police commission by the 1828 Manchester police act had given the 'high' party even more opportunity to monopolise key posts.[12] By 1832 many outside the police commission were complaining about the control of local affairs by a small select junto within the 'high' party. Much business was being dealt with by the improvement committee, and there was great collusion between this and other committees because the same individuals sat on several committees at the same time. Of the 30 men on the improvement committee, 18 were also on the gas committee, 11 were also on the finance and general purposes committee, and four were also on the paving and soughing committee.[13]

The growing number of townspeople in Manchester who demanded and campaigned for local reforms in the postwar period believed that local government would be cheaper and more efficient if it was made more representative. They disliked being excluded from any share in decision-making. Members of the band attempted to direct the energies and articulate the complaints of these people. They set out to increase public awareness of important local issues and to instigate confrontations with the ruling group on these issues. The band rose to new heights of activity, influence and effectiveness, and these controversies also demonstrated the importance of appeals to groups lower down the social scale. Numerical superiority at local meetings was to be essential to the respectable reformers in Manchester. They and their middling sort allies had to find and exploit what John Garrard has called 'access points', points at which the local opposition could confront the ruling party and attempt to influence the course of local events. Town, police and parish meetings were crucial 'access points' and the ruling party could not always guarantee success at these assemblies. This was why, in the 1820s, defenders of the established order would often resort to the voting system prescribed in the Sturges Bourne vestry act of 1818, which gave votes on a scale of one to six depending on rateable value, and therefore bestowed a decided advantage on leypayers assessed at high amounts. In Manchester this system was used (or there was an attempt to use it) even when its applicability was open to serious question. The liberals' *Gazette* had seen the dangers even before the 1818 act was

---

[12] *Times*, 6 Nov. 1830.
[13] *Times*, 14 April 1832.

passed, and Richard Cobden was to condemn the act in his 1837 pamphlet 'Incorporate Your Borough!'[14]

V. A. C. Gatrell has argued that Manchester's local government was based on 'uncontaminated middle-class influence' and that Manchester was the setting for an 'apartheid society', with the wealthy competing for power without reference to or concern for their social inferiors.[15] This gives an incomplete and misleading picture. Pressure from below could be a reality and could force the ruling oligarchy into precautionary or reactionary steps, as during the war years and in 1816–17 and 1819–20. Members of the band, moreover, made clear appeals to the lower classes in search of allies, particularly to the middling sort of shopkeepers, petty traders, publicans, small manufacturers, clerks and craftsmen, lesser ratepayers and the very people who would listen when they were told that public money was being wasted and that public bodies were unrepresentative and self-seeking. These assertive Manchester traders and men of small means are in some ways analogous to R. S. Neale's 'middling class': unstable, lacking in deference, dynamic, active and wanting to share in the privileges and authority of the locally dominant.[16] It is not surprising that the band often tried to tap the energy source represented by this stratum in the local political struggles of the 1820s and 1830s. The political activity of the middling sort was a crucial factor in the affairs of many towns, and the cleavage between large and small property and between ruling groups and 'economy' parties has been a recurrent theme in the historiography of nineteenth-century urban politics.[17]

---

[14] *Gazette*, 25 April 1818; R. Cobden, 'Incorporate Your Borough!' (1837), in W. E. A. Axon, *Cobden as a Citizen* (1907), pp. 30–61.

[15] Gatrell, 'Incorporation and liberal hegemony', pp. 19, 22.

[16] R. S. Neale, *Class and Ideology in the 19th Century* (1972), pp. 29–40.

[17] e.g. T. J. Nossiter, *Influence, Opinion and Political Idioms in Reformed England* (1975), ch. 7; B. Barber, 'Municipal government in Leeds, 1835–1914', in Fraser, *Municipal Reform*, pp. 64–5; J. Garrard, *Leaders and Politics in 19th-century Salford: a historical analysis of urban political power* (1977), p. 30; T. J. Nossiter, 'Shopkeeper radicalism in the 19th century', in *Imagination and Precision in the Social Sciences*, eds T. J. Nossiter, A. H. Hanson, S. Rokkan (1972), pp. 407–38; G. Crossick, 'Urban Society and the Petty Bourgeoisie in 19th-century Britain', in *The Pursuit of Urban History*, eds D. Fraser and R. Sutcliffe (1983), pp. 307–26; R. J. Morris, 'Class, power and social structure in British nineteenth century towns', in Morris, *Class, power and social structure*, pp. 2–22; see also discussion on 'The Middle Class in 19th-century politics', by Nossiter and Fraser, in Garrard *et al.*, *Middle Class in Politics*, pp. 67–84, 85–91.

In Manchester the middling sort provided invaluable aid to the incorporators of the later 1830s, and 18 of the 64 members of the first town council were from retail trades.[18] But it is important not to exaggerate the independence and radicalism of the middling sort. It was not only the liberal reformers in the Manchester business community who made appeals to the social groups below them. Conservatism and loyalism had their attractions and influence at various times, as may be seen from the anti-reform mob activity of the 1790s, the favourable response to the local volunteer movement of the war years, and the high number of middling sort applicants who offered to serve as special constables in 1817 and 1819. It cannot be denied that the main Tory organs themselves, the A.P.C.O. and the Pitt Club, were dominated by textile businessmen and professionals. But when local Toryism had to be active its more affluent and socially prominent leaders were quick to recruit allies from further down the social scale. About 76 per cent of the members of the Manchester and Salford Yeomanry on duty at Peterloo were drawn from the middling sort: publicans, butchers, petty traders and skilled workers.[19] Hence those of the middling sort (then and now a somewhat ill-defined stratum and only partially developing in self- consciousness, social identity and ambition during the 1820s) were not politically cohesive. Nor were their loyalties permanent and unchanging. They were open to persuasion; their support and approval had to be sought and won. Members of the band repeatedly made this effort, decisively shaping local Manchester politics in the process.

---

[18] A. Briggs, *Victorian Cities* (1963), p. 105.
[19] The social character of members of the A.P.C.O. and Pitt Club can be determined by comparing their membership lists with local commercial directories. Very few representatives of the middling sort are present, while the dominance of textile merchants and manufacturers is readily apparent. They formed by far the largest occupational group, 58 of a sample of 109 members of the A.P.C.O. and 141 of a sample of 345 members of the Pitt Club. For members of the Manchester and Salford Yeomanry, *Observer*, 11 May 1822.

2. OPPOSITION TO NEW CHURCHES,
CHURCH RATES AND TITHES

In view of the numerical strength and political assertiveness of Protestant Dissenters in Manchester, it is not surprising that the reformers' challenge against local Tory dominance was particularly powerful in the denominational sphere. Serious disputation arose in January 1816 when the local oligarchy backed a plan to establish a new Anglican church in Manchester with free sittings. This plan was championed by a strident Anglican-Tory amalgam led by such men as the Revd C. D. Wray of the collegiate church. After negotiations the Dissenters withdrew their opposition on the understanding that the Anglicans would bear all the costs involved.[20] But the probability of future collision was clear as pro-Church commentators claimed that there was a lack of Anglican accommodation in Manchester. A campaign to extend the pastoral care and influence of the Church of England in Manchester began after parliament established a £1 million grant for church-building in 1818. A parish meeting in the collegiate church on 27 January 1820 considered the purchase of suitable sites for new churches, but descended into arguments as members of the band raised objections. Richard Potter pointed to the high cost of sites and maintenance, and presented arguments that were used repeatedly against the local administrative and ecclesiastical establishment in subsequent years: there was no need for new churches, the existing ones were never full, and it was unjust to make Dissenters pay towards the building and upkeep of Anglican places of worship. Taylor contrasted the peaceful settlement of 1816 with

[20] *Gazette*, 6, 13, 20 Jan., 10 Feb. 1816; *Chronicle*, 23 Sept., 9 Dec. 1815; H. Wray, *Memoir of the Revd C. D. Wray* (1867), pp. 14–20; Revd C. D. Wray, *A Statement of Facts respecting the Population of the Parish of Manchester, showing the Want of a new Free Church* (1815); Prentice, *Sketches*, pp. 29, 59. On the perceived shortage of church accommodation, Wheeler, *History*, p. 375; R. G. Cowherd, *The Politics of English Dissent* (1959), p. 68; W. R. Ward, 'The Cost of Establishment: some reflections on church building in Manchester', *Studies in Church History*, 3 (1966), pp. 277–89. The balance in favour of Dissent was clear by the time of the Religious Census of 1851. Manchester Anglicans numbered 36,000 and had 38,000 sittings in 32 places of worship. Dissent had 44,000 adherents, 40,000 sittings and 78 places of worship. See Gatrell, 'Incorporation and liberal hegemony', p. 36.

the present attempt to lay heavy charges on the whole parish, Dissenters included, for the building of churches that were not needed. He also gave expression to a market theory of religion:

> Church of Englandism, like everything else (I do not use the term offensively), is a marketable commodity, by which I simply mean that the supply will always be equal to the demand. If more churches are wanted, more will be built; but it is not right, without looking to the necessity of them, or indeed under any circumstances, that Dissenters should be obliged to contribute to the support of an establishment, the doctrines of which they do not approve, and in the principles promulgated by which they do not coincide. Let the friends of the establishment build what churches they like; but do not let them force their Dissenting brethren to contribute thereto.

On a show of hands the meeting sided with Potter and Taylor, but the Tories invoked the Sturges Bourne vestry act and manufactured a victory. The reformers were outraged that the purchase of sites had been sanctioned in this fashion.[21] Another meeting was necessary to levy a rate, however, and this was arranged for 8 June 1820. As Richard Potter recalled, 'we immediately set to and made every exertion to induce the parish to attend'.[22] After speeches made by Potter, Taylor, Baxter and their allies, the meeting refused to approve a rate and even a scrutiny under the vestry act could not change this outcome. The reformers had evidently canvassed local opinion effectively and secured a formidable attendance of their own followers, and the result was warmly celebrated in their *Gazette*.[23] The Tories' desire for revenge after 8 June prompted them to issue a public notice a few days later:

> The members of the Established Church are requested to withdraw their subscriptions from, and to withhold their benefactions to, those Institutions connected with the Methodist and Dissenting Societies of all Denominations; and they are solicited to increase their subscriptions and to enlarge their

---

[21] *Gazette*, 29 Jan. 1820; Potter Collection, xi, p. 90; Hadfield, *Personal Narrative*, p. 66.
[22] Potter Collection, xi, p. 91.
[23] *Gazette*, 10 June 1820; Axon, *Annals of Manchester*, p. 161.

benefactions to all those Institutions promoting the interests of their own Apostolic Church.[24]

Though the meeting of 8 June 1820 had denied the necessity for new churches and refused to grant funds for the purchase of sites, the report of the parliamentary commissioners published in May 1821 stated that three churches would nevertheless be built in Manchester. The next parish meeting was on 6 June 1821, but the churchwardens argued that it was not competent to consider any matter other than their latest accounts. When Richard Potter demanded that all correspondence between the churchwardens and the parliamentary commissioners concerning new churches should be laid before the meeting, he was told that there had been no such correspondence. When he suggested that there should be a full investigation into the rate issue and the attendances at all places of worship in Manchester parish, he was told that such proposals were beyond the province of the present meeting.[25] This was to be the pattern at subsequent assemblies. The reformers were denied the chance to protest openly and formally about the new churches. It was difficult for them to gain a hearing at meetings which were concerned primarily with the passing of the churchwardens' quarterly accounts, and if they tried to introduce other topics for discussion they were ruled out of order.[26] Unable to make headway at parish meetings they turned to the newspapers. In letters to the *Guardian*, for example, Richard Potter presented statistics to show that attendances at local Anglican churches had actually been declining and that one, St John's, was hardly ever more than a quarter filled. The *Chronicle* disputed Potter's figures, but he was adamant that Manchester did not need new Anglican churches.[27] Despite this, the reformers had to accept that these churches were going to be built. The ruling party had somehow convinced the parliamentary commissioners that Manchester was short of church accommodation and that the motion passed on 8 June 1820 was irrelevant and unrepresentative. The disappointment of the liberal-Dissenting leaders was increased in March 1824 when they learned that the government was planning to

---

[24] *Gazette*, 10, 17 June 1820.
[25] *Gazette*, 2, 9 June 1821; Hay Scrapbooks, x, p. 119.
[26] e.g. Report of meeting in *Gazette*, 15 June 1822.
[27] *Guardian*, 6, 13, 20 July 1822; *Chronicle*, 13 July 1822; Potter Collection, xi, p. 92.

devote another £500,000 to the building of new churches. They organised a petition pointing out that the average Sunday attendances at five of the Anglican churches in Manchester (St Ann's, St Michael's, St Paul's, St Luke's and St George's) did not exceed 1,100 in total, while the total capacity of these five churches was 6,000.[28] Such protests against the building of new churches continued in the following years, but soon there were other matters to which the band had to attend.

Chief among these was the question of whether church rates could be used to pay for certain repairs, salaries and furnishings. In 1823 the churchwardens took legal counsel and gained the decision that they could resort to the church rates for these purposes. The reformers were not satisfied, and at a leypayers' meeting in June 1824 Richard Potter, Taylor, Baxter, Harvey and their allies carried a motion that the churchwardens should seek further counsel.[29] This the churchwardens did not do, and in June 1825 they provocatively included charges for plate and furnishings for two of the new churches in their quarterly accounts. Of course these churches, St Matthew's and St Philip's, were built in opposition to the recorded decision of the leypayers. There was a large attendance at the parish meeting of 30 June 1825. Prentice asserted that even if the churchwardens were bound to provide the items required for a decent administration of the sacraments, 'yet surely the parish was the best judge as to what *was* decent and what should be the scale of expenditure'. Richard Potter moved that the charges for plate be disallowed, but this was rejected.[30] As the Tory newspapers condemned the reformers for their stance,[31] there was talk of an appeal to the courts. That the band and such middling sort allies as the radical draper, P. T. Candelet, were considering this course was made clear at a parish meeting in July 1827. The churchwardens eventually agreed to take further counsel, that of J. W. Nolan, the premier parochial lawyer in the kingdom. In September 1827 Nolan ruled that the earlier decision had been sound: the churchwardens were bound to provide all the articles necessary for the celebration of services. Nevertheless, the reformers were encouraged by resistance to new churches and the necessary rates in Sheffield, Clerkenwell,

[28] *Guardian*, 27 March 1824; *Gazette*, 22 May 1824.
[29] *Gazette*, 5 June 1824.
[30] *Gazette*, 25 June, 2 July 1825.
[31] e.g. *Courier*, 2 July 1825.

Birmingham and Leeds. The Leeds ratepayers' decision (July 1827) to pay none of the costs incurred during the erection of new churches was given great publicity in Prentice's *Gazette*, which was in fact the only local paper to report and discuss it. Prentice also wrote to Edward Baines of the *Leeds Mercury* for further information.[32] Richard Potter made use of the Leeds decision at a Manchester parish meeting on 22 September 1827, and his 'small but clamorous faction' was attacked by the *Courier*.[33] For all the continuing protest and controversy, the band could not stop the churchwardens from proceeding with a policy that had received legal sanction and the backing of recent parish meetings. Potter, Prentice and their friends persistently stressed the injustice of the affair, and kept it before the public in speeches and newspaper articles. They were quick to condemn such statements as that of Bishop Sumner of Chester, who consecrated one of the new Manchester churches in December 1828 and declared that it was blasphemous to grudge the cost of a building where the name of God was to be praised.[34]

The ill-feeling produced by the struggles of the 1820s gave added force to the campaign against church rates as a whole in the early 1830s. Dissenters had resented having to pay church rates for many years, and their unease was only increased by the controversial uses the Church in Manchester had been making of its privileged position in recent times.[35] The parish meeting of 1 June 1832 took place at a time when the feeling against church rates had reached unprecedented heights, when respectable and middling sort reformers had some experience of working together, and when demands were rising for greater accountability on the part of officers who controlled the expending of public funds. At this meeting objections were raised to many items in the churchwardens' accounts, though Prentice attacked rating and the whole Church–state system rather than the churchwardens who, he acknowledged, had to make the payments they thought they were required to make. He recommended that the meeting should approve only a very low rate for the next year, to encourage

[32] *Gazette*, 14, 28 July, 4, 11 August, 8 Sept. 1827; *Chronicle*, 14 July 1827; Hay Scrapbooks, xii, pp. 19–20; Potter Collection, xi, pp. 93–4.
[33] *Gazette* and *Courier*, 29 Sept. 1827; Hay Scrapbooks, xii, pp. 11–12.
[34] *Times*, 12 Dec. 1828.
[35] e.g. 'Twenty Reasons why Dissenters should not be compelled to pay Church Rates and Tithes, or in any way support the Church of England', *Times*, 26 May 1832; Brotherton Scrapbooks, xi, p. 54.

greater economy and to register disapproval of the principle of church rates. Prentice's proposal for a rate of a halfpenny in the pound was approved. This was a victory for the Leypayers' Association which had been formed by middling sort reformers to keep a check on local expenditure.[36] The *Courier* condemned what had happened but Prentice's *Times* followed the victory with articles on pluralism, corruption and the need for ecclesiastical reform.[37] In 1833 he and his allies tried to wrest control of the parish offices from the local oligarchy. They were unsuccessful, but progress was made on the church rates issue. A parish meeting in July 1833 passed Richard Potter's motion that no rate was necessary. The churchwardens levied a rate anyway, but many Mancunians refused to pay. The same thing happened in 1834, and then in July 1835 the churchwardens bowed to the pressure of the opposition and announced that no rate would be sought.[38]

The liberal-Dissenting body was as ideologically opposed to tithes as to church rates,[39] but its leaders had little practical involvement in the celebrated Manchester tithe controversy of 1804 to 1829 because this was of most importance to the landowners, farmers and rural tenants of the parish. The reformers were highly interested in the affair, though, and it received much attention in the newspapers of Taylor and Prentice. The root cause of the dispute was the collegiate clergy's attempt to enforce payments in kind. Though widespread in the region, these had been dying out and in the Manchester parish had only applied to corn. The clergy secured a decision in the court of Chancery that the substitute payments which had long been made in lieu of tithes should be discontinued and all tithes of milk, potatoes, cattle and hay should be paid in kind. As the *Guardian* stated, this would mean that the income of the warden and fellows of the collegiate church would be 'prodigiously augmented'.[40] The Manchester reformers backed the opposition campaign and denounced the collegiate body's legal prosecution of recalcitrant parishioners.[41] Prentice did not want the tithe burden to be passed

---

[36] *Times*, 2 June 1832.
[37] *Courier*, 2 June 1832; *Times*, 23 June, 20 October 1832.
[38] Fraser, *Urban Politics*, pp. 37–9; S. D. Simon, *A Century of City Government: Manchester 1838–1938* (1938), pp. 64–5; *Times*, 11 July 1835.
[39] e.g. J. E. Taylor on 'Remarks on the Consumption of Public Wealth by the Clergy', *Guardian*, 13, 27 July 1822.
[40] *Guardian*, 22 March 1823.
[41] *Guardian*, 28 June 1823, 24 Jan. 1824; *Gazette*, 28 June 1823.

on to tenants by the landowners and, the odious corn laws never far from his mind, he argued that the tithe question affected everyone 'for this plain reason, that not only the rent of the land but all charges upon it, whether tithes or taxes, or in any other shape, ARE INCLUDED IN THE PRICE PAID FOR THE AGRICULTURAL PRODUCE'.[42] Eventually, in 1829, the churchwardens mediated and a settlement was worked out providing for financial payments per acre in lieu of all tithes, not just the ones in dispute.[43]

3. ACCOUNTABILITY, OFFICERS' SALARIES, MANORIAL RIGHTS AND COUNTY RATES

One of the best ways to highlight the need for reform and a more just distribution of local power was to launch determined attacks on the conduct of prominent local officers. If it could be shown that an officer was guilty of irregular conduct, both he and his allies in the ruling party could be subjected to great pressure and the willingness of townsmen to scrutinise officers' activities was appreciably increased.

The aforementioned Thomas Fleming, treasurer of the police commission from 1810 to 1819 and the holder of several other offices besides, came in for much accusation in the years following the end of the war. No officer was more prominent than Fleming in his day, and the fact that he achieved such a noticeable personal ascendancy served his critics because it made it easier for them to gain publicity. His chief antagonist from 1816 onwards was the middling-sort leader Thomas Chapman, who kept a fruit shop in Fennel Street and was also part-owner and editor of the radical *Observer* in the first half of 1819. He had to give this up when several libel actions were filed against him. One of these was brought by Fleming and resulted in Chapman being fined £250 in February 1820.[44] The campaign against Fleming was given great publicity in the liberals' *Gazette*. The main accusations against him were that he by-passed the normal procedures for conducting official business and took decisions without

[42] *Times*, 4 July 1829.
[43] *Guardian*, 11 July 1829; *Courier*, 4 July 1829.
[44] Leary, Periodical Press, p. 129; Timperley, *Manchester Historical Recorder*, p. 83.

waiting for the proper consultation. Chapman also suggested that he was corrupt. When Chapman was offered the chance to inspect Fleming's accounts, though, he declined.[45] Fleming took much of the blame for three major local government scandals in 1818–19: peculation in the provision of bran for police horses, the acceptance of a very high tender for work at the gas establishment from a firm with a partner on the gas committee, and irregular payments for cement used in the extension of the gas works.[46] Fleming was a target in the drive to make town officers more answerable. As 'J. B.' (probably J. B. Smith) warned in a letter of November 1818 to the *Gazette*: 'Perhaps Mr Fleming and his friends are not aware that if any money is paid for which the treasurer cannot produce vouchers, having the signatures of three Commissioners, *any nine* Commissioners . . . can procure the treasurer's commitment to jail unless the money is repaid or the receipts produced'.[47] Although nothing was ever proven against him, Fleming decided to resign as treasurer of the police commission at the end of 1818.

Another notorious local officer who was subjected to a tirade of accusations was Joseph Nadin, deputy constable of Manchester from 1802 to 1821. A principal executive agent of the local authorities and a highly successful thief-taker, his methods were regarded as oppressive and improper by many, and his participation in local political persecution on his masters' behalf made him particularly odious to both respectable reformers and plebeian radicals. Prentice called him 'the real ruler of Manchester', but though the deputy constable had a high public profile he was clearly a servant rather than a master.[48] Criticism of Nadin's conduct, and of local police in general, reached a crescendo after 1815. Nadin was often accused of conniving at crime, and this claim gained considerable strength after the Hindley affair of 1818. Nadin and one of his agents, William Hindley, tricked two youths named Hill and Lea into receiving stolen property and then arrested them for having this property in their possession. The *Observer* and the *Gazette* demanded an immediate inquiry, and further accusations against Nadin came thick and fast. He had

[45] *Gazette*, 8 June 1816, 1 Feb. 1817, 13 March 1819.
[46] Redford, *Local Government*, i, pp. 262–71; *Gazette*, 3 Oct. 1818, 13 March 1819.
[47] *Gazette*, 7 Nov. 1818.
[48] Prentice, *Sketches*, p. 34; Read, *Peterloo*, pp. 79–80; Marshall, *Public Opinion*, pp. 93–5.

refused to give back money taken from a Blanketeer. He had improperly accepted a reward for helping out when a warehouse caught fire; such was his cupidity that he later returned to the firm claiming that he had lost part of the money, and was paid a second time. The same thing happened when he assisted a merchant who had been robbed. In the face of such revelations the boroughreeve and constables agreed to hold an inquiry, but this only resulted in the dismissal of Hindley. Correspondents of the *Gazette* denounced this as a whitewash and cover-up: why had nothing been done about Nadin? The ruling party seemed to be protecting him because in so doing it was protecting itself. Every boroughreeve and constable of Manchester who had served between 1802 and 1818 signed a document expressing complete satisfaction with the ability, integrity and fidelity of Nadin during their own periods in office. The *Gazette* found this 'anything but satisfactory', but though the rumours and suspicions continued the authorities never allowed a full investigation into Nadin's conduct.[49] Other local officers were attacked at the time of the Hindley affair, particularly the Revd W. R. Hay. As chairman of the Salford Quarter Sessions Hay delivered an address on recent events to the grand jury in April 1818, and rejected the accusations which had been made against Nadin. The *Gazette* considered these remarks 'very improper', and a correspondent named 'Civis' argued that the allegations against Nadin were not the concern of the grand jury and that Hay had made an improper use of his position by publicising his own private opinions.[50]

In fact Hay was another prominent local official who came in for much criticism after the war, not for corruption and criminal conduct but rather for the political and party motivations behind some of his actions. At the time of the Hindley affair 'Civis' was not the only one who thought that Hay had overstepped the proper limits of his magisterial functions. Manchester liberals were always complaining that the administration of the law was in the hands of men who would readily use their privileged positions to defend the ruling party and its servants. Hay had taken an active part in implementing policies of restraint and social control during and immediately after the war. He and his fellow clerical magistrates had a reputation for

---

[49] Redford, *Local Government*, i, p. 90; *Gazette*, 7, 21, 28 Feb., 7, 14 March, 4 April 1818; Read, *Peterloo*, pp. 65–6; Hay Scrapbooks, viii, pp. 34–41, 42, 47, x, p. 32; *Chronicle*, 14 March 1818.
[50] Hay Scrapbooks, xi, pp. 145–6; *Gazette*, 18, 25 April 1818.

their hatred of reformers. Hay was sometimes criticised for the harsh sentences he meted out in court on the grounds that as a clergyman he should have been more temperate and charitable.[51] He was also at the centre of controversy late in 1818 when it was proposed that his salary should be raised. As chairman of the Quarter Sessions he already received £400 a year, for only about nine or ten days' attendance per quarter. This salary was ample, it was argued, and a further burden on the local rates would be unjustified.[52] Hay's role at Peterloo aroused much comment and tarnished his reputation for ever, and his appointment to the rich living of Rochdale soon after-wards only added insult to injury in the eyes of many local inhabi-tants.[53] Other magistrates besides Hay were condemned in these years for improper conduct. They included Ralph Wright, who prosecuted his Methodist gardener in 1811 for stealing potatoes which were actually part of the latter's wages,[54] the Revd C. W. Ethelston who in September 1819 shouted in court at one defendant 'some of you reformers ought to be hanged',[55] and Manchester stipendiary James Norris, who wrongly imprisoned an epileptic in December 1824 for vagrancy. Of the latter affair Richard Potter was to recall: 'We regretted exceedingly not being able to proceed against Mr Norris . . . but were advised not; as the courts always leaned so much to the magistrates, it was almost impossible to punish them however ill they behaved'.[56]

Nadin's successor as deputy constable was Stephen Lavender, formerly of the Bow Street Runners,[57] and he was to be a controver-sial figure in the 1820s and early 1830s because of his salary and conduct. At leypayers' meetings in the mid-1820s Prentice, Baxter and Richard Potter often protested that Lavender's salary of £600 a year was too high, and that extra privileges such as the paying of his rent and medical costs would be inappropriate.[58] Then in 1830 a former beadle named Jefferson accused Lavender of inefficiency,

[51] e.g. *Gazette*, 13 June 1818.
[52] *Gazette*, 7 Nov. 1818.
[53] *Gazette*, 4 Dec. 1819, 8 Jan. 1820; Prentice, *Sketches*, p. 178; Axon, *Annals of Manchester*, p. 158.
[54] Hadfield, Personal Narrative, p. 49.
[55] Taylor, *Notes and Observations*, pp. 172–3.
[56] Potter Collection, xi, pp. 85–6.
[57] Slugg, *Reminiscences*, p. 237. Lavender was deputy constable from 1821 to 1833.
[58] e.g. Reports of meetings in *Gazette*, 24 April 1824, 30 Dec. 1826.

ineptitude and laziness and recommended that Lavender's salary, now equivalent to about £800 a year, should be split and given to three executive officers appointed for different parts of the town. Prentice's *Times* agreed that £800 a year was scandalously extravagant and was bound to impair Lavender's efficiency, though Prentice dissociated himself from Jefferson's personal abuse of the deputy constable. The economy-conscious smaller ratepayers flocked to the next leypayers' meeting on 27 October 1830, and passed a motion cutting Lavender's salary to £400 a year.[59] The *Guardian*, by now an ally of the 'high' party in local affairs, blamed Prentice for this 'unjust' treatment of Lavender and hoped that the matter would be reconsidered. It was not right, said Taylor, to allow a settlement to be imposed 'by a convocation of the readers of the *Times*'.[60] The two sides in the dispute attacked each other as the weeks passed, with frequent recourse to the correspondence pages of the local papers.[61] In August 1831 Prentice informed his readers that Lavender's salary had still not been amended.[62] Further acrimonious leypayers' meetings followed, with Prentice, Richard Potter, P. T. Candelet and a radical shopkeeper named James Nightingale speaking for those who insisted on a reduction in Lavender's salary. The town officers proposed a compromise of £500 a year, but the meeting of 5 October 1831 decided on £400 a year and free accommodation. This success for Prentice and his allies did not last. Much to the pleasure of the *Guardian* and *Courier*, the appeal to the Sturges Bourne vestry act at the meeting of 3 October 1832 brought the 'high' party a crushing victory and Lavender's salary was fixed at £600 a year.[63] The differences which now existed between Taylor and other members of the band were highlighted by the former's comments on the vestry act. Taylor admitted that he had formerly disliked the voting system laid down in the act, but said that his views had been modified. It was unfair to allow smaller contributors to the rate as much influence over its disposal as that enjoyed by larger contributors, he explained, and it was also necessary for there to be some countervailing influence to that of numbers. This would ensure that the men of

[59] *Times*, 23, 30 Oct. 1830.
[60] *Guardian*, 30 Oct. 1830.
[61] e.g. *Times*, 6, 13, 27 Nov. 1830, 22 Jan. 1831; *Guardian*, 4 Dec. 1830.
[62] *Times*, 6 Aug. 1831.
[63] *Times*, 13 Aug., 8 Oct. 1831, 6 Oct. 1832; *Guardian* and *Courier*, 29 Sept., 6 Oct. 1832.

intelligence and station who paid the bulk of the rate were not subjected to the dictation of the more numerous smaller ratepayers. Recent meetings had been very large and it was difficult to get through business when assemblies were packed and excitable. It was necessary that leypayers' meetings should be run on a 'representative' basis.[64]

Among the other local disputes in which the band was involved was that relating to the lord of the manor's rights, particularly the right to regulate the markets. Complaints about inconveniences and obstructions connected with market regulation often commanded the attention of the police commission in the 1820s and 1830s. From 1825 Prentice, Atkinson, Baxter and Richard Potter led a campaign within the police commission for an inquiry into the lord's rights and for some settlement guaranteeing the proper provision of space, stalls and access in the markets. Several committees were appointed, but many police commissioners disliked the idea of interfering with manorial rights and the local ruling party tried to avoid any confrontation with the lord, Sir Oswald Mosley, for as long as possible. Mosley did promise to do something about the nuisances brought to his attention, but the situation did not improve. The whole affair was marked by procrastination, both from the lord of the manor and from Manchester's ruling group, despite the reformers' eagerness to bring about a much-needed local improvement.[65] The manorial rights were not purchased until after incorporation, for £200,000 in 1846. An earlier attempt to buy Mosley out had failed in 1808–9 because his asking price of £90,000 was deemed excessive. That disappointment had seriously damaged the police commission's hopes for a more efficient system of local government, as had the lord's decision in 1808 to sell Manchester's waterworks to a private company.[66]

The band was also involved in a campaign to reform the system of county rates. Richard Potter, Baxter and Prentice brought this matter up at several parish meetings in the 1820s, pointing out that

[64] *Guardian*, 6 Oct. 1832.
[65] *Gazette*, 9 April, 18 June 1825, 16 June, 24 July, 11 Aug., 13 Oct. 1827; Archives Dept. M.C.L., Boroughreeve's Papers, (2 vols), i, pp. 283–4.
[66] N. J. Frangopulo, 'The Growth of Manchester' and 'A Story of Municipal Achievement', in *Rich Inheritance. A Guide to the History of Manchester*, ed. Frangopulo (1969), pp. 46, 58; Redford, *Local Government*, i, pp. 233–8; Marshall, *Public Opinion*, pp. 82–8.

Mancunians paid an immense contribution to the county rate but had no influence over or even knowledge of the way it was spent. As with the manorial rights, this affair was marked by long delays interspersed with activity only when the respectable reformers could actually force the ruling party to do something. In October 1823 and July 1826 the churchwardens agreed to look into the matter, and accepted the reformers' argument that ratepayers had a right to examine county expenditure. But it was difficult to get the county authorities to provide copies of their accounts. The reformers did not think that the churchwardens were trying hard enough. Prentice's *Times* kept the pressure up and on one occasion calculated that the county magistrates were spending £100,000 a year, of which 10 per cent came from Manchester alone. Since none of the contributors had any say in the way this money was being used, there seemed to be no means of preventing wasteful or illegal expenditure. In 1827 Prentice and Richard Potter pressed for an inquiry into county expenditure and a consideration of ways to reduce it, but progress was slow and it was not really until incorporation in 1838, and Manchester's separation from the county, that the reformers could rest satisfied.[67]

Closely connected with the county rates issue was the unsuccessful campaign of 1823–24 against the magistrates' decision to provide new accommodation for judges sitting at the Lancaster assizes. Members of the band were involved, as were men of all parties, and ratepayers in Liverpool also joined in. The people of Manchester and Liverpool wanted the assizes to be transferred to their own towns, and in any case objected to the cost of a new judges' mansion in Lancaster. But the scheme went ahead, prompting Richard Potter to tell a leypayers' meeting in April 1824 that it was 'a most singular state of things that a set of magistrates should be suffered to act, and expend the money of the county of Lancaster after the leading towns of Manchester and Liverpool had publicly protested against the measure'.[68]

---

[67] *Gazette*, 1 Nov. 1823, 29 April, 29 July, 16 Sept. 1826, 28 July 1827; Potter Collection, xi, p. 133.
[68] *Gazette*, 8, 22 Feb. 1823, 24 April 1824; *Guardian*, 8 March, 30 Sept. 1823; Hay Scrapbooks, xi, pp. 204–5; Boroughreeve's Papers, i, pp. 100–1.

4. LOCAL RATES, LOCAL EXPENDITURE
AND STREET IMPROVEMENTS

The different branches of local government in Manchester suffered from a lack of funds during this era. Two of the most important rates levied to pay for local government were the poor's rate and the police rate, and insufficient yields from both caused disputation as attempts were made to change assessments and to increase exactions from groups hitherto largely exempt or rated only at low amounts. The poor's rate was used for so many different purposes that its low yield was particularly worrying. Its assessments were also used for other local rates (the police, highway and county rates).[69] Therefore to solve the problem of low yields generally meant the reform of the poor rate assessments as an essential first step. In March 1817, when a House of Commons committee was considering the state of the poor laws, the Manchester churchwardens recommended that the owners rather than the occupiers of tenements valued at under £12 a year should make the contribution due for their property. This would mean a return to the system which had prevailed before the 1790s, and would also mean higher yields and the removal of a serious burden from the poorer classes. But the owners of low-value housing would not agree to this 'invidious, unjust and oppressive' proposal, and the liberals' *Gazette* sympathised. A long dispute ensued.[70]

Arguments over the poor's rate were succeeded by controversy relating to the police rate. Ever since its creation in 1792, the police commission had experienced serious financial difficulties and was more often in debt than out of it. Complaints were often made about wasteful expenditure, lax management of public funds, too high a number of exemptions from the rate, and gross neglect on the part of rate collectors.[71] After the remodelling of the police commission by the 1828 Manchester police act, the problem of the police rate grew in magnitude not least because one of the promised advantages of this act had been greater police efficiency. When debts continued

[69] Simon, *City Government*, pp. 61–5.
[70] See below, chapter IV, section (3), pp. 178–86.
[71] e.g. Report of police meeting in *Gazette*, 3 Oct. 1818.

to rise it was natural that questions should be asked and changes proposed. Taylor, by now an ally of the ruling party and a member of several police committees, favoured a hard-line approach. In 1830, for instance, he welcomed the police body's attempt to enforce payments of arrears dating back to 1825. Prentice wondered if coercion and legal proceedings were really justified, but Taylor had no doubts. The *Guardian* condemned the old unreformed commission, which had included representatives of the groups Prentice often praised for their vigilance and efficiency in public affairs: shopkeepers, publicans and small traders. The old commission had left its accounts in such a disorganised state that the reconstituted commission had a duty to sort out a mass of arrears, Taylor stated, and summonses for non-payment (after due warnings) were the only means of doing this.[72]

Some police commissioners wanted to rationalise and simplify the collection of the rate, most obviously by drawing a clear line between those who should and should not be exempt. Between 1830 and 1832 the case for exemptions was made most forcefully by Richard Potter, the respectable carver and gilder Thomas Hopkins, and the radical draper P. T. Candelet. Prentice's *Times* provided newspaper backing. Here was another contest involving the rights of small property. Potter, Hopkins and Candelet argued at successive police meetings that small cottage dwellers should be exempted from the police rate on account of their penury and because the cost of collecting their rates was sometimes higher than the resulting income. Hopkins recommended that no rate contribution should be exacted for houses assessed below £6 a year.[73] But progress was slow and most police commissioners seem to have agreed with Taylor that everyone who could pay something should do so. The town could ill-afford to forego payments for low-assessed property, Taylor insisted. The policy of the collection was clear, what about the humanity of it? Was payment being unjustly forced from persons who could not afford it?

> We know of no reason for arguing the matter with reference to that feeling, as regards assessments below £6 per annum, which would not equally apply to those of a higher grade. No doubt there are many persons rated at less than £6 to whom

---

[72] *Times*, 19 June 1830; *Guardian*, 26 June 1830.
[73] *Times*, 17 July, 28 Aug. 1830.

the payment of the police rate is very difficult. But there are
also many rated at £7 or £8 to whom it is equally so, and we
do not see the justice or propriety of a general exemption in
one case any more than in the other.[74]

Potter, Hopkins and Candelet were soon complaining about the
harsh methods used to exact payments from cottage occupiers, such
as court cases and confiscations of personal property. At a police
meeting on 31 August 1831 they managed to secure the promise of
a full inquiry into the rates question, but the ruling party was just
buying time and a little respite from reformist agitation. Three
months later, on 30 November 1831, the police commissioners voted
in favour of continued exactions by a large majority. Taylor argued
on this occasion that many people living in low-assessed houses had
good incomes and were able to pay the police rate, and he added that
they ought to contribute in view of the commission's programme to
extend street paving and cleaning services and the fact that the poorer
parts of town would benefit most from this.[75] The reformers did not
give up. In 1832 it was pointed out that the rate on some large houses
amounted to only 2.5 per cent of their value while the rate could be
as much as 7 per cent on some small dwellings. It seemed only fair
to alter assessments.[76] But the decision of 30 November 1831 was
solid and unchanging, and continuing protests did not cause the
ruling party much concern. Potter, Hopkins and their allies were not
a large enough group within the remodelled police commission to
win many contests in the early 1830s against the determined opposition of the local rulers. This was one of the reasons why incorporation was to be so important for Manchester's respectable reformers.

The reformers' involvement in disputes concerning local expenditure gained them great publicity and, if only for one particular
protest at a time, a good deal of general support. It was quite an
achievement on their part to raise public awareness about and interest in the uses made of the town's funds, and in time the *Gazette*'s
wish that the passing of accounts should be 'something more than a
mere matter of form, without any inquiry or investigation' [77] was
repeatedly fulfilled. From an early stage the reformers would make

---

[74] *Guardian*, 11 Sept. 1830.
[75] *Times*, 3 Sept., 3 Dec. 1831.
[76] *Times*, 14 April 1832.
[77] *Gazette*, 25 April 1818.

an issue even of rather trivial charges in order to gain publicity and draw attention to local expenditure in general, as in 1817 when they objected to the inclusion in the constables' accounts of fees for the ringing of church bells on the anniversary of Waterloo.[78] Members of the band could present themselves as the advocates of economy and the guardians of the public purse, doing the ratepayers a valuable service by trying to make sure that the town's money was not wasted. Sometimes they played this role so well that their opponents were shown up in a most unfavourable light. Two rival deputations were sent to parliament at the time of the police bill controversy of 1827–28. Baxter, Brotherton, Prentice, Shuttleworth and Richard Potter were all appointed to the reformist deputation, and after the terms of the bill were finalised they declared that they would make no claims upon the town for expenses. The deputation of the 'high' party made no such statement.[79]

It is clear that members of the band were at their most threatening when circumstances favoured some cooperation, however loose or fleeting, between respectable reformers and men from humbler social ranks. If a large number of people from labouring and middling backgrounds could be motivated to attend important meetings, the band's leadership capabilities would come into play and grievances could be forcefully and effectively articulated. About 1,500 people attended the parish meeting of 30 April 1818 at the height of the Hindley affair, a time of great public agitation when the ruling oligarchy seemed vulnerable. At this assembly Richard Potter protested about boroughreeve, Joseph Green's, refusal to allow him to examine past constables' accounts (Green called the request 'a sly Presbyterian trick'), and Taylor objected when he found that a recent advertisement defending the conduct of Nadin had been charged to the town: 'the expense of Nadin's justification and defence ought to fall upon himself and not upon the leypayers, who were quite unconcerned in it'. The meeting opposed the passing of the latest accounts on a show of hands. Then the ruling party conducted a scrutiny and overturned this decision. The Tory *Chronicle* approved, but the resulting controversy only helped the band's campaign for more accountability.[80]

[78] *Gazette*, 21 March 1817.
[79] *Gazette*, 21 June 1828.
[80] *Gazette*, 2, 16, 23 May 1818; Hay Scrapbooks, x, pp. 70–9; *Chronicle*, 2 May 1818.

Further opportunities to attack the ruling party came during the long-running dispute over local military barracks which began in 1820. Members of the band claimed that Manchester's rulers were guilty of improper expenditure of public money, and that the town had been far more peaceful in recent times that its rulers had claimed, making extra troops unnecessary. Baxter and Richard Potter led the attempt to have barrack charges removed from the constables' accounts in April 1820, but were unsuccessful. Taylor drew attention to the use of troops for political purposes in May 1820, when he objected to the sum charged to the town in the third quarter of 1819 for paying soldiers who had assisted in the arrest of Middleton radical leader Samuel Bamford.[81] As controversy continued the town officers took legal counsel on the matter of barrack charges, and found that the town did not in fact have any obligation to pay them. After discussion with the magistrates it was decided that application should be made to the county rate, but Richard Potter reminded the leypayers at a meeting of 5 January 1821 that the county rate was something 'over which we have no control whatever'. Application to the county rate was fraught with dangers for public liberty, the band believed, and its legality was by no means clear.[82] Since the magistrates had approved it, though, it apparently went ahead on this occasion. Potter, Harvey and Taylor brought the barracks issue up again on subsequent occasions and managed to force the repayment of a portion of the barrack charges already paid out.[83] Further arguments occurred in the spring of 1823. Taylor, Prentice, Shuttleworth, Baxter and Richard Potter claimed that some of the military quarters previously established in the town had caused financial losses and inconvenience to the public, and had represented an improper use of town property.[84] In July 1826, a time of commercial hardship when the town officers evidently feared civil disorders, a large sum was included in the constables' accounts to pay for the accommodation of extra troops. Potter told a leypayers' meeting on 27 July that this was an improper use of the poor's rate and that the central government should pay all costs relating to the military forces under its direction. But the meeting sided with the boroughreeve

---

[81] *Gazette*, 22 April, 3 June 1820.
[82] *Gazette*, 27 Jan. 1821.
[83] *Gazette*, 4 Aug., 27 Oct. 1821, 20 July 1822.
[84] *Gazette* and *Guardian*, 10 May 1823; *Chronicle*, 17 May 1823; Shuttleworth Scrapbook, p. 42; Hay Scrapbooks, xi, p. 205.

William Lomas, who said that the charges were justified in the present circumstances of the town.[85] Lomas and his fellow town officers were under pressure at this time from another direction. The ordnance board wanted the town to pay for arms and equipment supplied to the civil authorities in recent years but not returned or accounted for. Town officers complained about this to the Home Secretary, Robert Peel, and pointed out that even though a compromise had been worked out to cover some of the barrack charges (they would be allowed, provided they formed no precedent), as for the lost arms and ordnance 'a successful application on that subject to the leypayers is quite out of the question'.[86] The band was quick to draw attention to many other items of expenditure that could be deemed questionable. These included charges 'for useful information' in April 1820 and January 1821, and charges with clear party motivations, as in May 1820 when the band managed to get some of the expenses incurred by loyalist meetings in the summer of 1819 removed from the constables' accounts.[87]

For years members of the band kept up their attempts to check the expenditure of public bodies, and to remind such bodies that they were answerable for their conduct. In May 1829 Prentice declared that local government was becoming more and more unsatisfactory. Control over expenditure was lax, and he scorned the recent decision to spend yet more money on the town hall, with plans for its future enlargement, when even the present edifice was not yet properly completed. The 1828 police act had remodelled the commission and given firmer control to the men of 'gentlemanly habits' (a *Guardian* phrase) by depriving the shopkeepers, publicans and small traders of influence. The change had been sought by the 'high' party on the grounds that it would improve the standard of local government, but this had not been the case.

> Instead of plodding, industrious, keen-sighted men, whose business occupations, requiring much attention to detail, peculiarly fitted them for the economical administration of public affairs, and who were gratified by holding office and made it a matter of conscience to discharge its duties, we have gentlemen

---

[85] *Gazette*, 29 July 1826.
[86] Boroughreeve's Papers, i, pp. 107, 182–3, 184–8.
[87] *Gazette*, 22 April, 3 June 1820, 27 Jan. 1821.

of wealth and respectability, well-educated and gentlemanly-habited no doubt, but who have neither time nor inclination to dive into the mysteries of lamp-lighting, street-scavenging or watch inspecting, and who, so far from exercising that rigid economy which characterised their predecessors and saved our pockets, scruple not to pay unexamined accounts to the amount of three or four thousand pounds . . . and while they profess to be unable to plaster the Hall in which they meet, lay out a thousand pounds to secure the power of enlarging it twenty years hence![88]

Prentice attempted to curb excess in local expenditure in March 1829 when a leypayers' meeting considered the Manchester and Liverpool Railway Company's plan to build a bridge over Water Street. Several speakers pointed to the problems of dirt, smoke and noise, and stated that the bridge should be higher than the level proposed. A committee was appointed to secure this change, but Prentice argued that the meeting should not assume the power to appoint a committee that might spend thousands of pounds on a relatively unimportant matter. 'I have seen enough of such committees to make me desirous to have limits set to their power'. Argument followed, with Prentice proposing a spending limit of £200 and then £500 when he was pressed, but the meeting eventually decided that no limit would be set.[89] Disputes about the accuracy and accessibility of local accounts went on into the 1830s. In 1834 the senior overseer of the parish, Nehemiah Gardiner, admitted the need for more thoroughness and publicity to satisfy local opinion. Gardiner informed the Poor Law Commissioners that Mancunians wanted better accounting: 'nothing is calculated to satisfy them but a rigid yearly investigation by legal powers, and a summary of the accounts made public'.[90] The efforts of the band had not been unavailing.

Street improvements provoked a great deal of discussion during this period. Such improvements were long overdue, but problems of financing, authorisation and compensation perplexed the town for many years. An earlier scheme in the 1770s to improve the St Ann's Square–Market Place area of town had been complicated by

[88] *Times*, 2 May 1829.
[89] *Times*, 14 March 1829.
[90] *Report from H. M. Commissioners on the Poor Laws* (1834), P.P. 1834, xvi, Appendix B2, parts 3–5, 68k.

arguments over finance, and had eventually depended on voluntary subscriptions.[91] The most ambitious project of the 1820s was the improvement of Market Street, a central and much-used thoroughfare long noted for its narrowness and obstructions. An improvement act was obtained in 1821, and this provided for the establishment of a Market Street Commission to oversee the improvement and the raising of necessary sums through bonds, mortgages and a contribution from the highway rate. The commission consisted of both reformers and conservatives, and included five of the band. These were Baxter, Shuttleworth, the Potters and Taylor, though the latter increasingly distanced himself from his former friends. The participation of reformers did not threaten the dominance of the 'high' party. Criticism of the project and of the commission came primarily from Prentice, Atkinson, P. T. Candelet and a prominent middling-sort spokesman, Nicholas Whitworth, a radical corn dealer.[92] These commentators pointed to the massive costs incurred, the lack of consultation with the general body of leypayers, and the methods employed by the commission in dealing with complaints and claims for compensation.[93] The promoters of the improvement scheme claimed that it would be near completion by the summer of 1826, but in fact it was still being finished off in the mid-1830s. Prentice used his newspapers to draw attention to the unsatisfactory manner in which the project was being managed. He also spoke out in leypayers' meetings, along with Whitworth and others. A meeting of 15 September 1824 saw Prentice speak on behalf of the residents and shopkeepers of Market Street, who were complaining about the piles of rubbish often left outside their properties. In December 1824 he wondered if certain individuals stood to profit by particular improvements and the contracts they involved, and he contrasted Manchester's methods with those of Glasgow. In Glasgow a joint stock company was managing street improvements, which meant no outlay of public money and good profits for stockholders. A meeting in April 1825 heard allegations that some Market Street tenants were being forced into agreements relating to the improvement, and in November 1826 Whitworth and Prentice

[91] C. W. Sutton, 'Manchester Improvements 1775–6', *T.L.C.A.S.*, 31 (1913), pp. 63–8.
[92] Nicholas Whitworth was the brother of William, mentioned above, p. 100.
[93] e.g. *Gazette*, 10, 24 March, 7 April 1821, May to June 1823; Hay Scrapbooks, x, pp. 116–19.

attacked Taylor for accepting £250 in compensation for moving the *Guardian*'s Market Street office when a solicitor who had been forced to move received only £40. In April 1829 Prentice contrasted the generous award to Taylor (who was a member of the Market Street Commission) with the forced eviction from its Market Street premises, without compensation, of a long-established coach company.[94] Prentice persistently condemned the commissioners for their high-handed approach to compensation claims. Time and again they forced tenants and landlords to go to the courts, only to lose the actions and have to pay legal costs as well as compensation. 'Arrangements which might have been effected by friendly bargaining between the parties became the subject of bitter contest and expensive litigation'.[95]

The enormous cost of the Market Street project meant that when further and related street alterations were proposed in 1830 there was a strong desire to keep expenditure as low as possible. The new plan was to link Market Street with Cannon Street, but immediately there was concern about the likely cost. It was pointed out during a police commissioners' meeting of 26 May 1830 that the Market Street improvement had already produced debts of £100,000, and that a further £200,000 would be needed before the project was completed.[96] The town officers complied with a requisition to call a town meeting to discuss the new scheme, signed by men of all parties including Shuttleworth, Watkin and Taylor. Taylor had already recommended the new plan to the readers of the *Guardian*.[97] Prentice believed that most people would agree on the utility of the proposed alterations, but feared that the cost would be much higher than the promoters claimed. He hoped that the town meeting would come to a fair and clear decision about how much could be spent.[98] Prentice got his wish. The meeting of 21 June 1830 decided that the limits on expenditure should be £8,000 if the new street was ten yards wide, and £10,000 if it was twelve yards wide.[99] But there was still opposition. Some argued that local taxation was already too

[94] *Gazette*, 18 Sept., 4, 11 Dec. 1824, 14 May 1825, 18 Nov. 1826; *Times*, 25 April 1829.
[95] *Times*, 24 Oct. 1828, 25 July 1829.
[96] *Times*, 29 May 1830.
[97] *Guardian*, 1 May 1830.
[98] *Times*, 5, 19 June 1830.
[99] *Times*, 26 June 1830.

high and that no new exactions were acceptable, and others said that those who resided away from the improved area should not have to pay anything towards the new scheme.[100] The Tory *Courier* could not accept that the public value of the improvement would justify the expenditure, which it estimated at £18,000 or more when property purchases, compensation claims and other matters were added.[101]

5. GAS, POLICE AND THE STRUGGLE FOR MASTERY

It was a source of pride in Manchester that the town was the first place in which the use of gas for economic purposes was successfully tested. This occurred at a cotton mill in 1805. The successful application of gas aroused the interest of police commissioners. It was thought that gas could be used for street-lighting and that the commission could even engage in the profitable manufacture of gas. From 1807 gas was used to light the police office and streetlamps in the most frequented parts of town. Soon an increasing number of townspeople were asking that gas be made available for private consumption, and meanwhile street-lighting by gas was extended. A leypayers' meeting on 30 April 1817 resolved to increase the police rate from 1s. 3d. to 1s. 6d. in the pound, in order to finance street-lighting by gas in the whole of the central district. The management of the gas works was entrusted to a gas committee of police commissioners. By 1823 there were deepening disagreements about whether or not the police body had the right to manufacture gas and sell it to private consumers. It therefore became necessary to obtain a parliamentary act to legalise what had been done and to permit the further extension of the gas works. The matter was brought to a head in September 1823 when a new joint stock venture, the Manchester Imperial Gas Company, gave notice that it was going to seek parliamentary authority to allow it to light the streets of Manchester. This was the first that had been heard of the company, and its chief

---

[100] e.g. See printed sheets signed 'A Publican' and 'An Extensive Cotton Spinner', in Atkinson Papers (political tracts), M 177/7/9 (dated 25 May, 2 June 1830).
[101] *Courier*, 19 June 1830.

promoters were completely unknown in Manchester. A special police meeting on 5 November 1823 decided that the plan of this new private concern had to be opposed, that the position of the town's gas works had to be regularised and its profits put towards town improvements, and that the 1792 Manchester police act would have to be revised to allow speedy and efficient improvements in the supply of gas for homes, businesses and street lamps. These were the aims of the 'high' party, and it was on the related gas and police issues more than any other that the old Tory rulers were joined by such respectable and moderate Whig-reformers as Taylor and the prominent merchant G. W. Wood. Taylor, indeed, was to be an outspoken advocate of town-owned gas works. He and others continually stressed the lesson to be derived from the waterworks episode of 1809, when control of the water supply had been lost to a private concern. This company was inefficient, soon became bankrupt, and did nothing to enlarge Manchester's appallingly insufficient water supply. The same thing, it was declared, should not be allowed to happen again. Members of the band were not against the idea of formally municipalising the gas works, but warned the public to pay attention to the details of any such scheme. Baxter spoke in favour of applying the gas profits to useful public transactions, such as the purchase of the manorial rights. Taylor and Baxter were on the committee appointed on 19 November 1823 to supervise the application to parliament for a Manchester gas act.[102]

Over the coming weeks the local newspapers were deluged with correspondence on the question. One contributor to the liberals' *Gazette* thought that the Imperial Gas Company should be allowed to compete for customers with the police commission, since competition would mean lower prices and gas of good quality. This writer complained that interested parties were trying to dictate to the townspeople and deny them choice. In February 1824 another correspondent attacked the gas committee of police commissioners for failing to act in the interests of the town as a whole. Plenty of gas was available for public use, particularly for the lighting of streets, but the desire for profit was prompting the committee to give preference to private consumers. This represented a strange set of priorities.[103] By March 1824 parliament was considering the draft bills of both the

---

[102] Shuttleworth, *Gas Works*, pp. 5–9; *Gazette*, 8, 15, 22 Nov., 6 Dec. 1823; *Guardian*, 29 Nov., 6 Dec. 1823; Fraser, *Urban Politics*, pp. 95–8.
[103] *Gazette*, 22 Nov., 6 Dec. 1823, 7 Feb. 1824.

proposed gas company and the police commission. The placing of advertisements and the writing of letters continued. Some agreed that the company would be a private interest group unconcerned with the general good and opposed to the sentiments of most inhabitants, while others insisted that it was dangerous and impolitic to allow the police commissioners to enjoy a monopoly. As a parliamentary committee discussed the matter it became clear that the company was guilty of frauds in its petitioning campaign.[104] The parliamentary committee eventually adjourned without making any report, but the company's bill had been lost by the end of March, and the feeling provoked against it helped to secure the passing of the police commissioners' bill. The company's fraudulent petitioning may have been decisive. Parliament took a serious view of such misuses of constitutional privilege, and this was partly why Manchester got its act. M.P.s were not decidedly against the idea of private utility companies at this time, for April 1824 saw the passing of an act instituting a private concern to control gas supplies in Dublin.[105] Members of the band played an important role in the gas affair of 1823–24. Baxter, Taylor and Richard Potter had all been involved in meetings called to oppose the gas company's plan. The *Gazette* and *Guardian* had provided coverage and comment. Shuttleworth was one of the auditors of the gas accounts appointed after the passing of the act.[106]

By the Manchester gas act of 1824 the existence and future management of the town's gas works were fully legalised and regularised. Early municipal ownership of the gas works in Manchester aroused the envy of governing bodies in other towns. In Leeds, for instance, during the many years of negotiation between the ruling body and the two local gas companies, councillors and improvement commissioners repeatedly pointed to Manchester as a precedent for municipal ownership and looked jealously at the funds municipal ownership made available for other purposes. But in Leeds the purchase of the gas works was not accomplished until 1869, over forty years after municipal control in Manchester was confirmed by the 1824 act.[107] Local companies controlling such utilities as gas, water and the markets could sometimes be centres of influence in

---

[104] *Guardian*, 27 March 1824.

[105] Manchester gas act is 5 Geo IV c. 133. Dublin act is 5 Geo IV c. 42.

[106] Shuttleworth, *Gas Works*, pp. 6, 8; *Guardian*, 3 April 1824; *Gazette*, 20, 27 March, 10 April 1824.

[107] Barber, 'Municipal government in Leeds', pp. 85–9.

rivalry to municipal governments, particularly when liberals controlled the governments and Tories dominated the companies. This was
true of Rochdale and Bolton, where companies fought long and hard
to resist attempted public takeovers.[108] It was therefore most fortunate for Manchester's respectable liberals, who won the battle for
incorporation in the later 1830s and then dominated the new town
council, that gas was already in public hands and that water soon
would be. It was also fortunate for the town itself, because many
local improvements would have been impossible without the help of
the gas profits. This is especially true of the extension and improvement of Manchester's water supply.[109]

Although the 1824 Manchester gas act settled the questions of the
ownership, legality and future expansion of the works, matters could
not rest there. The act had not explicitly stated what could and what
could not be done with the gas profits. By the second half of 1827
the profits realised by the gas establishment were rapidly increasing.
The average yearly profit from 1819–24 was £3,000, but from 1825–
39 it rose to £11,500.[110] At a police meeting on 5 September 1827 the
act of parliament committee recommended that a new act should be
sought to allow the gas profits to be used to help pay for street-wid-
ening and other local improvements. The 'low' party leader, William
Whitworth, protested that the gas profits should go towards reducing the police rate, and that it would be unfair to force gas consumers
to foot the bill for street improvements. He demanded that gas prices
should be reduced and the act of parliament committee dissolved.
Bitter arguments followed Whitworth's outburst, and the meeting
came to no clear decision. The position of the band, as outlined by
Baxter, was that the report of the act of parliament committee should
be fully discussed, since this would not necessarily bind the police
commissioners to anything. Prentice agreed, though he went further
than his friend and denounced the plan to use gas profits to pay for
local improvements. In the *Gazette* he stated that no trust could be
placed in those individuals who would be given the management of
such improvements.[111]

---

[108] J. Garrard, *Leadership and Power in Victorian Industrial Towns* (1983),
pp. 119–20, 123, 166, 170.
[109] On the Longendale Valley project of the 1840s and 1850s, Frangopulo,
'Municipal Achievement', pp. 57–8.
[110] Shuttleworth, *Gas Works*, pp. 13–14.
[111] *Gazette*, 8, 15 Sept. 1827.

Prentice printed a long address on the front page of his *Gazette* of 20 October 1827. This address asserted that it would be scandalous to make gas consumers pay for local improvements, because they would thereby be subjected to a perpetual and unjust burden. Those proposing an application to parliament had argued that the gas works were originally paid for out of the police rate, that most payers of the rate were not gas consumers, that the gas works were therefore the property of non-consumers of gas, and that the gas directors (the executive body of thirty established by the 1824 act) had the right not only to charge what prices they thought proper, but also to apply their profits to local improvements. It was also said that gas prices in Manchester were no higher than in other towns, and that gas consumers could not claim to be the victims of 'oppression' since nobody was forcing them to take gas. All these arguments, claimed the address, were easily refuted. The gas consumers did not owe the town anything. The profits arising from the gas supply since 1817 had been much greater than the sums expended in establishing it, so in fact it was the town that was indebted to the gas consumers. Manchester's gas prices, moreover, were not on a par with prices in other towns. In fact they were up to 45 per cent higher. Though nobody was forced to take gas, it was most necessary for some people to do so. If the neighbours and competitors of a shopkeeper or small businessman had gas, it was important to him that he had it too. The address concluded by acknowledging that town improvements were needed. But the point was that everyone should pay and that burdens should be equal. One particular group should not be singled out and forced to pay a disproportionately heavy share.[112]

In the *Guardian* of the same date, Taylor argued that the clamour against the use of gas profits for town improvements was based on erroneous ideas. This was not a question of effecting improvements at the expense of gas consumers, but concerned 'a mode of applying to one public purpose that fund which is now applied to another, namely aiding the police rates'. Taylor continued: 'If improvements are to be effected it will not make a farthing of difference to the gas consumer whether the profit arising from the sale of gas to him be directly expended in these improvements, or applied in the reduction of one rate while another is raised . . . for improving the town'. Some

---

[112] *Gazette*, 20 Oct. 1827.

consumers were saying that the gas works should make no profit at all, that the price of gas should be so far reduced as to pay only for the cost of production. But the gas establishment was a commercial speculation, Taylor insisted. The police body had run risks and was entitled to profits, and it was fitting that these profits should be used to benefit the whole town. Taylor emphasised that the gas establishment had not been equally beneficial to all inhabitants.

> Many persons finding it to their advantage to consume gas have become customers of the Commissioners, and have benefited beyond the other inhabitants of the town inasmuch as they have been enabled to substitute a better and cheaper light for the one they had previously used; and that advantage the consumers of gas now possess over those who cannot consume it.

It was clear that gas consumers could not expect to be free of town charges for improvements, but Taylor did concede that if gas prices were unnecessarily high consumers had reason to call for a reduction.[113]

By now party and social divides were becoming ever more pronounced on the gas issue. The majority of gas consumers were of the middling sort. They were shopkeepers, craftsmen, traders and publicans, men concerned about frugality in both public and their own private spheres, men who if they were not reformers were at least willing to be guided in the gas dispute by respectable liberals like Prentice and other members of the band. They were opposed by the dominant group in the police commission, the larger manufacturers and merchants who were led by wealthy and socially prominent Tories, Whigs and moderates. This body upheld the established network of local influence, biased as it was in favour of conservatism and large property.

The next police meeting, on 24 October 1827, was predictably large and noisy. Whitworth's motion to dissolve the act of parliament committee was carried by a large majority, to the disgust of the *Guardian* and *Courier*. In November a police meeting decided by 147 votes to 110 that gas profits should not be applied to town improvements. The gas controversy now became more closely entwined with a wider struggle over the proposed reconstruction of the police

[113] *Guardian*, 20 Oct. 1827.

commission. Leaders of the 'high' party wanted to restrict membership of the commission because numerical advantage was increasingly enjoyed by their opponents, and police meetings were becoming more tumultuous and noisy by the month. Both sides were actively urging their friends and supporters to present themselves for qualification, and meetings were very much larger than in the past. Under the 1792 act any inhabitant who wanted to serve, had paid all his rates, and owned or occupied premises valued at £30 a year could qualify as a police commissioner. 'The men of "gentlemanly habits" will qualify to put down the shopkeepers', said Prentice, and 'shopkeepers will qualify to protect their own rights'.[114] An agitated and crowded police meeting took place on 30 January 1828 after a good deal of active canvassing and propaganda by both sides. The gas consumers were ready to compromise, but all negotiation was rendered impossible when the boroughreeve, manufacturer and 'high' party stalwart Charles Cross, tried to take the chair and fell back into the crowd. There were scuffles, several persons were injured, and the radical William Whitworth was accused of assault and inciting violence. The meeting had to be abandoned. It provided excellent propaganda material for the 'high' party and its press allies in their campaign to raise the qualification for police commissioners. The 'high' party soon sent an account of recent police affairs to the Home Secretary. Prentice attacked this communication as an attempt to prejudice Peel's mind and make it easier for the ruling oligarchy to secure a new police act. About 150 police commissioners signed a counter-memorial to Peel containing the liberals' observations about recent events. A fund was also opened to finance resistance to any attempt to remodel the commission or appropriate the gas profits to town improvements without making all inhabitants liable to pay towards street lamps.[115]

The 1828 Manchester police act (9 Geo IV c. 117) failed to end the gas controversy, not least because it did not provide for the statutory regulation of the gas profits. But the 'low' party was able to secure a reduction in gas prices in June 1828, from 14s. to 12s. per thousand cubic feet, before the new act robbed it of its recent influence in police affairs. The 'low' party also managed to get some of its nominees elected as gas directors, and Prentice and others pressed to

[114] *Gazette*, 27 Oct., 24 Nov., 15 Dec. 1827; *Courier*, 24 Nov., 8, 29 Dec. 1827; *Guardian*, 1 Dec. 1827.
[115] *Gazette*, 2, 16 Feb. 1828; Prentice, *Sketches*, pp. 312–15; Boroughreeve's Papers, i, pp. 278–83, 285–9.

ensure that the gas accounts would be accorded a regular and wider publicity. Hence the gas struggle at least promised to bring about greater accountability in the future.[116] Argument over gas prices went on, and in November 1828 Prentice's *Times* carried an address announcing that a new application was to be made for a gas bill that would break down monopoly and deliver shopkeepers, innkeepers and other consumers from injustice. It pointed out that Leeds, Birmingham, Liverpool and other large towns had two gas companies each, and competition there meant a fair deal for customers. The address added that the financing of town improvements had also to be satisfactorily settled.[117] Nothing came of this scheme. Instead the police commissioners formulated their own plans for applications to parliament, for statutory powers not sought in 1828 but now regarded as necessary or desirable. By May 1830 a new Manchester police and gas bill was well on its way through parliament. The 'low' party had hoped for a limitation in the price of gas. As Richard Potter pointed out during a police meeting in December 1829, gas was charged at only 10s. per thousand cubic feet in such towns as Bury, Rochdale, Huddersfield, Leeds and Halifax, while Manchester had only just recently seen a reduction from 14s. to 12s. A further reduction was required.[118] The *Times* was hopeful, but the leaders of the police commission were sure to avoid any price limitation and this matter was not covered in the new act (11 Geo IV c. 47). The clauses relating to the gas establishment enabled the police commission to borrow up to £25,000 for the further extension of the gas works, and to use gas profits for general improvements under the direction of the improvement committee.[119] Thus the majority of gas consumers and their respectable spokesmen were defeated on the question of the appropriation of gas profits. Subsequent years saw them concentrate on the campaign for price reductions. Prentice and Richard Potter provided effective leadership, and their pressure paid off in November 1830 when the gas directors agreed to cut the price to 10s. 6d. per thousand cubic feet.[120] Further reductions were secured over the next decade. In 1839 the price stood at 7s. 6d.[121]

---

[116] Redford, *Local Government*, i, p. 309; *Gazette*, 28 June 1828.
[117] *Times*, 7 Nov. 1828.
[118] *Times*, 2 Jan. 1830.
[119] Redford, *Local Government*, i, pp. 319–23; *Times*, 15 May 1830.
[120] *Times*, 6 Nov. 1830.
[121] Shuttleworth, *Gas Works*, pp. 13–14.

The 1828 Manchester police act could have been much worse for the local liberals than it actually was. Even so, in its early operation it was rather less favourable to them than they had anticipated. After the riotous meeting of 30 January 1828 and the alleged assault on boroughreeve, Charles Cross, the *Exchange Herald, Courier, Guardian* and *Chronicle* were all in favour of a considerable increase in the property qualification required of police commissioners.[122] The ruling party rapidly drew up a bill which provided for a great change in the constitution of the police body. Occupiers assessed at £25 a year to the police rate would be eligible to vote in the election of 240 commissioners, who would qualify for this office if assessed at £35. One-third of this main body would go out of office each year but be eligible for re-election. The main body would appoint an executive of 48 commissioners, and again one-third of the executive would go out of office each year but be eligible for re-election. The main body of 240 commissioners would control all appointments and accounts, and would have to approve any town improvement costing over £500. Members of the band led the opposition to this scheme. Baxter feared that Manchester would come to be controlled by a 'closed corporation', and Prentice found it extraordinary that some townsmen could wish to see power taken from the whole body of police commissioners (of whom there were now over 1,700) and given to 'a little junto of FORTY-EIGHT'. In his correspondence on the question Baxter argued that the qualification for voters should be £15 a year. Then local government would at least have a much more representative and popular basis even if commissioners themselves had to be assessed at £35 a year. He also thought that all accounts should be sanctioned by the leypayers as a whole, not just the main body of 240 commissioners.[123] But Manchester's rulers quickly pressed the matter forward and tried to prevent all discussion. They invoked the Sturges Bourne vestry act at the public meeting of 28 February 1828, despite its doubtful applicability, and this gave the bigger ratepayers a convincing victory. The application to parliament went ahead at once. In fact it had already been decided upon at a private meeting before the public was even consulted.[124]

---

[122] e.g. *Exchange Herald*, 31 Jan. 1828; *Courier, Guardian, Chronicle*, 2 Feb. 1828.
[123] Prentice's editorial and Baxter's letter in *Gazette*, 23 Feb. 1828.
[124] Boroughreeve's Papers, i, pp. 285–9; *Gazette*, 1, 8 March 1828; Prentice, *Sketches*, pp. 318–19.

The polarisation of parties proceeded apace, and was also affected by disagreements within the Manchester Representation Committee. This body was concurrently campaigning to secure for the town the parliamentary seats of Penryn, a notoriously corrupt Cornish borough. The men on either side of the local government debate were often the same ones arguing over Manchester's parliamentary representation.[125] Members of the band carried the local government contest into the newspapers and town assemblies, and in April 1828 Baxter and Brotherton went as a deputation to parliament to oppose the 'high' party's bill in committee. Shuttleworth, Prentice and Richard Potter soon joined them, as did the radical corn dealer William Whitworth.[126] The band made useful contacts with Joseph Hume, Henry Brougham, Lord Holland and other reformist politicians, and a favourable impression was made on the parliamentary committee, chaired by Lord Stanley (M.P. for Lancashire from 1812 to 1832, succeeded as thirteenth earl of Derby in 1834). On 25 April Baxter wrote to Richard Potter with important news: 'We have seen Mr Peel and we think neutralised him'. Prentice kept up the appeal for funds from supporters back in Manchester, and Harvey did his best to solicit further donations. Both Peel and Stanley, with the majority of M.P.s on the committee, wanted the rival deputations to reach a negotiated settlement, but the representatives of Manchester's ruling party (who included Taylor) would not agree to any of the proposals put forward. A compromise was finally worked out as the leading members of the parliamentary committee pressed for a settlement. The assessment for police commissioners would be £28, and that for electors £16.[127] The *Courier* was disappointed and complained that the qualification for voters was too low.[128] Prentice's *Gazette* found the measure acceptable, but far from perfect.

> We must not look upon the bill as the best which could be framed but as the best which could be passed; and although it

---

[125] On the Penryn affair, see below chapter 6 section (2), pp. 279–89.

[126] Whitworth's presence caused great friction. Baxter disliked him personally, and all the respectable reformers believed that he wanted too many concessions and would endanger their chances of modifying the bill and getting parliamentary sanction for it.

[127] Prentice, *Sketches*, pp. 316, 320–27; Potter Collection, iv, pp. 40; xii, pp. 135–8, 141–4, 149–51, 153–7, 159–61, 167–8, 181, 187–9, 192–3, 195–6, 199–200, 203, 205–9, 217–21, 225, 235–6, 245–8.

[128] *Courier*, 14 June, 4 July 1828.

is very far from being one deserving unqualified approbation, and though it may be doubtful how it will work, there can be no difference of opinion amongst the independent and thinking part of our community, that we are likely to have much more useful Commissioners at a qualification of £28 than at one of £35, and that the control exercised over those Commissioners will be much more effective when their election is in the hands of persons assessed at £16 than if it had been in the hands of persons assessed at £25.[129]

The 'high' party had been taught a lesson and members of the band were pleased that they had secured lower qualifications than those originally proposed. They and their allies celebrated the passing of the new act at a police meeting on 16 July 1828, but they were soon left wondering whether or not any victory had really been won. It was difficult to tell how much the new act would alter the local balance of power, but it *was* clear that it could not be classed as a particularly liberal measure. The following years saw agitation in favour of extending the municipal vote to all ratepayers, as was the case in neighbouring Salford after 1830. The exclusive nature of the Manchester police act was brought home in August 1828 when the churchwardens issued the lists of persons meeting the new qualifications. About 2,000 townsmen were able to vote, 1,200 of whom were eligible to serve on the commission of 240 members.[130] This meant that only 2.5 per cent of adult males[131] had any say in who became a commissioner or what the commission did with its authority. By 1835 the electorate had risen to about 8.5 per cent of adult males,[132] but the representation was heavily biased in favour of the wealthier districts. The more rates a district paid, the more commissioners it elected. The early elections under the 1828 Manchester police act were decisive victories for the ruling party, much to the satisfaction of the *Courier* and *Guardian*.[133] The influx of convinced reformers was slow. Richard Potter and Shuttleworth were elected in October 1829, Thomas Potter in October 1830, Brotherton in October 1831.[134] Gradually more of their respectable and middling

[129] *Gazette*, 14 June 1828.
[130] *Gazette*, 9 Aug. 1828.
[131] Fraser, *Urban Politics*, p. 97.
[132] Gatrell, 'Incorporation and liberal hegemony', p. 22.
[133] e.g. *Courier* and *Guardian*, 30 Aug. 1830.
[134] *Times*, 4 Oct. 1829, 23 Oct. 1830, 29 Oct. 1831.

sort allies joined them, but real progress had to wait until the later 1830s. Prentice continually attacked the exclusive commission in his *Times* and contrasted its performance with that of the old police commission, in which men of humbler social strata had enjoyed a taste of minor office and had begun to effect a more economic and efficient administration. It was often argued that only the wealthier inhabitants could be expected to possess the time, money and breadth of view necessary for public service, but one of the premises of the criticism of the 1828 act was that the wealthy did not necessarily make the best local rulers. Continued ill-feeling about the exclusive nature of police affairs led to the formation in May 1832 of the Manchester Leypayers' Association, whose stated aims were the protection of rights and the redress of local grievances.[135] This body was the organ of the middling sort allies of Prentice and the band, and continuing cooperation between these two reformist groups was the basis for the successful incorporation campaign of the later 1830s.

---

[135] *Times*, 5, 12 May 1832.

IV *Social Questions*

I. EDUCATION AND IMPROVEMENT

Members of the band were extremely active in the causes of education and improvement. Their own educational experiences shaped their approach to these questions. All became educated due primarily to individual effort. Some had a basic elementary schooling, and used this to advance by themselves in their teens and early twenties. They were substantially self-made men in this respect, and rose because of their own perseverance, self-discipline and resourcefulness. These were the habits they later attempted to encourage among the lower classes, an attempt which involved members of the band in a wide range of educational and improving ventures.

Prentice spent six years attending a parish school in Lanarkshire and later recalled that the teaching there was poor. He considered the parochial school system to be far behind the requirements of the time, and like his friends he argued that British educational provision was inadequate both in extent and quality. Prentice owed most to his own father who helped him with his early reading. Then he was able to borrow books from the parish library, of which his father was a founder. As was the case with others in the band, Prentice had to reach high intellectual attainments through resolute personal effort. He was an avid reader and enjoyed the benefit of moving in cultured literary and political circles while a manufacturer's apprentice in Glasgow.[1] Taylor received some early education from his schoolmaster father, and when he was fifteen he was able to take lessons in mathematics from the renowned Manchester scientist John Dalton. The young Taylor was especially interested in the rise of the Lancasterian school movement, and after the Manchester school was established (1809) he became its secretary while still a manufacturer's

---

[1] Details in Dunlop, 'Archibald Prentice', pp. 435–8; Somerville, *Free Trade and the League*, ii, pp. 382–3.

apprentice.[2] Brotherton also lacked formal education, and was working in his father's mill from about fourteen years of age. He studied in his free time, though, becoming adept in shorthand and French, and he often attended evening lectures on sciences and engineering. This desire for improvement hastened his rise in business and later in public life.[3] Smith received an elementary education, attending a school in Warwick until he was fourteen. Then he entered the office of his uncle, a Manchester cotton merchant, so here was another whose future intellectual advancement depended on personal effort and initiative.[4] Watkin attended a school as a young child, until the death of his father forced him to leave at the age of thirteen. Soon he began to work at his uncle's Manchester warehouse, but continued to read and learn by himself. When he was 23 he resolved to spend three hours a day in study. He believed in the value and necessity of self-education and training oneself in good habits of order and regularity. He enjoyed books and lectures, especially on literary topics, and in his mature years was renowned in Manchester for his refinement and education.[5] So was Atkinson, who exhibited wide literary tastes from his youth and was to be a keen collector of books. He enjoyed a reputation in Manchester as a man of superior literary attainments, a thoughtful researcher and extremely well-read in biography, French literature, constitutional questions and curious historical topics.[6] Richard Potter was another of the band who lacked formal education but was determined to improve himself. In his youth he was helped by his elder brothers, and then moved on alone to books and poems. He would write out long extracts as a rewarding educational exercise. He learnt to speak French and wrote one of his diaries entirely in French, and he greatly enjoyed travel books. In 1797 he noted: 'I generally employ my leisure hours in reading'. During the late 1790s, while working in a Birmingham draper's shop, Potter began to collect volumes of poetry and hymns and items in French. Increasingly committed to personal educational advancement, he joined a newsroom and library and helped to form a

---

[2] Mills, *Guardian History*, pp. 6–7.
[3] O'Brien, 'Joseph Brotherton', p. 19; Costley, *Lancashire Poets*, pp. 64–5.
[4] Smith, Memoranda and Letters, short biography by J. E. Cornish (1887).
[5] Watkin, *Journal*, pp. 7–12, 20, 23, and *Fragment No. 1*, pp. 5, 9.
[6] *Examiner and Times*, 5, 17 May 1858, 12 July 1859; *Guardian*, 10 May 1858; also details in Atkinson Papers, M 177/7.

debating society. Such activities were continued when he moved to Manchester in 1801.[7]

The personal educational experiences of these reformers shaped their views on education, and they may also have been influenced by the example set in the late eighteenth century by the circle of public-spirited rational Dissenters collecting around Dr Thomas Percival of Manchester. These scientists, physicians, enlightened masters and reformers (mostly Unitarians) interested themselves in education and other social questions, and gave life to the Literary and Philosophical Society (established 1781), Board of Health (established 1795), and Warrington and Manchester Academies. A leading motive behind their activity was dissatisfaction with prevalent ideas and existing services; they were committed to finding alternatives.[8]

Members of the band were also convinced of the inadequacies of existing educational provisions. They wanted to encourage a desire for knowledge and improvement, and stressed the need to provide more opportunities and institutions so that people could act on this desire. Prentice was always ready to praise individual effort and was particularly proud of the progress being made in his home district of Covington in Lanarkshire. In 1815 he wrote that knowledge brought in its train self-respect, morality and the habits of industry and frugality. Such features elevated the individual and so produced better workers and better citizens. Prentice attacked the opponents of popular education and denied that it would encourage the lower ranks to lose respect for their betters.[9]

Prentice and his allies were not slow to act on their concern about educational provisions. In some ways they were themselves

---

[7] Potter Collection, i, pp. 1, 8, 79; ii (French diary); iii (diary 1801–23); v (account book); Meinertzhagen, *Potters of Tadcaster*, p. 116.

[8] *The Works of Thomas Percival M. D.*, (4 vols, 1807); S. E. Maltby, *Manchester and the Movement for National Elementary Education* (1918), ch. 2; 'A Historical Account of the Warrington Academy', *Monthly Repository*, viii (1813), pp. 1–5, 86–91, 161–72, 226–31, 287–94, 427–33, 576–9, ix (1814), pp. 201–5, 263–8, 385–90, 399, 487, 525–30, 594–9, x (1815), pp. 91–2, 215, 286–9; B. Simon, *Studies in the History of Education* (1960), pp. 25–6, 29–30, 32–6, 56–62; L. Burney, *Cross Street Chapel Manchester and its College* (1983); R. A. Smith, *A Centenary of Science in Manchester* (1887), pp. 186–7, ch. 2, appendix B; M. E. Sadler, 'The Story of Education in Manchester', and C. L. Barnes, 'The Manchester Literary and Philosophical Society', both in Brindley, *Soul of Manchester*, pp. 44–8, 142–9.

[9] Prentice, *Letters from Scotland*, pp. 150–54.

'educators'. The writings and lectures of Prentice were often directed at groups who wanted (or were thought to want and need) improvement. When Brotherton became the minister of the Bible Christian church he helped to establish a day school for children, night classes for working adults, and a lending library and reading room attached to the King Street premises. In 1820 Thomas Potter established a day school in Irlam at his own expense. In September 1829 he helped to establish a mechanics' institute in Pendleton; he was chairman of the subscribers and remained a generous benefactor for many years. In 1829 he also helped to found a library and library society in Pendleton, and was one of the earliest subscribers to the fund for the library's support.[10] The band eagerly encouraged the establishment of libraries. Prentice was convinced that no matter how small or where located, libraries were always of great use. The provision of libraries for the working population was a special interest of Brotherton. Even before he became Salford's M.P. (in 1832) he had helped to establish a subscription library in the town, and in later years he was at the forefront of the public library movement.[11]

Shuttleworth was another who was keen to further the cause of education. He wrote the article on schools in Manchester which appeared in the first issue of the *Guardian*. This painted a bleak picture and was partly intended as a spur to action. Shuttleworth thought that the provision of schools in Manchester was insufficient and the standard of instruction generally poor. In the *Guardian* Taylor regularly publicised valuable work in educational fields. He was especially interested in the moral and social effects of education, and in February 1827 expressed his belief that better education was producing perceptible changes in the conduct of working people.[12] The social value of education also interested Prentice, who thought that the provision of education was closely related to justice and social order. He advocated popular instruction, the offer of books and classes and the cultivation of the mind as the best way to lift labourers out of the degrading ignorance to which they had long been

---

[10] O'Brien, 'Joseph Brotherton', p. 21; *Sir Thomas Potter, first Mayor of Manchester*; *Times*, 5 July 1829, 2 Oct. 1830.

[11] Prentice, *Letters from Scotland*, pp. 45, 115; O'Brien, 'Joseph Brotherton', pp. 21, 31–2; J. S. Cowan, 'Joseph Brotherton and the Public Library Movement', *Library Association Record*, 59 (1957), pp. 156–9; R. D. Altick, *The English Common Reader 1800–1900* (1957), pp. 214–16, 223–6.

[12] *Guardian*, 5 May 1821, 10 Feb. 1827.

condemned. He also believed that tyranny could not be exercised over an educated people, and another such self-evident truth was that the educated man was peaceful and law-abiding. Prentice was optimistic enough to opine that popular education could mean better social relations. The workers would be grateful if they were given instruction and if their dignity and talents were recognised. Humane sympathy on one side would be met with grateful esteem on the other.[13] Throughout his newspaper career Prentice gave continuing support and publicity to the cause of education. He covered Henry Brougham's speeches and activities, the work of new educational institutions (often looking to his native Scotland for exemplars), and prevalent fashions in teaching and educational theory. One of these was phrenology, in which he became interested during the 1830s. Manchester had a Phrenological Society from 1829.[14] Like his friends, Richard Potter promoted and supported several educational establishments in Manchester in the early decades of the nineteenth century. He was also able to draw the attention of the House of Commons to educational issues while M.P. for Wigan (1832–39), and was one of those who forced the government to take action in 1833. He had joined in the campaign for a national system of education; the government preferred to offer annual Treasury grants. (Salford M.P. Brotherton voted against the first grant of 1833 in disgust.) From the mid-1830s Potter was involved in the work of the Central Society of Education, a lobbying body that published papers on teaching methods, child psychology and foreign educational systems. The society pressed for the abandonment of monitorial methods, more government action in educational fields, and the separation of secular and religious training.[15] Smith had a lifelong interest in education and participated in many efforts on its behalf. One of his most important contributions was his role in the establishment and early life of Owen's College, founded in 1851. After his death a chair in English Literature was endowed and named in his honour.[16]

[13] *Times*, 30 Dec. 1831.
[14] *Times*, 2 Oct. 1830, 13, 20 Aug., 1 Oct. 1831. Prentice was a friend of the renowned phrenologist George Combe; see correspondence in National Library of Scotland, Combe Papers MSS. 7243 f. 136, 7387 ff. 318, 345. These letters relate to a plan for lectures in Manchester during the spring of 1837.
[15] D. G. Paz, *The Politics of Working-Class Education in Britain 1830–50* (1980), pp. 5, 11–25, 69–70.
[16] Cornish's short biography in Smith, Memoranda and Letters, p. 9.

The Unitarians in the band were also active in educational work through their congregations. The Cross Street chapel had a library and schoolrooms attached, and classes were also organised in connection with the Mosley Street chapel. The Unitarians' most lasting and impressive venture was the establishment of the Lower Mosley Street schoolrooms in 1836. These survived until 1942.[17] Manchester Unitarians' interest in 'useful knowledge' led them to support societies for tract distribution and to involve themselves in the efforts of the Society for the Diffusion of Useful Knowledge (S.D.U.K.), which was established in 1826. The Unitarians were well-represented on the first council of the Manchester Institution, and 11 of the 22 men on the founding committee of the Manchester Mechanics' Institute were Unitarians.[18] Members of the band were prominent supporters of both these establishments, but do not appear to have been closely involved with the work of the S.D.U.K. They were not, however, unsympathetic towards the aims of this body. Brougham's seminal pamphlet of early 1825, *Practical Observations Upon the Education of the People*, was well-received by Prentice and Taylor.[19]

Though there continued to be complaints about Manchester's educational and cultural shortcomings, the town did develop an impressive range of educational, diffusionist and improving institutions in the pre-Victorian era. Men of all parties and sects participated, and the local ruling establishment and Tory newspapers were

[17] *General Regulations of the Library belonging to Cross Street Chapel* (1812); L. Burney, *Cross Street Chapel Schools Manchester, 1734–1942* (1977); R. Wade, *Sketch of the Origin and History of the Lower Mosley Street Day and Sunday Schools* (1898).
[18] Seed, 'Unitarianism and liberal culture', pp. 5, 12; Holt, *Unitarian Contribution*, ch. 6.
[19] *Gazette*, 19 March 1825; *Guardian*, 5 Feb. 1825. See also H. Brougham, *Practical Observations Upon the Education of the People. Addressed to the Working Classes and their Employers* (1971). This book emphasised that working people had to be given the resources, time and independence necessary for self-improvement and the acquiring of useful knowledge, and Brougham urged the wealthier classes to offer advice and assistance. 'I would say that the question no longer is whether or not the people shall be instructed – for that has been determined long ago, and the decision is irreversible – but whether they shall be well or ill taught – half-informed or as thoroughly as their circumstances permit and their wants require' (p. 32). In 1825, the year his *Practical Observations* were first published, Brougham helped to establish the University of London, and he later involved himself in the work of the S.D.U.K. He was Whig M.P. for Winchelsea during the 1820s.

occasionally as enthusiastic about these facilities as were the liberal-Dissenting leaders and their press organs. Nevertheless, the main impetus for educational and improving work usually came from the liberal-Dissenting body. As leaders of this body the band's members were prominent supporters and allies of Manchester's developing educational institutions.

The Manchester Sunday school movement began in the 1780s. There was some interdenominational cooperation at first, but this broke down amidst the fears and controversies created by the French Revolution and subsequent wars. By 1821 the Dissenters had taken a clear lead, with twice as many Sunday schools and pupils as the Church in Manchester. The schools normally taught only reading and religious instruction, but they did so successfully. Many observers commended them for instilling basic skills. The 1834 educational report of the Manchester Statistical Society showed that the Sunday schools were serving over 33,000 pupils, considerably more than all the other classes of school in Manchester put together, and praised the Sunday schools for the quality as well as the quantity of their work.[20] Prentice also praised their work, and called their teachers 'quiet but effective labourers for the production of thought'. By teaching their pupils to think, he explained, the Sunday schools were providing a crucially important preparation for the proper exercise of social and political responsibilities. Prentice was convinced of the social and educational value of Sunday schools, and like many others in this era he appreciated their useful restraining influence. He believed that the efforts of Sunday school teachers had assisted in preventing revolution in 1817–19. Watkin was similarly interested in Sunday schools and the problem of correcting idle and disorderly children. This was an interest he had first cultivated as a young man when he attended lectures on the work of Sunday schools.[21]

Members of the band were strong supporters of the Manchester Lancasterian School. Prentice praised its early operations while Shuttleworth was closely involved with the opening of a fund in 1815 to purchase an annuity on behalf of Joseph Lancaster. He wrote an

---

[20] A. P. Wadsworth, 'The First Manchester Sunday Schools', *B.J.R.L.*, 33 (1950–51), pp. 299–320; Maltby, *Manchester and Elementary Education*, pp. 36–8, appendix V (b) and (c); P. H. Butterworth, 'The Educational Researches of the Manchester Statistical Society 1833–40', *British Journal of Educational Studies*, 22 (1974), pp. 340–59.

[21] Prentice, *Sketches*, pp. 116–17; Watkin, *Journal*, p. 19.

influential circular that was sent to potential sympathisers, strongly commending the Lancasterian system and urging a good response to the appeal:

> To rescue the unfriended poor from the sad and lamentable evils that result from a want of instruction, to impart to their untutored minds a knowledge of their duties, to teach them to adore God and to love virtue, must ever have been the object of anxious desire to the wise and good. But to extend the blessings of education to *all* the destitute was an undertaking far beyond what even the most sanguine philanthropy deemed practicable; the time and expensiveness of regular instruction were fatal obstacles to the establishment of any general plan until, by the persevering application of an unsupported individual, that system of education was matured which, in reference to its founder, is denominated THE LANCASTERIAN.[22]

The governing body of the school remained a mixture of Anglicans and Nonconformists, though with a rising number of respectable liberals and Dissenters over time. Some Anglicans withdrew their support because of the controversy surrounding the establishment of two National Schools in June 1812.[23] Taylor had been appointed as secretary of the Lancasterian School by January 1813, and Atkinson and Shuttleworth were on its executive committee by 1814. An especially gratifying occasion for the promoters and supporters of the school came on 25 October 1815, with the celebrations marking its sixth anniversary. There was an exhibition at the Exchange, followed by the reading of a congratulatory letter from the school's royal patron the Duke of Kent. Among the speakers at this event were Taylor and Shuttleworth.[24] Though the Tory papers sometimes covered the school's affairs, they were more concerned with the National Schools in Manchester and the main publicity organ for the Lancasterian continued to be the liberals' *Gazette*.

---

[22] Prentice, *Letters from Scotland*, p. 222; Shuttleworth Scrapbook, p. 11.
[23] H. Wray, *Memoir of Revd C. D. Wray*, pp. 9–14; M. Sanderson, 'The National and British School Societies in Lancashire 1803–39: the roots of Anglican supremacy in English education', in *Local Studies and the History of Education*, ed. T. G. Cook (1972), pp. 1–36; *Exchange Herald*, Dec. 1811 to Feb. 1812.
[24] *Gazette*, 28 Oct. 1815.

The liberals also played a key role in the beginnings of the infant school movement in Manchester in the 1820s. The first important step came in August 1825 when it was decided to establish an infant school in Chorlton Row. Richard Potter went on to be an active member of the Chorlton Row infant school committee and was one of the organisers of the 1825 meeting. Prentice was a regular visitor at the school and joined Potter on the committee in 1827. He continued to publicise the school in his newspapers, particularly when the pupils were examined or meetings were held at which he or his allies were speakers. During the unrest and commercial depression of 1826–27 he pointed to the beneficial social and moral effects of the school. He was sure that infant schools improved conduct and created responsible adults, citizens and workers: 'These schools make characters rather than scholars, and train the dispositions rather than the intellect, and thus fit and prepare the mind for the duties of life in the station in which the individual may be placed'.[25] An infant school was established in Salford following a public meeting on 27 December 1826. Prentice was a speaker. He emphasised the advantages not only of early tuition but also of sectarian rivalry; this rivalry was a useful motivating force and would ensure continual and effective exertions in the field of infant schooling. In later years Prentice gave the Salford school continuing praise and publicity, and was a regular visitor.[26] Prentice publicised the infant schools in the St Michael's, Newton and Ancoats districts of Manchester in the later 1820s.[27] In addition he was a leading member of the educational committee of the St Andrew's Society, which held meetings on infant schooling and established a school in March 1832 near Lees Street chapel in Ancoats.[28] By the autumn of 1830, when Prentice began to tour around the Manchester region delivering lectures on infant schooling, he had been advocating the cause for over five years. His lectures went well and he followed them with a pamphlet offering guidelines about the establishment and curricula of infant schools. Published in December 1830, the sixpenny pamphlet was much in demand and reached its third edition within two

[25] *Gazette*, 22 April 1826. For further coverage of the school, *Gazette*, 1 July, 16 Dec. 1826; *Times*, 2 Jan., 26 Dec. 1828, 26 Feb. 1831.
[26] *Guardian* and *Chronicle*, 30 Dec. 1826; *Gazette*, 30 Dec. 1826, 12 April 1828; *Times*, 26 Dec. 1828, 28 Feb., 11 April 1829.
[27] e.g. *Gazette*, 27 Oct. 1827, 12 April 1828.
[28] *Times*, 25 June, 10, 17 Sept. 1831, 3 March 1832.

years. A fourth edition appeared in 1847. Prentice was glad that his efforts had been of some use. With other campaigners he had helped to make many schools self-supporting and had interested a large section of local opinion in early instruction.[29] The Statistical Society's report of 1834 lamented that there were so few infant schools in Manchester, because they seemed to be well-managed, well--designed and effective in their work.[30]

The Manchester Mechanics' Institute began operations in March 1825. The preparatory work was completed by an executive committee appointed at the inaugural meeting of 7 April 1824. Brotherton and Shuttleworth were on this committee, and Baxter, Harvey and Taylor were speakers at the inaugural meeting. The *Gazette* backed the project, as did the *Guardian*: 'We cannot too strongly recommend it to the liberal support of our townsmen'.[31] Over the following years the Tory papers reported the meetings, proceedings and lectures at the Institute and seemed generally sympathetic (apart from the *Courier*), but the main newspaper support continued to come from Prentice. The Potters, Brotherton and Shuttleworth were among the earliest financial benefactors of the Institute, and in December 1824 Brotherton made a gift of sixteen volumes to its library.[32] Brotherton, Shuttleworth and Richard Potter were all on the board of directors at various times from the mid-1820s to the mid-1830s. Potter and Shuttleworth were among the honoured guests at the ceremony held to open the new Cooper Street building in May 1827, and such was the value placed on Prentice's constant publicity that he was regularly offered free tickets for the Institute's functions and exhibitions.[33] Taylor noticed certain lectures in the *Guardian*, particularly when the speaker was a celebrity.[34] Prentice's coverage of lectures was

[29] Prentice, *Sketches*, pp. 340–42; Somerville, *Free Trade and the League*, ii, pp. 394–7; *Times*, 4, 18 Sept., 23 Oct., 13 Nov., 4 Dec. 1830, 29 Jan., 12 Feb., 10 Sept. 1831; *United Trades Cooperative Journal*, 11 Sept. 1830; Prentice, *Remarks on Instruction in Schools for Infants* (1830).

[30] Butterworth, 'Educational Researches', p. 346.

[31] *Gazette*, 10 April 1824; *Guardian*, 19 June 1824; M. Tylecote, *The Mechanics' Institutes of Lancashire and Yorkshire before 1851* (1957), p. 129; J. W. Hudson, *The History of Adult Education* (1851), p. 125.

[32] *Gazette*, 22 May, 11 Dec. 1824.

[33] *Times*, 22 May, 5 June 1830; Brotherton Scrapbooks, xii, p. 28; *Chronicle*, 9 May 1827; Hay Scrapbooks, xiv (unpaginated); Archives Dept. M.C.L., Manchester Mechanics' Institute, Letter Books, 1828, p. 73.

[34] e.g. William Cobbett: *Guardian*, Jan.–Feb. 1830.

impressive and, as he pointed out, his detailed reports meant that even those who did not attend a particular lecture could still benefit from it.[35] Prentice regretted that politics and religion were excluded from the Institute, for these were the very topics in which working men were most interested,[36] but he remained quick to defend it when it was criticised. In July 1825 he rejected the *Courier*'s claim that the Whig and radical promoters of mechanics' institutes were using them as political organs while presenting them as a laudable means of enlightening the lower orders.[37] The government of the Mechanics' Institute was originally exclusive, and in time the ordinary members pressed for more influence. Prentice was one who welcomed the gradual relaxation of the control of the wealthy and respectable directors. In 1832, for instance, the number of directors was reduced from 21 to 18 and it was agreed that half of these would henceforth be elected by the whole body of subscribers. Prentice had advocated this reform back in May 1831: 'There is no doubt that the arrangement will give mechanics a great deal of additional interest in the institution'.[38]

Dissatisfaction with the way the Manchester Mechanics' Institute was being governed was a main impulse behind the founding of the New Mechanics' Institute (N.M.I.) in March 1829. The promoters were a group of radicals and educators collecting around Rowland Detrosier, the commercial clerk, lecturer and radical leader whose rise to celebrity owed much to the band.[39] The new establishment

[35] Lectures were covered in *Gazette*, 2 April 1825, 15 April, 13 May 1826, 27 Oct. 1827, 26 Jan., 14 June 1828; *Times*, Nov.–Dec. 1828, 11 April, 5, 26 Dec. 1829, 9, 30 Jan., 19 June 1830, 4, 11 June, 24 Dec. 1831, 21 April, 5, 12 May 1832.

[36] *Gazette*, 19 March 1825.

[37] *Courier*, 16 July 1825; *Gazette*, 23 July 1825.

[38] Tylecote, *Mechanics' Institutes*, pp. 134–7; Hudson, *Adult Education*, pp. 127–8; *Times*, 28 May 1831.

[39] Shuttleworth, Brotherton and Prentice gave Detrosier a good deal of help, finding him work, providing financial gifts, encouraging his reading and lecturing, publicising his activities and later arranging for the publication of his lectures. Detrosier came to the attention of Bentham, Place and Mill, and moved to London in 1831. Both the band and the Bentham circle used him as an exemplar – the archetypal 'improved working man'. Shuttleworth, *Memoir of the late Rowland Detrosier* (1834), and *A Sketch of the Life of Rowland Detrosier* (1860); Shuttleworth Scrapbook, p. 135 and loose leaves; G. A. Williams, 'Rowland Detrosier, working class infidel, 1800–34', *Borthwick Papers*, 28 (1965), pp. 3–23; *Times*, 30 Jan., 6 Feb., 10, 24 April 1830, 1 Oct., 31 Dec. 1831; Glen, *Urban Workers*, pp. 267–70.

was designed specifically for working people, many of whom had
for nearly four years been complaining about the cost of membership
of the original institute, its ban on political and religious topics and
newspapers, and the social gulf between the sponsors and intended
members. The N.M.I. began operating in Pool Street in March 1829.
Detrosier was elected president. Members of the band were involved
too, for Thomas Potter agreed to act as treasurer and Prentice gave
the project press support:

> We regret that the exclusion of ordinary members from any
> share in the management of the Mechanics' Institute should
> have rendered a new school necessary; but with our notion that
> they who contribute to the support of a public institution
> should take part in its direction, we heartily wish the new
> Institute success.[40]

The *Times* covered the lectures, meetings and general affairs of the
new Institute while continuing its publicity for the original. About
100 members of the latter left to join the new establishment. The
involvement of members of the band in the affairs of the N.M.I.,
though, does show that it was not entirely an unsponsored institution. Thomas Potter's treasurership, Prentice's publicity and his
readiness to lecture there (on infant schools, for example, in September 1830), and other marks of approval and help from middle-class
reformers, did not rob the N.M.I. of independence but did mean that
this independence was not complete. Members of the N.M.I. recognised their debt to these respectable allies, as can be seen in the
presence of Prentice and Richard Potter as honoured guests and
speakers at the supper of March 1832 which marked the Institute's
third anniversary.[41]

A new and ambitious project in adult education for the lower
classes was announced at the end of 1831. This was the Mechanics'
Hall of Science, again intended specifically for the use of working
people. The total cost was estimated at £4,000, and shares of £1 each
were offered to all interested parties. The Potter warehouse was one

[40] *Gazette*, 7 Feb. 1829; R. G. Kirby, 'An early experiment in workers'
self-education: the Manchester New Mechanics' Institution', in *Artisan to
Graduate* ed. D. S. L. Cardwell (1974), pp. 88, 90; Detrosier, *Address delivered at the New Mechanics' Institution* (1831); Slugg, *Reminiscences*, pp.
270–1; *Times*, 28 March 1829.
[41] *Times*, 31 March 1832.

of the places where applications for shares could be made.[42] A long list of subscribers appeared in November 1832. The Potters, Baxter and Prentice were among those who had already purchased shares, as were their respectable friends the merchant Mark Philips, manufacturer J. C. Dyer and lawyer George Hadfield. Detrosier himself took six shares, and P. T. Candelet (the draper, a leader of the band's middling-sort allies) five.[43] But the whole project quickly lost momentum, and the plan for a Hall was not revived until the local Owenites took it up in 1839. Meanwhile the N.M.I. had declined and been dissolved, partly due to Detrosier's departure for London and the failure of the Hall project.[44]

Those respectable Mancunians who were interested in the evolution of their town's cultural and educational facilities envisaged the Mechanics' Institute as a service primarily designed for selected sections of workers and lower sections of the middle classes. Another important establishment was intended primarily for the wealthier sections of the middle classes. This was the Royal Manchester Institution for the promotion of Arts, Literature and Science, inaugurated at a public meeting on 1 October 1823. Prentice later recalled that the response to the opening of a subscription fund was most impressive: it was not long before £14,000 had been donated. Baxter was one of the leading advocates of an institution for the arts in Manchester and was an early contributor to the fund, as were the Potters and such allies as Hadfield. The *Gazette* backed the project, declaring that it was sure to provide useful opportunities for enlightenment and improvement. Taylor expressed his approval in the *Guardian*.[45] Members of the band were among the supporters and patrons of the Institution in the following years. Watkin enjoyed its exhibitions of painting and sculpture, as did Prentice. In his younger days Prentice had been greatly impressed by collections he had seen in Edinburgh, and judging by payment records in the early ledgers of the Manchester Institution he was a regular user of its facilities during the 1820s.[46]

---

[42] Detrosier, *An Address on the Advantages of the intended Mechanics' Hall of Science* (1832); Kirby, 'Early experiment', pp. 93–5.
[43] *Times*, 24 Nov. 1832
[44] Kirby, 'Early experiment', pp. 96–7.
[45] R. F. Bud, 'The Royal Manchester Institution', in Cardwell, *Artisan to Graduate*, pp. 119–20; Prentice, *Sketches*, p. 243; *Gazette*, 27 Sept., 4, 11, 18, 25 Oct., 1 Nov. 1823; *Guardian*, 4 Oct., 29 Nov. 1823, 8 Jan. 1825.
[46] Watkin, *Journal*, p. 134; Prentice, *Letters from Scotland*, p. 80; Archives Dept. M.C.L., Royal Manchester Institution, Ledgers, 1825, 1827–9.

Baxter was an art lover and of course a keen collector, and was closely involved with the activities of the Institution. On one occasion he was asked to select paintings for its exhibition of ancient masters.[47]

The Manchester Institution was dominated by the most wealthy and cultured members of the local business community.[48] The Manchester Athenaeum, established in 1836, was designed for younger professionals, clerks, retailers, mercantile servants and men of small means, social groups slightly below those that formed the bulk of the Institution's membership. The Athenaeum project was often discussed during the early 1830s, but it was Thomas Potter who took the matter up, proposed the erection of a grand new edifice worthy of the plan, and opened a fund with a gift of £500. Watkin was also an early contributor. The government of the Athenaeum combined openness with oligarchy. All subscribers paying their 30s. a year and aged over 21 were eligible to serve on the board of directors. In practice, though, directors were normally drawn from the wealthiest and most respectable section of the membership. The Athenaeum was democratic in form, but with continuing business elite control. This may have been the model most favoured by respectable and liberal-minded Mancunians, not only for local cultural organisations but also for the wider society and polity. Here was an open system with participation for all members, but with effective control in the hands of the wealthy and respectable. Of all Manchester's educational and improving organs, the Athenaeum perhaps approached most closely to the band's view of how these establishments should be organised and managed.[49]

In his remarks on education Prentice often gave expression to one of his abiding obsessions: no system could work properly or be of any use unless it had a prominent religious content. Religious teaching had to form the basis of any education for the lower ranks. He often complained, for example, that the exclusion of religion from

---

[47] Royal Manchester Institution, Letter Book, Baxter to Winstanley (secretary of the Institution), 25 March 1834.

[48] Bud, 'Manchester Institution', p. 122.

[49] Hudson, *Adult Education*, pp. 110–24; Wheeler, *History*, p. 416; Simon, *City Government*, p. 35; H. M. Wach, 'Culture and the Middle Classes: Popular Knowledge in Industrial Manchester', *Journal of British Studies*, 27 (1988), p. 380; R. J. Morris, 'Voluntary societies and British urban elites', *H.J.*, 26 (1983), pp. 95–118.

mechanics' institutes was a mistake. 'We think that every system of popular education which does not provide for religious instruction is essentially defective'.[50] Nor did Prentice believe that religious education would be wasted on the young, for nine or ten was not a premature age for serious religious impressions.[51] Prentice condemned secular education. This was a matter on which he could not agree with his idol Bentham (though he did agree with the Benthamite notion that education could and should open the door to full political participation for the mass of the people). Prentice thought that schools should be controlled by the sects and opposed state control. A strong voluntaryist in the 1840s and unenthusiastic about public funding, he slightly modified his position after visiting the U.S.A. in 1848 and admitted that public funding might be less objectionable in certain circumstances.[52] There was heated debate in Manchester over funding, state action and the role of the sects. In 1837 the National Education Society was founded in the town to press for a secular and non-sectarian system based on a mixture of government and voluntary support. Prentice had to agree to disagree with some of his friends, for Richard Potter, Watkin and Brotherton were among the leaders of this movement. In 1847 Brotherton was one of the founders of the Lancashire Public School Association, which advocated a measure of local control and local taxation. In 1850 this body was renamed the National Public School Association. Its first conference was held in Manchester, and Brotherton, Harvey and Shuttleworth were all involved in its work.[53]

One of the reasons why members of the band were so interested in education was their belief in the connection between education and political rights. They understood the complaint made by Thomas Walker in the 1790s, that ignorance created an indifference

---

[50] *Gazette*, 19 March 1825.
[51] e.g. Prentice, *Life of Alexander Reid*, p. 3.
[52] See Read, introduction to Prentice's *Sketches*, p. xiii; Ziegler, 'Archibald Prentice', p. 422; Prentice, *Tour in the United States*, pp. 123–4.
[53] Maltby, *Manchester and Elementary Education*, pp. 49–56 and chs. 5–9; Archives Dept. M.C.L., National Public School Association, Records (M 136); Butterfield, 'Educational Researches', pp. 354–6; C. B. Dolton, 'The Development of Public Education in Manchester 1800–1902', in Frangopulo, *Rich Inheritance*, pp. 77–80; Fraser, *Urban Politics*, pp. 272–4; A. Howe, *The Cotton Masters 1830–60* (1984), pp. 216–18, 220–27; F. W. Hirst, *Free Trade and Other Fundamental Doctrines of the Manchester School* (1903), pp. 479–87.

to reform, and claimed that better education would mean more backing for respectable liberalism. Their *Gazette* made this point in the aftermath of Peterloo.[54] They were probably also influenced by Bentham and the philosophic radicals, who emphasised the independence and responsibility that were (or should be) corollaries of full citizenship and political rights. Citizens had a duty to use their education and exercise their votes sensibly; they were not merely to accept conclusions without thinking for themselves. Perhaps Bentham's circle and the band misjudged the 'reasonableness' of the people and the speed at which the masses could be made ready for full rights. The optimism of the philosophic radicals and their provincial emulators seems excessive, but it is to this optimism that much of the band's educational activity is attributable. Certainly it helps to explain Prentice's enthusiasm for infant schools. In March 1832 he published the third edition of his pamphlet on the subject, adding a new preface which pointed to the likelihood of parliamentary reform and emphasised that education not only made a man deserving of the vote, but also ensured that this vote would be used properly and responsibly.

> The probability of a great extension of the elective suffrage makes it the duty of all who have the welfare of their country at heart, to promote the means of enabling those to whom the right is to be extended, to exercise it for the public good. I know of nothing to effect so desirable an end than the establishment of schools that not only instruct the child, but make it a most influential teacher of the parent, by awakening a perception of social relations and the obligation of social duties.[55]

There was an unmistakable and genuine spirit of philanthropy among the Manchester middle classes. This prompted activity on a whole range of social issues (which tells against V. A. C. Gatrell's thesis about 'the stranglehold of political economy' and the unyieldingly self-referential psyche of the Manchester middle classes).[56] A generous and humanitarian concern for the education of the labouring ranks was at least as important as the desire for social control in

[54] *Gazette*, 2 Oct. 1819.
[55] Prentice, *Remarks*, preface to 1832 edition, and *Sketches*, p. 342.
[56] V. A. C. Gatrell, 'A Manchester Parable', in *Studies in Local History*, ed. J. A. Benyon (1976), pp. 28–36.

the prompting of educational work in the town.[57] Benevolent, moral and religious impulses existed alongside considerations of sectional interest and social order. In the statements and activities of the band the philanthropic impulse comes through as clearly as anything else, although it is true that concern about control was also expressed. As well as philanthropy there were motivations stemming from the voluntary ideal and a view of contemporary society that owed something to Benthamism, developing Mancunian liberal thought, and the respectable reformers' conviction that urgent steps had to be taken to tackle the social problems created or exacerbated by industrial progress. Many contemporaries thought that educational improvements were closely related to several other necessary social and economic reforms, and all of these were part of the concern about the quality of life and what was to become known as the 'condition of England' question. The band and other educators and liberals shared an approach to education that was rooted in certain assumptions and predilections. The most important were the antipathy towards authoritarianism, conservatism and obscurantism, faith in progress and in human rationality (which led some to exaggerate the speed at which results could be achieved), and belief in the worth of the individual and in the need for self-improvement and rational recreation. It was believed that one's potential, merit, dignity and ability to share in culture and society should not rigidly be set by birth, rank or employment. It was also believed that success in turning people away from objectionable pursuits depended on offering them continual guidance and better alternatives.

[57] On education as social conditioning, J. M. Goldstrom, *The Social Content of Education* (1972); J. Foster, *Class Struggle and the Industrial Revolution* (1974), pp. 188–9, 191–2, 194; E. P. Thompson, 'Time, Work Discipline and Industrial Capitalism', *P.&P.*, 38 (1967), pp. 56–97; R. Johnson, 'Notes on the Schooling of the English Working Class', in *Schooling and Capitalism. A Sociological Reader*, eds R. Dale, G. Esland, M. McDonald (1976), pp. 44–54, and 'Really Useful Knowledge: radical education and working class culture, 1790–1848', in *Working Class Culture: studies in history and theory*, eds. J.Clarke, C. Critcher, R. Johnson (1979), pp. 75–102; F. Engels, *The Condition of the Working Class in England* (1973), pp. 149–53.

2. HEALTH AND SOCIAL WELFARE

Early nineteenth-century Manchester suffered from all the problems attendant on rapid industrial development and uncontrolled urban expansion. It was many years before concern about public health, housing, sanitation, food and water supply and basic social services resulted in any effective improvements. The local government apparatus (especially before incorporation in 1838) was out-dated and inefficient, and official meliorative measures achieved little. This placed heavy burdens on Manchester's charities and philanthropic societies. Despite the pessimism of some contemporaries the early nineteenth century did see some progress in the fields of health and welfare; problems were recognised, opinion was formed and converted into action, and the organisational and institutional basis for health and welfare improvements began to appear. If the situation was still alarming in the mid-1830s at least a useful beginning had been made, and members of the band helped to bring this about. Like many of a similar social standing they were concerned about the quality of life in Manchester's streets and houses. Manchester's respectable reformers were increasingly prominent among those who discussed and analysed prevalent social problems, and they joined wholeheartedly in activities adopted to deal with them.[58]

Much attention was given to the perceived causes of social ills. Some blamed the factory, others the character failings of the workers. Many believed that reformation should begin in the home rather than the workplace, and sometimes the comments made were flavoured by prejudice and didacticism. Members of the band often contributed to these debates. Brotherton and Prentice favoured factory reform and did not regard the factory or the employer as entirely

---

[58] Contemporaries were fascinated by Manchester and its social problems: J. P. Kay, *The Moral and Physical Condition of the Working Classes Employed in the Cotton Manufacture in Manchester* (1832); P. Gaskell, *The Manufacturing Population of England* (1833); L. Faucher, *Manchester in 1844. Its present condition and future prospects* (1969); W. Cooke Taylor, *Notes of a Tour in the Manufacturing Districts of Lancashire* (1842); Engels, *Condition of the Working Class*; Reach, *Manchester and the Textile Districts; Visitors to Manchester. A selection of visitors' descriptions of Manchester c.1538–1865*, ed. L. D. Bradshaw (1987).

without blame for Manchester's social problems. But even Prentice – genuinely concerned about the working and living conditions of the lower ranks, an advocate of generous aid for the unfortunate and needy, and a critic of the more heartless aspects of orthodox political economy – nevertheless assumed that the workers themselves were partly responsible for the conditions in which they lived. They needed to be hard-working and sober, he insisted, and to take a pride in themselves and seek after education, sound religion, domestic economy and good morality.[59] Prentice welcomed J. P. Kay's *Moral and Physical Condition* in 1832, and thought it a valuable, accurate representation of the evils suffered by working people. He reproduced extracts in his *Times* to direct attention to the need for remedies. As for the causes of social malady, he emphasised the effects of heavy taxation and the corn laws and agreed with Kay that the manufacturing system was not culpable by itself. In the *Guardian* Taylor argued that Kay had been too pessimistic, that the moral and social circumstances of the people were not as bad as Kay was claiming. For Taylor the merit of Kay's study was not the description of lower class life in Manchester but the two central arguments: that improvement was possible, and that social complaints had more to do with commercial restrictions than with the factory system.[60]

For years local government was disorganised and ineffective in its responses to pressing health and welfare issues. The liberals sometimes put this down to the political dominance of Tories and the 'high' party, but this was not only or mainly a party issue. The very extent of Manchester's health and welfare problems was a significant factor, as were general apathy, increasing argument about the pros and cons of interfering with private property, a confusing overlap of authorities and jurisdictions, and a lack of power to do anything even if the will was present.[61] Eventually some important advances were made. The Manchester police acts of 1828 and 1830 vested the police commissioners with wider prerogatives and enhanced their ability to effect change. Manchester had its first statutory improvement committee from September 1828; this was to be an active if at times controversial agency. Taylor rose to be its deputy chairman in the 1830s. The local authorities' growing concern for the health and

---

[59] e.g. Prentice, *Letters from Scotland*, pp. 72, 74, and *Tour in the United States*, pp. 153–4.
[60] *Times*, 28 April 1832; *Guardian*, 21 April 1832.
[61] Redford, *Local Government*, i, chs. 5–7.

welfare of the inhabitants during the 1830s and 1840s was firmly encouraged by members of the band, notably Prentice, who was a councillor for New Cross ward after incorporation. His proposal in the summer of 1844 led to a new and important initiative: the improvement committee was instructed 'to make arrangements with the owners of property for the purchase of such buildings as obstruct the thorough ventilation of small courts and allies, with the view of promoting the health and comfort of the working classes who reside therein'. In 1845 Prentice helped to draw up drastic proposals for sanitary improvement, and he continued to be concerned about the lack of public walks, playing fields and open green spaces for the healthy enjoyment of local people. He was one of the original members of the public parks committee established by the town council in 1846.[62]

Such later improvements may be seen as the corollary of earlier activities in Manchester, unofficial and voluntary as well as official. An important pioneering role was played by the circle of educated professionals, physicians, scientists and influential cotton masters (most of them rational Dissenters and members of the Literary and Philosophical Society), who came together to form the Board of Health in 1795. Two leading members were the Warrington graduate, Dr Thomas Percival, an enlightened social commentator, medical luminary and correspondent of French philosophers, and Dr John Ferriar, originally from Roxburghshire, a physician at the Manchester Infirmary. The board set out to inform and educate, but it lacked authority to implement the improvements it favoured and local government was not yet ready to act on the advice offered. Opinion is divided on the value of the board's work.[63] It would be unfair to judge the board simply on what it achieved during its short lifetime; it should also be remembered that the propagandists of the Chadwick era deliberately painted the worst possible picture of the social welfare situation and minimised the achievements of the past in order to prompt reforms in the present. One lasting achievement

---

[62] Redford, *Local Government*, i, ch. 13, pp. 346, 354, ii, pp. 28–9, 41, 152, 213–14, 219; Briggs, *Victorian Cities*, p. 107.

[63] B. Keith-Lucas, 'Some influences affecting the development of sanitary legislation in England', *Ec.H.R.*, 6 (1953–4), pp. 290–6; E. P. Hennock, 'Urban sanitary reform a generation before Chadwick?', *Ec.H.R.*, 10 (1957–8), pp. 113–20; C. H. Hume, 'The Public Health Movement', in *Popular Movements 1830–50*, ed. J. T. Ward (1970), pp. 183–200.

of the board was the foundation of the House of Recovery for fever
patients (1796),[64] but the body was probably of greatest impact in
providing encouragement, avenues of inquiry, and examples for
later social reformers to follow. Some of the methods and ideas it
established became relevant again during the cholera scare of 1831–
32. New boards were established in Manchester and Salford in
November 1831. Brotherton and Harvey were involved in the work
of the Salford body, Baxter, Watkin, Taylor, Prentice and the
Potters in the work of the Manchester board.[65] The measures
adopted by the latter were designed to meet a specific threat and in
themselves were of little long-term effect in improving welfare
provisions in Manchester. Pamphlets were distributed, the worst
streets were drained and cleaned and the worst habitations white-
washed, but real advances still waited on an extension of the functions and powers of local government. The activity of the board
nevertheless weakens the notion that the town's respectable classes
washed their hands of Manchester's social problems and abdicated
their urban responsibilities. The board of 1831–32 was also important in providing an opening for J. P. Kay, its secretary, who went
on to have a long and distinguished career as a social reformer. The
Manchester and Salford boards gave members of the band an outlet
for their health and welfare concerns, providing them with more of
the experiences, knowledge and encouragement they needed to
satisfy their taste for good works, to exert themselves for the
material benefit of the lower ranks, to make their names as prominent philanthropic townsmen and to push themselves further into
Manchester's public life generally. As an M.P., moreover, Brotherton was later to further the cause of health and welfare improvements nationally as well as locally. He was a persistent supporter of
the public health movement and the calls of Chadwick, Kay and
their social reform party for legislative action, and acted as mediator

---

[64] W. P. Povey, 'The Manchester House of Recovery 1796, Britain's first
general fever hospital. The Early Years', *T.L.C.A.S.*, 84 (1987), pp. 15–45;
Mercury, 23 Feb., 12 April, 7 June 1796; Marshall, *Public Opinion*, pp. 60–64;
Exchange Herald, 7 Feb., 1 Aug. 1815, 10 Nov. 1825; *Guardian*, 1 Oct. 1825.
[65] Boroughreeve's Papers, ii, pp. 46–7, 215–18; *Guardian*, 5, 19 Nov. 1831,
11 Feb. 1832; *Times*, 5, 12, 19 Nov., 3, 31 Dec. 1831, 7 Jan., 11, 18 Feb., 10
March, 7 April, 7 July, 4 Aug., 6, 20 Oct. 1832; Potter Collection, xi, p. 188;
Simon, *City Government*, pp. 23, 26.

between the local authorities and the promoters of the 1848 public health act.[66]

In early nineteenth-century Manchester there was a great expansion of interest in social investigation and particularly social statistics. The Manchester Statistical Society was established in 1833, but the local interest in this approach to social questions can be traced back to Percival, Ferriar and the pioneers of the 1790s.[67] Many of the founders and members of the Statistical Society were educated Unitarians and members of the Literary and Philosophical Society, so the body was very much part of the social and cultural milieu in Manchester that produced the town's most significant improving ventures.[68] Though members of the band were not involved in the Statistical Society's foundation, they belonged to the same circle as the founders and Thomas Potter and Shuttleworth joined the society within a year or two of its establishment. Shuttleworth became an active member, delivering papers on such topics as temperatures in cotton factories, and acting as one of the society's delegates at an assembly of the British Association for the Advancement of Science in August 1838.[69]

Conscious of the need to provide social reformers and legislators with information, the Statistical Society conducted a range of surveys into housing, education, crime, factory conditions and popular morality. The position on many issues was strongly interventionist, though not on the poor law or factory conditions. M. J. Cullen has detected in the society's activity a tension between moralism and environmentalism, 'between a moralistic attitude of condemnation of laziness, lack of self-reliance and improvidence, and an environmentalist appreciation of the effects of lack of education and atrocious living conditions'.[70] Such a tension existed in the approach of many Mancunians to the social problems of the age. There *was*

---

[66] U. R. Q. Henriques, *Before the Welfare State* (1979), pp. 126–31; Redford, *Local Government*, ii, p. 167.

[67] T. S. Ashton, *Economic and Social Investigations in Manchester 1833–1933* (1934), p. 2.

[68] M. J. Cullen, *The Statistical Movement in Early Victorian Britain* (1975), pp. 105–9; Ashton, *Economic and Social Investigations*, pp. 4–12.

[69] Shuttleworth Scrapbook, p. 148 and loose leaves; Cooke Taylor, *Notes of a Tour*, p. 261; F. Smith, *The Life and Work of Sir James Kay-Shuttleworth* (1923), p. 26; Ashton, *Economic and Social Investigations*, p. 48; J. Morrell and A. Thackray, *Gentlemen of Science* (1981), pp. 396–411.

[70] Cullen, *Statistical Movement*, p. 110.

genuine concern and a desire to help others, but there was also an analysis of the causes of health and welfare problems which placed some responsibility for them on those who suffered most. Perhaps the targets of philanthropy had brought suffering on themselves because they knew no better; this was why such emphasis was given to education and the training of minds. Many respectable towns-people, though, refused to be so dominated by rigid dogmas that they lost their benevolent impulses or failed to act upon them. Orthodox political economy and *laissez-faire* may have suited their commercial interests, but many decided that these ideas had less to offer when it came to a consideration of social issues.

Certainly the band was ready and willing to act in charitable and philanthropic causes, often helping out with relief funds and other benevolent projects. These reformers subscribed to and helped to collect and manage funds opened for the Peterloo wounded, the Manchester poor, the Irish poor, the casualties of a serious factory accident in October 1824, Spanish and Italian refugees in London in 1825, and the Salford poor.[71] They acted in other ways. Harvey, for instance, sank a well near his mill in Canal Street, Salford, for the use of his workers. They paid a penny a week and the proceeds went towards a mill library fund.[72] Members of the band were keen philanthropists who gave much time, money and attention to worthy causes. They had a sense of the responsibilities that went with wealth and position, a zeal for the welfare of the community, and a passion-ate belief that the worship of God should also mean the service of man. Richard Potter could have been speaking for the whole of the band when he wrote in his diary of his sense of duty and belief that it was a luxury to do good.[73]

Among the philanthropic institutions in which the band took a close interest was the Deaf and Dumb Institute established in 1823. The Potters and Baxter gave money for the foundation, and Prentice was among the subscribers from 1825.[74] Richard Potter was a foun-der of the Chorlton Row Dispensary, established in December 1825. Prentice gave the scheme newspaper support and was among the

[71] *Gazette*, 16 Nov., 28 Dec. 1816, 11 Sept. 1819, 22 Jan., 19 Feb. 1820, 18 May 1822, 23 Oct. 1824, 5 Feb. 1825, 11, 18 March, 1, 29 April 1826; Brotherton Scrapbooks, ii, p. 17; Prentice, *Sketches*, pp. 167–71.
[72] Reach, *Manchester and the Textile Districts*, pp. 9–10.
[73] Potter Collection, iii, p. 261.
[74] *Gazette*, 14 June 1823, 5 Feb. 1825.

earliest benefactors, as were Richard Potter and Shuttleworth. Brotherton was one of the trustees of the Salford and Pendleton Dispensary established at about the same time.[75] Prentice and Taylor interested themselves in the problem of juvenile delinquency and the need for an institution to rehabilitate young offenders, and Prentice also wrote articles on the sound supervision of workers' children.[76] One of Brotherton's most important achievements was his campaign to reform the Salford Charities. By the early nineteenth century these were being totally mismanaged. Brotherton found out about this problem while an overseer of the poor in 1812–13. He then spent several years in patient investigation of the abuses of local trusts and funds, and wrote a long history of the Salford Charities. This brought so many irregularities to light that Salfordians began to demand an inquiry. In March 1826 Brotherton wrote an open letter to Salford's town officers, calling for closer checks on the handling of trust money and recommending that the receipts and disbursements of all local charities should be published annually. He asserted that it was up to the town officers to take care of this, because they distributed much of the charity on offer and were in a position to gain the attention of the trustees of the funds in question. Following much argument and negotiation the trustees eventually agreed to publish the accounts each year after a parish meeting of April 1829 had approved this step.[77] The Unitarians in the band were also philanthropically active through their congregations. This was part of their ethic that public service was a religious duty, that chapels were really associations for beneficial ends, and that wealth was a gift from God and should be used to serve one's neighbours. In addition to these moral impulses, good works were motivated by the desire for prestige and authority. They were part of the process by which respectable Unitarians became well-known, identifiable social leaders. The Unitarians organised home visits, tract distribution and savings clubs, all of which were normally centred on their Sunday schools, and also promoted social reform through the Domestic

[75] *Gazette*, 10 Dec. 1825, 14 Jan. 1826; *Chronicle*, 10 Dec. 1825; Brotherton Scrapbooks, vii, p. 25.

[76] *Gazette*, 20 Aug., 1 Oct. 1825, 8, 15 Dec. 1827; *Guardian*, 17 Sept. 1825; *Times*, 13 Aug. 1831.

[77] Brotherton, Commonplace Book; O'Brien, 'Joseph Brotherton', pp. 22–3; *Gazette*, 5, 12 April 1828; *Chronicle*, May – June 1828, 25 April 1829; Brotherton Scrapbooks, xi, pp. 19, 34–5.

Mission Society founded in January 1833. The Potters and Taylor were among its members.[78]

One of the band's most important contributions to social thought in early nineteenth-century Manchester was the notion that the worker should be regarded as a person and not just an economic adjunct of the factory unit. Among the many palliative measures that were discussed at this time was the need to promote the reformation of the individual. Members of the band were keen to spread sound moral and religious principles, and this involved them in such ventures as the encouragement of a better observance of the Sabbath. In the summer of 1825 Prentice called for the establishment of a Manchester society to promote Sabbath observance. Many Mancunians agreed that the gambling, drunkenness and idle lounging from which working-class areas of town suffered each Sunday had to be curtailed, and Prentice advanced his proposal as a suitable response to this problem. As well as the moral rectitude of Sabbath observance, he emphasised its practical service to working people: 'We have shown with respect to many subjects that we have the welfare of the working classes at heart . . . we wish not to abridge their pleasures. But we do wish to see them weaned from courses which in many instances lead to jail and the gallows'.[79] Prentice was proud that Sabbath observance was so widespread in his native Scotland, and he linked this with the admirable religious zeal of his countrymen.[80] Sabbath observance was one of his favourite subjects as a lecturer. He believed that Sunday was an essential day of rest and one that the worker should put to good use. It was a time not for sluggish idleness but for reflection, exercise and self-improvement. Prentice argued that working people should be ready to defend their right to a day of rest. Without it they would be slaves, prey to perpetual physical exhaustion. There were therefore sound moral and physical reasons to observe the Sabbath and it made sense to use the free time in a responsible way, to make proper use of recreation opportunities.[81] Others in the band shared Prentice's attitude. Watkin was convinced of the usefulness and rectitude of Sabbath observance, and in the later

[78] Seed, 'Unitarianism and liberal culture', pp. 6, 12–19; H. E. Perry, *A Century of Liberal Religion and Philanthropy in Manchester. A History of the Manchester Domestic Mission Society 1833–1933* (1933).
[79] *Gazette*, 25 May, 1 June 1825.
[80] Prentice, *Letters from Scotland*, pp. 132–3.
[81] Prentice, *One Day's Rest in Seven*, pp. 2–4, 8.

1830s opposed the opening of the Zoological Gardens on Sundays. Harvey was to be an active member of the Sunday Closing Association in his later years.[82]

Band members were also concerned about Manchester's serious and noticeable lack of parks, green open spaces and pleasant rural walks where the hardworking populace could go for fresh air, exercise and healthy recreation. Prentice opposed the Irwell bridge project of 1817 because the charging of a toll would restrict the workers' access to the countryside.

> The vindication of a right in small things keeps alive the spirit of resistance to greater unjust encroachments; and the man who preserves a footway where the humble mechanic can take his wife and children through fresh and verdant fields is as much a benefactor as he who gives the public a path or an arboretum.[83]

Members of the band were steadfastly opposed to the obstruction of paths and encroachments on parks. Prentice loved the countryside and in some of his writings included fond descriptions of impressive rural scenery.[84] Watkin also enjoyed the countryside and was a keen rambler, while Richard Potter was remembered for his 'love of the land and outdoor life'.[85] Potter was a vice-president of the Manchester Floral and Horticultural Society established in 1824, and the treasurer of the Botanical Society established in 1827. Both bodies were partly a demonstration of the growing interest in healthy recreation and approval for the provision of places where local people could enjoy space, fresh air, greenery and flowers. The Botanical Society opened some gardens in Old Trafford in 1831 and encouraged the study of flora and plant life. The opening of the Zoological Gardens in 1838 was another step in the attempt to remedy Manchester's deficiency in such facilities.[86] One of the band's most important contributions in this sphere was the part it

---

[82] Watkin, *Fragment No. 1*, p. 20; *Guardian*, 31 Dec. 1870.
[83] Prentice, *Sketches*, pp. 119–21.
[84] See especially his *Letters from Scotland* and *Tour in the United States*.
[85] Watkin, *Journal*, especially part 1, chs. 4, 5, 9, 13; Meinertzhagen, *Potters of Tadcaster*, preface, p. x.
[86] 'Amusements' and 'Literary and scientific institutions', in B. Love, *Manchester as it is* (1839), pp. 110–26, 138–44; *Gazette*, 18 June 1825; Slugg, *Reminiscences*, p. 266.

played in the foundation and campaigns of the Manchester Society for the Preservation of Ancient Footpaths. This body was established in November 1826 at a time of rising controversy, as local people protested about the closure and obstruction of public paths. The Potters, Prentice, Atkinson, Baxter, Taylor, Smith, Shuttleworth and Harvey all involved themselves in the work of the society, and it soon acquired great local influence. Smith recorded that 'such a wholesome fear of its power and influence was established as to lead landowners not to attempt any alteration in ancient footpaths without consulting the Society'.[87] The footpaths society became involved in many disputes with farmers, landowners and magistrates, and was extremely successful in upholding the public's right of way. Soon it was asked for its help in disputes over pathways in other parts of Britain. The society's activity combined a concern about the public's opportunities for healthy recreation with a reformist disposition against the selfish exercise of power by those who traditionally possessed political and social influence.[88]

Temperance was another health and welfare issue which interested the band. The two Bible Christians, Brotherton and Harvey, turned teetotal (and vegetarian) after 1809 when their minister, William Cowherd, proclaimed the spiritual necessity of such self-restraint. The Manchester Cowherdites, indeed, played a leading role in the developing temperance movement despite their small number.[89] Harvey was a founder and the chairman of the U.K. Temperance Union established in 1853, and president of the Manchester and Salford Temperance Union established in 1851.[90] In 1849, when the *Morning Chronicle* reporter A. B. Reach visited the

[87] Smith, Reminiscences, p. 30.
[88] *Gazette*, 8 May, 24, 31 July, 20, 27 Nov. 1824, 22 Jan., 23 April, 7 Oct. 1825, 14 Oct., 11, 18 Nov. 1826, 16 June, 22, 29 Sept., 27 Oct., 3, 10 Nov. 1827, 14 June 1828; Prentice, *Sketches*, pp. 289–92, 359–61; Potter Collection, iv, p. 34, xi, pp. 140–1; H. E. Wild, 'The Manchester Association for the Preservation of Ancient Footpaths', *M.R.*, 10 (1963–5), pp. 242–50; *Chronicle*, 24 July, 27 Nov., 4, 11 Dec. 1824, 22 Jan. 1825, 18 Nov. 1826, 16 June, 27 Oct. 1827; *Guardian*, 8 May, 24, 31 July, 20, 27 Nov. 1824, 22 Jan, 23 April 1825, 7 Oct., 18 Nov. 1826, 16 June, 22, 29 Sept., 27 Oct., 3, 10 Nov. 1827; *Times*, 31 Jan., 6 June 1829, 23 Jan., 12 June, 18 Sept., 30 Oct. 1830; Shuttleworth Scrapbook, p. 77; Cooke Taylor, *Notes of a Tour*, p. 133.
[89] B. Harrison, *Drink and the Victorians. The Temperance Question in England 1815–72* (1971), pp. 100, 164, 225–6.
[90] *Guardian*, 31 Dec. 1870; *Courier*, 29 Dec. 1870; *Salford Weekly News*, 31 Dec. 1870.

Harvey and Tysoe mill in Salford, he noted that 'the partners are steady adherents of the teetotal system, and lose no opportunity of inculcating the advantages of temperance upon their workpeople'.[91] Brotherton was on the committee of the Salford Society for Promoting Temperance, founded in January 1830. He was an unyielding advocate of total abstinence. In 1810 he wrote that indulgence in drink was 'not to be conquered by half-measures; no compromise with it is allowable', and he supported this with references from the Bible and several religious tracts. He was in no doubt that abstinence was good for both the spiritual and physical health of the individual. His 1821 tract *On Abstinence from Intoxicating Liquor* attacked publicans, magistrates and central government for failing to act, and urged all Christians and reformers to set an example and give up alcohol.[92] Others in the band shared such sentiments. Moderation in all things was regarded as a sign of sound character. In March 1800 Thomas Potter told his younger brother Richard that public houses were to be avoided and that 'a rigid system of industry and sobriety' was the key to personal and commercial advancement.[93] Prentice exercised moderation and in his later years was converted to total abstinence from alcohol. He was a prominent local lecturer on temperance, and a founder and the treasurer of the Manchester and Salford Temperance League established in 1857.[94] His contact with drunkenness and excess as a young commercial traveller left a deep impression on him. He later warned potential emigrants to the U.S.A. to discipline themselves and, when they reached their new homes, to avoid drink in spite of its cheapness.[95] Watkin also condemned excess, and thought that respectable persons could personally benefit from temperance just as much as labouring people could.[96]

---

[91] Reach, *Manchester and the Textile Districts*, p. 13.

[92] *Times*, 23 Jan. 1830; Brotherton, Commonplace Book, entry for 2 April 1810; Brotherton, *On Abstinence from Intoxicating Liquor*; O'Brien, 'Joseph Brotherton', p. 20.

[93] Potter Collection, xii, pp. 1–4.

[94] Dunlop, 'Archibald Prentice', p. 443; Read, introduction to *Sketches*, p. xi; Ziegler, 'Archibald Prentice', p. 422; Prentice, *Sanitary and Political Improvement* and *Lecture on Wages*.

[95] Prentice, *Letters from Scotland*, pp. 31, 37, and *Tour in the United States*, pp. 15–16, 187–8.

[96] Watkin, *Journal*, pp. 96–7.

Manchester and Lancashire played an important role in the progress of the temperance movement.[97] One important impulse was a feeling of disgust caused by drunken disturbances in July 1821; these shameful episodes accompanied the ill-organised civic celebrations marking George IV's coronation.[98] By the later 1820s the temperance debate was becoming more prominent because of the attempt of brewers, publicans and free traders to reform the licensing system.[99] As the campaign for freer trade in spirits and beer began to advance, the *Guardian* lamented the direction which government policy was taking, and in November 1829 Taylor pointed to the rising consumption of alcohol and its detrimental effect on public morals.[100] Although they were all free traders, members of the band apparently thought that drink should be an exception. In his *Times* Prentice backed the temperance campaign, reported meetings and commended the Salford Society for Promoting Temperance and the Manchester Temperance Society (both established in 1830). He said it was a Christian duty to attack the evil of habitual drinking, and in December 1829 stressed the harm inflicted by drink on the individual, the family and society as a whole. Intemperance led to crime, arguments and violence, and inevitably to beggary, misery and ruin. 'What heart does not stand appalled at the progress of this many-headed monster!'[101] Prentice linked the drink question with the issues of education and political rights. Like ignorance, intemperance represented an obstacle that had to be overcome so that 'responsible' working men could be granted the vote. Temperance was also an attractive issue for the liberals because it would add to the dignity of the reform cause and help to combat drinking and hooliganism, identified as tools used by their opponents during elections. The use of drink as a bribe meant that many voters did not use their right in a responsible and acceptable way. This problem was brought home to Shuttleworth, Taylor and others when they assisted the local reformist manufacturer John Wood in the contested Preston election of 1826. Both the Cobbettites and the Stanley party offered free drink, 'and the effect is abominable'.[102]

---

[97] Harrison, *Drink and Victorians*, pp. 107–9, 139, 197–8.
[98] Watkin, *Journal*, pp. 93–4; Prentice, *Sketches*, pp. 216–18.
[99] Harrison, *Drink and Victorians*, ch. 3.
[100] *Guardian*, 14 Nov. 1829.
[101] *Times*, 19 Dec. 1829.
[102] Wood to Shuttleworth, 31 May 1826, Shuttleworth Scrapbook, loose leaves.

Always keen to show the lower ranks how they could best help themselves, the band energetically encouraged habits of thrift and providence by promoting savings banks, building societies and benefit and sick clubs. Brotherton's short pamphlet *Useful Information to Members of Friendly Societies*, written in the early 1820s, explained how to establish and organise such bodies and included a table demonstrating the relationship between monthly contributions and sick allowances.[103] In March 1825 Prentice wrote a long article on the aims and organisation of building societies, benefit clubs, savings banks and other such bodies, convinced that they would 'ultimately effect not only a favourable change in the condition of the working classes as regards their command over the necessaries and conveniences of life, but a decided improvement in their intellectual and moral state'.[104] Prentice often urged workers to save a little each week and use this money for education, clothing and furniture. To save was to improve one's standard of living. He also showed that savings could give workers something to fall back on during wage disputes.[105] Taylor advocated savings banks, sick clubs and benefit societies, but he argued that these institutions should be under respectable control, otherwise there would not be sufficient security for their funds nor guarantees of sound management.[106] Many observers believed that workers could not run sick and benefit clubs themselves, and there was also concern about the diverting of their funds to support combinations and turn-outs. This 'improper' use of funds remained an issue even after the repeal of the combination acts.[107] Members of the band helped to establish a savings bank in December 1828. This was a commercial as well as a philanthropic venture. Thomas Potter, Baxter and Smith were leading shareholders in the joint stock company behind the Manchester Savings Bank, and were among the bank's directors and trustees. Unfortunately the bank collapsed in 1842. Smith, by now its chairman, lost £12,000 in shares.[108]

[103] Brotherton Scrapbooks, v, p. 3.
[104] *Gazette*, 5 March 1825.
[105] e.g. Prentice, *Lecture on Wages*, p. 2.
[106] *Guardian*, 25 Sept. 1824.
[107] A. Aspinall, *Early English Trade Unions* (1949), docs. 140, 185, 213, 261–4.
[108] *Times*, 5 Dec. 1828; Brotherton Scrapbooks, x, p. 75; Archives Dept. M.C.L., Declaration of the Trusts upon which the Bank of Manchester is held (9 Jan. 1829), Mr Edward Burdekin and his sureties to the Trustees of the Company (31 Aug. 1829); Smith, Newspaper Cuttings, pp. 29–31; Grindon, *Manchester Banks*, ch. 19.

Of the other suggested solutions to the social and moral problems of the lower classes, two of the most controversial were birth control and Owenite cooperation. Among band members only Taylor came out clearly in favour of birth control, and he circulated printed bills on the subject. Prentice was against birth control on moral grounds and also because he believed it was unnecessary; free trade would produce plenty for the world's growing population. His disapproval of Francis Place's advocacy of birth control was made clear when he met Bentham in April 1831. Watkin shared Prentice's position. Speaking to the radical Richard Carlile when the latter was in Manchester in August 1827, Watkin admitted that too many births sometimes exacerbated social and health problems, but denied the wisdom of a general publication and recommendation of contraceptive methods. As Watkin put it, 'to teach the means of gratifying the sexual appetite with impunity was to loosen the bonds of moral obligation and to license an almost general prostitution'.[109]

Manchester's respectable reformers disagreed about Owenite ideas and practices. Watkin found them unrealistic and impractical, and was particularly condemnatory towards 'National Regeneration'. He did not think that 12 hours' wages could be given for an 8-hour day, and scorned theories about the reconstruction of society on 'scientific principles' with no religion, laws, prisons or marriage, and with children as the property of the state. Watkin doubted that any of this could truly benefit the labouring classes. Taylor was highly sceptical about cooperation, by which he meant the creation of small self-sufficient communities of workers who joined together, cut out middlemen and conducted their own affairs by themselves. Such experiments had all failed in the past, he explained. Abstract reasoning was against cooperation, because it ignored the principles of supply and demand and the division of labour. Furthermore, employment could not be found for *all* descriptions of labourers who might join a cooperative society, and such societies would not be controlled by men of any business acumen. Prentice was more sympathetic. He visited Owen's New Lanark in 1815 and was not impressed, but in later years he did express approval for certain aspects of the cooperative ideal. At least the Owenites were looking

---

[109] *Report of the Proceedings on the Trial of an action Taylor v. Cuff and others, for libel, Lancaster Spring Assizes, 25 March 1833* (1833); Ziegler, 'Archibald Prentice', p. 422; G. Wallas, *Life of Francis Place* (1918), pp. 81–2; Watkin, *Fragment No. 1*, pp. 5–10.

into ways of improving workers' living conditions and encouraging self-dependence, dignity and respectability. In December 1829 Prentice praised cooperative societies for instilling habits of prudence and foresight. He also used his newspapers to publicise lectures on cooperation at the Mechanics' Institute and N.M.I. Prentice refused to subscribe to any indiscriminate condemnation of cooperation. While he did not always praise the cooperators, he often pointed to the good they were doing and the commendable principles they were instilling.[110]

3. POVERTY AND POOR RELIEF

Poverty and the distribution of poor relief were matters that attracted great attention in Manchester, for the town was a magnet for migrant labour[111] and also had many thousands of settled workers who lived near or below bare subsistence level. The periodic depressions associated with the trade cycle inevitably accentuated the effects of what was in truth a continual presence of large numbers of poor and needy. Pity and philanthropic concern, a sense of public duty and an interest in the quality of life mixed with alarm about what poverty could lead to. There was some discussion of the connections between poverty and crime, for example, with Richard Potter arguing for leniency and patience towards the 'criminal' who acted out of harsh necessity; he was thinking particularly about half-starved pilferers of foodstuffs.[112] Some working people did reject the social arguments of their betters and occasionally also the aid that was offered, because they associated it with hypocrisy and patronising self-interest. A similar view could be taken of the middle classes' educational and other welfare efforts. This development had much to do with the radical politics and class-oriented appeals of the postwar era.[113] Band members often

---

[110] Watkin, *Fragment No. 2*, pp. 21–3; *Guardian*, 26 Dec. 1829; Prentice, *Letters from Scotland*, pp. 145–6; *Times*, 19 Dec. 1829, 14 June, 4 Sept. 1830, 4, 11 June 1831.
[111] e.g. Aston, *Manchester Guide*, p. 211; Gaskell, *Manufacturing Population*, pp. 288–9.
[112] Potter Collection, xi, pp. 106–10, 113–18.
[113] For plebeian radical views on poverty and 'respectable' aid, *Observer*, 7 Nov. 1818, and 'To the Land Proprietors, Fundholders and Large Capitalists of Great Britain' by JUSTITIA, Hay Scrapbooks, xviii, p. 118.

participated in activity designed to alleviate poverty and distress. They seem to have imbibed the notion that poverty should not be regarded merely as a natural condition but as a social problem worthy of organised collective (and perhaps state) action. Certainly the *Gazette* made much of the duty of 'universal sacrifice' in the summer of 1816.[114] Manchester liberals could still disagree, however, about the aims and methods of poverty relief.

It was not just the existence of poverty that aroused concern, but its seemingly unstoppable increase. In 1775–76 Manchester township paid out about 16.5 per cent of the poor rates for the whole of Salford Hundred. By 1802–3 the proportion was 22.5 per cent. Annual expenditure on poor relief in Manchester in 1802–3 was five times what it had been 26 years earlier, and in Salford Hundred only about three times what it had been, so Mancunians could easily notice the extension of local poverty in comparison with the surrounding area.[115] G. B. Hindle has shown that Manchester was a town in which the poor rate burden was 'generally bewailed and universally attacked', and in which the massive rise in relief expenditure after the mid-1790s encouraged the ideas that the poor were idle and immoral and that relief contributed towards this. But there was continuing concern for the needy, and the very men who complained about the poor rates were also the first ones to act on their benevolent impulses in times of distress.[116] Great importance, though, was placed on making relief discriminatory.[117] Manchester's rulers and leading townsmen did not want to see wasteful and slack liberality creating more dependency and a belief among the lower ranks that relief was automatic and unconditional. In December 1816 the *Exchange Herald* was horrified to find some workers expecting relief as if they had an incontestable right to it.[118]

---

[114] *Gazette*, 3, 31 Aug. 1816.
[115] These calculations are based on statistics in *Abstract of the Answers and Returns made pursuant to . . . An Act for Procuring Returns relative to the Expense and Maintenance of the Poor in England* (1804).
[116] G. B. Hindle, *Provision for the Relief of the Poor in Manchester 1754–1826*, Chetham Society 3rd series, 22 (1975), pp. 3–6, 8.
[117] As a county Lancashire was one of the most discriminatory in its provision of relief, and highly adept at cutting its relief bill when opportunities arose. See figures in *Report of the Select Committee on Poor Rate Returns*, P.P. 1824, vi. Appendices B, C, D and D2.
[118] *Exchange Herald*, 24 Dec. 1816.

Propertied Mancunians were usually generous when appeals for voluntary aid were made and when relief was well-administered and discriminatory. Compulsory benevolence in the form of poor rates was tolerated by many provided that demands were reasonable and fair. But this was a controversial matter and Manchester saw a long-running dispute over poor rate assessments. This bitter conflict also involved such related matters as the friction between small and large property-owners and the protest against the way local government was being conducted. In the late 1790s the parish authorities had agreed to a change in the local administration of the poor laws. The occupiers of all tenements were called upon to pay the poor rates instead of the bulk of the contribution being borne by the landlords and owners, as was 'formerly the established custom' in Manchester. In March 1817, however, the church-wardens and overseers complained that this change 'has ever since occasioned very serious losses', and they decided that the poverty of those occupying houses valued below £12 a year 'furnishes an irresistible ground of exemption from the payment of the poor's rate'. The authorities wanted the owners of this low-valued property to pay the contribution due for it; this would mean a greater levy and would remove a direct tax from the poorer classes.[119] The authorities' decision provoked several years of heated debate. The owners of low-valued property resisted, argued that contributions from larger property should be higher, and pointed out that the change in the 1790s had been necessary because of the difficulty they had experienced in collecting their rents from poorer tenants. Taylor sided with the churchwardens and those favouring the new assessments. He wanted an 'equalisation of charges upon property' – that is, he wanted the smaller property-owners to pay their share. So did the Tory papers. The liberals' *Gazette* wanted a fair, negotiated settlement, though was sympathetic towards the small property party and towards the view that the poor rate was and should remain a personal tax related to one's ability to pay. According to this view contributions should come from *all* inhabitants and occupiers, because the Elizabethan statutes said nothing about taxing property as such, and demands should depend on means. The *Gazette* also occasionally accused the churchwardens of attempting to tyrannise over the small property-

---

[119] *Gazette*, 8 March 1817.

owners.[120] The arguments continued through the 1820s and there were several acrimonious parish meetings on the subject. By the early 1830s it was regular procedure in Manchester for landlords to pay the rate due for small houses, though abatements were normally granted. The system for property valued at under £10 a year seems to have been that the payment could be made by either the occupier or the owner. The parish authorities were concerned only to receive some of the rate due; it did not matter to them who actually paid it.[121]

Many of Manchester's respectable reformers favoured poor laws, though there was disagreement about how they should be administered. The *Gazette* leaned in favour of a generous relief provision, especially after Prentice took over as editor, but even before this the paper had been for liberality rather than restriction, while emphasising the need for discrimination.[122] The latter point was taken further by Taylor, who was probably the least sympathetic towards poor laws of all the members of the band (and more receptive than some of them towards the tenets of orthodox political economy). He always insisted that precautions had to be taken to ensure that the undeserving received nothing. This applied to both voluntary and statutory relief. Taylor thought it an indignity for an individual to seek aid from the parish. This betrayed serious character failings, ignorance, wickedness and laxity, and was 'repugnant to every man of right feeling who knows it to be his duty, and feels it his pride to maintain himself and his offspring'.[123] In 1828 Taylor told the local weavers that they should do all in their power to avoid dependence on the parish. In 1831 he blamed agrarian unrest on the Speenhamland system, saying of the disturbances:

> They are undoubtedly attributable mainly to the pernicious custom which has been so prevalent in the southern and midland counties, of making up from the poor's rate the deficiency in wages, thus disconnecting subsistence from labour and

[120] *Gazette*, 8, 29 March 1817, 4 April 1818, 14 June, 30 Aug., 6, 13, 20 Sept. 1823; *Guardian*, 4 May 1822; *Mercury*, 20 April 1819, 16 Sept. 1823; *Chronicle*, 4, 11 May 1822, 13 Sept. 1823; *Exchange Herald*, 14 May 1822, 9, 16 Sept. 1823.

[121] *Report from H. M. Commissioners on the State of the Poor Laws*, P.P. 1834, viii, Appendix A, 922. xvi, Appendix B2 (Answers to Town Queries), 68, i.k.

[122] e.g. *Gazette*, 10 July 1819, 29 July 1820.

[123] *Guardian*, 11 March 1826.

thereby removing from the poor their natural and strongest stimulus to exertion and good conduct.

Taylor believed that excessive leniency sapped good sense and moral restraint. This encouraged a readiness to depend on parish allowances rather than the natural demand for labour, and also resulted in larger families which put more pressure on the labour market and helped to ruin the habits of industry.[124]

Taylor had displayed Malthusian tendencies years before, in May 1821 at the time of James Scarlett's proposal to amend the poor laws. Scarlett (Whig M.P. for Peterborough) wanted to abolish removal, fix a maximum to the amount paid in relief, and limit relief to men who were unmarried at the time the new rules came into operation. The *Gazette* declared that the measure was biased against the interests of the poor, but Taylor denied that it was cruel or unjust. Aston's *Exchange Herald* also backed the bill, commending reforms that would stop the relief system from demoralising the labouring classes. Public meetings in Manchester and Salford came out against the bill, which was withdrawn after its second reading. Prentice and Richard Potter addressed the Salford meeting and were appointed to the committee which organised a petition against Scarlett's plan. Many local people thought that a reform of the poor law system might be necessary, but doubted that this plan represented the right approach. In particular, to prevent removal would be to ruin populous towns like Manchester. But the *Guardian* defended Scarlett's bill, and it was after this that Taylor's relationship with Prentice began to deteriorate.[125]

A year later Scarlett introduced a poor removal bill, another attempt to serve the landed interests by preventing removal. Manchester opinion was decidedly against the measure. Prentice was a speaker at the collegiate church meeting of 23 May 1822, praising the principle of poor relief and criticising Scarlett's measure, especially the clause allowing magistrates to confine paupers who were suspected of idleness, extravagance or misconduct.[126] The ending of removal was opposed by Manchester's Tory papers, which feared the

---

[124] *Guardian*, 12 April 1828, 5 Feb. 1831.
[125] *Gazette* and *Guardian*, 26 May, 2 June 1821; *Exchange Herald*, 29 May, 5 June 1821; Prentice, *Sketches*, pp. 212–15.
[126] Prentice, *Sketches*, pp. 234–5; *Gazette*, 25 May, 1 June 1822; Hay Scrapbooks, xi, p. 94.

bankrupting of the parish.[127] Scarlett's proposal was doubly alarming at this time because of rising distress, especially in agricultural regions, which was bound to stimulate more migration to the big towns. These weeks also saw Richard Potter scorning the statements of government ministers that distress was only temporary, that nothing could be done to reverse the natural tendencies of the economy, that people should be patient and submit to the dictates of Providence, and that the present suffering was due to abundance. Potter was incredulous: 'in the estimation of these men the Blessings and Bounties of Providence are an *actual Evil*'.[128] Prentice was of a similar outlook,[129] but there were plenty of local Anglicans still expressing Paleyite ideas and urging the poor to be thankful for their lot and endure hardship with patience and resignation.[130]

The *Gazette* was a consistent advocate of generous relief provision after Prentice became editor in July 1824. He had been an anti-Malthusian for some time. His *Letters from Scotland* had attacked what he regarded as the cruel relief system in Scotland, and had displayed his hostility to strict discrimination: 'The wicked and extravagant must not look for charity. No! The object must be *deserving*. Curse on the heartless morality which prates about deserving when a fellow creature wants bread!'[131] Prentice did not believe that the poor themselves were primarily to blame for their predicament. His impressive leading articles of July 1826 'On the Causes and Cure of the Present Distress' argued that hardship could be traced to the

---

[127] *Chronicle*, 25 May 1822; *Exchange Herald*, 28 May, 4 June 1822; *Mercury*, 11 June 1822.

[128] Potter Collection, xi, pp. 31–2.

[129] Prentice, *Sketches*, pp. 231–3.

[130] Braidley, Diary, ii, pp. 55–6. In his famous *Reasons for Contentment* (1792), the archdeacon of Carlisle, William Paley, had warned the people against revolutionary principles, defended the Church-state system, and asserted that poverty brought pleasures rather than hardships because it encouraged hard work and frugality and safeguarded innocence and purity. Everyone in society had been given their status according to God's plan, said Paley, and it was wrong for an individual to complain or to compare his own condition with that of others. Obviously such a teaching had scant appeal for many groups in a society which was undergoing rapid industrial change and suffering continual disruption of customary styles of living and working. In particular, Paleyite opinion seemed to have little relevance to or attraction for large numbers among both the urban poor and the ambitious merchants and manufacturers of the commercial middle class.

[131] Prentice, *Letters from Scotland*, pp. 165–76.

corn laws, heavy taxation and interference with the currency. The *Courier* disputed some of Prentice's claims, but these well-written and forceful essays were reprinted in cheap pamphlet form and reached a wide audience.[132] Prentice thought that parochial relief was necessary and appropriate. Establishing a *right* to aid of some kind would mean that the poor would not be degraded by the acceptance of it. The poor would certainly retain their independence, morality and industriousness, Prentice insisted, and with a little self-denial they could also collect some modest savings in good times. The boon was that they would always have something to fall back on. In 1817 Prentice wrote a reply to an *Edinburgh Review* article by the Revd Thomas Chalmers, a Malthus-inspired piece on 'The Causes and Cure of Pauperism' which Prentice found ripe for refutation. Though the opinions of Chalmers gained some backing in Manchester, and Prentice was criticised for his reply to them, he was at least able to spur generous and humanitarian townspeople into action. 'My pamphlet was only a stone thrown into the strong stream, but the ripple it caused was seen by others able to throw stronger impediments into the current'.[133] In his *Gazette* and *Times* Prentice often wrote in favour of a liberal poor law administration, and complained that too many people were not covered by the parochial aid system. He made the latter point most strongly in periods of economic distress, when those who for various reasons did not qualify for official relief quickly became a hungry and desperate multitude. In his view the parochial system was inadequate. It needed to be extended, not subjected to new restrictions, and its weaknesses meant that the need for voluntary action could not be emphasised enough. Occasionally Prentice would claim that too many applications for relief were being denied. He praised certain magistrates for their benevolent attitude and their castigation of parish officers who had been high-handed and cold-hearted towards applicants for parochial aid.[134]

[132] *Gazette*, 15, 22 July 1826; *Courier*, 22, 29 July 1826; Prentice, *Sketches*, p. 284.

[133] Prentice, *Sketches*, p. 119; 'Archibald Prentice' (obituaries) in *Biographical References*; Somerville, *Free Trade and the League*, ii, p. 391. Chalmers, the Glasgow-based evangelical minister and lecturer, achieved wide renown in educated circles at about this time after several publications and a lecture visit to London. From 1828–43 he occupied the chair in theology at Edinburgh University.

[134] His clearest statements on the poor laws came in *Gazette*, 26 Aug. 1826; *Times*, 28 Nov., 26 Dec. 1829, 9 Jan. 1830.

At a leypayers' meeting of 27 January 1830 it was Richard Potter's turn to impress upon the parish officers the need for more compassion during this period of economic depression and cold weather. Potter said that the public would prefer the churchwardens to err on the side of generosity rather than parsimony. The churchwardens replied that they were willing to relieve all who were distressed, and would pay more attention to cases neglected by their subordinates. Prentice found this undertaking highly commendable. January 1830 also saw the Tory *Courier* adopt a characteristically paternalistic line on the prevalent distress. The *Courier* was in favour of poor laws and also recognised that statutory relief was not enough. It therefore called for more voluntary effort, particularly on behalf of the Manchester weavers. Food and fuel had to made available to this most vulnerable class of workers.[135]

Although it was to be known for its efficiency in the Victorian period, in the late eighteenth and early nineteenth centuries the poor law administration in Manchester was confused and disorderly. The responsibilities of particular officers and authorities were not clearly defined, and there were many local variations in procedure. The system was strained by such complicated matters as the assessment and collection of rates, laws of removal and settlement, officers' discretion on the giving or withholding of relief, the administration of the workhouse and decisions about outdoor relief, the treatment of different classes of pauper, policy on vagrants and bastards, and the problem of corruption within the parish government. In later times the situation was said to have improved. A detailed account of the Manchester system was included in the Poor Law Report of 1834. The author, assistant commissioner Henderson, was generally complimentary, though did point out that 'as admission is rather a matter of favour, little use can be made of the workhouse as an alternative to repel improper applications for relief'. Further pertinent points were revealed by the replies made to the Town Queries by Gardiner and Lings, two of Manchester's overseers. They made it clear that the fundamental features of the Manchester system, constant visitation and strict discrimination, were never abandoned.[136] Many Mancunians decided that, as far as their town and

---

[135] *Times*, 30 Jan. 1830; *Courier*, 16 Jan. 1830.
[136] Hindle, *Provision for Relief*, chs. 2–5; Redford, *Local Government*, i, ch. 8; *Report on the state of the Poor Laws*, P.P. 1834, viii, Appendix A, part 1, xv and xvi, Appendix B2, parts 1–5.

region were concerned, the poor law amendment act of 1834 was unnecessary. Some of the changes proposed in 1834 had already been implemented under the old system. Opposition to the reform also came on moral, political and economic grounds. But Manchester opinion was divided. Influential social commentators J. P. Kay and Peter Gaskell had condemned the old system, the Statistical Society was pro-reform, and J. P. Culverwell of the Manchester Athenaeum (the translator of Faucher's study of Manchester) was to argue in 1844 that the giving of relief was more creditable to the donor than beneficial to the recipient.[137] Yet *laissez-faire* did not enjoy intellectual and practical dominance in Manchester. Considerable numbers favoured the old system, including all of the band apart from Taylor. Taylor welcomed a fixed and discriminating system in which nothing would be given to the idle and undeserving, and he dismissed the opposition to the 1834 reform as the affair of a small and noisy minority. But humanitarians like Brotherton and Prentice, less tied to rigid doctrines, were against the reform.[138]

4. THE MANCHESTER IRISH

Manchester had a large Irish population. Estimates of its size during the 1830s and 1840s varied between 40,000 and 60,000 persons; according to the census Manchester had 142,026 inhabitants in 1831.[139] Contemporaries were clearly conscious of a substantial Irish presence. The Irish influx was a central topic in the discussion of health and welfare problems and the consideration of causes and effects of rapid urban growth. Attention was given to the living conditions of the Irish, their diet, appearance, health and habits. The evidence given to the parliamentary Poor Inquiry (Ireland) in 1835 was representative of contemporary observations and opinions.

[137] Kay, *Moral and Physical Condition*, pp. 45–54; Gaskell, *Manufacturing Population*, p. 216; Cullen, *Statistical Movement*, pp. 109–10; Culverwell, preface to Faucher's *Manchester in 1844*, p. xi.
[138] *Guardian*, 12, 26 April, 26 July 1834, 7 Feb. 1838, 26 Dec. 1840, 18 May 1842; *Mr Brotherton and the New Poor Law* (1834); *Times*, 21 June, 26 July 1834, 28 Jan. 1837, 28 Aug. 1841.
[139] Bradshaw, *Visitors to Manchester*, pp. 32–3; Wheeler, *History*, pp. 194, 246, 340; Engels, *Condition of the Working Class*, pp. 99–100, 128–31; *Times*, 11 June 1831.

Though it cannot be denied that the Irish presence was greeted with
alarmism, prejudice and misconception, Manchester witnesses in
1835 generally agreed that the Irish immigrants led depraved and
deprived lives.[140] Recent commentators have revised the older picture of slums, illness, improvidence and ghettoisation,[141] but it seems
that most of the Manchester Irish did live in the way that many
contemporaries and later writers of old-fashioned accounts said
they did.[142]
     The Irish presence in Manchester caused much controversy. There
were constant accusations about the immigrants' bad habits and
objectionable conduct. Many regarded the Irish themselves as responsible for the squalor, overcrowding, illness and other problems
of the areas in which they lived. Irish criminality was often emphasised; it was difficult to stamp out because it was tied in with old
habits and traditions of violence and feuding, and there was also a
link with the secret societies that formed an inherent part of the
immigrants' culture.[143] A prominent complaint was that the Irish
took too much of the public and private relief that was on offer, and
practiced widespread deceit to secure it.[144] The main concern,
though, was the effect the Irish seemed to have on wage levels and
the living standards of the host community. Even the humanitarian
Prentice joined in with the general tide of opinion which held that

[140] *Report on the State of the Irish Poor in Britain*, P.P. 1836, xiv. Poor Inquiry
(Ireland) 1835, Appendix G, part 3: Irish poor in Manchester and towns of
Lancashire and Cheshire.
[141] D. Fitzpatrick, 'Emigration 1801–70' and 'A Peculiar Tramping People.
The Irish in Britain 1801–70', both in *Ireland Under the Union*, ed. W. E.
Vaughan (1989), pp. 562–622, 623–60; D. Fitzpatrick, 'A curious middle
place: the Irish in Britain 1870–1921', C. Pooley, 'Segregation or Integration?
The residential experience of the Irish in mid-Victorian Britain', and G. Davis,
'Little Irelands', all in *The Irish in Britain 1815–1939*, eds. R. Swift and S.
Gilley (1989), pp. 10–59, 60–83, 104–33.
[142] e.g. J. Werly, 'The Irish in Manchester 1832–49', *Irish Historical Studies*,
18 (1972–3), pp. 345–58; M. O'Tuathaigh, 'The Irish in nineteenth-century
Britain: problems of integration', *T.R.H.S.*, 5th series, 31 (1981), pp. 149–73.
[143] Gaskell, *Manufacturing Population*, pp. 113, 125–7; *Report on the Irish
Poor*, pp. 48, 62, 75–7; R. Swift, 'Crime and the Irish in nineteenth-century
Britain', in Swift and Gilley, *Irish in Britain*, pp. 163–82; Fitzpatrick, 'Tramp-
ing People', pp. 646–9; Werly, 'Irish in Manchester', pp. 355–6; J. A. Jackson,
The Irish in Britain (1963), pp. 57–62, 67–8; G. P. Connolly, 'The Catholic
Church and the first Manchester and Salford Trade Unions in the Age of the
Industrial Revolution', *T.L.C.A.S.*, 83 (1985), pp. 125–60.
[144] *Report on the Irish Poor*, pp. 48–52, 54, 73.

the Irish influx meant more labour on the market and so a fall in wage levels. The way the Irish lived, he agreed, could also depress living standards generally.[145] Watkin believed that the 'bad example' set by the Irish had ruinous effects and that Manchester wages would rise if Irish immigration was ended. Other witnesses at the time of the 1835 inquiry told the same story,[146] and the idea that the Irish dragged the English down to their level was shared by such varied commentators as Kay, Gaskell, Cobden, Tocqueville, Wheeler, Engels and Reach.[147]

Although the Irish influx posed many problems, at first it was economically useful if not necessary to Manchester. The Irish were attractive to many employers because they were in plentiful supply and on the whole willing to take the lowest wages. The Manchester poor law authorities' relative generosity to the Irish before the late 1820s was partly a recognition of the immigrants' contribution to the local economy. It may also have been assumed that too many removals would mean a labour shortage when trade recovered after a depression. But by 1830 Manchester's masters had decided that the local economy could not absorb any more Irish. This was made clear in the evidence given to the 1835 inquiry (and casts doubts on Jeffrey Williamson's thesis about the absorptive capacity of the home economy). Some witnesses also said that the Irish were disruptive and refractory workers, more trouble than they were worth.[148] The cost of Irish pauperism was a pressing concern in early nineteenth-century Manchester. Parochial relief was given to Irish people who had been resident for ten years, but sometimes this qualification was waived, and in general Irish poor were not removed unless they were bad characters. This tolerant policy was expensive and Irish pauperism continued to rise, from 12.6 per cent of the Manchester total in 1827 to 21.5 per cent in 1831. Irish poor without settlement took 16.9 per cent of Manchester's expenditure on outdoor poor in

---

[145] *Gazette*, 10 Feb. 1827.
[146] *Report on the Irish Poor*, pp. 48–9, 61, 67–8, 72.
[147] Kay, *Moral and Physical Condition*, pp. 21–2; Gaskell, *Manufacturing Population*, pp. 113, 125–7; Cobden, 'Ireland', in Hirst, *Manchester School*, pp. 35–70; Tocqueville is cited in Bradshaw, *Visitors to Manchester*, pp. 32–3; Wheeler, *History*, pp. 194, 340; Engels, *Condition of the Working Class*, pp. 99–100, 128–31; Reach, *Manchester and the Textile Districts*, pp. 55–6.
[148] *Report on the Irish Poor*, pp. 51, 61–2, 64, 67–8, 72–3, 78–9, 82; J. G. Williamson, 'The impact of the Irish on British labour markets during the Industrial Revolution', in Swift and Gilley, *Irish in Britain*, pp. 134–62.

1831–32.[149] Manchester's Irish population was so large that extensive removals would have been difficult, impractical and expensive. The need for labour could not be ignored, and the authorities also saw that to be too parsimonious would mean sentencing thousands of Irish to starvation. Policy and pragmatism demanded relative liberality, but such a course began to create obvious pressures in the 1820s. As G. B. Hindle has shown, Manchester's leniency attracted 'baser elements who would not work and only made the town a depot for their wives and families'.[150] The directing overseer Nehemiah Gardiner expressed alarm about the rise in Irish pauperism in Manchester at the time of the 1835 inquiry: the numbers and expense of 'our own poor' had doubled in ten years, but Irish pauperism had increased fivefold in number and fourfold in expense. The governor of the Manchester poorhouse (W. Robinson) thought that Manchester's liberality had increased her Irish pauperism and formed an unfavourable comparison with 'her more politic neighbours'.[151]

The size, character and conduct of the Irish population of Manchester encouraged continual discussion. Concern about Ireland and the Irish who came to Manchester rose considerably. Richard Potter had first-hand experience of social and economic conditions in Ireland, and a long-standing interest in Irish affairs. The Potters were importers of Irish linens and Richard was often in Ireland on business after 1803, particularly in the 1820s. On one occasion (August 1824) he was accompanied by Shuttleworth. It is possible that the Potters' attention (and that of others) was drawn to Ireland's problems for commercial as well as humanitarian reasons.[152] It is also possible that Richard Potter's knowledge of Ireland's problems was used by the *Gazette* in its treatment of the Irish influx into Manchester. The *Gazette* appreciated that hardship in Ireland was bound to mean a rise in emigration. Hardship in Ireland therefore became newsworthy in Manchester,[153] and suggestions were made about

---

[149] These figures are based on the findings of *Report on the state of the Poor Laws*, P.P. 1834, viii. Appendix A, part 1, pp. 920–2.

[150] Hindle, *Provision for Relief*, appendix A.

[151] *Report on the Irish Poor*, pp. 44–7.

[152] Potter Collection, i, pp. 105–12, iii, p. 110, iv, pp. 7–9, 13–16, 38–9, 40–41; Meinertzhagen, *Potters of Tadcaster*, pp. 74, 173.

[153] e.g. *Gazette*, 2 March 1822, 18 Sept. 1824, 14 Jan. 1826; *Guardian*, 26 Jan. 1828, 8 May 1830.

possible social, economic and political reforms in Ireland. These, it was hoped, would make emigration from that land less desirable and necessary. Manchester's respectable liberals advocated reforms in Ireland on humanitarian grounds as well as in the cause of influencing more Irish to stay at home.

One matter given serious consideration in Manchester was Irish tithes. The *Gazette* argued that a tithe settlement was a cardinal requirement. Manchester's liberal-Dissenting leaders were against tithes in principle, for they objected to national church establishments. In Ireland the problem was exacerbated by the nature of social and economic relations there. These were based on 'extortion', a word the *Gazette* used frequently in its treatment of the Irish question.[154] In the early 1830s, by which time systematic resistance to tithes had become well-established all over Ireland, Prentice argued for abolition and attacked the Whig government's plan for commutation. He wanted the problem to be settled in such a way that tithes were not confused with private property; the proceeds should remain applicable to public purposes. Taylor was also in favour of abolition, and wanted the proceeds to go towards public improvements and the expansion of educational opportunities.[155] The Tory papers opposed abolition. They argued that if there was to be any tithe reform, this should not be designed to appease the Irish people but to give the Protestant clergy a secure and adequate provision.[156] The tithe act of 1832 brought little satisfaction. It made composition permanent and compulsory (voluntary composition had been permitted by an act of 1823), and transferred payment from tenants, reducing the number of tithe payers by over a third. But for the reformers, and for Ireland, it did not go far enough. The tithe issue was bound up with the campaign to reform the Established Church of Ireland. March 1823 saw the *Gazette* praising Joseph Hume's Commons speech on the matter. (At this time Hume was the radical-Whig M.P. for Aberdeen.) Taylor hoped that continuing discussion and pressure for change would eventually achieve something, and was in no doubt that reform was needed.

---

[154] *Gazette*, 21 Oct., 25 Nov. 1815, 3 Nov. 1821.
[155] *Times*, 29 Oct., 24 Dec. 1831, 11 Feb., 17 March 1832; *Guardian*, 24 Dec. 1831, 18 Feb. 1832.
[156] *Chronicle*, 17 March 1832; *Courier*, 24 Dec. 1831, 11 Feb. 1832.

That the Irish Church Establishment is replete with the grossest abuses, that it furnishes a most enormous income to a number of clergymen who perform no duties and have in fact no duties to perform, because their parishioners are almost exclusively of a different religion, and that its emoluments are bestowed as rewards for political services in and out of Parliament, are facts as notorious as any that could be mentioned.

Prentice also argued for reform, as did Richard Potter, who wanted Irish Church property to be placed at the disposal of the legislature. Potter was amazed at the abuses in the Irish Church, typified by the attempt in the 1820s of the clergy in the rich see of Derry to saddle the general public with the cost of repairing Derry cathedral.[157]

Among the reforms Prentice advocated for Ireland was the extension of education.[158] Some of Manchester's Tories advocated this too, though their views about the purposes of education no doubt differed from those of Prentice. The *Courier* often argued that the real answer to the Irish problem was a Protestant Reformation there, to be encouraged by Bible and education societies, discussion groups, writings and the circulation of sound religious tracts.[159] (The *Courier* did not make clear what social and economic improvements might come out of this so-called 'New Reformation'.) The most important development of this era in Irish education came in 1831–32 when the Whig government established a board of national education in Ireland to manage a parliamentary grant. This body included Protestants and Catholics, and the schools it administered were open to clergy of both faiths for religious instruction. Prentice, Taylor and Richard Potter agreed that the promotion of education and better sectarian relations in Ireland were much needed, but the reform aroused great controversy in Manchester.[160] This largely sectarian wrangling of early 1832 mirrored earlier Manchester disputes in the 1820s over the activities of Bible associations and the use of the Bible as a tool for education in Ireland.[161]

---

[157] *Gazette*, 8 March 1823, 26 Feb., 18 June 1825; *Guardian*, 15 March 1823, 9 Oct. 1824, 13 March 1830; Potter Collection, xi, pp. 45–7.
[158] e.g. *Gazette*, 11 Dec. 1824.
[159] *Courier*, 2 Dec. 1826, 27 Jan. 1827.
[160] *Times*, 24, 31 March 1832; *Guardian*, 3, 31 March 1832; *Chronicle* and *Courier*, 31 March 1832.
[161] *Chronicle*, 7 Dec. 1822; *Guardian*, 11 Dec. 1824; *Mercury*, 15 Feb. 1825.

The band often participated in voluntary relief activity on behalf of the suffering Irish. Baxter, Taylor and the Potters were on the committee established in May 1822 to supervise the collection of a fund following a poor potato harvest in Munster. They and their friends made donations, and Baxter, Taylor, Brotherton and the Potters were also among the district collectors.[162] The suffering of the poor in Ireland normally aroused the paternal instincts of the Tory papers. Though they were ready to advocate and excuse coercion in times of disorder, they also favoured voluntary aid. The Tory papers welcomed the relief fund of 1822 and also approved of later relief efforts.[163] Another fund was opened at a meeting in July 1831. The Potters, Smith, Prentice, Shuttleworth and Taylor were among the organisers of the event, which went ahead despite the lack of official sanction. The town officers had refused to convene a public meeting, possibly on account of the excitement of these weeks caused by the Reform Bill controversy.[164]

Prentice's first leading article as the new editor of the *Gazette* in July 1824 dealt with the Irish problem. In it he advocated three main remedial measures: a forceful policy to ensure that food reached the places where it was most needed, works of public utility to provide employment and improve the quality of life in Ireland ('self-interest and humanity in reciprocal action'), and finally that reform he was to advocate persistently in following years, poor laws for Ireland. He regarded poor laws as essential to any realistic attempt to improve social conditions in Ireland, and was sure they would help the Manchester labouring classes by encouraging and enabling more Irish to stay at home. Prentice attacked the Irish landowners for their unwillingness to support their own poor, and parliament for failing to act in a decisive manner. He knew his arguments were unfashionable, but nevertheless defended them tirelessly against so-called 'experts' of his day. In February 1827, for instance, he denounced the statistician and political economist J. R. McCulloch as a 'most mischievous political quack'. McCulloch's hard-line, pro-emigration approach to the Irish population 'surplus' was deemed inhuman by Prentice, who repeated his earlier calls for poor laws. He was to go

---

[162] *Gazette*, 18, 25 May, 1, 15, 22 June, 6 July 1822; Prentice, *Sketches*, p. 236; Boroughreeve's Papers, i, pp. 57–70.
[163] *Chronicle*, 18 May, 8 June, 6 July 1822, 11 June 1831; *Exchange Herald*, 21 May 1822; *Mercury*, 21 May, 9 July 1822.
[164] *Times*, 2, 9, 16 July 1831.

through the same arguments time and again, hoping to awaken, convince and prompt others into action. In the later 1820s he was glad to find his views quoted in some London papers.[165] Watkin also favoured poor laws for Ireland. He addressed a public dinner on the matter in 1833, engaged in regular correspondence and later planned to publish some of the papers he had written about Ireland in previous years.[166] Taylor was less convinced that poor laws could provide the solution to Ireland's ills, and more willing than Prentice to accept certain fashionable dogmas. Aid for the sick, aged and infirm was one thing, reasoned Taylor, but it would be impolitic and unjust to give an able-bodied man the right to claim support for himself and his family and thereby take the fruits of the labour of others. What was really needed was more education. This would teach men about the consequences of their actions, encourage moral restraint and self-improvement, and so check population growth in a country where the resources could not support it. Taylor stuck by these theories, though he did suggest after Catholic emancipation that selfish Irish landlords, ordering many tenants to quit now that they had lost the vote by the disfranchisement of 40s. freeholders, deserved to suffer the imposition of poor rates. (Taylor had accepted the disfranchisement on the grounds that the 40s. freeholders were not wholly independent as voters.[167]) Manchester's Tory papers were generally favourable towards poor laws for Ireland, as was the Irish-born radical and labour leader John Doherty, who advocated them in his *Voice*. But Taylor was not alone with his reservations. J. P. Kay opposed poor laws for Ireland, as did Cobden, and the

---

[165] *Gazette*, 10 July 1824, 10, 24 Feb., 3, 17 March, 23 June, 18 Aug. 1827, 12 April 1828; *Times*, 25 April 1829. (J. R. McCulloch held the chair in political economy at the new University of London between 1828–32.) Prentice's cousin David, of the *Glasgow Chronicle*, also argued in favour of poor laws for Ireland; Prentice's *Gazette* of 2 April 1825 commented on a recent *Glasgow Chronicle* article on the subject. For the wider debates on poor laws, emigration and public works, R. D. Collinson Black, *Economic Thought and the Irish Question 1817–70* (1960), chs. 4, 6, 8. When an Irish Poor Law was eventually passed in 1838 it did little to improve the situation because it contained no settlement rules, and in any case the Great Famine of 1845–49 prevented the new system from becoming fully operative. R. B. McDowell, 'Administration and the Public Services 1800–70', in Vaughan, *Ireland Under the Union*, pp. 538–61.
[166] Watkin, *Fragment No. 1*, pp. 19–20, 24–7, 32.
[167] *Guardian*, 19 April 1828, 23 May 1829.

Prentice school of thought was not well-represented among those Mancunians who gave evidence to the 1835 inquiry.[168] Manchester's respectable reformers were in favour of granting civil and political rights to Ireland's Catholics, and viewed emancipation as a central part of the wider Irish question, not least because the friction created by the emancipation issue was a cause of disorder in Ireland. Emancipation, it was hoped, would ease social and political relations in Ireland. The liberal-Dissenting leaders also favoured emancipation on principle: it would serve the ends of justice, freedom and equality. Opinion in Manchester was sharply divided on emancipation. Two anti-Catholic petitions in 1825 received 28,000 and 38,000 signatures.[169] The Tory papers were steadfastly opposed to emancipation,[170] while the *Gazette* and *Guardian* argued for concession all through the 1820s. The difference between Prentice and Taylor was that Prentice was not prepared (unlike Taylor) to accept any tampering with the Irish franchise as the price of concession. Taylor, Shuttleworth, Baxter, Prentice and Richard Potter organised and spoke at pro-emancipation meetings in the 1820s. Potter's visits to Ireland may have strengthened his desire to see emancipation granted. During one stay he joined Daniel O'Connell's Catholic Association, and he addressed two Association meetings in Ireland in 1827–28.[171] Another suggested solution to Ireland's social and political problems was the repeal of the Union, but this was something with which few of Manchester's politicians had any sympathy. The Anglican-Tory leaders were hostile, and the *Courier* feared that changing the system of Irish government would open the door for more attacks on the Irish Church.[172] In October

---

[168] *Exchange Herald*, 11 May 1826; *Courier*, 12, 26 June 1830, 21 May, 3 Sept. 1831; *Voice*, 11 June, 3 Sept. 1831; Kay, *Moral and Physical Condition*, pp. 83–4; Hirst, *Manchester School*, pp. 58–60; *Report on the Irish Poor*, pp. 48, 51, 78–83.

[169] *Courier*, 14 May 1825.

[170] *Courier*, 8 Jan., 23 April, 24 Sept. 1825, 29 April 1826, 15 March, 30 Aug. 1828, 7 Feb., 9 May 1829; *Chronicle*, 17 April 1819, 21 April 1821, 12 Feb. 1825, 4, 18 Oct. 1828, 21 Feb., 14 March, 11 April 1829; *Mercury*, 13 May 1817, 16 March 1819, 19 April 1825.

[171] *Gazette*, 30 June 1821, 6 April, 29 June 1822, 30 April, 7, 14 May, 19 Nov. 1825, 17 Feb. 1827, 12 July 1828; *Guardian*, 10 Nov. 1821, 2 Feb., 4, 18 May, 14 Dec. 1822, 30 April, 9 July, 15 Oct. 1825, 10 March 1827, 17 May 1828, 7 Feb., 14 March 1829; *Times*, 21 Nov. 1828, 7 Feb., 4 April 1829; Prentice, *Sketches*, pp. 338–9; Potter Collection, iv, pp. 38–9, xi, pp. 95–8, 100–2.

[172] *Courier*, 15, 29 Jan., 12 Feb. 1831.

1830 Taylor criticised O'Connell's repeal campaign as a clear threat to public order. Prentice told a meeting of 'Friends of Ireland' in January 1831 that a reformed parliament at Westminster would do more for Ireland than could a separate Irish assembly. It was folly to believe that Irish distress was solely attributable to the Union. At about this time he also renewed his call for poor laws for Ireland.[173]

Some commentators believed that Ireland's maladies would be eased by a relaxation of commercial restrictions. The *Guardian* argued in November 1821 that freer trade between Britain and Ireland would be greatly beneficial, though Taylor was as concerned about Manchester masters' ability to secure more business as about the removal of Ireland's social and economic troubles. Shuttleworth, Atkinson and Taylor all took part in a meeting of May 1821 which called for freer trade with Ireland.[174] The gradual freeing of the Irish trade in the 1820s was also welcomed by the Tory *Mercury*, which in September 1823 remarked upon the large increases in the amount of Irish calicoes sold in Manchester and Glasgow. It seemed that such trade was likely to increase further. This would enable Irish weavers to gain work at home, and in time wage levels in Ireland would rise. It was hoped that the influx into Manchester would be considerably reduced as a result.[175]

5. LABOUR ISSUES

The attitude of Manchester's respectable reformers towards strikes and combinations was often rather ambivalent. Many of them were themselves employers and had their own economic interests to protect, but their political and religious outlooks also made them sympathetic towards the claims of the working population and interested in the promotion of political and social justice. Like others of similar opinions and background, most of the band tended to adopt a middle ground in the matter of strikes and combinations, viewing industrial conflicts according to the circumstances of each case. There could be a mixture of sympathy, censure, praise and

---

[173] *Guardian*, 30 Oct. 1830; *Times*, 8, 22, 29 Jan., 19 Feb., 11, 18 June, 2, 9 July 1831.
[174] *Guardian*, 24 Nov. 1821; *Gazette*, 2 June 1821.
[175] *Mercury*, 9 Sept. 1823.

blame in the written and spoken statements of the band. Prentice was probably the most interested of his group in workers' issues. It was not unusual for his views to differ from those of Taylor and the *Guardian*. On labour relations Prentice's position was generally one of sympathy for the workers, provided their claims were reasonable and their conduct not illegal, and of support for those masters who were willing to listen to these reasonable claims. He preferred peaceful, negotiated settlements to trade disputes.

Manchester's liberals liked to give full and fair consideration to both sides in any trade dispute. When possible the *Gazette* tended to give coverage equally to employers and operatives, as in 1815 during a strike of journeymen calico printers.[176] By publicising the arguments of both sides, the *Gazette* was giving its readers the information they needed to form their own conclusions. During the long and bitter spinners' strike of 1818, the *Gazette* pointed to the rectitude of some of the operatives' claims but could not extend its sympathy to the point of approving of the strike, on the grounds that the state of trade did not justify the wage advances being sought.[177] Respectable reformers were more closely behind the workers when there was clear evidence that employers were conspiring to keep wages low, as in March 1823 when the master spinners of Bolton combined together and engineered a dispute to try and force wage cuts.[178] (Such apologists as E. C. Tufnell, of course, were to deny that masters combined to lower wages or for any other purpose.)[179] The local weavers seem to have been subjected to such mistreatment for many years, and their plight was a leading concern of social commentators. Their standard of living was threatened by an oversupply of labour and the introduction of machinery and new production techniques. The 'grinding system' caused problems too, as masters pushed down wages to enlarge profits and make themselves more competitive. J. B. Smith wrote replies to the reports of 1835 and 1841 which were published after parliamentary inquiries into the condition of the weavers. He emphasised the threat from machinery

---

[176] *Gazette*, 21, 28 Jan., 4 Feb. 1815.
[177] *Gazette*, 18, 25 July, 1 Aug. 1818.
[178] *Gazette*, 5 April 1823.
[179] E. C. Tufnell, *The Character, Objects and Effects of Trade Unions* (1834), pp. 98–101. Tufnell was one of the factory commissioners appointed in 1833.

and foreign competition, and the effects of the corn laws on the weavers' living standards.[180]

Prentice was steadfastly opposed to the combination acts and a convinced advocate of their repeal in 1824. The *Gazette*, very much under his influence once Taylor had gone to the *Guardian* in May 1821 and William Cowdroy junior had died in March 1822, strongly backed Joseph Hume's repeal motion of February 1824. There was no desire to inflame the minds of workers against their employers, 'we wish only that the poor man's property, his labour, may be equally protected with that of the rich man, whose wealth may lie in houses, land or money'. All men were supposed to be equal before the law, and yet masters formed their own associations at will. The repeal of the combination acts was vital for the cause of justice and for strengthening the pride and independence of the worker.[181] L. S. Marshall goes too far in his assertion that Manchester economic opinion at this time was purely liberal.[182] There were exceptions. Not only the workers but also such sympathisers as Prentice rejected the idea that the labour market ought to be left completely free. Some groups deserved protection. Hence Prentice's disagreements with Taylor. They both favoured repeal of the combination acts, but for different reasons. Prentice was concerned about justice and the dignity and welfare of workers, while Taylor's (Placean) position had more to do with his *laissez-faire* opinions and his view that the cotton masters had nothing to fear from repeal. According to Taylor, the combination acts contravened good principle because they restricted workers in the matter of wage adjustments and so prevented wages from finding their own natural level according to supply and demand. Combinations would not greatly inconvenience employers because in any dispute they could win by simply relying on their capital, whereas workers had nothing to fall back on. After repeal Taylor argued against the reimposition of the acts. Something had to be done to control the workers' conduct but *not* the commodity of

---

[180] Smith, Memoranda and Letters, pp. 29, 32–53. On the weavers see also D. Bythell, *The Handloom Weavers. A study in the English Cotton Industry during the Industrial Revolution* (1969); Glen, *Urban Workers*, chs. 7–10; P. Richards, 'The State and Early Industrial Capitalism: the case of the handloom weavers', *P. &P.*, 83 (1979), pp. 91–115.

[181] *Gazette*, 21 Feb., 6, 13, 27 March, 10 April, 10 July, 18 Sept. 1824; also Prentice, *Lecture on Wages*, for retrospective comments on the combination acts.

[182] Marshall, *Public Opinion*, pp. 211–19.

labour. The free movement and sale price of labour should not be subjected to 'legislative tinkering'.[183]

The repeal of the acts was followed by a new and powerful wave of trade union activity in Manchester.[184] By the end of 1824, for example, there were new general unions of weavers and fustian cutters.[185] Taking its familiar position as the ally of the cotton masters, the *Guardian* was unenthusiastic about the weavers' combination. Prentice was glad to see workers taking full advantage of their rights, but advised caution. There should be no intimidation or illegality.[186] He often defended combinations against their detractors, as in April 1825 when he criticised the anti-union stance of the Tory *Courier*.[187] His standing among some Manchester workers was high. He was a valued supporter and regularly publicised their activities, including the campaign against the reimposition of the combination acts. One meeting passed a vote of thanks to Prentice 'for his constant attention to the working classes'. It was carried 'by three simultaneous cheers'. In later years Prentice's newspapers carried pieces on the state of the law concerning combinations, showing workers what they could and could not do and enabling them better to avoid legal penalties.[188]

Combinations continued to have a bad reputation because they had been associated with violence, disorder and intimidation. Watkin was a little more equivocal about them than Prentice. As he said of the workers in 1833: 'When they associate for legitimate and proper purposes their Unions are not only lawful but praiseworthy, and will have the approbation of every right-minded man. But unfortunately they sometimes unite to forward schemes which tend only to inconvenience others and do mischief to themselves'. Watkin also rejected the argument that the working classes were the sole producers of wealth in the community; wealth was produced by the combined exertions of the whole, not by a part.[189] Through the 1820s and 1830s

[183] *Guardian*, 2 Aug. 1823, 15 Jan., 9 April 1825.
[184] For a detailed account of trade unionism in the Manchester area in the first half of the nineteenth century, R. A. Sykes, 'Popular Politics and Trade Unionism in South East Lancashire, 1829–42' (unpublished Ph.D. thesis, Manchester University, 1982).
[185] *Gazette*, 18 Sept., 6 Nov. 1824, 22 Jan. 1825.
[186] *Guardian* and *Gazette*, 25 Sept. 1824.
[187] *Courier*, 2, 16 April 1825; *Gazette*, 9, 23 April 1825.
[188] *Gazette*, 16 April, 30 July 1825, 2 Dec. 1826.
[189] Watkin, *Fragment No. 2*, p. 21.

Prentice continued to treat combinations in a sympathetic manner. His views on turn-outs did not change: workers should always follow only legal courses, if their arguments were reasonable they should be given a proper hearing, employers guilty of unfair practices should be censured and punished, and when possible disputes should be settled through negotiation. He also advocated thrift, temperance, 'improvement' and education, all of which could make workers better able to stand up to grasping masters. The *Guardian* tended to be hostile towards turn-outs while Prentice tried to help the workers in various ways. He printed communications from the associated spinners' secretary, John Doherty, in 1829, for example, and called for mediation and compromise, condemning workers' disorder but at the same time attacking such masters as H. H. Birley (of Peterloo fame) who had their factories guarded by armed men and sought to 'obtrude a fortification on the eyes of a suffering people'. In 1830–31 he publicised the activities of the new Doherty-inspired general union of trades, the National Association for the Protection of Labour. He soon quarrelled with Doherty, though, when the latter decided to establish a new workers' paper, the *Voice of the People*.[190]

Prentice's attitude towards strikes and combinations was closely tied in with his views on other aspects of labour relations, particularly wages. He agreed that in normal circumstances the forces of supply and demand controlled wage levels,[191] but he also believed that other factors were important and was not afraid to argue the point with men of formidable intellect and wide renown. In January 1825 he reviewed James Mill's *The Elements of Political Economy* and disputed Mill's view that wages were determined by the relationship of supply and demand and population and capital.

> There are circumstances which occasion a reduction in wages although the ratio which capital and population bear to one another remains the same. That these circumstances have been overlooked by the economists is obvious . . . In order to

---

[190] *Gazette*, 23 June, 30 July, 24 Dec. 1825, 11, 18, 25 Feb., 4, 11 March, 22, 29 April, 6, 13 May, 16, 23 Sept., 9 Dec. 1826, 27 Jan., 3 Feb. 1827; *Times*, 24 Jan., 28 March, 4, 11 April, 2, 9, 16, 23, 30 May, 6 June, 8, 25 July, 8, 15, 22, 29 Aug., 12, 19, 26 Sept., 3, 10 Oct. 1829, 3, 17, 24 Oct., 6, 13, 20, 27 Nov. 1830, 19, 26 Feb., 12, 19 March 1831; *Guardian*, 11 March 1826, 3 Feb. 1827, 10 Jan., 21 Feb., 8 Aug., 10 Oct. 1829, 23, 30 Oct. 1830, 26 Feb. 1831.
[191] e.g. See comments on Adam Smith in Prentice, *Lecture on Wages*.

account for the poverty and misery of the great mass of mankind, they have supposed that population has a tendency to
increase faster than capital and that the insufficient reward of
labour is the necessary consequence of that increase. They have
entirely lost sight of the difference in the conditions of the
employers and the employed which is sufficient to account for
a fall of wages when there is no diminution of demand.

Prentice argued that the dissolution of the contract between worker
and master inconvenienced the former far more than the latter, for
the worker lost his whole income while the master suffered only a
slight loss, which could be made up when he employed another
worker. Combinations could conceivably enable workers to leave a
master as a body, but even then the two sides were not on a par
because the master could fall back on his capital. Here were circumstances that influenced wage levels but had nothing to do with supply
and demand or population and capital. Though Francis Place publicly took exception to his comments, Prentice continued to take this
line on wages, notably in his April 1829 piece 'On the circumstances
which regulate the Wages of Labour'.[192] Prentice sought some future
industrial utopia in which peaceful wage settlements were the norm
and master-worker relations were cordial. To bring this about the
workers had to be stronger. Combinations would help them, but
more important was the need to improve their means of self-support
and sustenance (that is, they had to develop their own 'capital').
Prentice was also a paternalist, though, and put faith in humane
masters who were concerned about their hands. He favoured mutual
agreements within separate trades and the fixing of wage minimums.
In some cases, he said, legislative action would be necessary.[193]
Taylor, by now one of the most avid readers and popularisers of
orthodox political economy in Manchester, was wholly against legislation to regulate wages, and believed there could be no exception
when sound principle was at stake. Hence his opposition to the
Manchester weavers' campaign for parliamentary action on wages in
1823, and his criticism of a similar request by Macclesfield silk
weavers in 1828.[194]

[192] *Gazette*, 22 Jan., 19 Feb. 1825; *Times*, 4 April 1829.
[193] *Gazette*, 27 May 1826.
[194] *Guardian*, 17 May, 16 Sept. 1823, 27 Sept., 15 Nov., 6 Dec. 1828.

The introduction of machinery aroused much discussion in this period. Such was the alarm of weavers at the spread of the power loom that a meeting of November 1822 in Rossendale, north of Manchester, advocated a tax upon the extra profit produced by power looms. The *Gazette* sympathised, stating that although machinery was not evil in itself, exception could be taken to the way in which it was used. The pattern of mechanisation, and the motives behind it, had to be properly investigated. Mechanisation was enriching the few and harming the many.[195] Taylor wrote for the masters. He said that the workers should not fear machines, for they could only be introduced slowly and workers had time to prepare for the change. Machines created new work as well as superseding old kinds of work, and they cut production costs, which was good for labouring people as consumers. Taylor spoke of the march of progress and pointed to the beneficial results of mechanisation in spinning. (He apparently ignored the fact that circumstances in the spinning branches of the cotton trade were different from those in weaving.) Predictably, he dismissed the idea of a tax on profits produced by power looms. This profit had to be protected because it would add to the facility of production, enable more reductions in the price of articles, and make it easier for employers to fight off foreign competitors.[196] Prentice's position was that mechanisation, if in some ways objectionable, was nevertheless inevitable and had to be accepted. Machine-breaking was no answer to the workers' problems, he decided. It would increase unemployment and prompt masters to refuse relief. Attention would better be given to the need for corn law repeal, a sound currency, and a massive reduction in public expenditure and taxation.[197]

There were heated arguments in Manchester over the restrictions on the exportation of machinery. Many vested interests were involved. The desire to protect the productive powers of the south Lancashire cotton industry conflicted with the application of free trade ideas. This issue, in fact, demonstrates that self-interest lay behind the Manchester business community's advocacy of free trade. There was no theoretical consistency because ideas were abandoned when they came into conflict with practical commercial

[195] *Gazette*, 30 Nov., 7, 14 Dec. 1822.
[196] *Guardian*, 23 Nov. 1822.
[197] *Gazette*, 6 May 1826; *Times*, 1 Jan. 1831.

considerations.[198] Merchants, manufacturers and machine makers argued over machinery exportation for years. The Chamber of Commerce, always more concerned about its members' interests than about free trade ideology, favoured continued regulation.[199] Taylor sided with those who wanted the removal of restrictions.[200] This issue was one on which he could not agree with the chamber, which he supported and praised on so many other occasions. He was such a keen doctrinaire that when theory came into conflict with practical commercial considerations he almost always upheld the former. Prentice does not appear to have interested himself in the question.

Great ill-feeling was created by the truck system. Respectable liberals usually sided with labour spokesmen in the outcry against truck.[201] The matter was especially pressing late in 1830 as a truck bill was introduced in the Commons by E. J. Littleton, the reform-minded Whig M.P. for Staffordshire. Due partly to the extra-parliamentary campaign in its favour, the measure was passed in 1831. Prentice was quick to join in the agitation, used his *Times* to back it, and attended meetings like that in Bolton on 9 November 1830, when he told his audience of the mischief of truck and condemned those M.P.s who had voted against Littleton's measure. He also denied the validity of Joseph Hume's recent speech against 'intervention' in the relations between masters and workers.[202] Taylor welcomed Littleton's bill. Although masters and hands should be free to come to their own arrangements over wages, he argued, a bargain with goods was not the same as a bargain with money. In practice no bargain for payment in goods could be made on terms of equality.[203]

Among the various solutions proposed as a means of helping those workers displaced by machines or suffering unemployment in times of commercial depression, emigration was particularly prominent. It

---

[198] A. E. Musson, 'The Manchester School and the Exportation of Machinery', *Business History*, 14 (1972), pp. 17–50; Marshall, *Public Opinion*, p. 184. Marshall says little about attitudes towards machinery exportation, perhaps because the strong opposition to it in Manchester goes against his thesis that free trade opinion ruled the town by the 1820s.

[199] Local History Dept. M.C.L., Manchester Chamber of Commerce, Annual Reports of the Board of Directors (1820 onwards), especially 1825–8.

[200] *Guardian*, 28 Feb., 24 April 1824.

[201] e.g. *Gazette*, 21 March 1818, 1 May 1824.

[202] *Times*, 13 Nov. 1830.

[203] *Guardian*, 20 Nov., 18 Dec. 1830.

seemed a suitable answer to many social and economic ills, for removing people could help to remove problems. Prentice, however, was equivocal. He was not keen to see unemployed workers being forced by circumstances or encouraged by legislators to leave their homes, though he recognised that in some cases emigration could be necessary for survival. Emigration would not be necessary if there were reforms, if trade was freer and taxation lower, but until such reforms were achieved it had to be considered as a serious option. This was the stance he took on the Bolton weavers' petition of June 1826, praying for government aid for emigration to Canada. Emigration had to be properly organised, though, and Prentice repeatedly insisted that all arrangements should be taken care of before workers left their homes. He thought that 'a great deal of trash' was talked about emigration, and cited a report of October 1827 which estimated the total cost of shipping off the surplus population of Britain at £100 per family. The report claimed that the families would be able to raise this sum themselves, which Prentice found absurd. Nobody who had any knowledge of the conditions of cotton workers in south Lancashire could ever accept such an assertion.[204] Emigration was one of the topics on which Prentice lectured between the 1820s and 1850s. After his visit to the U.S.A. in 1848 he was in a good position to advise audiences about emigration to that particular country. While admitting that it was a land of opportunity, he stressed that he himself was not out to encourage emigration, only to help others make up their own minds for or against. Certain requirements were essential, especially taking up the right trade in one's new home, avoiding alcohol and bad habits, and saving about £30 before leaving Britain in order to provide the basis for a new life. Those workers whose labour was not in great demand in the U.S.A., he warned, should not think of going there.[205]

Emigration was hardly ever discussed in the *Guardian* at any length, and Taylor seems only to have concerned himself with the laws preventing the emigration of skilled artisans. These laws were rooted in concern about the security of Britain's manufacturing supremacy, but Taylor believed that such restrictions (like those on machinery exports) represented obstacles to free trade and violations of good policy. He was certain that removing the

---

[204] *Gazette*, 8 July 1826, 6 Oct. 1827.
[205] Prentice, *Tour in the United States*, pp. 197–210.

restrictions on artisans, and machinery, would not harm British manufacturing.[206]

The debates on factory regulation in this period focused mainly on the overworking of children, although it was clear to both factory reformers and their opponents that a limitation of the hours of work for children might also eventually mean a limitation of the hours for adults. The spring of 1825 saw a campaign in Manchester in favour of John Cam Hobhouse's factory bill, which aimed to reduce children's labour to 11 hours a day. (Hobhouse was the radical-Whig M.P. for Westminster.) Even before the measure was introduced in May, over thirty leading Manchester millowners and reformers had publicly expressed their readiness to concur with the wish of local spinners that the working week should not exceed 66 hours. Among them were Brotherton and Harvey. Prentice commended this declaration and hoped that it would influence parliament. He also welcomed it as a sign that industrial relations in Manchester were improving, and as an effective reply to the *Courier*'s recent remarks about the tensions caused by combinations and workers' meetings.[207] Prentice favoured a limitation of factory hours.

> We know that an argument may be raised against a compulsory limitation of the hours of labour on the ground that it would diminish the national wealth, and if wealth constituted the happiness of a state we would allow that the argument had some force. But if wealth is to be accumulated only by a great sacrifice on the part of the majority of the people, it becomes a question whether the acquisition is worth the price which is paid for it; and surely it will be conceded that a state of constant labour, unbroken by rest or recreation, and which leaves not a moment for the acquisition of knowledge, is not that in which a people has the greatest amount of enjoyment.

In response to those employers who opposed legislative regulation on principle, Prentice argued that its disadvantages had been exaggerated. Any reduction in output would not be in proportion to the reduction in hours. A worker who exerted himself for less time became less exhausted and individual output per hour was bound to rise. Of course legislation would not be necessary if masters and

[206] *Guardian*, 28 Feb. 1824.
[207] *Gazette*, 23 April 1825; *Courier*, 2, 9 April 1825.

employees could come to some voluntary agreement, but this was difficult to achieve and there could be no guarantee that *all* involved parties would stick to it.[208] Prentice had first visited a Manchester factory in 1815. Though he accepted the proprietor's point that cotton workers were not seriously unhealthy and were no more liable to illness than other types of worker, he noticed the factory hands' tired expressions and anaemic appearance. They did not have the ruddy faces of farm workers. 'When I experienced the heat of the factory and learned that everyone in it was employed fourteen hours a day, and saw the paleness of visage which unremitted toil in such an atmosphere occasioned, I could not exult in the prosperity of our manufactures'.[209]

Taylor's position in 1825 was that a reduction in hours was probably necessary, and he undertook to support Hobhouse's bill provided it covered *all* manufacturing activities. (In fact the bill was limited to cotton establishments.) Opposition to the bill in Manchester was headed by a group of master spinners who petitioned against it in mid-May.[210] The passing of the bill was celebrated by its supporters, and at the operative spinners' dinner of 9 July a toast was proposed to Archibald Prentice, 'our friend and advocate'. The greatest praise at this gathering was for Brotherton, who had been the most active supporter of the bill among Manchester's philanthropic reformers. He had procured many masters' signatures for the operatives' petition, had attended masters' meetings to argue in favour of protection for factory children, had gone to London to canvass M.P.s, had advised and assisted the operatives in every way he could, and throughout had given his time, attention and money without a second thought. The spinners' leaders Foster and McWilliams hailed him as 'a man who could not be too much praised'. Brotherton subsequently took part in activity to prevent evasions of the 1825 act, as did Prentice and Richard Potter, but an operative-led campaign of surveillance and prosecution was not very successful.[211]

Hobhouse introduced a new factory bill dealing with child labour in February 1831. Doherty's *Voice* backed it,[212] as did Prentice, who

[208] *Gazette*, 23, 30 April 1825.
[209] Prentice, *Letters from Scotland*, p. 223.
[210] *Guardian*, 16 April, 21 May 1825.
[211] *Gazette*, 28 May, 4, 25 June, 16, 30 July, 17 Aug. 1825, 30 Dec. 1826; Brotherton Scrapbooks, iii, p. 49; *Chronicle*, 15 Nov. 1828.
[212] *Voice*, 9 April 1831.

argued that parliament should prohibit *all* factories from working between 6 p.m. and 6 a.m. He therefore envisaged a limit on the adult working day as well as the child's. He welcomed the call of the spinners' leader, Foster, for philanthropic individuals, intellectuals, clergymen, writers and others to come forward and join the campaign on behalf of factory children. This was a cause which should be advocated by every class of Christians in the land, Prentice declared, for what was at issue was the health, morality and happiness of the labouring population. To persist in the working of children for 14 to 16 hours a day was to turn a healthy and robust population into 'a puny, degenerate, squalid, sickly and short-lived race of beings that will be a disgrace to the political and religious institutions of the country'. But even as the campaign for a new act gathered steam, cases of the overworking of factory children continued to come to light.[213] Hobhouse's measure received the royal assent in October 1831. It prohibited night work (between 8.30 p.m. and 5.30 a.m.) for persons aged under 21, and fixed the working day for persons under 18 at twelve hours. The *Guardian* welcomed the act and hoped that masters would obey it, not just because it would help improve the health and morals of the workforce but also because it would benefit the cotton industry in general. It would tackle overworking and thereby combat overproduction.[214] As usual Taylor had his eyes on what would serve the interests of the cotton masters. He was also, apparently, one of those champions of *laissez-faire* who thought that factory children presented a special case as 'unfree' agents.

In later years the Manchester liberal most actively involved in the struggle for factory reform was Brotherton. He was Salford's M.P. for 25 years, and during that time was at the forefront of the factory movement along with Lord Ashley and John Fielden.[215] Others in the band were interested too. Watkin spoke in favour of the ten hours bill of paternalist Tory, Michael Thomas Sadler, at the

---

[213] *Times*, 17 April 1830, 22 Jan. 1831.

[214] *Guardian*, 29 Oct. 1831.

[215] O'Brien, 'Joseph Brotherton', pp. 29–30; Brotherton, *Speech on the Ten Hours Factory Bill* (1857); J.R.L., Fielden Papers, Box 1, 'Some Reminiscences of the Ten Hours Factory Act' and 'Speeches of John Fielden and Joseph Brotherton'. Brotherton's activity can also be followed in J. T. Ward, *The Factory Movement 1830–55* (1962). The Tory evangelical Lord Ashley (later seventh earl of Shaftesbury) was M.P. for Dorset 1833–46, and John Fielden was a Todmorden cotton manufacturer and radical M.P. for Oldham 1832–47.

Exchange in 1833.[216] Extending protection for working children was part of the programme of the Manchester Anti-Corn Law Association formed in 1838, of which Thomas Potter, Smith, Watkin and Prentice were founder-members.[217] Prentice supported the ten hours campaign through the 1830s and 1840s on humanitarian grounds, but he did warn the workers that fewer hours would mean lower wages.[218] Taylor was more hostile and would not approve further intervention unless it could be achieved without affecting production, prices and the competitiveness of the home cotton industry.[219] Though in the past Richard Potter had favoured parliamentary action and wanted the acts preventing the overworking of children to be properly enforced, his position in the 1830s was probably closer to Taylor's than to that of Brotherton and Prentice. He does not seem to have been convinced of the need for and policy of further parliamentary action.[220]

It was not only the respectable liberals, and not only men who were active in local politics, who engaged in discussion of and remedial work related to social problems in Manchester. The band's role in this discussion and work was nevertheless a prominent one. Band members believed in self-reliance and hoped to instil in others an impetus for personal advancement. They were willing to provide help and wanted to extend opportunities so as to facilitate the rise of those who could not yet depend on themselves. One day these people *would* be self-reliant; they would take responsibility for their own actions and occupy their rightful place as citizens. But on their way up they had to adopt ideas and behaviour that would prevent their decline back into ignorance, poverty, immorality, ill-health and recalcitrance. Members of the band preached a gospel of social

[216] Fielden Papers, Box 1, 'Report of the Public Meeting in the Exchange Dining Room, 14 Feb. 1833'.
[217] *Address of the Manchester Anti-Corn Law Association* (1838).
[218] *Times*, 23 Feb., 23 March 1833, 9 April 1836, 20 April 1844, 19 Feb., 7 May 1847.
[219] *Guardian*, 19 Jan., 20 April 1833, 20 March 1844.
[220] Ward, *Factory Movement*, pp. 80, 108, 141, 143, 156, 167.

reformation which gave full scope to their religious zeal and moral premises. They acted on philanthropic and charitable impulses, on their commitment to 'good works' and the voluntary ideal. They were also interested in social conditioning, but usually placed more emphasis on kind encouragement, corrective remedies and benevolent guidance than on coercion and condemnation. The band wanted to extend educational, social and cultural provisions for all classes and age groups. This involved an increase in health and welfare facilities, an improvement in living conditions, the encouragement of preventive measures, the extension of relief and schooling, and the greater involvement of local government in all these spheres. Something had to be done about the quality of life in Manchester, and the respectable reformers were especially preoccupied with the need to show the lower classes how they could help themselves. Most of the band favoured a generous provision for the poor, and denied that relief encouraged poverty and idleness. Here was a clear humanitarian insistence that the distressed should have something to fall back on. This idea also shaped the band's thinking on the Irish problem. Concern about the habits and conduct of immigrants, and the effects of the influx on the host community, led to the discussion of reforms that might enable and encourage more Irish to stay at home. The band also engaged in discussion of industrial relations, combinations, wages, machinery, truck, emigration and factory regulation. Manchester's respectable reformers were concerned about those in the lower ranks both as workers and as citizens. If society was to be reformed, attention had to be given equally to the workplace, to homes and to streets. This notion of reform existed alongside an interest in the working population that was based on economic considerations. Members of the band seem to have believed that it would be both inhuman and impolitic to pay insufficient attention to the health, dignity, morality and conduct of working people.

The band's consideration of all these social issues featured an obvious conflict on the matter of how perceived social problems could best be solved. There were important disagreements, particularly between Prentice and Taylor. The latter was fond of theory and evinced a strict *laissez-faire* approach to most social questions, notably poverty and industrial affairs. Prentice's position, more characteristic of the band as a whole, was infused with a paternalistic and humanitarian outlook. If there could be agreement about what was wrong and about the need for action, there could also be antagonism on matters of analysis, aims and preferred solutions.

v Commercial Affairs and the Campaign Against the Corn Laws

I. THE BAND AND COMMERCIAL ISSUES

Manchester's importance as a centre of manufacturing and trade grew enormously in the late eighteenth and early nineteenth centuries. Many commercial campaigns and discussions took place in Manchester in the years after 1815, stirring up local opinion on all the relevant issues. Among these various views and activities those of the band were often of great influence. The Chamber of Commerce was established at this time as the representative body of the local business community, and importance was attached to its statements and agenda. Close attention was paid to regulations and duties affecting local trades, and such controversies as the struggle over the exportation of yarns and twist demonstrated that there could be divisions within the business community on some commercial matters. Local business people avidly discussed economic theory, foreign trade and Manchester's access to foreign markets, government policies and the perceived need for local commercial interests to be properly represented, advanced and defended in parliament. Other crucial debates related to commercial practices, particularly the problems of fraud, credit, liability and speculation, and to currency and taxation.

The decision to establish the Manchester Chamber of Commerce was taken at a meeting held in the police office in May 1820. Manchester's merchants and manufacturers had long felt the need for some organisation in which they could join together for mutual benefit. There had been some cooperation on commercial questions in previous times, notably in 1784–85 to oppose Pitt's fustian tax, and many committees had been formed to defend specific local interests. But all of this lacked permanency. Even the Manchester Commercial Society, founded in 1794, had ceased operations by

1801.[1] The chamber gave the needs and desires of the Manchester business community proper institutional form, continuity and collective weight. Its membership was eclectic, consisting of cotton masters, other businessmen and public figures, as well as men who were not prominent or active in local trade and politics. The first board of directors included individuals of varying political and religious creeds, but the majority was in cotton and drawn from Manchester's ruling establishment. Members of the band were highly interested in the foundation of the chamber. Most of them were or had been engaged in trade, and all of them were now heavily involved in Manchester's public affairs. Indeed some of the band were to be among the chamber's most outspoken members. The Potters and Smith joined soon after its foundation. Baxter, Taylor, Shuttleworth and Prentice were also members during the 1820s, 1830s and 1840s, intermittently if not continually. Thomas Potter was a director from 1823 to 1826, Smith from 1837. Smith was president of the Chamber of Commerce from 1839.[2] Thomas Potter, Taylor and Baxter were among the speakers at a town meeting on 30 January 1822, which was called to consider the support and expansion of the chamber, and Baxter was on the special committee appointed to assist the directors in extending the body's activities.[3] These activities, particularly the meetings, reports and representations to government, received regular coverage in the local newspapers, Tory as well as reformist. The Manchester papers were all ready to promote and publicise the chamber's efforts, though Prentice was to be a prominent critic of the chamber's equivocal stance on the corn laws.

Controversy was created in the early decades of the nineteenth century by taxes and duties of special concern to the Manchester business community. There had been agitation on these questions even before the chamber's foundation. In the spring of 1815, for

---

[1] E. Helm, *Chapters in the History of the Manchester Chamber of Commerce* (1901), pp. 1–60; A. Redford, *Manchester Merchants and Foreign Trade* (1934), chs. 1–5; Marshall, *Public Opinion*, pp. 184–5; Howe, *Cotton Masters*, pp. 191–206; E. R. Street and A. C. Walters, 'The Beginnings of the Manchester Chamber', *Manchester Chamber of Commerce Monthly Record*, 32 (1921), pp. 223–5, 287–9, 293.
[2] *Gazette*, 16 Dec. 1820, 15 Feb. 1823, 14 Feb. 1824, 19 Feb. 1825; Redford, *Manchester Merchants*, pp. 69–72; Street and Walters, 'Beginnings of the Chamber', pp. 393–4; Chamber Annual Reports (1820 onwards).
[3] *Gazette*, 2 Feb. 1822.

instance, there were protests against a proposed tax on the rents and windows of warehouses, factories, shops and other commercial premises. Taylor and Shuttleworth were among the speakers at a town meeting in March 1815, though the opposition campaign was mainly the affair of the ruling party. Newspaper support came from the *Gazette*, *Exchange Herald* and *Mercury*, and there was celebration when the ministry abandoned its plan. The *Mercury* concluded that such replacements for the income tax were bound to be unpopular and that it would be best if income tax was retained, though with modifications to make it work better.[4] The early months of 1815 also saw a campaign against the introduction of new duties on cotton wool imports, in conjunction with pressure for the removal of the existing ones. There was also alarm because of the government's notion that a duty on cotton exports could be imposed as a substitute for the duty on imports of the raw material. In fact the chancellor of the exchequer, Nicholas Vansittart, decided that the import duty should remain in force, though it was modified in subsequent years. The Potters and Baxter took part in this Manchester campaign of 1815, endorsing arguments that were often repeated in local businessmen's subsequent communications with policy-makers: duties and restrictions could only benefit foreign manufacturers; Europe already had the capital and the local advantages to pose a threat to Manchester's cotton trade; the continental cotton industry had expanded fivefold between 1808 and 1815, while Britain's had been 'stationary'; labour abroad was about half the price of labour in Britain; commercial duties led to depression and a loss of markets.[5] In the spring of 1818 concern in Manchester about duties on cotton imports and exports was raised again by Vansittart's plan for customs regulation. The *Gazette* reminded readers of Vansittart's previous schemes and encouraged opposition.[6] Another scare came in May 1822 when it was rumoured that the tax on cotton wool imports was to be increased. A committee of the Chamber of Commerce investigated, and was glad to report that the rumour was

---

[4] *Gazette*, 11 March 1815; *Exchange Herald*, 7, 21 March 1815; *Mercury*, 7, 14, 21 March 1815; Marshall, *Public Opinion*, pp. 197–8.
[5] *Gazette*, 6, 13, 20 May, 3 June, 8, 15 July 1815; *Exchange Herald*, 2, 9, 16, 23, 30 May, 27 June 1815; *Mercury*, 18, 25 April, 2, 16, 23, 30 May 1815; Marshall, *Public Opinion*, pp. 196–7; Helm, *History of the Chamber*, pp. 69–70; Timperley, *Manchester Historical Recorder*, p. 77.
[6] *Gazette*, 11 April 1818; Hay Scrapbooks, xi, p. 142.

groundless.[7] In these years the liberals' *Gazette* often argued that parliament's understanding and treatment of commercial matters left much to be desired. By adopting such positions, Cowdroy and the respectable reformers behind the *Gazette* could gain credit for pointing to the need for the better representation of commerce and for defending the interests of local businessmen. In addition, by highlighting the legislature's lack of attention to these interests they thereby made a case for parliamentary reform that was likely to appeal to moderates as well as liberals among Manchester's men of affairs.

The 1820s saw the gradual spread of free trade opinion in Manchester. Though there was some enthusiasm for the doctrines of free trade, however, this should not be exaggerated. More important were arguments rooted in self-interest and a belief in the practical advantages of freer trade. For a combination of ideological and pragmatic reasons there was concern about duties which did not fall directly on the cotton trade and its requirements, but which affected foreign trade and so were potentially damaging to Manchester's own commercial prospects. This partly explains the interest in the question of East Indian sugar. The chamber was active on the issue in the 1820s and 1830s, sometimes cooperating with the Liverpool East India Association.[8] Shuttleworth made a forceful speech in favour of freer trade with the East Indies at a town meeting on 31 May 1821. The argument soon spread to cover the objectionable privileges of the East India Company, and much was also made of the fact that West Indian sugar was given preferential tariff treatment over East Indian sugar. This latter issue involved the strong anti-slavery lobby in Manchester, in which members of the band were prominent, because British consumers were having to pay more for sugar produced by free labour than for sugar produced by slave labour. Such regulations were said to serve the interests of slave owners and perpetuate the heinous system of slavery. There was also general concern about Britain's Eastern trade and the chances for Manchester men to gain good returns for their activities in the East.[9] Taylor always considered the matter to be simple. It was so obvious that freer trade could benefit all, and that the merchant's interest was everybody's interest, that the answer to the East India sugar question was the same as the

---

[7] *Exchange Herald*, 14 May 1822.
[8] Chamber Annual Reports, 1820, 1821, 1828, 1830, 1831.
[9] *Gazette*, 19 May, 2, 30 June 1821.

answer to all other commercial questions. Restrictions were harmful and should be abolished. He wrote in 1823:

If it be desirable for every consumer to supply himself with articles of the best possible quality at the lowest possible rate, it is alike desirable, as regards us all, that we should derive those comforts and luxuries for which we are dependent on other countries, from those markets where, as they are most cheaply produced, they may be most advantageously acquired.[10]

Here was one of Taylor's clearest statements on the absolute necessity of buying in the cheapest market, later to be a fundamental doctrine of the Manchester School. The Tory *Mercury* was also in favour of reducing the duties on East Indian sugar, and on South American sugar, because these were burdensome for home consumers and represented a harmful restriction of Britain's foreign trade.[11]

Complaints were often voiced in Manchester about stamp duties relating to commercial transactions. Members of the band played a prominent role at public meetings on this issue, and the merchants among them could always give impressive speeches based on their own commercial knowledge. The attorney Atkinson often spoke about the legal aspects of the problem, while Taylor's *Guardian* constantly complained about the restrictive tendencies of the stamp regulations. At town and chamber meetings Atkinson, Taylor, Baxter, Shuttleworth and Richard Potter were among those expressing the business community's concern about expenses and inconveniences relating to transactions involving rents, title deeds, mortgages, land sales, sea, fire and other insurances, bills of exchange, receipts and legacies. Manchester men persistently advocated the reduction of stamp duties, on which several petitions were organised by the Chamber of Commerce during the 1820s and 1830s.[12]

[10] *Guardian*, 19 April 1823.
[11] *Mercury*, 1 Nov. 1825.
[12] *Gazette*, 2 June 1821, 1 June 1822, 18 Feb. 1826; *Guardian*, 2 June 1821, 8 May 1830; *Chronicle*, 12 Jan. 1828; *Exchange Herald*, 4 June 1822; Redford, *Manchester Merchants*, ch. 15; Boroughreeve's Papers, i, pp. 72–7; Chamber Annual Reports, 1820, 1826, 1827, 1830, 1831; 'The Chamber a hundred years ago', *Manchester Chamber of Commerce Monthly Record*, 33 (1922), pp. 104–5.

A prominent concern of sections of the business community was the excise duty on printed calicoes. The chamber advocated repeal throughout the 1820s, as did the *Guardian*, and the various short-lived campaigns of the decade also had the backing of the Tory papers. But no progress was made despite the effective articulation of arguments that duties were in themselves vexatious and against good principle, and that the calico duty pressed severely on the poor and was more expensive to collect than the net income warranted. A new campaign was launched late in 1830. Deputations from Manchester, Liverpool and Glasgow were in London in November. The Manchester representatives included Brotherton. On 25 November there was a pro-repeal meeting in the town hall. Shuttleworth was among the speakers and was also named on the committee appointed to further the purposes of the meeting. The chamber was active again, as were the master calico printers as a body. It was soon discovered that the government was considering the abandonment of the excise duty on printed goods in exchange for an increase in the tax on raw cotton imports to one penny per pound weight. The tax then stood at about a halfpenny per pound, and was levied in the form of a 6 per cent *ad valorem* duty. The chamber protested that the cotton trade would experience only a change in the form of its taxation while for years the general trend had been to remove or reduce commercial duties. Eventually the chancellor of the exchequer, Viscount Althorp, and Charles Poulett Thomson, vice-president of the Board of Trade, agreed to a compromise. The excise duty on printed calicoes would be removed, and raw cotton imports would be subjected to a fixed tax of five-eighths of a penny per pound (and three-eighths for cotton grown in the colonies). The *Guardian* welcomed the settlement as the best that could be expected.[13]

Another matter of special concern, particularly in the immediate postwar years, was the income or property tax. Opinion in Manchester was generally in favour of its removal once the war was over, but gratitude for repeal in 1816 was tempered in succeeding years by the fear that the tax might be reimposed. The business community's resentment against the tax was undoubtedly strong, and

---

[13] Chamber Annual Reports, 1823, 1826, 1830, 1831; *Guardian*, 2 Sept. 1826, 27 June 1829, 20, 27 Nov. 1830, 26 Feb. 1831; *Chronicle*, 18 Nov. 1826, 27 Nov., 11 Dec. 1830, 5, 19, 26 Feb. 1831; *Exchange Herald*, 17, 31 Aug. 1826; *Times*, 27 Nov. 1830, 19 Feb., 5 March 1831, 18 Feb. 1832; Boroughreeve's Papers, ii, pp. 1–5; Helm, *History of the Chamber*, p. 70.

this may have been one of the factors making the 'middle class'.[14] It seems that merchants and manufacturers were not as badly affected by income tax as were the landed interests, because it was easier to get away with low claims in trade and industry.[15] But Manchester businessmen still regarded the tax as a burden, a restriction and an insulting inquisition into a trader's private concerns. It was also argued that trade and industry were being asked to pay too great a share of the nation's revenues. The *Gazette* came out in favour of repeal in January 1816. So did the *Exchange Herald* in February, though with more caution.[16] The respectable reformers took the lead in Manchester's repeal campaign, but when a requisition was presented to the town officers they refused to call a public meeting, possibly because of the large number of reformers' names among the signatures. A meeting was nevertheless held, in the Exchange on 7 March. Baxter was in the chair and he, Atkinson and Taylor were the main speakers. It was resolved that the income tax was 'peculiarly repugnant to the feelings of Englishmen' and that if the government exercised economy, reduced the military establishment and abolished sinecures and unnecessary pensions, income tax would not be needed. The *Gazette* commended the meeting and its resolutions, while the *Exchange Herald* upheld the town officers' right of veto. The *Mercury* had already suggested that local businessmen might be reconciled to the continuation of income tax if ministers spread its burden more equally.[17] The facts that the *Mercury* could take this line, that some Manchester businessmen actually signed a petition in favour of an income tax that was efficiently and fairly administered, and that the town officers refused to call a public meeting demanded mainly by respectable reformers who favoured the removal of the tax, lend credence to L. S. Marshall's view that this became a party political

---

[14] A. Briggs, 'The Language of Class in early nineteenth-century Britain', in his *Collected Essays* (2 vols, 1985), i, pp. 3–33, also his 'Middle-class consciousness in English Politics 1780–1846', *P.&P.*, 9 (1956), pp. 65–72; c.f. J. C. D. Clark's argument that the essence of middle-class identity and ideology was not new and forward-looking but traditional: Clark, *English Society*, pp. 83, 92. These aspects are also discussed in M. J. Daunton, 'Gentlemanly Capitalism and British Industry 1820–1914', *P.&P.*, 122 (1989), pp. 119–58; M. J. Wiener, *English Culture and the Decline of the Industrial Spirit* (1981).
[15] Harvey, *Britain in the Early Nineteenth Century*, pp. 336–7.
[16] *Gazette*, 27 Jan., 17 Feb. 1816; *Exchange Herald*, 27 Feb. 1816.
[17] *Gazette*, 9 March 1816; Potter Collection, xi, p. 8; *Exchange Herald*, 12 March 1816; *Mercury*, 21 March 1815, 12 March 1816.

issue in Manchester.[18] It is possible that some of Manchester's Tories were prepared to accept the income tax in peacetime because this was what the government wanted. In the event the government bowed to pressure from inside and outside parliament, and income tax was abolished. There was continuing concern that it might be reimposed. The *Gazette* steadfastly opposed this, but in 1822 the *Exchange Herald* suggested that reimposition would help to alleviate distress by allowing the government to reduce other forms of exaction.[19] Some plebeian radical pamphleteers also wanted reimposition, provided the tax was fairly based on ability to pay. One writer stated in 1816 (correctly) that the removal of the income tax stemmed from ruling-class self-interest.[20] When Peel reintroduced income tax in 1842 Prentice was an outspoken critic. In one lecture he condemned Peel as a 'slavish serf of the aristocracy', and repeated some of the arguments current in 1815–16. This was an anomalous, tyrannical and unjust tax, he explained. It favoured landowners, harmed commercial and manufacturing men, and forced individuals to suffer the humiliation of having to reveal their private affairs.[21]

One of the most divisive issues discussed by Manchester's cotton masters during these years was the exportation of yarns and twist. Master spinners wanted to sell their products abroad so that they did not have to depend on the home market and could be assured of customers even when home demand was slack. But those engaged in other branches of the cotton trade opposed the exportation of yarns and twist. They claimed that exportation gave a huge and dangerous advantage to foreign manufacturers. The matter had often been debated in the past,[22] but took on a new urgency in the second half

[18] Marshall, *Public Opinion*, pp. 198–9.
[19] *Gazette*, 13 Dec. 1817; *Exchange Herald*, 29 Jan. 1822.
[20] 'The Wonders of the Magic Lantern . . . the distress of the country and . . . consequences of the late war' (1816), pp. 12–14, in C.L.M., Wray Pamphlets.
[21] A. Prentice, *The Pitt-Peel Income Tax and the Necessity of Complete Suffrage* (1842). Norman Gash has praised Peel's bold measure and argued that 'the paralysing grip of post-war siege economics' was only broken by Peel's income tax and corn law repeal. Gash, 'After Waterloo: British society and the legacy of the Napoleonic Wars', *T.R.H.S.*, 5th series, 28 (1978), pp. 145–57.
[22] e.g. autumn 1794, spring 1800: Marshall, *Public Opinion*, pp. 180–3; Redford, *Manchester Merchants*, p. 130; Hay Scrapbooks, xiv (unpaginated). This matter was one of those prompting some merchants and manufacturers to regard parliament as indifferent to their interests and so in need of reform. G. Whale, 'The influence of the Industrial Revolution on the demand for Parliamentary Reform', *T.R.H.S.*, 4th series, 5 (1922), pp. 101–31.

of 1816 as the trade in piece goods began to slow down. Many blamed this situation on the free exportation of cotton twist, legalised by the government in 1815. In these months the correspondence pages of the local papers were full of comment, and for as many arguments in favour of exportation there were arguments against. The band may have been equivocal on the subject since it included men engaged in both the spinning and the merchanting sides of the cotton trade. Most of the local newspapers adopted a neutral editorial position, apart from the *Mercury*, which opposed exports.[23] The campaign in favour of restrictions was unavailing, but there was less urgency as the trade in piece goods picked up. The matter was discussed again in 1820, primarily because of rising concern about the plight of the handloom weavers. In February 1820 a correspondent of the *Gazette* claimed that the prohibition of cotton twist exports would be the best way to improve the weavers' condition.[24] The arguments over exports were closely tied in with a general lack of sympathy between the two business units of factory and warehouse. Before the 1820s there was a schism in the Manchester cotton trade as these two interests struggled for control over the direction of local economic advancement. Factory and warehouse represented different modes of production and followed different patterns of growth, but the rift was overcome during the 1820s. Some problems were common to both business components and growing cooperation allowed for the rise of a more united cotton interest.[25]

Manchester men traded with all parts of the globe and were always concerned about safeguarding and extending their foreign commerce. The cotton industry was markedly export-oriented but also had a significant role as an importer. By 1820 Britain was the largest consumer of raw cotton in the world, and remained so until

[23] *Gazette*, 5, 12, 19, 26 Oct., 2, 9, 16, 23, 30 Nov., 7, 14, 21, 28 Dec. 1816, 11 Jan., 1 Feb., 31 May, 28 June 1817; *Chronicle*, 12, 19, 26 Oct., 2, 9, 16, 23, 30 Nov. 1816; *Exchange Herald*, 15 Oct., 31 Dec. 1816, 4, 11, 18 Feb., 13 May 1817; Prentice, *Sketches*, pp. 117–18; Hay Scrapbooks, vii (unpaginated); *Mercury*, 1 Oct. 1816.
[24] *Gazette*, 12, 19, 26 Feb., 4 March 1820.
[25] See Lloyd-Jones and Lewis, *Manchester and the Age of the Factory*, for a useful study of the relations between factory and warehouse. The book is perhaps flawed by insufficient attention to political and religious divisions in Manchester. These meant that despite the growing unity of factory and warehouse interests within the business community, 'class' cohesion was never likely to be complete.

1897.[26] The remarkable expansion of the cotton industry is also signified by the growth of capital investment in it. Under £2 million in the 1780s, it rose to over £52 million by the 1850s.[27] It is not surprising to find the merchants and manufacturers of Manchester so preoccupied with foreign trade, and in particular with the Eastern trade. Promising markets seemed to be available in the vast and wealthy regions of India and China, and Manchester men wanted more access to them.[28] This desire involved Mancunians in the debate over the status and monopolies of the East India Company. Interest in the Eastern trade was expressed forcefully during the 1820s. Mancunians demanded the East India Company's agreement to a liberalisation of this trade, beginning with free entry for Manchester goods into Canton and Singapore. Shuttleworth spoke on the matter at a town meeting in May 1821.[29] As the directors of the chamber had said, India 'promises a market for our manufacturers more extensive than anything we have hitherto known'. The Chamber of Commerce energetically joined in the demands for freer trade with the East,[30] but progress was slow. Although the renewal of the company's charter in 1813 had been followed by the opening of certain ports and stations, the China monopoly remained and Indian trade was subjected to a complicated licensing system. The exportation of cotton piece goods to the East did increase, but more reforms were demanded.

In 1823 trade with India (except in tea) was freed. The China monopoly was maintained, however, and in practice it could still be difficult to gain access to India. In November 1826 the *Guardian* claimed that parliament could look at no more important question

[26] D. A. Farnie, *The English Cotton Industry and the World Market 1815–96* (1979), ch. 1 and pp. 17, 82; Timperley, *Manchester Historical Recorder*, p. 88; R. Smith, 'Manchester as a centre for the manufacturing and merchanting of cotton goods', p. 53; J. Clapham, *An Economic History of Modern Britain* (3 vols, 1950), i, pp. 478–9; W. H. Chaloner, introduction to Prentice's *League* (2nd edn, 1968), p. ix.

[27] S. Chapman and J. Butt, 'The Cotton Industry 1775–1856', in *Studies in Capital Formation in the United Kingdom*, eds C. H. Feinstein and S. Pollard (1988), p. 122.

[28] On Manchester's commercial relations with the East, Redford, *Manchester Merchants*, ch. 9. On the growing importance of India to Manchester's cotton trade, Farnie, *Cotton Industry*, ch. 3.

[29] *Gazette*, 24 June 1820, 2 June 1821.

[30] Chamber Annual Reports, 1820; Street and Walters, 'Beginnings of the Chamber', p. 395; 'Chamber a hundred years ago', p. 135.

than the need to remove restrictions on commercial relationships with the East.[31] Early in 1829 Prentice advocated an assault on the privileges of the East India Company, an end to all monopolies and the equalisation of duties on goods imported from India and the West Indies (including sugar: Prentice was one of the most outspoken critics of that system of duties which rendered slave-produced sugar cheaper than sugar produced by free labour).[32] The *Guardian* gave its readers statistical evidence to demonstrate the harm done by the company's restrictions. Taylor compared the extent and value of cotton exports to the East Indies going through the company with those exports not subjected to company regulation. The figures for 1828 were particularly instructive: 630,639 yards of manufactured cotton worth £21,513 had been handled by the East India Company, along with 412 pounds of yarn worth £37. But over 42 million yards of cotton worth £1,594,123, and 3 million pounds of yarn worth £273,990 had been exported under 'free trade'. Taylor's point was clear: the demand for Manchester goods would increase remarkably if not for the East India Company.[33] The Tory *Chronicle* also favoured freer trade with the East, and even the *Courier* accepted the need for some revision of the company's charter. The Chamber of Commerce stirred itself again on this issue, and Prentice pointed to the valuable example given by a recent Glasgow meeting which resolved to petition for the entire abolition of the company's monopolies in every branch of the India and China trade.[34]

An important town meeting on 27 April 1829 came out strongly against the company, much to Prentice's approval. Pride of place in his long report went to the speech delivered by Shuttleworth, and judging by this Shuttleworth fully deserved his reputation for skilful oratory and commercial expertise. He spoke with a great grasp of detail and with clarity and force, mixing in humorous asides and quotations from classic literary works. He was certain that the company's monopoly should be abolished. He stressed the need for unanimity and persistence, explaining that pro-monopoly interests were extremely well-entrenched in parliament and in business circles.

[31] *Guardian*, 4 Nov. 1826.
[32] *Times*, 31 Jan. 1831. The point about the perpetuation of slavery had also been made by Taylor, e.g. *Guardian*, 25 Aug. 1827.
[33] *Guardian*, 31 Jan., 7 Feb. 1829.
[34] *Chronicle*, 7 April 1827, 7 Feb., 25 April 1829; *Courier*, 31 Jan., 7 Feb. 1829; *Times*, 4, 25 April 1829.

Shuttleworth also spoke of inefficiency within the company, the misuse of privileges and revenues, the opposition to reforms and narrow desire to perpetuate its system of patronage. He accused the company of costing the nation a fortune in lost trade and emphasised that the East, especially China, had the potential to be an enormous and vital market for British goods.[35] The *Courier*, which gave the meeting a mixed reception and questioned some of Shuttleworth's comments, was keen to promote local economic interests but remained unenthusiastic about free trade doctrines when they were pushed too far, and cannot have been pleased to see Manchester's reformers and free traders taking such a prominent role in local affairs. The *Courier* had criticised them in the past, and also attacked William Huskisson and the 'new school' which had influenced economic policy in recent years.[36] After the April 1829 meeting the campaign for freer trade with the East grew in strength. The *Guardian*, *Chronicle* and *Times* provided publicity and support, the chamber continued its efforts, and another important town meeting on 21 January 1830 (at which Shuttleworth was again a speaker) reaffirmed the views previously expressed. It was also pointed out that India could be a new supplier of raw cotton. This was significant because Manchester men were conscious of their dependence for raw cotton on the U.S.A. The Tory government was applauded for promising a committee of inquiry, but Prentice and Taylor were disappointed by its first report (July 1830), which was favourable to the East India Company. The pressure from Manchester and elsewhere was eventually rewarded when the India Act of 1833 arranged for the reorganisation of the company's commercial business.[37]

Another region of special interest to the Manchester business community was Central and South America. There were important markets in this subcontinent, though Mancunians often complained about the trade restrictions imposed in Spanish-controlled areas. Spain's

[35] *Times*, 2 May 1829; Shuttleworth Scrapbook, pp. 63, 67; *Guardian* and *Chronicle*, 2 May 1829; Chamber Annual Reports, 1829; Boroughreeve's Papers, i, pp. 358–65, 376–81.

[36] *Courier*, 25 April, 2 May 1829. Huskisson was president of the Board of Trade 1823–27 and Colonial Secretary 1827–28.

[37] *Times*, 23 May 1829, 9, 23 Jan., 20 Feb. 1830; Shuttleworth Scrapbook, p. 67; Smith, Reminiscences, p. 34; Boroughreeve's Papers, i, pp. 399–403; *Courier*, 23 Jan. 1830; Prentice, *Sketches*, p. 354; *Guardian*, 23 Jan., 6, 13, 27 Feb., 6, 20 March, 24, 31 July 1830, 11 Feb. 1832; *Chronicle*, 23 Jan. 1830; Chamber Annual Reports, 1830, 1831, 1832.

domestic problems and weakening control over her American colonies were welcomed in Manchester. It was thought that trade with new independent states would be more plentiful and profitable than it had been when those states were under Spanish rule. In the early 1820s the local newspapers and the chamber pressed for prompt diplomatic recognition of the newly independent states. The liberal *Gazette* welcomed developments in South America on commercial grounds, and also because it was keen to support the cause of freedom.[38] Manchester's trade with the region continued to expand, but alarm was raised in 1830 when it became clear that Spain intended to regain control of Mexico. An Anglo-Mexican commercial treaty had been concluded in 1825, and the importance of the Mexican trade to Manchester was highlighted by the *Guardian* in the summer of 1829.[39] At a special meeting on 21 April 1830, the Chamber of Commerce decided to cooperate with Liverpool merchants in lobbying the government and urging it to deter the Spaniards from ill- advised action. Prentice agreed that commerce would be endangered if Spain invaded Mexico, but he was more concerned about the threat to the liberties of a free people. The government replied to representations with a promise to do what it could.[40] Subsequent months saw discussions in Manchester on matters such as the port duties at Montevideo, naval protection for merchant shipping to South America, and Brazilian customs. European markets were also highly valued by Manchester traders, and were often the subject of meetings and correspondence. They included towns and territories in Russia, Turkey, Germany, Italy, Greece, Portugal and Spain. Concerns included the internal political instability of these areas, as this had obvious implications for commerce, and access to and passage through the Baltic.[41]

[38] *Gazette*, 12, 19 June 1824; *Guardian*, 5, 12, 19 June 1824; *Chronicle*, 19 June 1824; *Exchange Herald*, 6 Nov. 1821, 23 Dec. 1823; *Courier*, 8 Jan. 1825; *Mercury*, 2 May 1820, 7 May 1822; Redford, *Manchester Merchants*, pp. 99–100; Chamber Annual Reports, 1823.

[39] Redford, *Manchester Merchants*, p. 103; *Guardian*, 20 June 1829.

[40] *Times*, 24 April 1830; Chamber Annual Reports, 1829, 1830.

[41] Chamber Annual Reports, 1820, 1821, 1825, 1826, 1827, 1829, 1830, 1831; Redford, *Manchester Merchants*, pp. 87–8, 90–92 and chs. 7–8; *Gazette*, 18 Feb. 1826; Street and Walters, 'Beginnings of the Chamber', p. 395; *Exchange Herald*, 16 Jan. 1816, 1, 8 Aug. 1820, 27 March, 1, 8, 15 May 1821, 6 Aug., 2 Oct., 13 Dec. 1822; *Guardian*, 22 Jan. 1825, 13 Sept. 1828; 'Chamber a hundred years ago', p. 81; *Courier*, 10, 17, 24 Oct., 7, 14, 21, 28 Nov. 1829; *Mercury*, 19 June 1821.

The desire of Manchester's merchants and manufacturers to defend and extend foreign trade involved them in debates about the government's commercial policies, and these debates were particularly animated during the 1820s when reforms and liberalisation seemed to be the order of the day. Attention was increasingly drawn to such matters as 'reciprocity', rules of navigation, tariff policy and commercial treaties.[42] The minister responsible for many of the reforms of these years, William Huskisson, had no firmer supporter in Manchester than Taylor. From early 1825 Taylor constantly praised and defended Huskisson's policies, and was often astounded that the opponents of freer trade could claim that the Huskisson school had ruined commerce.[43] The *Exchange Herald*, before Aston sold it in October 1826, also approved of Huskisson and the liberal-minded members of the Tory ministry who were advancing the cause of commercial freedom.[44] The *Courier* initially seemed to favour the relaxation of commercial regulations, but before long began to argue that Huskisson was going too far. In February 1826 the *Courier* opposed the commercial treaties being negotiated with Colombia, France and the Hanseatic towns on the grounds that Britain was giving too much for what she would receive. 'Freedom', 'reciprocity', 'enlightened policy' and similar notions were all very fine, suggested the *Courier*'s editorials, but they were too often incorrectly applied and uncritically appraised. The *Courier* blamed free trade doctrines for rising commercial confusion and hardship, and was soon an avid champion of the shipping interests and others who wanted the return of the old protective barriers.[45] The directors of the chamber were more favourable towards Huskisson and the commercial reforms of the 1820s, and in May 1828 passed a vote of thanks to Huskisson on his retirement from office.[46] A new round of arguments accompanied Huskisson's visit to Manchester in

---

[42] On contemporary commercial policy, C. R. Fay, 'The Movement towards Free Trade', in *Cambridge History of the British Empire*, (8 vols, 1961), ii, pp. 388–414; A. J. Boyd Hilton, *Corn, Cash and Commerce. The Economic Policies of the Tory Governments 1815–30* (1977), possibly the most valuable conclusion of which is that the main purpose of theory was not to originate measures but to justify them.

[43] e.g. *Guardian*, 26 March 1825, 17 Feb. 1827, 13 Dec. 1828, 4, 18, 25 July, 26 Sept. 1829, 17 April, 15 May 1830.

[44] *Exchange Herald*, 9 Dec. 1823, 29 March 1825.

[45] *Courier*, 26 March 1825, 11 Feb. 1826, 3 March, 12 May 1827.

[46] Chamber Annual Reports, 1825, 1828.

August 1829. The *Chronicle* and *Courier* assailed his principles and previous policies, while the *Guardian* defended them.[47] The *Courier* went on to attack the whole system of the 'new economists' and to praise the ideas of such Tory protectionists as M. T. Sadler, M.P. for Newark and future leader of the factory reform movement, who had recently declared that the national wealth and the people's welfare should not be sacrificed to capital, 'the mammon of political economy'.[48] Taylor regretted Huskisson's death in 1830 and Prentice also mourned the loss of a useful public figure, though he had previously attacked Huskisson's conduct on the corn law issue.[49]

Manchester's business community was very concerned to secure for local trade an effective and influential parliamentary representation. The petitioning and commercial campaigns of the chamber and previous committees of merchants and manufacturers had certainly been useful, and local commercial interests had been served by the Lancashire county M.P.s and other M.P.s who had some acquaintance with Mancunian men and affairs. But the prospect of parliamentary seats for Manchester in 1827–28 during the Penryn affair, and more importantly in 1831–32, made Manchester businessmen think increasingly in terms of sending their own representatives to sit in parliament. As their oracle, the *Guardian*, stated at the end of 1827, the real problem with the representative system was not the exclusion of the lower orders but that of the commercial middle classes.[50] The desire for parliamentary seats had been strong for years. One of the earliest acts of the Chamber of Commerce was to send parliament a petition in June 1820 in favour of transferring the Grampound franchise to the freeholders of Salford and Blackburn Hundreds.[51] There was much discussion in 1831–32 about the effects the Reform Bill might have on local commerce, and many thought that the vote should go to as many Manchester businessmen as possible. A meeting of the chamber on 18 April 1831 heard complaints that the Reform Bill gave the vote to resident householders and not to gentlemen who conducted their business in Manchester but resided beyond the proposed borough boundaries. This was in

---

[47] *Chronicle*, 29 Aug., 12 Sept., 10 Oct. 1829; *Courier*, 22 Aug., 5, 12, 19 Sept. 1829; *Guardian*, 5, 19 Sept. 1829.
[48] *Courier*, 26 Sept. 1829.
[49] *Guardian* and *Times*, 18 Sept. 1830.
[50] *Guardian*, 22 Dec. 1827.
[51] Street and Walters, 'Beginnings of the Chamber', p. 394.

contrast to the 1827 measure to give Manchester the seats of Penryn, which had proposed to enfranchise householders *and* occupiers of warehouses and other property. Richard Potter, Prentice and Smith were members of the Chamber of Commerce at this time and attended the April 1831 assembly. They argued that the chamber should not act on the question of the franchise, for the body had not been founded to consider political subjects and political debate would only destroy unanimity among members. They may have suspected that the chamber was bound to favour a higher voting qualification than they themselves were hoping for, though they did not mention this. After some argument their objections were overruled. The Reform Bill was soon altered in any case. Warehouses and counting houses were included among the voting qualifications, and agitation by the chamber was not necessary.[52] As the voice of the business community the *Guardian* had been eager for the franchise to include business premises. By the autumn of 1831, moreover, Taylor was hoping that the Reform Bill would be passed without delay because the suspense and agitation were harming trade.[53] Meanwhile thoughts were turning to the parliamentary candidates who should be returned by commercial constituencies like Manchester. Many commentators, including Taylor, argued that merchants would make excellent M.P.s. This was disputed by radical journalist and labour leader John Doherty, while Prentice declared that commercial knowledge was only one of several qualities required in a suitable representative of Manchester.[54]

There was a great deal of discussion in Manchester about those commercial practices which unsettled local business or seemed to threaten the rights and welfare of the honest trader. A strong movement arose in the town against fraudulent debtors, for example, and many petitions were organised demanding that parliament should improve the laws on bankruptcy and insolvencies. October 1822 saw the establishment of the Manchester Society for Opposition to Fraudulent Debtors, of which Taylor was a founder member. His *Guardian*, indeed, was a consistent advocate of parliamentary action on the matter, and other local newspapers shared this concern. In December 1822 Taylor and Thomas Potter involved themselves in a

---

[52] *Times*, 16, 23 April 1831, 18 Feb. 1832; *Chronicle*, 23 April 1831; Chamber Annual Reports, 1831.
[53] *Guardian*, 19 March, 29 Oct. 1831.
[54] *Guardian*, 8 Sept. 1832; *Voice*, 9 July 1831; *Times*, 18 June 1831.

public campaign for the repeal of the insolvent debtor laws, which were said to be too mild and an encouragement to malpractice. Manchester businessmen wanted more protection against the unscrupulous or inept trader.[55] In May 1823 the *Guardian* welcomed a parliamentary inquiry into the laws affecting the liability of merchants and factors. A prominent complaint relating to the law of principal and factor was that a person who purchased goods in the hands of an agent who had no authority to sell them could be sued by the owner, even though the purchaser had no way of knowing that the goods he bought were not the property of the seller. This was an anomaly emphasised by Taylor in April 1824, when he welcomed Huskisson's decision to have the law repealed.[56] In the following month the *Guardian* came out strongly in favour of Althorp's bill to facilitate the recovery of small debts.[57] Members of the band who were still engaged in trade must have had plenty of experience of the problems created by lenient laws. In November 1825, for instance, the Potters had to arrange to 'look after' the affairs of a London customer who could not meet his engagements.[58] The chamber was active on these issues during the 1820s and 1830s.[59] The unsettling and damaging effects of speculation were also of concern, and members of the band participated in public discussions of this problem. Local newspapers were highly condemnatory towards rash speculatory activities and the carrying on of business without secure foundations.[60] It is interesting, though, that in the winter of 1829–30 when local trade was depressed, the *Guardian* suggested that speculative buying of cotton would be advantageous. This was a curious reversal of policy for Taylor, prompted by his observation that the consumption of cotton was increasing faster than imports. Prentice and others doubted that speculation could ever be advantageous, while a meeting of Manchester manufacturers on 26 January 1830

[55] *Gazette*, 28 Dec. 1822, 11 Jan. 1823; *Guardian*, 11 Jan. 1823; *Chronicle*, 11 Jan. 1823; *Exchange Herald*, 3, 31 Dec. 1822, 14 Jan. 1823; *Mercury*, 9 March, 18 May 1819; Boroughreeve's Papers, i, pp. 83–7; Chamber Annual Reports, 1820.
[56] *Guardian*, 24 May 1823, 17 April 1824.
[57] *Guardian*, 8 May 1824.
[58] Potter Collection, iv, pp. 21–2.
[59] Chamber Annual Reports, 1825, 1828, 1832.
[60] Prentice, *Sketches*, p. 248; Smith, Reminiscences, pp. 26–7; *Guardian*, 18 June, 19 Nov. 1825, 5 April 1828; *Courier*, 15 Jan., 9 April, 3, 17 Dec. 1825; *Exchange Herald*, 27 Oct., 15 Dec. 1825, 9, 16 Feb. 1826.

opposed any speculative buying of cotton. Prentice's *Times* was soon claiming that Taylor's commercial advice was faulty, and that the *Guardian*'s usefulness on this score had been greatly overrated.[61] Manchester businessmen were continually concerned about the safety and efficiency of the circulating medium used in trade, and evinced a decided preference against the issuing and use of local banknotes and more generally the use of any paper not backed by specie.[62] Members of the band were prominent in the debates and activities relating to the currency question. An important public meeting in the Exchange on 23 August 1821 set the tone for many that followed. Baxter, Taylor, Shuttleworth, the Potters, Atkinson and Harvey were all among the requisitionists, and Taylor, Baxter and Atkinson were among the movers and seconders of resolutions. The meeting decided that a secure currency could not involve any reliance on individual credit, and that bank failures and general distress would be the inevitable results of the issuing of local notes. Alarm was expressed about the issue of local notes elsewhere in the region, and it was decided that Manchester banks should issue no notes at all, lest they be regarded as having sanctioned and encouraged the practice. Notes that had already been issued were to be confined in circulation and not used for distant payments. They were not to be regarded as legal tender nor accepted as payment for rent or debts, and they could not be used as a basis for loans. Baxter emphasised the dangers of this latter practice, pointing out that it could lead to overtrading and improvident speculation. Finally the meeting resolved that the issuing of local notes was particularly dangerous in times of commercial hardship, and would mean potential disaster for the whole district. Therefore local business would continue to be based as far as possible on gold coin and Bank of England notes. Security was to be the watchword, and a special committee was appointed to prevent the introduction into Manchester of dangerous and unsatisfactory currency.[63] Further steps were taken after another meeting on 24 October 1822. This time Taylor,

---

[61] See *Times* and *Guardian*, Jan.–Feb. 1830; *Chronicle*, 30 Jan. 1830; Shuttleworth Scrapbook, p. 37.
[62] Grindon, *Manchester Banks*, for a useful account of local banking activities and ideas in this era.
[63] *Gazette*, 18, 25 Aug. 1821; *Observer*, 1 Sept. 1821; *Chronicle*, 25 Aug. 1821; *Mercury*, 28 Aug. 1821; Boroughreeve's Papers, i, pp. 33–55; Hay Scrapbooks, x, p. 121; Prentice, *Sketches*, pp. 218–23.

Atkinson and Baxter were named on the committee appointed to further the purposes of the assembly. The chamber approved these steps and in October 1822 recommended the local fixing of a recognised basis of values between notes of different amounts, coin and bills of exchange.[64]

The business depression and financial crisis of 1825–26 excited renewed concern. The chamber called for legislative restrictions on the circulation of local notes, and in March 1826 Prentice was glad to report that local notes had been almost entirely excluded from the town and district.[65] There was also much discussion of the government's withdrawal of small notes from circulation (provided for in an act of March 1826, but not to take full effect until April 1829), the establishment of branches of the Bank of England, and the provision that joint stock banks could be established beyond a 65-mile radius of London. The *Guardian* was enthusiastic about these reforms and welcomed the establishment in Manchester of a branch of the Bank of England in September 1826.[66] There were some dissentient voices, though, including those of the *Exchange Herald* (which preferred joint stock banking)[67] and of country bankers who feared competition. (Taylor pointed out that his approval of Bank of England branches did not mean that he approved of its monopoly. He opposed monopolies in principle, but argued that the Bank's charter was a *fait accompli* and could not justly be interfered with while it was in force.) Members of the band soon became involved in joint stock banking schemes. Thomas Potter, Baxter and Smith were among the founders and directors of the new Manchester Savings Bank established in December 1828.[68] Concern about local financial arrangements continued unabated. A meeting in December 1828, attended by Taylor, Prentice and Richard Potter, decided on new regulations to prevent the circulation of local notes. It was believed that such circulation was likely to increase after the suppression of small notes under the 1826 act.[69] There was a rising amount of

---

[64] *Gazette*, 2 Nov. 1822; *Chronicle*, 26 Oct. 1822; 'Chamber a hundred years ago', pp. 320–21.

[65] *Gazette*, 17 Dec. 1825, 18 Feb., 18 March 1826.

[66] *Guardian*, 3, 17, 31 Dec. 1825, 21 Jan., 11, 18 Feb., 4 March 1826, 6 Oct., 15 Dec. 1827; Grindon, *Manchester Banks*, ch. 18.

[67] *Exchange Herald*, 3 Aug. 1826.

[68] See above, chapter IV section (2).

[69] *Times*, 5, 19 Dec. 1828; Boroughreeve's Papers, i, pp. 340–54; *Chronicle*, 20 Dec. 1828; *Courier*, 20 Dec. 1828.

currency analysis in the local papers, especially the *Guardian*. In January 1829 Taylor argued against the financial views of Thomas Attwood, the Birmingham banker and currency reformer who favoured inflationary policies and the paper system. Taylor also rejected the Potter-Prentice argument (expressed at a meeting on 18 December 1828) that if small notes were withdrawn the value of money would rise and render many people unable to pay their taxes, which meant that the withdrawal of small notes would have to be accompanied by a considerable cut in taxation. Taylor denied that the nation could not pay the taxes being exacted. Business was expanding, he said, and all that was needed was an issue of coin to make up for the withdrawn small notes. There was no reason why the pressure of public burdens should increase. In January 1830 Taylor discussed the views of William Cobbett, then lecturing in Manchester, and decided that Cobbett had exaggerated the ill-effects of the withdrawal of small notes. Since Cobbett's premise was wrong it followed that the rest of his argument was wrong too, particularly his view that economic distress was caused by a change in the value of currency and could not be relieved except by reducing taxation to its 1791 level. Various suggestions from landed men, Tories and others at this time, that small notes should be reintroduced and the currency depreciated, were met by Taylor with derision.[70]

On general matters relating to currency there was a good deal of bullionist orthodoxy in Manchester. Paper was forcefully condemned by the *Gazette*, for example, during the troubled weeks of late 1825. Prentice often wrote of the dangers and inconvenience of paper money and of the need to restrict the circulation of paper in favour of 'true coin'. Harvey criticised the 'paper system' at a public meeting in August 1826. In June 1829 Prentice approved of Peel's stand against a Birmingham demand for an issue of banknotes. Prentice argued that such an issue might for a time stimulate trade, but this would produce a false prosperity which would soon disappear. This was no time for such stimulants. What was required was a specie-based currency along with tax cuts and corn law repeal.[71] Taylor also advocated a metallic circulating medium: specie meant confident and sound business dealings, paper meant confusion and artificiality. In the later 1820s he often condemned Attwood's

---

[70] *Guardian*, 6, 13, 20 Sept., 22 Nov., 13, 20, 27 Dec. 1828, 3 Jan., 25 April 1829, 9, 16, 23 Jan., 6, 20 Feb., 4, 18 Dec. 1830.
[71] *Gazette*, 10, 17 Dec. 1825, 19 Aug. 1826; *Times*, 13 June 1829.

demands for reflationary policies and the repeal of Peel's 1819 act restoring cash payments.[72] The Tory *Chronicle* was hostile towards paper, wanted secure policies instead of stopgap measures, and chided Attwood. Aston's *Exchange Herald* was also in favour of a specie-based currency.[73]

Currency matters, taxation, corn laws and such other issues as parliamentary reform were regarded by the band as closely related. They were not usually discussed in isolation from each other. Prentice's leading articles of July 1826, 'On the Causes and Cure of the Present Distress', argued that corn law repeal, a stable currency and a reduction in taxation were the three essential and interconnected reforms necessary to solve the nation's ills, provide inexpensive food and ensure cheap government.[74] A meeting to consider the prevalent distress on 17 August 1826 decided to petition for the twin reforms of corn law repeal and lower taxation. Baxter, Shuttleworth, Richard Potter, Harvey and Prentice were among the organisers (in the absence of any cooperation from the churchwardens) and speakers. Harvey dwelt on the evil effects of paper currency, Baxter attacked the churchwardens and Shuttleworth spoke on the corn laws. Prentice and Potter discussed taxation. Potter argued that the government could reduce taxation if it was more efficient and economical. Prentice thought that if the government abandoned 'the not palpable juggle of the sinking fund' and exercised retrenchment, the nation would be relieved of £10 million in taxes per year. This meeting was an important event for the band. It was reported and discussed all over the kingdom. The band had taken the leading role and can be said to have spoken to a truly national audience, perhaps for the first time since Peterloo. Richard Potter later recalled that 'the proceedings excited much attention', and soon after the event Prentice was rejoicing that 'no meeting held in Manchester ever created so general an interest or received so general an approbation'.[75]

Prentice had much respect for Cobbett's views on taxation and the financial system, and gave extensive coverage to the latter's lectures in Manchester early in 1830. Two of Cobbett's arguments seemed to

[72] *Guardian*, 12 Jan., 2 Feb. 1822, 16 May, 20 June 1829.
[73] *Chronicle*, 9 Jan., 12 June 1830; *Exchange Herald*, 7 Oct. 1817, 15 May 1821.
[74] *Gazette*, 15, 22 July 1826.
[75] *Gazette*, 5, 12, 19, 26 Aug. 1826; *Chronicle*, 5, 19 Aug. 1826; Shuttleworth Scrapbook, p. 42; Potter Collection, iv, p. 29; Prentice, *Sketches*, pp. 284–7.

be particularly sound: that high expenditure and high taxation were prominent causes of social and economic distress, and that it was wrong to separate the questions of currency and taxation as if they were unrelated, for in truth they were branches on the same rotten tree.[76] A public meeting on the state of the nation in February 1830 heard more speeches by members of the band, and decided to petition for a reduction in taxes and government spending, the repeal of the corn laws and other commercial restrictions, and an end to the disturbance of commerce by alterations in the currency.[77] Prentice repeatedly made the connection between parliamentary reform, taxation, currency issues and the corn laws, as had many plebeian radical leaders (to judge by their meetings during these years). Prentice often commended them for their sound opinions on these related subjects.[78]

The Potter–Prentice argument that the withdrawal of small notes should be accompanied by a reduction in taxation was elaborated at the town hall meeting of 18 December 1828. But Taylor, G. W. Wood and others carried the majority with them when they retorted that discussion should be confined to the currency issue and that taxation would have to be considered on some other occasion.[79] Soon the Times was complaining about the harmful effects of the withdrawal of small notes. Many traders, businessmen and manufacturers were experiencing difficulties in carrying on their transactions, and the

[76] *Times*, 16, 23, 30 Jan. 1830; Prentice, *Sketches*, p. 353. At the end of January 1830 Prentice published a 3d. pamphlet entitled 'Opinions on the Currency Question, with a review of Mr Cobbett's lectures', based partly on his newspaper editorials.

[77] Boroughreeve's Papers, i, pp. 403–7; *Times*, 20, 27 Feb., 13 March, 3 April 1830; *Chronicle*, 20, 27 Feb. 1830; *Guardian*, 13, 20 March, 10 April 1830; Shuttleworth Scrapbook, pp. 75–6; Prentice, *Sketches*, pp. 354–8; Smith, Reminiscences, pp. 34–5. Smith considered the most memorable part of the meeting to have been the speech of Richard Potter, 'who in describing the wretchedness of the poor man's cottage became so overpowered by his feelings as to be unable to proceed'.

[78] On the workers' meetings, *Gazette*, 28 Oct. 1826, 24 March 1827; *Times*, 19 Sept. 1829, 22 May 1830; *Chronicle*, 28 Oct. 1826, 24 March 1827; *Courier*, 28 Oct. 1826. A good sample of Prentice's comments can be found in *Gazette*, 2 Dec. 1826, 13 Jan. 1827; Prentice, *Sketches*, especially ch. 22; *Times*, 16 May, 25 July, 29 Aug. 1829, 28 April 1832.

[79] *Times*, 19 Dec. 1828. Prentice estimated that the 1820s saw the amount of paper currency in circulation fall by £11 million in a five-year period. Prentice, *Sketches*, p. 220.

latest depression was deepening all the time. In February 1830 Prentice repeated that economic distress would not be so bad had the government reduced taxation when it withdrew small notes from circulation.[80] Prentice's argument with Taylor on the matter in December 1828 indicates only one of the many issues on which they disagreed. It followed an earlier argument over taxation in August and September 1826, when Prentice drew attention to Taylor's remarks on the ability of the nation to pay the taxes required of it. Taylor's view was that the level of taxation was supportable. Yet he had ignored the fact that the value of money had been altered in recent times. As Prentice said, the weight of taxation was not to be estimated by referring to the amount of money paid but rather to its worth. Taylor replied that he had purposefully left depreciation out of his calculations because he wanted to test the *Gazette*! The argument went on for weeks and soon involved the problem of the national debt. Taylor accused Prentice of favouring a Cobbettite 'equitable adjustment' and 'the robbery of the public creditors'. Prentice denied this. All he wanted was justice, he explained, which meant that the burden of taxation should be shifted from those who had suffered most to those who had suffered least. Economic conditions dictated that the fundholders could no longer be indulged as formerly. Prentice did not make it clear precisely what he advocated with regard to the national debt. Apparently he was in favour of some alterations, but not to the degree that Cobbett was demanding.[81]

Prentice's views on taxation were probably more representative of the opinions of Manchester's reformers than were Taylor's, and certainly more representative of the band's opinions. 'What a fine country England would be', he once wrote to Richard Potter, 'were it taxed less heavily'.[82] The consensus was that taxation was too heavy and that the burden had been increased by changes in the value of the currency. Special attention was sometimes given to those taxes pressing disproportionately on the commercial middle classes. Prentice focused on these in February 1824.[83] In 1826 he said that the anomalous and unjust system of direct taxation diminished the profits of the shopkeeper, merchant and manufacturer, but left the

[80] *Times*, 14 March 1829, 6 Feb. 1830.
[81] *Gazette*, 12 Aug., 2, 16, 30 Sept. 1826; *Guardian*, 26 Aug., 9, 23 Sept., 7, 21 Oct. 1826.
[82] Prentice to Potter, 27 April 1828, Potter Collection, xii, pp. 153–6.
[83] *Gazette*, 28 Feb. 1824.

demands on them unchanged. Nor did Prentice forget those taxes on necessaries which burdened the labouring ranks. The taxes on malt, soap, beer, tea, tobacco, leather and other items meant that the poor worker paid out a full 50 per cent of his meagre earnings each week in indirect taxation. In reality he was handing his pennies over to the fundholder, sinecurist, placeman and pensioner.[84] Again the need for parliamentary reform was clear. Tax cuts, currency improvements and a more representative system of government were inseparable.[85] Taylor occasionally made this point too. In the early 1820s he condemned the financial management of the government and regularly discussed budget proposals and the state of the revenues. He considered the interest on the national debt an unbearable burden, though he could not approve of adjustments that would unduly disadvantage the public creditors (so he disagreed with Cobbett). Anyone who lost out through some tampering with the national debt would have to be compensated, Taylor insisted, but there should be no interference with the national debt at all until a programme of rigid economy had first been properly implemented. Hence Taylor wanted the dismantling of the sinking fund, the reduction of taxation and possibly some minor interference with the national debt involving compensations. Such reforms were bound to be resisted, and this was where parliamentary reform came in. According to the *Guardian* a more representative legislature would be willing to adopt the bold remedial policies that were necessary.[86] Taylor's views on the national debt changed little over the coming years. After his argument with Prentice in August and September 1826, he wrote a long piece for the *Guardian* in February 1827 in which he stated that the nation's contract with its creditors had to be kept and that they could

---

[84] *Gazette*, 15 July 1826. These remarks were scorned by local Tories: *Courier*, 22, 29 July 1826.

[85] See N. Gash, 'Cheap Government 1815–74' in his *Pillars of Government and other Essays on State and Society* (1986), pp. 43–54. Belief in the connections between parliamentary corruption, high government spending, heavy taxation, the national debt and currency regulations had a long intellectual ancestry behind it, but became all the more relevant because of the strain of the French Wars.

[86] *Guardian*, 9, 16 June 1821, 2, 16 March 1822, 18 Jan., 1 March 1823. Gash has called the sinking fund 'the final economic futility'. Meant to reassure the public that it was still the government's intention to pay off the debt, it involved the borrowing of sums at a high rate of interest to maintain a fund yielding a lower rate. Gash, 'After Waterloo', p. 155.

not be paid less than they had been promised.[87] The *Chronicle* and *Exchange Herald* also opposed the breaking of contracts with the public creditors. The *Courier* condemned Cobbettite 'spoilation' and was against any tampering with the sinking fund: the fame of Pitt rested in large measure on the wisdom of his financial measures, and they should not be abandoned.[88]

2. THE BAND AND THE CORN LAWS

Manchester opinion was generally hostile towards the corn laws but formal declarations usually fell short of demanding repeal, betraying the caution of the majority and its sense of policy and expediency. Prentice later recalled that feeling in Manchester on the 1815 law had been rather lukewarm. In these years members of the band led the campaign for full repeal, and played a crucial role in converting many others to this position. They were later to be among the founders and most active leaders of the Anti-Corn Law League. But it did take a long time to educate Manchester opinion on this question, for the corn laws represented an emotive and complicated problem that seemed to defy simple solutions. Many agreed about the injustice and evil effects of the corn regulations, but there was disagreement about what could and should be done about them in prevalent political and economic conditions. There were also heated arguments over several related issues, especially food prices, wage levels and the prospects for the export trade in Manchester goods. Before the time of the League, when opinion in favour of repeal had achieved a measure of ascendancy, the tasks of keeping the corn laws before the public, stimulating debate and influencing local opinion were performed primarily by members of the band. It was due to them that the main theoretical and practical arguments for repeal had been advanced and elaborated long before the founding of the League.[89]

---

[87] *Guardian*, 10 Feb. 1827.
[88] *Chronicle*, 9 Jan. 1830; *Exchange Herald*, 7 Jan. 1823; *Courier*, 19 April 1828, 9 Jan., 20 Feb. 1830.
[89] See also W. H. Chaloner, 'The Agitation against the Corn Laws', in Ward, *Popular Movements*, p. 136; T. S. Ashton, 'The Origins of the Manchester School', *The Manchester School of Economics, Commerce and Administration*, i (1931), pp. 22–7; D. G. Barnes, *A History of the English Corn Laws from 1660 to 1846* (1930), p. 216.

The law of 1815 was strongly condemned by Manchester's respectable reformers. Their *Gazette* argued that the first object of government should be to feed the people at the cheapest rate, and that ministers should not be swayed from this task by the demands of the landed interest, a tiny minority of the population. One key to the problem seemed to be land rentals. The *Gazette* stated that a restriction on corn imports would be unnecessary (even had landed men been justified in asking for it) if rents could somehow be abated. It had also to be remembered that 'on the price of corn depends that of almost every other article of consumption. It is the standard by which the price of everything, even of daily labour, is regulated'.[90] But the town meeting of 27 February 1815, predominantly a local establishment affair, was a disappointment to the band. The resolutions had more to do with Mancunian businessmen's self-interest than with free trade principles, and the matters most discussed were Manchester's export trade and the cotton industry's need for cheap labour.[91] The meeting was one of the most important events in the early history of the band. Prentice had only just settled in Manchester, and the others were still only beginning their careers as local politicians. The meeting served to draw these men closer together. They shared a common outlook on contemporary affairs and an enthusiasm for rational and sensible reform, and in February 1815 they openly disagreed with some of the statements made at the corn law meeting. They thought that opposition to the corn laws could not be based merely on cheap labour and Manchester export trade arguments. This was too narrow an understanding of the issue. The corn laws affected the whole community, employer and worker alike, and were bound up with such matters as rent, agricultural production and farming practices, as well as the needs and desires of manufacturing and commercial regions.

The reformers' views were made clear by Shuttleworth in his 'Plain Observations on the Corn Laws', inserted as an anonymous advertisement in some of the local newspapers after the 27 February meeting. Shuttleworth argued that it was natural and right for land rents to fall in peacetime, because the circumstances causing rent increases were now altered. The high price of subsistence necessarily raised that of labour and all commodities, but the link was variable

---

[90] *Gazette*, 21 Jan. 1815.
[91] *Gazette*, 25 Feb., 4, 11, 18, 25 March 1815.

rather than fixed: 'it is a delusion to hold out to the lower classes that wages or the price of labour can or will rise in the same extent with the proposed rise in the price of food'. Britain's foreign trade would cease if it could not be carried on more cheaply than that of her economic rivals. Less trade would mean unemployment and a general fall in the rate of wages. Workers had patiently submitted to high provision prices in wartime, and it would be scandalous if these were artificially continued. Moreover, 'the complaint of the landholders, that they are oppressed by protecting duties favouring our manufacturers, is a misapprehension; for the manufacturers furnish better markets for the products of agriculture than could otherwise be found for them'. Agriculture already benefited from various protecting duties anyway, far higher than those protecting manufactures. Shuttleworth was convinced that corn laws 'can only be effectual when accompanied by legislative restrictions extended to rent, and as this cannot perhaps be practically enforced, the free importation of foreign corn alone can keep down prices'. Some lands should be taken out of cultivation, he explained, and if only the best land was used this would promote a rise in output. 'The only equitable increase of rent must be drawn from the increase of the quantity of produce, and not from the increase of the price of it'. Artificial rent increases would be an injustice to all classes in the community and would only serve the landowners. If the high price of food was to be continued by legislative interference, this should at least wait until rents had fallen to their just level.[92]

Shuttleworth's arguments were those that the band advanced for years to come. Prentice's 'open and strong expression' of support for them in February 1815 led to a visit from Baxter and Taylor, and after this he immediately joined the circle of respectable liberals that Richard Potter was soon to dub the 'small but determined band'.[93] Smith was another reformer who was animated by the February 1815 meeting; he joined the band soon afterwards. An avid free trader from youth and a disciple of Adam Smith, he believed that wage levels depended on the demand for labour and rejected the notion that high food prices occasioned by the corn laws would have the effect of raising wages.[94] Members of the band also approached the

[92] *Gazette*, 11 March 1815.
[93] Prentice, *Sketches*, pp. 69–74; Somerville, *Free Trade and the League*, ii, pp. 385–90.
[94] Smith, *Reminiscences*, pp. 1–2, 9–11.

question as one of humanitarian and moral idealism. Corn laws were immoral, monopolies unrighteous, and the movement for free trade should be a religious and emotive crusade. Free trade was not just a matter of commercial self-interest, but also concerned moral obligations. Hence the 1815 law was objectionable on three counts (as Prentice put it):

> in the first place as an impious attempt to intercept, for the profit of a few, the gifts which God had bestowed for the benefit of all; in the second place, as an impolitic and impoverishing interference with the liberty of exchanging the surplus produce of other lands; and in the third place, as a gross injustice to the working classes, the great mass of the nation, tending at once to lower their wages and raise the price of food.[95]

There was some equivocation on the part of Manchester's Tory press towards the 1815 corn law and the town meeting. It was stated that protection for agriculture was necessary and justified, but that the measure passed was too harmful to the commercial and manufacturing interests. The arguments relating to cheap labour and Manchester's export trade were lauded, and the Tory papers said little about free trade theory.[96] Once the 1815 corn bill was passed the discussion about it subsided. Most local businessmen and politicians became inactive on the question. Prentice asserted that Manchester's opposition to the 1815 measure was faint and ineffectual, largely because it was based on erroneous principles (that high prices would raise wages, for example) and rooted in sectional interest rather than free trade doctrines. Free trade took a long time to gain a hold over Manchester middle-class opinion (and many workers saw the 'truths' about the operation of the corn laws long before their employers did). As Prentice said: 'I did not find many persons of my own class in Manchester whose opinions on free trade in corn were in accordance with my own'.[97] It should also be remembered

---

[95] Prentice, *Sketches*, pp. 61–5, 68. The links between free trade and moral idealism are also stressed in Prentice, *League*, especially preface and i, p. 230; N. McCord, *The Anti-Corn Law League* (1958), p. 104; Cowherd, *Politics of Dissent*, ch. 10.

[96] *Chronicle*, 25 Feb., 4, 11 March 1815; *Exchange Herald*, 21, 28 Feb., 7 March 1815; *Mercury*, 28 Feb., 7 March 1815.

[97] Prentice, *Sketches*, pp. 69, 74–6.

that the February 1815 meeting did not represent an attack on the corn laws generally, for what was at stake was not the corn duty itself but its proposed increase. The relative lack of interest in the question in 1815 is partly to be explained by Manchester businessmen's preoccupation with other burdens falling more directly on them, particularly the import duty on raw cotton and the proposed tax on the windows and rents of commercial premises.[98] Nothing much changed with the establishment of the Chamber of Commerce, which gave Mancunian businessmen an important forum for debate. It was many years before the chamber shook off its moderation and hesitancy on the corn issue and came out clearly for repeal.

Some historians have obviously exaggerated Manchester's devotion to liberalism and free trade. G. B. Hertz and L. S. Marshall have argued that economic and political liberalism dominated Manchester thought by about 1820, while V. A. C. Gatrell writes that *laissez-faire* came to have an unchallenged intellectual and practical hegemony over the Manchester business community. Similar claims have been made by Donald Read and John Seed.[99] Yet this interpretation seems far too neat and simple. Could one body of doctrines really gain such ascendancy, and could there be such uniformity of opinion? Although W. D. Grampp rather oversimplifies the Manchester School as 'a group of businessmen who forced Britain to repeal its corn laws and thereby to commit itself finally to free trade', he does at least make it clear that the school was never a uniform body. It was heterogeneous, containing a number of distinct interest groups, lacking in consistency and coherence and only really united by a feeling against the corn laws.[100] It seems that wholesale commitment to a body of economic doctrines was far less important than hopes and expectations about the possible *results* of free trade policies. There was far more interest in practice than in principles, and the advance of free trade opinion in Manchester was slow. The real characteristic of the Manchester businessman was self-interest, not adherence to doctrine. If the

[98] Redford, *Manchester Merchants*, pp. 134–5; Marshall, *Public Opinion*, pp. 192–9.
[99] G. B. Hertz, *The Manchester Politician 1750–1912* (1912), chs. 3, 4; Marshall, *Public Opinion*, chs. 8, 10; Gatrell, 'Manchester Parable', pp. 28–36; Seed, 'Unitarianism and liberal culture', p. 2; Read, 'Reform newspapers and Northern opinion', pp. 306–7.
[100] W. D. Grampp, *The Manchester School of Economics* (1960), preface and pp. 1–15.

relaxation of restrictions suited his interest he favoured it. If it did not he opposed it, as demonstrated by the disagreements over the exportation of machinery and yarns and twist. Few Mancunians were convinced that free trade could provide all the answers. Even Watkin, a keen free trader, admitted that Cobbett had a point when he said that free trade could do harm because it would allow foreigners to supply articles previously supplied by fellow Englishmen. This would increase home unemployment and there was no guarantee that the foreigners would buy English manufactures with their new profits.[101] As for the corn laws, W. Cooke Taylor's observation is well worth bearing in mind: 'It is absurd to say that Manchester was either the birthplace or the cradle of free trade; it can only claim the merit of reviving the demand for the repeal of an impolitic law which had been allowed to slumber during a period of great political excitement and some commercial prosperity'. This fits in with Prentice's picture. Free trade opinion did not achieve dominance in Manchester for many years, and even then it did not enjoy a permanent or secure ascendancy. And its fundamental purpose was actually self-protection and self-preservation, to prevent or delay foreign industrial competition and give Manchester manufacturers a commanding position in existing and future foreign markets.[102] Clearly there was considerable indifference to free trade doctrines and corn law repeal in Manchester for a long period. Agitation on the corn laws was in any case noticeably dormant during times of low wheat prices. At such times it was more difficult for campaigners like the band to influence people. Prentice later recalled that there had been 'seven years' sleep' on the corn law question in Manchester before the League appeared.[103]

After 1815, in the knowledge that there was a distinct lack of commitment on the corn issue in Manchester, it was up to the more advanced reformers to keep the matter before the public in readiness for a time when a new campaign could be launched. Hence the *Gazette*'s surveillance of grain prices and occasional warnings about potential food shortages.[104] The *Guardian* also played its part in

[101] Watkin, *Fragment No. 1*, pp. 80–81.
[102] Prentice, *Sketches*, pp. 74–5; Somerville, *Free Trade and the League*, ii, pp. 389–90; the Cooke Taylor quotation (which both Prentice and Somerville cite) is from his *The Life and Times of Sir Robert Peel* (1846–8).
[103] Prentice, *League*, i, pp. 88; Chaloner, 'Agitation against the Corn Laws', p. 137.
[104] e.g. *Gazette*, 11 May 1816.

keeping the issue alive, while Smith recorded his view that the agricultural problems of the early 1820s proved not only that the corn laws were useless, but that the interests of farmers, landowners and agricultural labourers were not the same. This contradicted the claim made by defenders of the corn laws. The fall in the price of corn after a run of good harvests enabled the labourers to buy more food with their wages, so they had no reason to join in the alarmism and complaints of landlords and farmers.[105] In the summer of 1824 the U.S.A. imposed new tariffs on imported British manufactures. The Manchester liberals blamed the corn laws. Foreigners' reactions to British policy were bound to interest Manchester businessmen, and the *Gazette* pointed to the continuing economic retaliation Britain was likely to suffer because of the corn laws: 'This is a measure to which the States have been impelled by our exclusion of their agricultural produce from our market; and we have thus drawn upon ourselves the double evil of paying a high price for food, and lessening the number of those who could afford to purchase our manufactures'.[106] Taylor made a similar point, and these arguments were repeated in 1828 when Manchester businessmen were again threatened by increased American protective tariffs.[107] Concern about Britain's commercial relations with the U.S.A. rose considerably in early nineteenth-century Manchester because of America's importance as a source of raw cotton; 77 per cent of Britain's raw cotton imports came from U.S. suppliers during the period from 1815 to 1859.[108] Of course the American government had home industries to protect and would probably have done so whatever Britain's agricultural policy, but it is understandable that the band used American tariffs as a propaganda weapon at this time. Another powerful argument was that by preventing foreign states from taking Britain's manufactures, the corn laws encouraged these states to develop their own manufacturing industries. This was bound to raise alarm in Manchester. Many Mancunian businessmen, indeed, saw for themselves the extent of foreign industrial progress while on their commercial travels abroad. Shuttleworth was often in Europe on business, for example. Knowledge about the development of foreign

---

[105] *Guardian*, 30 June 1821, 12 Jan., 2 Feb., 11 May 1822; Smith, Reminiscences, pp. 25–6.
[106] *Gazette*, 26 June 1824.
[107] *Guardian*, 19, 26 June 1824, 31 May, 14, 28 June, 16 Aug. 1828.
[108] Farnie, *Cotton Industry*, p. 15.

industry was rapidly built up during the 1820s and 1830s, and became a leading topic of conversation.[109]

After Prentice became the editor of the *Gazette* in July 1824 that paper was hardly ever silent on the corn law question. He believed that he had a duty to keep it constantly before his readers and to improve the public's understanding of all the issues involved. Convinced that the corn laws made grain prices artificially high, he often compared British prices with those abroad. Early in 1825 he gave the average prices for grains in England and France for October 1824. While wheat had been 58s. a quarter in England, it was 32s. 3d. in France. At the same time rye was 32s. a quarter in England and 18s. 8d. in France, and oats 20s. a quarter in England and 13s. 2d. in France. This begged the question: how long could such a large difference in prices be tolerated?[110] Other points stressed in Prentice's articles were the false premises and mistaken direction of government tariff policy, the failure of the corn laws to do what their supporters had hoped and expected of them, the need for an energetic repeal campaign and for class unity in that campaign, the fact that all social ranks suffered from the operation of the corn laws and would benefit equally from repeal, and the effect repeal would have in promoting a general and cumulative prosperity. In November 1824 he called for masters and workers in the manufacturing regions to unite. They seemed to have forgotten the corn question. Controversies over wages and combinations meant that employers and operatives 'are forgetting in the struggle the operation of laws which are manifestly injurious to the interests of both'.[111]

The problems inherent in the 1815 system became increasingly apparent as time passed. There was too much rigidity. There was also a great deal of confusion, with ports alternately opened and closed according to price averages which were not in themselves a sound guide by which to judge Britain's need for corn. Another problem was the unpredictability of prices. There were growing

---

[109] See remarks in Prentice, *Tour in the United States*, p. 147; R. Cobden to W. Neild, 30 Sept. 1838, in E. Hughes, 'The development of Cobden's economic doctrines and his methods of propaganda: some unpublished correspondence', *B.J.R.L.*, 22 (1938), p. 412; J. Aikin, *A Description of the Country from Thirty to Forty Miles around Manchester* (1795), p. 184. See Shuttleworth Scrapbook, loose leaves, for some of Shuttleworth's European passports.

[110] *Gazette*, 8 Jan. 1825.

[111] *Gazette*, 27 Nov. 1824.

calls for reform. In his *Protection to Agriculture* (1822), the influential economist David Ricardo recommended a fixed duty beginning at 20s. a quarter, to be lowered by a shilling each year down to 10s. a quarter. Huskisson, the leading advocate of commercial reforms in the government after 1823, also came to favour corn law revision. His support for a fixed duty and his dissatisfaction with the system of averages were given great emphasis by the *Chronicle* in May 1824.[112] Opinion in favour of corn law amendment was quite strong in Manchester by early 1825, and the reformers continued to argue that agitation was needed to urge the government forward in its liberalising commercial policies. A town meeting was held in the Exchange on 3 March 1825. Thomas Potter, Taylor, Shuttleworth and Baxter were among the participants. It was decided to petition for the revision of the corn laws, but Prentice later recorded his disappointment that in 1825 Manchester's merchants and manufacturers were still clinging to the fallacy that high food prices would compel them to pay higher wages. There had been little advance on the selfish and unenlightened position of 1815. Smith was as disappointed as Prentice.[113]

In later years, of course, Friedrich Engels was only one among many commentators who accused Manchester businessmen of demanding corn law repeal on the assumption that repeal would enable them to reduce wages.[114] In 1901 Elijah Helm argued that the League had not wanted repeal in order to pay lower wages,[115] but this historian and former president of the Chamber of Commerce was a great admirer of the League, and his reading of the League's propaganda and records was unquestioning. Many of the Leaguers were

---

[112] *Chronicle*, 22 May 1824. On the operation of the 1815 law, Barnes, *History of the Corn Laws*, pp. 157–79; C. R. Fay, *Corn Laws and Social England* (1932), pp. 78–81. On Ricardo's opinions, Dinwiddy, *Luddism to Reform Bill*, pp. 13–14. I am also grateful to A. D. Macintyre for a copy of an unpublished piece on 'Classical Political Economy', which deals with the Ricardian position. Ricardo, possibly the most influential political economist of the time, achieved wide renown with his *Principles of Political Economy and Taxation* (1817), and was M.P. for Portarlington 1819–23.

[113] *Guardian*, 30 April 1825; *Gazette*, 19 Feb., 5 March 1825; *Chronicle*, 5 March 1825; Boroughreeve's Papers, i, pp. 141–4; Prentice, *Sketches*, pp. 251–2; Smith, Reminiscences, pp. 27–8.

[114] Engels, *Condition of the Working Class*, pp. 312, 315–16.

[115] Helm, *History of the Chamber*, pp. 73, 79–80; c.f. Grampp, *Manchester School of Economics*, ch. 3.

strong-willed and self-interested cotton masters who did expect that repeal would benefit them, and they were hardly likely to complain if it did so at the expense of labour. Cumulative prosperity and Cobdenism might have been favoured creeds by the 1840s, but what about before this time? It is clear from the complaints of Prentice, Smith, Shuttleworth and their friends that agitation against the corn laws was for many years based on the cheap labour argument. It was the band's self-appointed task to bring about a conversion. This began to occur, albeit very slowly.

Through 1825 the *Guardian* and *Gazette* kept up their coverage of the corn law issue. Taylor attacked the aristocracy, and Prentice wondered why Huskisson was not doing more to extend his liberalising programme to the corn regulations. It is noticeable that Taylor was thinking more about revision than repeal, and more about the need for cheap labour and the relationship between food prices and wages than about cumulative prosperity and the way in which all classes would benefit from freer trade in corn. In these important respects Taylor and Prentice were following different courses. Their tasks were to get people interested in the corn question and to inculcate sound opinions. Theory was not enough, for not everyone accepted or understood free trade doctrines. Exploiting the individual's sense of self-interest was thus the key to a successful campaign. Prentice and agitators of his ilk recognised this as well as Taylor did, but were more concerned to stress collective interests and the public good alongside sectional interests. Meanwhile the Tory *Chronicle* argued in favour of the government's wait and see policy, suggesting that there should be no changes until all relevant information had been collected and considered.[116]

In the distressed months of 1826 Prentice continued to berate the stubbornness of those resisting full repeal. He later said of George Canning's May 1826 proposal to allow the temporary entry of foreign corn at a duty of 12s. a quarter: 'there was not a single argument used in favour of a temporary suspension of the corn laws that would not have been applicable to their total repeal'. At the time he also continued to stress that the government's policy on corn was out of step with the liberalising trend of its other commercial measures. Ministers were displaying 'a disposition to cling to office at a

---

[116] *Guardian*, 26 Feb., 26 March, 16 April, 11 June, 10 Dec. 1825; *Gazette*, 5, 26 March, 30 April, 12 Nov. 1825; *Chronicle*, 30 April 1825.

considerable sacrifice of consistency'. In July 1826 his articles 'On the Causes and Cure of the Present Distress' identified the corn laws as one of the fundamental problems that had to be tackled before there could be any improvement in Britain's social and economic conditions. Meanwhile the *Guardian* continued its detailed criticism of the arguments of the agriculturalists, and even the Literary and Philosophical Society discussed the corn question. This occurred on 7 April 1826, at a meeting attended by Watkin, and was unusual in view of the society's customary avoidance of public controversy.[117] Due mainly to the persistence of the band, a public meeting on the prevalent distress was held on 17 August 1826. Baxter was in the chair, and among the speakers Shuttleworth made a strong case for corn law repeal. Anticipation mounted early in 1827 as it became clear that the ministers were at last going to do something about the corn regulations. The *Chronicle* hoped for a fair compromise that would be acceptable to both agriculturalist and manufacturer.[118] Canning introduced a corn bill in March 1827 (just weeks before his appointment as prime minister). It provided for a sliding scale of duties to operate around the pivot point of 60s. a quarter, ceasing entirely at 70s. a quarter. It was an advance on the 1822 act, which had introduced a scale of duties on foreign corn between 70s. and 85s. a quarter. The 1822 act had aroused only limited discussion in Manchester and was in fact a redundant measure, because it did not repeal the 1815 clause prohibiting the entry of corn until the home price reached 80s. This price was never reached while the 1822 act was in force.[119] Prentice regarded the 1827 bill as wholly inadequate, and blamed the manufacturing districts for remaining too quiescent and placing too much reliance on ministers' firmness. Then the duke of Wellington carried an amendment in the Lords to prevent bonded corn from coming to market until the price reached 66s. a quarter, and Canning abandoned his measure in June. Prentice had expected such an outcome and was not sorry. The measure would have done little for consumers, he argued, and government ministers were clearly at fault for remaining too half-hearted in their readiness to

[117] *Gazette*, 1, 29 April, 13, 20 May, 15, 22 July 1826; Prentice, *Sketches*, p. 281; *Guardian*, 31 Dec. 1825, 21 Jan., 11 Feb., 15, 29 April, 13 May 1826; Watkin, *Journal*, p. 108.
[118] *Chronicle*, 10 Feb. 1827.
[119] *Exchange Herald*, 9 July 1822; Barnes, *History of the Corn Laws*, p. 174; N. Gash, *Aristocracy and People. Britain 1815–65* (1979), pp. 120–21.

effect reforms. Taylor had welcomed the sliding scale as a step in the right direction. He stated that it did not go as far as it should have, but at least its moderation would give it a good chance of gaining parliamentary approval. He was outraged by Wellington's amendment, and claimed that it had an immediate effect on Manchester's foreign trade. Orders had been cancelled and there had been a serious loss of business, especially for the calico printers. The *Chronicle* had approved of Canning's scheme on the grounds that protection was better than prohibition, and opined that the abandonment of the corn bill was a misfortune for the commercial interests.[120]

A town meeting was held on 5 July 1827 to discuss what had happened. All parties were represented among the requisitionists, who included Harvey, Taylor, the Potters, Prentice, Watkin, Smith, Atkinson and many of the band's allies. Shuttleworth, Taylor and Richard Potter were among the speakers. They asserted that the corn laws had to be removed and that the abandoned bill would at least have been a beginning. But members of the band were again disappointed by the meeting. As before the resolutions dwelt on Manchester's need for cheap labour and the harmful effect of the corn laws on foreign demand for Manchester goods. These were familiar arguments, but seemed to have relevance only for the merchants and manufacturers. The meeting advocated 'modification', apparently along the lines suggested by Canning's sliding scale. The advanced reformers had hoped for something more, though one slight consolation was that they were able to use the town meeting to give further expression to liberal sentiments. The Tory *Courier* and *Chronicle* did not approve of the meeting, claimed that many respectable townsmen had stayed away, and complained that speakers had been disrespectful towards the House of Lords. The *Courier* also printed some observations from London papers in which Manchester merchants and manufacturers were condemned as hypocrites. They would not allow agriculture its just protection, but had grown rich due to the protection of the cotton industry. The *Guardian* rejected this 'compound of twaddle and falsehood'.[121]

---

[120] *Gazette*, 10, 31 March, 16, 23, 30 June 1827; Prentice, *Sketches*, pp. 296–9; *Guardian*, 9 Dec. 1826, 10, 17 March, 9, 16, 23 June 1827; *Chronicle*, 17 March, 16 June 1827.

[121] *Gazette*, 30 June, 7 July 1827; Boroughreeve's Papers, i, pp. 242–51; Shuttleworth Scrapbook, p. 42; Prentice, *Sketches*, p. 302; *Chronicle*, 7 July 1827; *Courier*, 7, 14 July 1827; *Guardian*, 21 July 1827.

In the next parliamentary session the corn question was taken up by Huskisson. A new sliding scale was proposed which respected the wishes of Wellington (now prime minister) and the more conservative members of the government, who did not want to anger the landed interests. The duties in the scale were higher than in Canning's, and foreign wheat was not to be admitted 'free' (subject only to a nominal duty of 1s. a quarter) until the home price reached 73s. a quarter. Prentice attacked Huskisson, and suspected that too much had been made of the 'guarantees' Huskisson claimed to have been given by Wellington concerning the moderate policies to be pursued by the government. The new corn bill was too favourable towards the corn growers, said Prentice, and Huskisson was being inconsistent in advocating the new scale when he had approved of the abandonment of Canning's after it was modified. 'These resolutions show how little the people have to expect from the present ministry, and what value is to be attached to Mr Huskisson's guarantees'. The *Guardian* blamed Wellington rather than Huskisson, but Taylor was still as dissatisfied with the new measure as was Prentice. The *Chronicle* welcomed the new scale as a fair compromise, arguing that free trade was inadvisable, problematic and unlikely to bring the boons that repealers were claiming. Despite objections from both reformers and protectionists the bill passed quite easily. Ministers were probably influenced most by reports that foreign grain production was not at a level that could mean the flooding of the British market. The 1828 system was not without its drawbacks, for it encouraged speculative buying of corn and led to excessive price fluctuations. Nevertheless, it seems to have worked well. Certainly the end of the 1815 system meant that supplies could be brought in more easily, as after the bad harvests of 1828–29. The harvests of 1830–35 were better, and the repeal campaign only really revived with the return of hard times in the later 1830s.[122]

Members of the band did not cease their efforts in the aftermath of the 1828 act. Prentice continued his regular articles on the corn laws, hoping to spread opinion in favour of repeal or at least to make people more aware of their effects. In May 1829 he praised Perronet

---

[122] *Gazette, Guardian* and *Chronicle*, 5 April 1828; Gash, *Aristocracy and People*, p. 113; E. L. Woodward, *The Age of Reform 1815–70* (1962), pp. 61–2; Chaloner, introduction to Prentice's *League*, p. xii–xiii; Chaloner, 'Agitation against the Corn Laws', pp. 138–9; Fay, *Corn Laws and Social England*, pp. 84–6; Barnes, *History of the Corn Laws*, pp. 199–201, 208–10.

Thompson's 'exceedingly able' *Catechism of the Corn Laws*, which had recently been published in sixpenny pamphlet form. In all its essentials it represented the ideas and arguments Prentice had been advancing for several years. Soon Prentice made an arrangement with the publishers whereby copies of the *Catechism* would be delivered without charge around the Manchester region by the newsmen who distributed his *Times*. Later he gained permission to print copies of the pamphlet on his own presses, and he gave away a copy free with every sale of the *Times* on 29 August 1829. This was costly, but Prentice had always believed that when the public good was at stake the honest reformer should put all other considerations aside. His editorials continued to demand corn law repeal, sometimes in conjunction with a cut in taxation and radical parliamentary reform.[123] The *Courier* expressed the views of those who were unsympathetic towards repeal. The owner-editor, Thomas Sowler, wanted security for agriculture and mistrusted 'free trade'.[124] Such historians as Betty Kemp and Susan Fairlie have doubted that the corn laws had the effects claimed by their opponents, and also suggest that repeal failed to bring all the benefits that the free traders had hoped for.[125] It should be remembered, though, that the true effects of the corn laws (which can be discussed now with the benefits of reflection and a mass of assembled historical data) are perhaps less important than what contemporaries thought and claimed were the effects.

---

[123] *Times*, 16, 23 May, 11, 25 July, 22, 29 Aug. 1829; Prentice, *Sketches*, p. 352; T. Perronet Thompson, *A Catechism of the Corn Laws* (1827); L. G. Johnson, *General T. Perronet Thompson 1783–1869. His military, literary and political campaigns* (1957), ch. 8. Thompson emerged as one of the leading philosophic radicals during the 1820s, edited the *Westminster Review* from 1829 to 1836 and was M.P. for Hull (1835–37) and Bradford (1847–52, 1857–59). On repeal and free trade as the promoters of the 'identity of interests' between rulers and ruled, see E. Halevy, *The Growth of Philosophic Radicalism* (1952), pp. 4, 153, 313–14, 487–98. Bentham's views on the corn laws were given in his *Observations on the Restrictive and Prohibitory Commercial System* (1821). See discussion in Dinwiddy, *Luddism to Reform Bill*, pp. 14–17. The similarities between the positions taken by Prentice, Thompson and Bentham are striking, as one would expect.

[124] *Courier*, 26 March, 9 April 1825, 13 May, 22, 29 July, 9 Sept. 1826, 10 March 1827, 5 April 1828.

[125] B. Kemp, 'Reflections on the Repeal of the Corn Laws', *Victorian Studies*, 5 (1962), pp. 189–204; S. Fairlie, 'The 19th century Corn Law Reconsidered', *Ec.H.R.*, 18 (1965), pp. 663–74, and 'The Corn Laws and British Wheat Production 1829–76', *Ec.H.R.*, 22 (1969), pp. 88–116.

While Prentice continued to press for repeal, Taylor's position in 1829 was that the time was not right for repeal nor for a major repeal campaign. There had to be a proper opportunity for full parliamentary deliberation on the matter, he stated. A demand for repeal so soon after the passing of the 1828 act would be inadvisable, moreover, because the protectionists would simply argue that the new system had not been given a fair trial. But Taylor did agree that the 1828 system was unsatisfactory. Business was still being restrained, and despite the sliding scale there were times when the duties were entirely prohibitory, due to delays before home deficiencies in grain were signified by a rise in price. By the time Britain was ready to buy foreign corn, the suppliers were aware of her shortage and commanded higher prices. There had also been speculation among British corn dealers, Taylor added, and this gambling spirit was not healthy for the trading community as a whole.[126] Prentice and Taylor continued their discussions through 1829–32 making use of statistics, items from other newspapers and extracts taken from *Westminster Review* articles. They also used pamphlets by such writers as the former Manchester banker Thomas Crewdson (who was becoming an influential advocate of repeal), physician and social reformer J. P. Kay, and Viscount Milton, a liberal-minded Whig magnate with substantial manufacturing interests (who succeeded as fifth Earl Fitzwilliam in 1833).[127] By now Taylor was spending much of his time arguing for a moderate fixed duty. In a discussion with local corn merchant Edward Swanwick he said that the fixed duty should be no more than 10s. a quarter, and if possible as low as 7s.[128] Arguments in favour of a fixed duty became louder after 1828, and the views of provincial commentators like Taylor were given more force by the agitation for a fixed duty by prominent politicians and economists. Meanwhile Prentice suggested that corn law repeal would be the first task of the reformed parliament, and he often introduced the subject at meetings he attended even if they had been called for other purposes. Notable examples of this are the December 1830 meeting called to celebrate and pay for Henry Hunt's successful

[126] *Guardian*, 17 Jan., 23 May, 22 Aug. 1829.
[127] *Times*, 12 Sept., 31 Oct., 21 Nov., 26 Dec. 1829, 27 Feb., 19 June, 17 July 1830, 21 Jan., 28 April 1832; *Guardian*, 19 Sept., 26 Dec. 1829, 23 Jan., 17 July 1830, 6 Oct. 1832.
[128] *Guardian*, 2, 9, 16 Oct., 13 Nov. 1830. For information on Swanwick I am grateful to R. Carr of the Local History Dept. M.C.L.

Preston election campaign, a meeting organised soon afterwards by John Doherty and the Manchester trades in support of the striking spinners of Ashton, and a meeting in January 1831 called by Ashton shopkeepers to discuss parliamentary reform. By this time Prentice was convinced that parliamentary reform would have to precede corn law repeal. He argued that parliament was too exclusive and unrepresentative to grant repeal, and would have to be thoroughly reconstituted. Prentice examined the links between the corn and parliamentary reform issues in his speech at a public meeting on distress in February 1830. The boroughreeve, who was in the chair, told him to stick to the matter in hand and he replied that he had done so, since social and economic hardship, the corn laws and the corrupt system of representation were inseparably bound together.[129] According to Prentice a growing number of Manchester reformers regarded parliamentary reform primarily as a means to gain freer trade. The Reform Bill was seen as a necessary instrument and the end in view was corn law repeal.[130] He may have been unduly influenced in this interpretation by what followed the Manchester parliamentary reform campaign of 1830–32, but it is true that the band and its allies did regard this campaign in part as a protest against monopoly, and did place importance on the need to secure the return of two liberal, free trade candidates at Manchester's first parliamentary election (and secure it they did).

Prentice's speeches at meetings attended by workers and middling sort Mancunians were all part of his attempt to enlighten the lower ranks on the corn question. It has already been mentioned that he wanted a repeal campaign based on class cooperation. This campaign would need the strength of numbers and popular support. It would have to be led by respectable and thoughtful reformers, of course, but they could not get far by themselves. Hence Prentice's desire to drum up support from the Manchester Huntites, the local trade clubs and the shopkeepers of Ashton. For years he had been trying to influence and educate the workers, encouraging their self-expression and publicising their meetings, and he was especially pleased when he heard working men uttering sound statements on the corn laws. Smith was another who made much of the fact that the workers' spokesmen were for repeal, not just revision, which

---

[129] *Times*, 1, 8, 29 Jan., 2 April 1831; Prentice, *Sketches*, pp. 275, 354–8.
[130] Prentice, *League*, i, chs. 1, 2; c.f. Barnes, *History of the Corn Laws*, p. 216.

was too often the demand of 'respectable' meetings.[131] Throughout the 1820s Prentice's newspapers covered workers' meetings on the corn laws, addressed by John Doherty and such contacts of the band as the lecturer Rowland Detrosier, spinner Jonathan Hodgins and radical draper P. T. Candelet.[132] Even before these meetings a good number of plebeian radicals had not been slow to join in the call for repeal. In 1818–19 the *Observer* had declared that the repeal of the 1815 law was essential. It was a 'Bill for Starving the People', an audacious folly, and represented a blasphemous disregard of God's will by denying the poor all access to the earth's produce merely in order to enrich the ruling class.[133] This critique could have come straight from Prentice, so similar was it to his own. He was sure that the workers adopted sound opinions on the corn laws long before their employers did: 'I can safely aver that in 1815, exclusive of the working classes, there were not more persons right as to the manner in which wages could be affected by that enactment than were wrong when the successful agitation for its repeal commenced in 1838'.[134]

Hoping for class cooperation in a repeal campaign, and convinced that the respectable reformers could not get far unless they attracted the interest and support of the workers, Prentice was bound to make a case for repeal that did not depend on cheap labour arguments. He and his allies advocated repeal with arguments that attracted both employers and workers. They explained that repeal would increase the masters' profits and the workers' wages because it would mean more foreign demand for British manufactures in exchange for corn. Repeal would benefit everyone, and all classes would enjoy a general prosperity if the odious corn laws were removed.[135] This was to be the position of the leaders of the League. They have been accused of calculation, dissembling, self-interest and presenting their own sectional desires as if they represented the whole community. But judging by Prentice's own statements, writings and activities, the

[131] Smith, Reminiscences, p. 29.
[132] e.g. *Gazette*, 21, 28 Oct., 2 Dec. 1826, 13 Jan., 24 March, 11 Aug., 1 Sept. 1827; *Times*, 8 Aug. 1829, 22 May 1830, 1 Jan., 9 July 1831.
[133] *Observer*, 7 Nov., 5 Dec. 1818, 9 Jan., 6 Feb., 26 June 1819.
[134] Prentice, *Sketches*, pp. 74–6.
[135] Prentice, *League*, i, p. 94; c.f. his *Lecture on Wages*, pp. 1–2, in which he points out that the corn laws had raised the price of food while keeping wages down, because they limited foreign demand for British manufactures and thus limited Manchester employers' demand for labour.

argument for 'cumulative prosperity' was not a mere tactic. He really did believe that the workers would benefit from repeal, and that they would benefit as much as their masters. Others in the band agreed, and focused on the well-being of the labouring ranks alongside that of other social groups. Brotherton, for instance, was to attack the New Poor Law (1834) on the grounds that such an enactment was wholly unjust when the corn laws were still in force. It was outrageous to deprive the poor working man of both food and relief.[136] To Prentice, Shuttleworth, Brotherton and others in the band, the corn issue had humanitarian as well as commercial importance. They made this clear during the 1820s, and it was partly their humanitarianism that led them to seek the cooperation of the lower ranks in their repeal agitation. But not everyone shared Prentice's desire to have workers involve themselves in prominent public questions. Prentice himself, and the workers' meetings of the time, were frequently condemned by local Tories.[137]

As well as attempting to get a favourable response from the workers, Prentice and his friends tried to secure unequivocal statements and determined actions from the Chamber of Commerce. But the body that was the voice and forum of the Manchester business community was not as responsive as members of the band would have liked. For much of the time the chamber was silent on the question. It tended to act only after much agitation by the free traders among the membership, and usually the action fell short of what they had hoped for. In 1820 the directors only interested themselves in the corn laws when they heard that the agriculturalists wanted to raise the price limit set in the 1815 measure from 80s. to 82s. a quarter. There was no criticism of the corn law itself.[138] Repealers were a minority among the members for many years. All they managed to secure in 1825 was an undertaking that the chamber would petition for revision, and a statement in the annual report in favour of a lowering of duties.[139] For the band the chamber was not persistent or unequivocal enough to be a useful ally. A resolution at the 1826 annual meeting favoured a 'material reform' in the corn law

---

[136] Brotherton, *Speech on the Corn Laws*, and *Mr Brotherton and the New Poor Law*, (part 2).
[137] e.g. *Chronicle*, 28 Oct. 1826, 24 March, 11 Aug., 1 Sept. 1827; *Courier*, 28 Oct. 1826.
[138] Chamber Annual Reports, 1820.
[139] *Gazette*, 19 Feb. 1825; Chamber Annual Reports, 1825.

system, but added that the membership 'abstains from urging the subject on the immediate notice of Parliament, in consideration of the other important questions with which their attention is already engaged'.[140] Most members do seem to have believed that the corn laws had 'injurious consequences', but the free traders could not shake them from their ineffectual stance. Baxter told a special chamber meeting on 8 November 1826 that full repeal was necessary and that 'the very existence of manufactures depended on the people having cheap bread', but the majority (which included Taylor) thought that too rapid a change would lead to worse distress, and it was decided to petition for a moderate fixed duty. Prentice condemned the majority for its caution, but Taylor asserted that repeal would be too drastic in prevalent circumstances and would ruin many agriculturalists. A fixed duty was preferable, to be lowered over time. The chamber's annual report for 1826 would say no more than that the corn laws were 'impolitic'.[141]

When the chamber discussed Canning's corn bill of 1827 it was resolved that: 'Though the Bill proposes a scale of protecting duties higher than sound policy suggests, and the welfare of the general interests of the country requires, it is nevertheless founded upon just and salutary principles and tends to mitigate the evils of the existing corn laws'. Prentice protested that the wording made it seem as if the chamber fully approved the principles of the bill. He suggested that the wording be changed to: 'it is nevertheless founded upon more just and salutary principles than the existing corn laws, and tends in some measure to mitigate them'. Richard Potter seconded Prentice's amendment, which was lost by a single vote. Surprised by the closeness of this margin Prentice tried again shortly afterwards, but again lost by one vote. He had secured the conversion of one of those present who had previously voted against him, but now his erstwhile ally Taylor switched his vote away from Prentice on the grounds that, if amended, the resolution would not agree with the petition which had been prepared in favour of Canning's measure.[142] Why Taylor had not said this at the time of the first vote is not clear. Perhaps he thought, as he did on many other issues, that Prentice wanted to go too far too quickly. The directors' report for 1828

[140] *Gazette*, 18 Feb. 1826.
[141] *Gazette* and *Guardian*, 11 Nov. 1826; Chamber Annual Reports, 1826.
[142] *Gazette*, 30 June 1827; Prentice, *Sketches*, pp. 297–8, 301; Smith, Reminiscences, p. 32.

praised the new corn law of that year, but still there was no demand for repeal nor even radical revision, and there was also an acceptance of agriculture's right to some form of protection. In 1833 and 1835 the chamber expressed itself in favour of a fixed duty, but it was said that 'no favourable opportunity' had presented itself for action on the matter. In 1836, when wheat prices were about 50 per cent higher than they had been in 1835, the directors called for 'thorough revision', nothing more.[143]

The Chamber of Commerce was not a free trade organ, nor was it ever intended to be. Cobden said in 1835 that both Manchester and England lacked societies to promulgate 'the beneficent truths of the Wealth of Nations'.[144] He spoke for many, including the band, who wanted to promote the spread of free trade principles. Clearly the chamber did not fit the bill in 1835, otherwise Cobden and others would have said so. Elijah Helm, the historian of the chamber, was led by his own predilections into a slanted view of the chamber's early history when he stated that it was a truly liberal commercial body, animated by the same spirit present in the commercial policy of Pitt the Younger and the writings of Adam Smith.[145] This view is credible up to a point, but only with the provisos here discussed. The members of the band who belonged to the chamber constantly attempted to secure its support for an unequivocal demand for corn law repeal, but all through the 1820s and 1830s they were up against the hesitancy of the majority of directors and members. Prentice left the chamber in disgust in 1834. Smith introduced a repeal motion at every annual meeting between 1828 and 1835. His singlemindedness earned him the nicknames 'Mad' and 'Corn Law' Smith. A breakthrough finally came in December 1838. Smith, Cobden and their allies managed to get a repeal resolution passed at a chamber meeting. Some directors resigned, and this opened the door for the rise to prominence of free traders within the chamber. Meanwhile Smith, Watkin, Prentice, Taylor and Thomas Potter helped to form the Manchester Anti-Corn Law Association, the forerunner of the League. Smith then became the president of the chamber in February 1839. In the following years the election of directors and officers became hotly

---

[143] Chamber Annual Reports, 1828, 1833, 1835, 1836.
[144] R. Cobden, 'England, by a Manchester Merchant' (1835), in Hirst, *Manchester School*, pp. 23–4.
[145] Helm, *History of the Chamber*, pp. 63–4.

contested, and the chamber split in 1845 when conservatives left and formed the Manchester Commercial Association.[146] Once the free traders had achieved dominance in the chamber, and Smith had become president, only then could the chamber be described as more avowedly a free trade organ, though there remained a substantial group of conservative members until 1845. Although the chamber had congratulated Huskisson and favoured the liberalising commercial reforms of the 1820s, there was far more intellectual commitment to free trade after the December 1838 meeting, Smith's promotion and then the secession. In any case the commitment to the ideal of free trade was more obvious from the late 1830s and the rise to ascendancy of doctrinaires like Smith.[147]

It is clear that campaigns and discussions in Manchester relating to commercial affairs were characterised by self-interest and moderation for much of this period. Mancunian businessmen and politicians of different parties did feel strongly about certain issues and policies, but their activity on these questions was normally intermittent and limited in extent. Once a specific goal had been achieved, once the government or parliament had been made aware of Manchester's views on the corn laws or cotton wool imports, once a duty had been reduced or the circulation of local banknotes curtailed, then the majority of campaigners rested satisfied until the next major controversy arose. It usually fell to the band to keep issues before the public, to advocate new campaigns and prompt the more moderate majority into action. Members of the band had some success. They were certainly responsible for making sure that interest in the corn question did not disappear. They were equally active on other

[146] Cornish, 'John Benjamin Smith', pp. 7–9, in Smith, *Memoranda and Letters*; *An Authentic Report of the late Important Discussions in the Manchester Chamber of Commerce, on the destructive effects of the Corn Laws upon the Trade and Manufactures of the Country* (1839); Redford, *Manchester Merchants*, p. 72; Helm, *History of the Chamber*, pp. 74–7; Grampp, *Manchester School of Economics*, ch. 4; Fraser, *Urban Politics*, pp. 243–4.
[147] e.g. Smith, *Report of the Directors to a special meeting of the Chamber . . . on the injurious effects of Restrictions on Trade, March 11th 1841* (1841).

questions, and fully participated in the local debates about commercial policies and theory, the currency system, taxation, and the image that Manchester – through the chamber and the many town meetings on economic issues – was presenting to the outside world. There could be disagreements within the band on matters of theory and practice, with Taylor once again the most obvious promoter of discord, but there remained agreement on many questions and on the general matter of what was best for Manchester business and for the whole nation's economic wellbeing. All of the band were free traders. Many Mancunians also favoured freer trade, but not necessarily for the same reasons as the band, and this helps to explain why the band had to be so active in informing, agitating and discussing. What is clear is that those who wanted more energetic commercial campaigns and a more widespread and solid commitment to freer trade faced an uphill struggle in the years before 1839. Such a struggle was an indispensable prelude to the politics of Manchester, and hence of the nation, in the 1840s and beyond.

VI *The Band and Parliamentary Reform*

I. THE POSTWAR YEARS, PETERLOO AND ITS AFTERMATH

The parliamentary reform movement in the postwar years was primarily the affair of radicals and reformers from the labouring ranks. Charismatic heroes such as Hunt and Cartwright rose to provide leadership on the national stage, and both were popular in Manchester, but the reform movement in the town lacked substantial respectable participation. Respectable reformers, including the band, did provide commentary, guidance and also direct help, but they were not true leaders during these years. They were consistent and benevolent allies of a movement which gained its main direction and numerical support from other social groups. Not surprisingly, the respectable reformers' own social and political preferences occasionally made them equivocal in their attitude towards popular radicalism.

One of the largest reform meetings of 1816 took place in Manchester on 28 October. This led to the establishment of a new plebeian Union Society (or 'Reform Union'), with veteran radical, John Knight, as secretary. Baxter was one of several liberal merchants who were asked to preside at the assembly, but he declined. Some respectable sympathisers attended, though, including the writer of the report which appeared in the *Gazette* (probably Taylor or Shuttleworth). The two themes stressed in this report were to become familiar over the coming years: the need for the popular radicals to conduct themselves peacefully, and the need for men of status to come forward and lead a decisive campaign for parliamentary reform. Meanwhile the Tory press condemned and ridiculed the popular meetings.[1] Some

---

[1] *Gazette*, 28 Sept., 5, 12 Oct., 2 Nov. 1816; Hay Scrapbooks, vii, pp. 142, 244; informant's report in H. O. 40/3, cited by H. W. Davies, 'Lancashire Reformers 1816–17', *B.J.R.L.*, 10 (1926), p. 67; *Chronicle*, 23 March, 31 Aug., 2 Nov. 1816; *Exchange Herald*, 15, 29 Oct., 12 Nov. 1816, 7 Jan., 4, 11, 18 Feb. 1817; *Mercury*, 5 Nov., 31 Dec. 1816.

middle-class reformers were prepared to help the Union Society. When it sent out circulars to wealthy local liberals in December 1816, asking for contributions to finance petitioning and missionary activity, Baxter's warehouse was one of the collection points.[2] It is possible that members of the band were involved on the fringes of the popular movement, offering press coverage, money and encouragement, though it is unclear how influential they were. They may have hoped that by being cooperative they could keep the plebeian campaign sane and judicious. Yet this wave of activity was to culminate in the Blanket affair, which the respectable reformers regretted, so any influence they did have was distinctly limited.

As the reform campaign gathered momentum with its petitions, meetings, delegate networks and radical associations, the Manchester Tories and loyal ministerial supporters decided on precautionary steps. Arrangements were made for the enrolment of additional special constables, implementation of watch and ward, and in January 1817 a new Association in Support of the Civil Authority was established. The Pitt Club and the Orange Institution also became more active.[3] The Blanket scheme was devised and acted upon in this atmosphere of radical assertiveness and rising Tory hostility.

The *Gazette* covered the Blanket meeting of 10 March 1817 with a mixture of sympathy for the 'dreadful misery' of the workers, condemnation for the heavy-handed manner in which the authorities had dispersed the assembly and pursued the marchers, and regret that the cause of reform 'has here devolved, through the lukewarmness of its opulent friends, into the hands of those whose station and character afford, it must be admitted, scarcely a sufficient guarantee of the purity and wisdom of their proceedings'. Prentice later reflected that the meeting and march were understandable demonstrations of popular suffering, but were not likely to convince the respectable classes that the mass of the people was ready for

---

[2] Circular is in H. O. 40/9; Hay Scrapbooks, xviii, p. 187; W. W. Kinsey, 'Some Aspects of Lancashire Radicalism 1816–21' (unpublished M.A. thesis, Manchester University, 1927), p. 79.

[3] *Gazette*, 18, 25 Jan., 1 Feb. 1817; Hay Scrapbooks, vii, pp. 148–9, 151; Wheeler, *History*, pp. 108–9; Wray Pamphlets, for letters and addresses, especially 'Manchester Political Register' Jan.–March 1817, Police Office resolutions (13 Jan. 1817), 'Petitioning Weavers Defended' 1817, and 'A Letter to the Inhabitants of Manchester' (21 Jan. 1817); *Exchange Herald*, 14, 21 Jan. 1817; *Chronicle*, 18 Jan., 22 Feb. 1817; *Mercury*, 14, 21 Jan., 4 Feb. 1817; Pitt Club, i, p. 73.

enfranchisement. The Blanket affair was soon followed by the so-called Ardwick Conspiracy. The local authorities convinced themselves that an insurrection was planned for 30 March. Arrests were made and suspects taken to London for secret examinations at the Home Office. Rumours circulated about entrapment by agents in the pay of the civil powers. When the 30 March passed off without incident, and all those arrested were later released without a single indictment or trial, it became clear that no plot had ever existed (at least not on the scale claimed by the Manchester authorities). Prentice reported at this time that all was quiet and would remain so if only the people were left alone. Some local Tories seemed to be convinced that Manchester was gripped by sedition and insurrectionary intentions, and this was one primary cause for a continuing propaganda battle in these months. The conservatives had some of their most effective spokesmen in local clergymen. Tory writers made regular use of the spectre of 'Jacobinism' in 1817 to recreate the conservative mentality of the 1790s and to ascribe un-English characteristics and intentions to the reformers.[4]

Revelations about the activities of spies reached epidemic proportions around the time of the Pentridge Rising in Derbyshire in June 1817. The *Gazette* called the trial and conviction of the Pentridge leaders 'a solitary example of success in the midst of the numerous attempts which have recently been made to prove the existence and to inflict the consequences of treasonable designs'. Prentice believed that it was largely due to the efforts of his circle that more damage was not done by spies and informers in Manchester. By putting workers on their guard the band ensured that there was no Pentridge-style conspiracy in the local area. The Tory press rejected

---

[4] *Gazette*, 15, 29 March, 5 April, 13, 20, 27 Sept. 1817; W. D. Evans (presiding magistrate), *Address . . . on discharging the prisoners apprehended on account of an illegal assembly at Manchester on 10 March 1817* (1817); Prentice, *Sketches*, pp. 92–102; Wheeler, *History*, pp, 110–11; Hay Scrapbooks, vii, pp. 160–83; Bamford, *Early Days*, pp. 317–63, and his *Passages in the Life of a Radical* (2 vols, 1844), i, chs. 6, 13–19, 23; *Chronicle*, 15, 29 March, 5, 12, 26 April, 3 May 1817; *Mercury*, 11, 18 March, 1, 8 April 1817; *Exchange Herald*, 4, 11, 18, 25 March, 8, 15, 22, 29 April, 10 June 1817; Revd C. D. Wray, *The Street Politicians* (1817), and *The Speech of Mr John P., schoolmaster, lately delivered before a crowded assembly of his neighbours, to take into consideration the Expediency of Parliamentary Reform* (1817); Revd C. W. Ethelston, *Patriotic Appeal to the Good Sense of all Parties* (1817); Revd M. Horne, *A Word for My Country* (1817).

the claims being made about spies and entrapment, and argued that Pentridge arose from revolutionary aims rather than provocation by government agents.[5] In the autumn of 1817 the *Gazette* ran a series of articles on parliamentary reform addressed 'To the Labouring Classes'. They were written by 'The Poor Man's Friend', who was probably one of the band. Its members were by now Cowdroy's chief assistants and contributors, and this was the kind of political essay writing at which they excelled. These pieces attacked the 'spy system' and asserted that the plebeian radicals would never involve themselves in revolutionary schemes. Such was the controversy created by the Ardwick Conspiracy, however, that it was deemed advisable for the radical leaders to cooperate with the authorities and put the public mind at rest. The author (or authors) of these addresses extolled the virtues of 'moderate' over 'revolutionary' change. Clearly the respectable reformers were keen to restrain the popular radicals and turn them away from extreme aims and methods. What was needed, declared the articles, was a respectful and conciliatory call for the correction of obvious abuses.[6]

The first *Gazette* of 1818 rejected the accounts of Manchester given by provincial and London Tory papers during 1817. They had singled the town out as a hotbed of treason, but the band now wanted to set the record straight. If events in Manchester had been the grounds for parliament's suspension of constitutional liberties, there were no grounds at all for such a suspension. The band opined that repression was unjustified and had more to do with the prejudices of those in authority locally and nationally than with alleged threats to order posed by plebeian radicals. With more calmness in Manchester, and the restoration of *habeas corpus* early in 1818, members of the band decided to act. They organised a petition to the Commons calling for a full inquiry into the events of the early part of 1817, and particularly into the conduct of the local authorities. This petition was presented by George Philips, previously active

[5] *Gazette*, 5, 19 July, 6 Sept., 1 Nov. 1817, 21 Feb., 14, 21 March 1818; Bamford, *Passages*, i, chs. 12, 24; Hay Scrapbooks, xi, pp. 130–40; Prentice, *Sketches*, chs. 6–7, p. 112; Kinsey, 'Aspects of Lancashire Radicalism', ch. 8 (a rather uncritical view of available documentary evidence, which upholds the reliability and value of informers' reports and doubts the reformers' claims about provocation and invention); *Chronicle*, 14, 28 June, 1 Nov. 1817; *Mercury*, 24 June, 1 July, 11 Nov. 1817; *Exchange Herald*, 17, 24 June, 4 Nov. 1817.

[6] *Gazette*, 20, 27 Sept., 4 Oct. 1817.

with the Manchester Constitutional Society in the 1790s, who was Whig M.P. for a succession of boroughs after 1812 under the patronage of the twelfth Duke of Norfolk, to whom he lent large sums of money. (He became a baronet in 1828.) The House of Commons refused to grant an inquiry. The petition had been signed by twenty-six of Manchester's leading respectable and middling sort reformers. There were only twenty-six of them because they had undertaken to spend time and money in urging and aiding an inquiry, and not all of their friends could make such an undertaking. Five of the band were signatories: Prentice, Baxter, Taylor, Shuttleworth and Harvey. Of the remaining signatories whose occupations can be traced there were six manufacturers, four merchants, two corn dealers and a coal dealer, an attorney, a hatter, a dyer, a calico printer and a commercial agent. The names of the Twenty Six were not given in the *Gazette* but they were posted in places of business by Tory opponents, a not-so-subtle suggestion that loyal friends of social order should not soil their hands by doing business with any critic of the local authorities. Some of Manchester's plebeian radicals were glad to hear of this effort by respectable liberals. The recently-established *Observer* commended Philips and the Twenty Six, and argued that the alarmism of 1817 had been wholly fatuous. The Tory papers were hostile, and listed the petitioners in an attempt to create feeling against them and discourage them and others from similar activities in the future. But Prentice and the others were not put off; indeed their indignation made them even more determined to press for justice and redress. They were outraged when Tory Lancashire M.P. John Blackburne (of Hale Hall) told the Commons that the Twenty Six were not respectable men. 'To have any sympathy, then, with the poverty-stricken multitude', Prentice wrote, 'was to forfeit all claim to the name of gentleman'.[7]

The respectable reformers were soon expressing more protests when it was found that the government had proposed an indemnity bill to excuse ministers and local authorities from responsibility for actions they took in 1817 while constitutional rights were suspended.

---

[7] *Gazette*, 3 Jan., 7, 14 Feb., 7 March 1818; Prentice, *Sketches*, pp. 122–7, 129–31; Potter Collection, xi, pp. 9–10; Hay Scrapbooks, viii, pp. 30, 43–4, 48–9; Howe, *Cotton Masters*, pp. 91–2 on George Philips, and see also chapter I section (2) above; *Pigot and Dean Directory*, 1818, for the occupations of the Twenty Six; *Observer*, 14 Feb. 1818; *Chronicle*, 21, 28 Feb., 14 March 1818; *Mercury*, 24 Feb., 3 March 1818; *Exchange Herald*, 3 March 1818.

The *Gazette* repeated that there had been no grounds for these actions, and again the respectable reformers attempted to use the force of moral protest to strengthen their position and win more support for 'rational and necessary' reforms. But they remained anxious to restrain the popular radicals from unwise courses; hence their lack of enthusiasm for the St Peter's Field meeting of 9 March 1818. Those involved with the *Gazette* argued that a meeting was not appropriate at this time. The subsequent 'REMARKS, By one of the Twenty Six Petitioners' (signed 'B', probably Edward Baxter) urged the plebeians to keep within the strict bounds of propriety. The 'Remarks' also pointed out that extremism only gave an excuse for repressive policies, harmed the cause of reform, and dissuaded respectable liberals from coming forward and taking the leading role for which they were fitted. These were becoming familiar and oft-repeated arguments, and once again they demonstrated equivocation in the ranks of Manchester's respectable reformers.[8] The Tory papers continued to attack both plebeian radicals and respectable reformers, and the Pitt Club went on with its dinners, meetings and anti-reform pronouncements, but the 1818 general election did give the reformers another opportunity to reflect on the faults of the representative system. The *Gazette* condemned the electoral control exercised by such landed families as the Tory Lowthers in Westmorland, while Taylor and others worked on behalf of the reform-minded Lord Sefton in Liverpool (who was unsuccessful). All reformers lamented the continued lack of contests in the county of Lancashire, where the representation had long been shared by the Stanleys and the Tory interests.[9]

Members of the band continued to progress in standing and influence, however. The trial of Taylor for libel was significant in this respect, and represents an important event in the liberals' rise to a higher public profile and a more assertive role in local affairs. The matter began in the summer of 1818 at a meeting of the Salford police commissioners. Taylor was proposed for a minor office, but his name was rejected by one John Greenwood, a quilt and muslin

[8] *Gazette*, 14 March 1818; Hay Scrapbooks, viii, pp. 44, 48; *Observer*, 14 March 1818.

[9] *Chronicle*, 14 March 1818; *Mercury*, 10, 24 March 1818; *Exchange Herald*, 10 March, 21 April 1818; Pitt Club, i (entries for 1817–18); Hay Scrapbooks, vii, pp. 367, 376–9, viii, pp. 31, 33; *Gazette*, 4 April, 6, 13, 20 June, 4 July 1818; *Observer*, 27 June 1818.

manufacturer, member of the Pitt Club and a stalwart of the local government oligarchy. Greenwood said that Taylor was a radical and the author of the placard 'Now or Never' which, according to local Tories, had caused the Exchange Riot of April 1812. Taylor demanded that Greenwood explain this accusation, but repeated requests were unavailing and so he publicly castigated Greenwood as a 'liar, slanderer and scoundrel'. Taylor's stand demonstrated the reformers' readiness to defend their cause and to protest against discrimination on the grounds of political opinions. They were probably aware, moreover, that if the matter achieved notoriety it could serve as a useful rallying point. Greenwood and the Tories aimed to teach the reformers a lesson, but this strategy failed when the libel trial at Lancaster in March 1819 resulted in Taylor's acquittal, a victory that bred increased confidence.[10]

The *Gazette* began 1819 by reminding its readers of the activities of Thomas Walker and the Constitutional Society in the 1790s, and praised that body for its heroic attempt to lead and coordinate an energetic campaign for reform.[11] But the *Gazette* was wary about the proliferation and character of the workers' reform meetings during the summer of 1819. The band and its allies mistrusted independent working-class political activity, and doubted that reform of the kind desired by some extremists could bring an automatic remedy to economic distress, as some were claiming. They were also concerned, as usual, that plebeian assertiveness might harm the cause of reform and frighten away respectable, propertied men who would otherwise be keen to participate in a responsible and well-conducted campaign. As the *Gazette* put it:

> It is impossible to regard without deep commiseration the sufferings of our manufacturing population, arising from the inadequate wages and the scarcity of labour; and our pity for them is augmented by perceiving that they are pursuing measures which will infallibly aggravate their distress. It must be obvious to anyone who can reason at all, that the interference of the labouring classes in political matters has almost

[10] *Gazette*, 25 July 1818, 3 April 1819; Prentice, *Sketches*, ch. 9; *Observer*, 3 April 1819; *Chronicle*, 31 Oct. 1818, 10 April 1819; *Mercury*, 4 Aug. 1818; *Trial of Mr J. E. Taylor*, especially Taylor's preface pp. 3–10, and speech to the jury pp. 15–23. See also chapter II section (2) above.

[11] e.g. *Gazette*, 13 Feb., 20 March 1819.

invariably an effect contrary to that which is intended. Harsh
as it may appear, we must say that poverty incapacitates for
public usefulness, for the poor man has no influence otherwise
than by the exertion of physical strength, to which it would be
absurd as well as treasonable to have recourse . . . We can
account for the apathy of the rich in the cause of reform, which
it is most palpably *their own interest* to obtain, no otherwise
than by supposing that it originates in an undefined fear of the
designs of the poor.[12]

The Tory press condemned the mass reform meetings of 1819. On
9 July a police office meeting established a new Committee to
Strengthen the Civil Power, and recommended the swearing in of
extra constables. Advertisements soon appeared encouraging volunteers to join armed associations. The local magistrates approved of
this, as did the Tory papers. Another aspect of anti-radical activity
was the continuing campaign against the *Observer*. Its conductors
faced indictments for libel and fines for failure to meet stamp charges
in the spring and summer of 1819, but the *Observer* continued its
coverage of workers' meetings and advocacy of the radical cause.[13]
The Peterloo meeting of 16 August 1819 took place in this period of
mounting panic and bellicosity. The rival groups in the struggle,
radicals and anti-reformers, seemed to feel that a decisive coup was
needed to tip the balance in their favour, and confrontation of some
kind was desired and expected by the more uncompromising elements on both sides.

The crucial question after Peterloo was: who were the aggressors?
For the *Gazette* the aggressors did not come from the ranks of the
reformers but from the holders and allies of civil authority. Although
the regular troops had displayed 'coolness and comparative moderation', the Manchester and Salford Yeomanry had '*charged* up to the
hustings' (my emphasis) and the officers effecting the arrests had
subjected Hunt in particular to unjustifiable mistreatment. Clearly
the peace had been broken by those who ordered yeomanry and then
regular cavalry into the crowd. This was the position taken up by

---

[12] *Gazette*, 19 June 1819.
[13] *Chronicle*, 26 June, 3, 10, 17, 24, 31 July 1819; *Exchange Herald*, 22 June,
13 July, 10 Aug. 1819; *Gazette*, 17, 24, 31 July, 7, 21 Aug. 1819; Hay
Scrapbooks, xi, p. 190; J.R.L., English Ms. 1197/3, 9; *Mercury*, 13, 20, 27 July
1819; *Observer*, 13, 27 Feb., 8 May, 3, 10, 17, 24 July, 7, 14 Aug. 1819.

reform newspapers and protest meetings all over the country, of course, and the *Gazette* devoted a good deal of space to this press and platform activity over the following weeks.[14]

This 'radical version' of Peterloo was energetically disseminated by Prentice. His *Sketches* explain that he and Taylor wrote reports of the meeting and sent them to the London papers to take the place of the account John Tyas (of *The Times* of London) would have sent had he not been arrested on the hustings. Robert Walmsley has pointed out with some justification that Taylor's view of Peterloo mellowed over time. In effect there were two Taylors, says Walmsley, an imperfectly-informed one who believed the radical version and a better-informed one who did not. It is also interesting that Taylor never admitted that he had sent a report to London, nor claimed that anything he had written on Peterloo was ever used by the London papers. It must have been Prentice's report that appeared in *The Times* of London, telling of an unlawful attack on a peaceful crowd. Prentice said that Tyas later corroborated this report, but in fact Tyas stated that the crowd parted to let the cavalry through, while in Prentice's account the cavalry charged into the crowd. It is also important to remember that Tyas was an eyewitness and Prentice was not; nor was Taylor. By Prentice's own account he had slipped away from the meeting intending to return later, and it was during his absence that the yeomanry arrived on the scene. Then again, Tyas was on the hustings and possibly did not have the best of vantage points. He can only have seen part of the crowd. Another significant matter is the enmity that developed between Taylor and Prentice from the mid-1820s. It had various causes, but it could be that a disagreement over the authenticity of the radical version of Peterloo was one of them. Even if Walmsley is correct in assuming that Prentice's account of Peterloo was and is misleading, however, there can be no doubt as to the validity of Prentice's view of the underlying factors behind the 'massacre'. The real problem was a total absence of sympathy and understanding between the authorities and reformers, and none of the local magistrates was acquainted with the real condition and opinion of the labouring ranks. However unreliable Prentice might be on the events of 16 August themselves,

[14] *Gazette*, 21, 28 Aug., 4, 11 Sept. 1819. The idea of wilful wounding is supported by evidence in M. & W. Bee, 'The Casualties of Peterloo', *M.R.H.R.*, 3 (1989), pp. 45–6. For the yeomanry's and magistrates' version of events, see narrative and reports in English Ms. 1197/26, 67, 86, 89.

moreover, he is certainly accurate in his estimation of the effect Peterloo had on many respectable Manchester reformers:

> It was the breaking up of a great frost. The middle classes had appeared as if they were bound up in the icy chains of indifference to the demands of their humble fellow-countrymen for their fair share of representation; but the sudden outburst showed that whatever opinions they might hold as to how far the elective franchise might be safely extended, they were not disposed quietly to witness death inflicted on men whose only crime had been that they asked for universal suffrage, vote by ballot, annual parliaments, and the repeal of the corn laws.

This is a highly suggestive analysis and reflects some of Prentice's strongest views on reform, especially the desirability of some class cooperation and the need for active middle-class involvement in any reform campaign, in the form of rational and respectable leadership.[15]

The band played a prominent role in the evolution and dissemination of the radical version. Prentice was one of the most uncompromising writers on Peterloo, and even claimed that the assault on a peaceful crowd had been planned beforehand. Shuttleworth's account survives in the form of the evidence he gave at Hunt's trial and during the case of *Redford v. Birley*. He was an eyewitness, and as firm in his belief in the radical version as his friend Prentice. Shuttleworth was active in the aftermath of Peterloo, corresponding with reformers around the country and keeping in almost constant communication with H. G. Bennet, the liberal Whig M.P. for Shrewsbury and one of the band's parliamentary contacts. He provided Bennet with much information on Manchester affairs, some of which was used by Bennet and also by Henry Brougham and Lord Holland during the parliamentary debates on Peterloo. It is not clear if Watkin was an eyewitness, but he certainly believed that the yeomanry had charged a peaceful crowd. Before Taylor's later retreat from the radical version he gave it forceful backing in his *Notes and*

---

[15] Prentice, *Sketches*, pp. 152, 157, 159, 163, 166. Walmsley's views are best followed in his *Peterloo. The Case Reopened*, chs. 15, 16, 19, 27, 28; but see also his two unpublished pieces 'Peterloo Magistrate', pp. 203, 225, 234, 237, 300; 'The Peterloo Reopener and his Critics', pp. 9–10, 32–3, 35, 54–5. On the general breakdown of communications between the Manchester authorities and the local populace before Peterloo, Bohstedt, *Riots and Community Politics*, chs. 3–7.

Observations of 1820, though (as has been noted) he was not an eyewitness. Smith, who was present, stressed at the time and long afterwards that the crowd had been peaceful and that aggression came from the cavalry. The attorney Atkinson does not seem to have been an eyewitness, but he did take part in the post-Peterloo protests and was also in touch with Hunt. Atkinson's reputation as a reformer who had given legal advice to and represented other reformers in the past prompted Hunt to write to him for assistance on 17 August 1819. Atkinson was prevented from seeing Hunt by the magistrates, and could not wait in Manchester because he had to go on business elsewhere.[16]

The respectable reformers' main concern in the aftermath of Peterloo was to utilise the local sense of grievance and so strengthen their own position *vis-a-vis* their Tory opponents. Controversy followed the Star Inn resolutions of Thursday 19 August, which thanked and commended the town officers, yeomanry, special constables, magistrates and military for their conduct at Peterloo. The reformers rightly claimed that these were not the sentiments of the town but proceeded from a closed and unrepresentative assembly of partisans, summoned by circulars sent around to carefully selected persons. The *Gazette* had first-hand information from Smith, who had been in attendance at the Star Inn by accident or design, and who did not approve of what had been resolved.[17] While the respectable

[16] Prentice, *Sketches*, pp. 157, 159–60; Shuttleworth Scrapbook, loose leaves for correspondence on Peterloo, especially letters to Shuttleworth from J. Lowe of London, 1 Sept. 1819, J. Strutt of Derby, 19 Aug. 1819, T. Preston of Ambleside, 7 Nov. 1819, G. Young of Shrewsbury, 27 Sept., 6, 10 Oct., 18, 22, 26 Nov. 1819, 6 March 1820, and H. G. Bennet M.P., 2, 21 Oct., 3, 15, 18, 19, 25, 26, 27, 30 Nov., 1, 2, 4, 6, 9, 15, 16, 27 Dec. 1819, 30 Jan., 6 April 1820; *The Trial of Henry Hunt esq. (and others) for an alleged conspiracy . . . at the York Lent Assizes*, 1820, published by T. Dolby (1820), pp. 198–204; Report of the Proceedings in the cause Redford v. Birley and others . . . at Lancaster. Taken from the shorthand notes of Mr Farquharson (1822), pp. 153–63; Watkin, *Journal*, pp. 78–9; Taylor, *Notes and Observations*, especially pp. 164–84 which focus on the Peterloo meeting itself; Smith, Reminiscences, pp. 15–19, Memoranda and Letters, pp. 4–5, and Parliamentary Elections, pp. 2–8; Bruton, *Three Accounts of Peterloo*, pp. 59–74; Archives Dept. M.C.L., BR 942. 73071 for the Hunt-Atkinson correspondence: Hunt to Atkinson, 17 Aug. 1819, Atkinson to James Norris (stipendiary magistrate), 18 Aug. 1819, and Atkinson to Hunt, 19 Aug. 1819.

[17] *Gazette*, 21 Aug. 1819; English Ms. 1197/93; Smith, Reminiscences, pp. 19–20.

reformers began to conduct energetic protest activity, attempting to win converts and direct opinion into anti-establishment channels, the Tory papers gave excuses and explanations for recent events, praising and defending the conduct of the military and civil authorities. The radical *Observer* was as indignant about Peterloo as the *Gazette*.[18]

The Star Inn resolutions prompted members of the band into a more decisive gesture. Early in September they and their allies issued the *Declaration and Protest*. This was composed by Watkin and received over 4,800 signatures, including those of men who had never before involved themselves in local politics. Among the earliest signatures were those of Baxter, Harvey, Shuttleworth, Taylor, Richard Potter, Atkinson and Prentice. The *Declaration and Protest* stated that the Peterloo meeting was 'perfectly peaceable', that if the riot act had been read it was done so 'privately or without the knowledge of the great body of the meeting', that 'unexpected and unnecessary violence' had been used to disperse the assembly, that the Star Inn proceedings were 'exclusively private' and that 'no expression of dissent from the main object of the meeting was there permitted'. Two meetings followed the publication of the *Declaration and Protest*, both chaired by Baxter. The first approved the document and the second established a subscription fund to relieve the Peterloo wounded. The committee appointed at this second meeting included Baxter, Harvey, Prentice, Brotherton, Taylor, Shuttleworth and Richard Potter.[19] The most obvious immediate effects of Peterloo, therefore, were to encourage the band to confirm its position at the head of Manchester's respectable reformers, and to enable it to make use of the growing number of sympathisers who had previously been lacking but who had now been made available by the spread of moral outrage after 16 August. Members of the band took advantage of these circumstances to enhance their local credibility and standing. Aside from tactical considerations, they also believed in what they were fighting for. Their commitment, courage

[18] *Chronicle*, 7, 14, 21, 28 Aug., 4, 18, 25 Sept. 1819; *Exchange Herald*, 10, 17, 24, 31 Aug., 14, 28 Sept., 12 Oct., 16, 23 Nov. 1819; *Mercury*, 3, 10, 17, 24 Aug., 21, 28 Sept., 12 Oct., 9 Nov. 1819; *Observer*, 7, 14, 21, 28 Aug., 4, 11, 18, 25 Sept. 1819.

[19] Prentice, *Sketches*, pp. 164–5; Watkin, *Fragment No. 1*, p. 19; a copy of the *Declaration and Protest* can be found in Archives Dept. M.C.L.; *Gazette*, 21 Aug., 4, 11 Sept., 4 Dec. 1819; Hay Scrapbooks, ix. 169; Smith, Reminiscences, pp. 20–2.

and honesty made their protests and demands that much more persuasive, and since their own preferences were for rational ends and respectable means, this also helped them to appeal more successfully to an expanding constituency of potential supporters.

The main requirement was to keep the momentum going. The *Gazette* continued to discuss the meetings being held across the kingdom, and to encourage attempts to have the aggressors at Peterloo identified and punished. These attempts, however, met with little success. Even when precise accusations could be made against certain individuals for 'cutting and maiming', the magistrates argued that the cases were not strong enough for the granting of warrants. The reformers were also angered by the obstruction of the Oldham inquest on the body of John Lees, a Peterloo victim. This inquest was repeatedly adjourned and then finally discontinued in December 1819 because of a technical irregularity. The coroner and the jury had not inspected the corpse together at the same time. It was claimed that the coroner and his superiors would have used any excuse to stop the inquest.[20] By mid-November the respectable reformers were ready to organise another formal expression of representative Manchester opinion. This was to be a direct appeal to the House of Commons for an inquiry into what had happened at Peterloo. The *Gazette* backed the move and the petition lay for signature in Cowdroy's office for about a fortnight. It was presented by H. G. Bennet on 29 November.[21] Like the *Declaration and Protest* it was a forceful and precise exposition of the views of the respectable reformers. As with their other efforts, though, it did not achieve its main object. There was no inquiry. But at least the band had created and perpetuated a protest movement, and had gained valuable experience in the arts of political campaigning and challenging the holders of local and national power. The attack on the ministers was particularly heated in November and December 1819 at the time of the parliamentary debates on Peterloo and the measures that were to become known as the 'Six Acts'. Prentice's *Sketches* suggest that the main effect of the post-Peterloo reaction was to make radicalism more thoughtful and deliberative. The silencing of the

[20] *Gazette*, 11, 18, 25 Sept., 2, 9, 16, 23, 30 Oct., 6, 13, 20, 27 Nov., 4, 11, 18, 31 Dec. 1819, 8 Jan. 1820; Prentice, *Sketches*, pp. 174–5; English Ms. 1197/79, 80; Bamford, *Passages*, ii, ch. 5; G. Young to Shuttleworth, 27 Sept., 1, 6, 10 Oct. 1819, in Shuttleworth Scrapbook, loose leaves.
[21] *Gazette*, 20, 27 Nov., 4 Dec. 1819.

extremists gave respectable middle-class men an interval of calm in which they could quietly consider the defects of the representative system undisturbed by agitation.[22] There is probably some truth in this, though Prentice wrote in 1850 in the knowledge that the reformers had eventually been successful. In 1819–20 he and his friends could not have been so sanguine.

Soon the Tory cotton master Francis Philips, a prominent member of the Pitt Club and the local ruling party, had published a twopenny pamphlet in defence of the local authorities and their conduct at Peterloo. The *Gazette* found it 'most licentious', but the most effective reply was Taylor's *Notes and Observations*, published early in 1820. Praise for Taylor's work came from near and far. It consisted of more than 200 pages of clear analysis, justification, explanation and refutation, and was dedicated to H. G. Bennet. Taylor had written a coherent and detailed account of Peterloo, its background and aftermath which, though biased, was also persuasive. Certainly many reformers were glad that their case had now been put with such skill and clarity. Shuttleworth urged Bennet to read the work. Bennet promised he would do so, and discuss it with Brougham and other allies. Meanwhile the Tory papers praised Philips's pamphlet, and also approved of the promotion of the Revd W. R. Hay, chairman of the Salford Quarter Sessions, to the living of Rochdale. The reformers argued that this was a reward for Hay's role at Peterloo and his consistent service against the cause of progress. In the Pitt Club it was business as usual. At the eighth annual dinner in May 1820 all the familiar speeches and toasts were made, but they took on a new significance because this was the first annual gathering since Peterloo.[23]

In the spring of 1820 attention turned to Hunt's trial at York. The *Gazette* devoted more than 23 columns to the trial over three weeks in March and April. Despite a 'brilliant defence' Hunt and the local radical leaders tried with him were convicted of unlawful assembly.

[22] Prentice, *Sketches*, pp. 178, 199–200.
[23] F. Philips, *An Exposure of the Calumnies circulated by the Enemies of Social Order* (1819); *Gazette*, 5 Feb. 1820; Bennet to Shuttleworth, 30 Jan. 1820, Shuttleworth Scrapbook, loose leaves; Hay Scrapbooks, x, pp. 12, 19–20; *Chronicle*, 27 Nov. 1819, 8, 22 Jan. 1820, 28 Sept. 1822; *Mercury*, 4, 18 Jan. 1820, 24 Sept. 1822; *Exchange Herald*, 4 Jan. 1820, 1 Oct. 1822. On Hay see also *Gazette*, 4 Dec. 1819, 8 Jan. 1820; Prentice, *Sketches*, p. 178; J. M. Wilson, *The Vicars of Rochdale* (1905), pp. 59–60; Axon, *Annals of Manchester*, p. 158. On the Pitt Club see Pitt Club, ii, entry for Exchange dinner and toasts, 29 May 1820.

Bennet emphasised to Shuttleworth that the verdict did not necessarily mean that the Peterloo meeting itself had been illegal, only that
Hunt and others had acted illegally. No doubt this was of some
comfort to the band, and provided a justification for continuing
protests. Manchester Tories were naturally satisfied with the way the
trial had gone, while the radical *Observer* had expected an acquittal
and was shocked by the verdict.[24]

It has been suggested that the York verdict owed more to outside
factors than to the evidence itself, and that the verdict was not
particularly unwelcome, even to some reform-minded people.[25] The
latter point is interesting. Perhaps some of Manchester's respectable
liberals were glad that Hunt had been removed from the scene for a
while. They may have believed that this would be better for the cause
of reform and better for the kind of reform campaign that they, as
men of property and standing, wanted to conduct. In any case,
Hunt's trial provided an opportunity for the further dissemination
of the radical version of Peterloo. Shuttleworth was called as a
witness on the sixth day. His evidence stressed that nothing about
the coming together of the Peterloo crowd could have excited alarm
about the safety of Manchester, that Hunt's language had been
moderate, and that the people did nothing to resist the yeomanry as
the latter tried to ride up to the hustings.[26]

Meanwhile the band was making difficulties for the local government oligarchy at leypayers' meetings, questioning the authorities'
conduct in the second half of 1819, objecting to financial burdens
relating to the quartering of extra troops in Manchester, and advocating the rejection of expenses incurred by loyalist meetings. The
troops were unnecessary and had been used improperly, said Taylor,
Baxter and Richard Potter, while the loyalist meetings had been
private, party affairs for which the public funds should not have been
used.[27] Another way of keeping these issues before the townspeople

[24] *Gazette*, 25 March, 1, 8 April 1820; Prentice, *Sketches*, pp. 180–92; Bamford, *Passages*, ii, chs. 12–30; Bennet to Shuttleworth, 6 April 1820, Shuttleworth Scrapbook, loose leaves; *Chronicle*, 18, 25 March, 1 April 1820;
Exchange Herald, 28 March, 4 April 1820; *Mercury*, 14, 21, 28 March, 4 April
1820; *Observer*, 18, 25 March, 1, 8 April, 20 May 1820.
[25] L. Webley, *Across the Atlantic: eight comparable episodes treated from the
legal aspect in the history of Britain and the U. S. A* (1960), p. 275.
[26] *Trial of Hunt*, pp. 198–204.
[27] e.g. see reports of meeting of 31 May 1820 in *Gazette*, 3 June 1820, and
Exchange Herald, 6 June 1820.

was to give constant reminders of the need for an inquiry into Peterloo. The *Gazette* often did this in the early 1820s, as did the new *Guardian*.[28] Some of the band were given the freedom of the city of Nottingham in 1820 and 1821, in recognition of their efforts to gain redress for Peterloo. Taylor, Baxter, Smith, Atkinson and Richard Potter gained this mark of respect.[29]

Another attempt to apportion blame for Peterloo and to gain redress for the innocent victims of aggression came in April 1822 with the trial of *Redford v. Birley and others*. Thomas Redford, a journeyman hatter wounded at Peterloo, brought an action for assault against the yeomanry commander, H. H. Birley, and three other yeomen (Withington, Meagher and Oliver), and the case was heard at Lancaster between 4–9 April 1822. The *Gazette* of 13 April gave the trial seven and a half columns (nearly a third of all available space), and relished the chance to discuss Peterloo again. But the *Gazette* was not too surprised by the outcome, a victory for the defendants (whose costs were paid by the Tory government). Hunt and the *Observer* denounced the trial as a sham, and condemned the prosecution for being so ineffectual. Richard Potter blamed the lack of funds and the difficulty in getting witnesses to attend. In the *Guardian* Taylor argued that many people connected with Peterloo were afraid of having their conduct properly investigated, but he also claimed that the trial harmed the cause it was supposed to help. It was ill-timed and ill-directed. (Here, perhaps, was an early sign that Taylor was beginning to reassess his earlier attitude towards Peterloo, as Walmsley suggests.) The Tory papers thought the outcome laudable. The evidence given by Shuttleworth on the second day of the trial is of special interest. His Lancaster statement was basically the same as the one he had given at Hunt's trial, but he did say things that he had not said at York. He suggested that there might have been a plan behind the yeomanry's manoeuvres, and he was certain that the horsemen had struck out at the crowd on their way to the hustings. Walmsley, who thinks the jury came to the correct verdict, emphasises that Shuttleworth was the only witness to say that there was striking and cutting on the way to the hustings, and points out that this was contradicted by other witnesses. But this does not necessarily mean that Shuttleworth was wrong. Walmsley also says

---

[28] *Gazette*, 19 Aug. 1820, 19 May 1821; *Guardian*, 9, 16 May 1821.
[29] Potter Collection, iii, p. 283; Smith, Memoranda and Letters, p. 3; Atkinson Papers, M177/7, letter from Town Clerk of Nottingham, 1821.

that Prentice left *Redford v. Birley* out of his *Sketches* because he knew it would weaken the radical version of Peterloo. There is no way of knowing if this is true. As for Shuttleworth's remarks, these were made two years after Hunt's trial at York, and two and a half years after Peterloo. If we accept the accuracy of Shuttleworth's memory we still face the problem of why he had not said these things at York. One explanation is that he was not asked the kind of questions at York that he was asked at Lancaster, so his answers were bound to be different. It could also be true that the upholders of the radical version felt the need to be more definite, insistent and precise by the time of *Redford v. Birley* in view of their failure, so far, to gain any real redress for the events of 16 August 1819. Shuttleworth admitted that he had refreshed his memory by looking at his York evidence before he testified in *Redford v. Birley*. Now he went beyond his York evidence, and when cross-examined he made his position as clear as possible, and as favourable to the radical version as possible.[30]

After *Redford v. Birley* the campaign to set right the wrongs done at Peterloo became far more intermittent and lacklustre. Plebeian radicalism was not as strong as it had been, and the respectable reformers were preoccupied with other matters. Peterloo was still discussed in the *Gazette* and occasionally in the *Guardian*, but less often than before. Under Prentice the *Gazette* and then the *Times* were never to mention Birley or the magistrates Hay and Hulton, or any of the other chief villains, without reminding readers of their association with Peterloo. But the 'massacre' did not become an issue again until the reform crisis of 1831–32. As the Reform Bill made its way through parliament, and as reformers of all shades were looking for arguments to strengthen their own position and discredit that of their opponents, the causes and results of Peterloo became useful for morale and propaganda purposes.[31] At the end of 1831, controversy was aroused by Viscount Althorp, when he made unfavourable comments in public about the conduct of the authorities at Peterloo.

[30] *Gazette*, 1 Dec. 1821, 13 April 1822; Hay Scrapbooks, xi, p. 158; Axon, *Annals of Manchester*, pp. 163, 165; Wheeler, *History*, p. 121; *Observer*, 6 April 1822; Potter Collection, xi, p. 25; *Guardian*, 1 Dec. 1821, 16 Feb., 6, 13, 20 April 1822; *Chronicle*, 16 Feb., 6 April, 4 May 1822; *Exchange Herald*, 9, 16 April, 14 May 1822; *Mercury*, 16 April 1822; *Report of Redford v. Birley*, pp. 153–63; Walmsley, 'Peterloo Magistrate', pp. 186, 383.
[31] e.g. *Times*, 20 Aug. 1831; *Voice*, 20 Aug. 1831.

William Hulton, who had presided over the magistrates at Peterloo, protested and later resigned his commission of the peace. Francis Philips, author of the *Exposure* in 1819, also protested against Althorp's comments. Soon Prentice was discussing the affair, as were others in the band. The Tory papers regretted Hulton's resignation and accused Althorp of inappropriate conduct.[32] Prentice brought the Peterloo saga before his readers again in March 1832 when Hunt (now M.P. for Preston) introduced an unsuccessful motion into the Commons for an inquiry into the 'massacre'. Prentice repeated the opinion he had often expressed in the past: the lapse of time was no excuse for refusing an inquiry, and the offenders of 16 August 1819 should not be allowed to remain unpunished. Taylor disagreed. Perhaps this was another sign that his views on Peterloo had changed. The *Guardian* did not approve of Hunt's call for an inquiry so long after the event, and doubted that any advantage could come of a re-agitation of the question. The *Chronicle* opposed Hunt's motion, and the *Courier* asserted that the responsibility for the deaths and injuries at Peterloo would always rest with those who had made the interference of the authorities necessary.[33]

The early and mid-1820s saw members of the band continue their efforts to inform and direct local opinion on the matter of parliamentary reform. Manchester's liberals were swimming against the tide for much of the time, but they were rising in individual confidence and group assertiveness. Their determination and perseverance ensured their advance as principal actors on the Manchester political stage. Sometimes they could do nothing positive and had to rely on protest and complaint. On meeting the tenth duke of Hamilton in 1820, Prentice complained to this nobleman that he and his Whig friends were too cautious and should identify themselves more closely with the cause of reform. At this time Prentice was advocating the abolition of rotten boroughs, a transfer of seats, shorter parliaments and an extension of the suffrage. He wanted franchise qualifications that would bestow the vote on 'the intelligence of the county' and go beyond the payment of direct taxes. Meanwhile Richard Potter complained that of the 658 members of the House of

---

[32] *Times*, 24, 31 Dec. 1831, 14 Jan. 1832; Brotherton Scrapbooks, xi, pp. 40–1; *Guardian*, 24, 31 Dec. 1831; Potter Collection, xi, p. 87; *Chronicle*, 24 Dec. 1831; *Courier*, 12 Nov. 1831.

[33] *Times*, 24 March 1832; *Guardian*, 18 Feb., 24 March 1832; *Chronicle*, 24 March 1832; *Courier*, 18 Feb., 24 March 1832.

Commons, 307 were returned by only 154 borough proprietors. The Grampound affair was a disappointment to the band because, inevitably, it did not represent the first stage in a programme of sweeping reform. The matter aroused interest in Manchester because there was a chance that the seats might be given to the Hundreds of Salford and Blackburn. In the end they went to augment the representation of the county of Yorkshire. Some local Tories were prepared to accept such cautious, piecemeal improvements, but the *Gazette* and *Guardian* were disgusted.[34]

At the time of the Cato Street Conspiracy the *Gazette* discussed the role of spies and emphasised that Manchester men had nothing to do with Arthur Thistlewood and his party of extremists. The *Exchange Herald* was not so sure while the radical *Observer*, though not approving of revolutionary designs, stated that violence was bound to increase in reaction to misrule and oppression.[35] During the Queen Caroline controversy the band attacked the government for its high-handed and irresponsible course, and also condemned the town officers for rejecting requests for a public meeting. This did not dissuade the band from giving the townspeople an opportunity to air their views, though, and Baxter chaired a meeting in the manor court room on 4 December 1820. Taylor, Richard Potter and Shuttleworth were the main speakers. In the summer of 1821 Baxter and Potter objected to the organisation of civic celebrations to mark George IV's coronation, pointing to the way the queen had been mistreated, and at a parish meeting in October 1821 the band opposed the customary vote of thanks to the outgoing town officers on the grounds that they had denied the townspeople an official meeting to discuss the queen's trial.[36] The queen's staunchest supporters in Manchester were the plebeian radicals and the men behind the

---

[34] Prentice, *Sketches*, pp. 172–4; Potter Collection, xi, p. 18; *Gazette*, 18 Dec. 1819, 27 May, 17 June 1820; *Exchange Herald*, 21 Dec. 1819, 20 Feb. 1821; *Mercury*, 22 May 1821; *Guardian*, 7 July 1821.

[35] *Gazette*, 26 Feb., 4, 11 March, 6, 13, 27 May 1820; *Exchange Herald*, 29 Feb., 7 March, 25 April 1820; *Observer*, 26 Feb. 1820.

[36] *Gazette*, 17, 24 June, 8 July, 19, 26 Aug., 2, 9 Sept., 7, 21 Oct., 4, 11, 18, 25 Nov., 2, 9, 16, 23 Dec. 1820, 27 Jan., 30 June, 14, 21, 28 July, 27 Oct. 1821; Hay Scrapbooks, x, pp. 179, 183, xi, p. 15; Hadfield, Personal Narrative, pp. 66–7; Brotherton Scrapbooks, ii, pp. 18–20; Watkin, *Journal*, pp. 81–3; Potter Collection, xi, pp. 26–7; Shuttleworth Scrapbook, p. 11; *Guardian*, 7 July, 11, 18, 25 Aug., 3 Nov. 1821; Prentice, *Sketches*, pp. 216–18.

Observer. The Tories were critical of Queen Caroline and her allies, and keen to demonstrate their loyalty to king and ministry.[37]

To the reformers the use of, and access to, printed matter was absolutely essential if they were to make any progress in the fight for political justice. The 'free press' remained an ideal to be jealously guarded against all encroachment. In the early and mid-1820s members of the band were active in this sphere. The *Gazette* was subjected to a libel accusation in May 1820. Atkinson rendered legal assistance and in the end no indictment was forthcoming.[38] More serious were the activities of the Constitutional Association, a body designed to harass and prosecute radical publications and writers. Local Tories welcomed this but the band's circle and the *Gazette*, *Guardian* and *Observer* were extremely alarmed and hostile. Members of the band came to the assistance of several newsmen, booksellers and pamphleteers in this period, notably David Ridgeway of Manchester and Joseph Swann of Macclesfield.[39]

The *Gazette* and *Guardian* kept parliamentary reform before Mancunians with articles and comment, and also gave coverage to the reform proposals submitted in parliament. There was enthusiasm for J. G. Lambton's unsuccessful scheme of April 1821 for triennial elections, a franchise including all copyholders, leaseholders, resident householders and payers of direct taxes, and the redrawing of constituency boundaries in England and Wales. Two years later the

---

[37] *Observer*, 5 Feb., 1 April, 10, 24 June, 1 July, 2, 9, 16 Sept., 14 Oct., 18, 25 Nov., 2, 9, 16 Dec. 1820, 13, 27 Jan., 3, 10 Feb. 1821; Revd M. Horne, *The Political and Moral Crisis of England* (1820), pp. 22–7; *Chronicle*, 2, 9, 30 Sept., 18, 25 Nov., 9, 16, 23 Dec. 1820; *Exchange Herald*, 13, 27 June, 25 July, 8 Aug., 14, 28 Nov., 12, 19 Dec. 1820, 9, 30 Jan., 20 Feb., 3 July, 14, 21 Aug., 30 Oct. 1821; *Mercury*, 14 March, 25 July, 19 Sept., 21, 28 Nov., 5, 19 Dec. 1820, 13 March, 15 May, 3 July 1821.

[38] The report in question concerned the conduct of the local military commander. *Gazette*, 29 April, 6 May 1820; *Mercury*, 9 May 1820; Leary, *Periodical Press*, p. 144.

[39] *Chronicle*, 15 Jan. 1820, 13 Jan., 26 May 1821, 9 March, 31 Aug. 1822; *Mercury*, 11, 18 Jan. 1820, 8 May 1821; *Exchange Herald*, 29 May, 3 July 1821; *Gazette*, 12 May, 2 June, 4 Aug., 27 Oct., 17 Nov. 1821, 15 May, 24 July 1824; *Guardian*, 5 May, 9 June, 28 July, 22 Sept. 1821, 11 Feb., 9 March, 31 Aug. 1822, 15, 22 May, 26 June, 17 July 1824; *Observer*, 20 Oct., 14 Sept. 1822; Hay Scrapbooks, x, pp. 158–9, 170–71; Leary, *Periodical Press*, pp. 137, 148; Meinertzhagen, *Potters of Tadcaster*, pp. 209–14; Potter Collection, xi, pp. 14, 19–20, 42, xii, pp. 91–4, 95, 97, 99–101, 103–5, xiiA, pp. 143, 154, 155; Prentice, *Sketches*, pp. 237–8.

Gazette had to accept another defeat, this time of Lord John Russell's proposal for gradual reform through the disfranchisement of rotten boroughs. Taylor welcomed this plan, though he was not in favour of pecuniary compensation for disfranchisement. He had previously regretted Russell's concentration on rotten boroughs and opposition to a uniform franchise. In the early 1820s the *Guardian* (before it began to shake off its youthful vigour and radicalism, at least in the eyes of its critics) was keen most of all for a substantial extension of the franchise to cover the 'wealth and mind' of the nation.[40]

Manchester's respectable reformers lacked the kind of institutional basis for organisation and action that was enjoyed by their conservative opponents. Though they had their religious congregations, they did not have Pitt Clubs or Orange societies or loyalist associations, and they were also substantially excluded from the direction of police affairs and the parish government. One possible compensation was the Cheshire Whig Club, founded in 1820 to maintain the principles of 1688 and, in the political environment of the 1820s, to further the cause of moderate and sensible reform. The club was dominated by local Whig landed notables, M.P.s and other public men, and also drew in reformers of respectable but more modest standing in the north-western counties. Four of the band, Richard Potter, Baxter, Atkinson and Taylor, seem to have belonged to the club. Prentice found it too cautious and aristocratic. He was pleased by a declaration of principles prepared by a special committee of members in October 1824, which called for the repeal of the septennial act, the exclusion of placemen from the Commons, better regulation of elections and the enfranchisement of direct taxpayers, but this declaration went too far for the majority of members and was never ratified. Prentice disliked compromise and was not keen on a taxpaying franchise in any case, because it bestowed or withheld the vote without reference to the character and competency of the individual. It therefore seemed an 'absurd' limitation. The Tory *Exchange Herald* used the dispute over ratification to ridicule the club and point to the split between 'old' and 'new' Whigs. Taylor was more favourable towards the club than Prentice. The *Guardian* was a firm supporter, and Taylor addressed the annual meetings of 1824 and 1825. Meanwhile Prentice continued to attack the club as a tame and useless ally, and he

[40] *Gazette*, 28 April 1821, 3 May 1822; *Guardian*, 7 July, 4 Aug. 1821, 4 May 1822, 3 May 1823.

contrasted the moderation of George Philips, the Manchester Unitarian who was now an M.P. and a leading member of the club, with Philips's radical stance back in the 1790s when he had acted with Thomas Walker and the Constitutional Society. Manchester's Tory press derided the club as a foolish and harmless exercise.[41]

Taylor made much of the political changes of the mid-1820s, the rise of 'liberal Toryism' and the redefining of political parties. At the time of Viscount Goderich's short premiership the *Guardian* was to state that 'our proper place is no longer amongst opposition journals',[42] but even before this Taylor had expressed approval for the policies followed by the more progressive Tory ministers. Prentice was not blind to political developments, but in March 1826 he pointed out that until something was done about the corn laws and the representative system 'we must not go too far in our laudation of the ministers'. He was also amused by the problem posed for Tory editors by the new situation: they did not know whether to praise or condemn the 'whig' measures proceeding from a Tory government.[43] The new situation seems to have perplexed members of the Pitt Club. The rise of 'liberal Toryism', locally as well as centrally, marked the beginnings of self-analysis and even internal disagreement among some Manchester conservatives. There are signs that interest in the Pitt Club was declining. The attendance at the annual dinner of May 1826 was much smaller than on previous occasions, and back in April 1825 it was said that only about a quarter of members paid much attention to these events. Resolutions were passed condemning this apathy and imposing fines for non-attendance. Hard-liners complained that too many members were showing a lack of respect for the Pitt Club and its principles.[44]

Although the policies of the Tory government might have been less objectionable to the band than in the past, the state of the representative system still caused complaint and resentment. The 1826 general election gave Prentice the opportunity to print a series of diatribes on this matter, and he calculated that of all the members of the Commons only 171 were returned independent of nomination.

---

[41] *Gazette*, 9, 16 Oct. 1824, 12 Nov. 1825; *Exchange Herald*, 12, 26 Oct. 1824; *Guardian*, 13 Oct. 1821, 12 Oct. 1822, 11 Oct. 1823, 16 Oct. 1824; Hay Scrapbooks, x, p. 125, xi, p. 167; *Chronicle* and *Courier*, 15 Oct. 1825.
[42] *Guardian*, 5 Jan. 1828.
[43] *Gazette*, 18 March 1826.
[44] Hay Scrapbooks, xiv, p. 290; Pitt Club, ii, p. 40.

Peers nominated 300 and commoners 187 members of the lower House.[45] Members of the band were involved in the 1826 Preston contest, as indicated in the surviving correspondence between Shuttleworth and the reform-minded local manufacturer John Wood, who took one of the seats. The other went to the Whig Edward Stanley (later fourteenth earl of Derby), and Cobbett trailed in third. Wood's success was achieved despite much bribery and treating by supporters of the other two candidates.[46]

The annual meeting and dinner of the Cheshire Whig Club in October 1826 was attended and addressed by Richard Potter. He shared Prentice's view that the club was too timid and should be doing more to promote the cause of reform, but Potter was normally more restrained in his language than his friend. He discussed his speech beforehand with Prentice, however, and used information Prentice had previously inserted into the *Gazette*. He also had a copy of Prentice's list of 100 boroughs which returned two M.P.s each and yet had a combined population less than that of unrepresented Manchester parish. Potter's speech emphasised that parliamentary reform had become absolutely essential and that the principles of the Whig Club 'should lead to a correspondent practice'. The *Gazette* and *Guardian* covered the event, and the Tory *Courier* used the occasion to scorn 'Whiggery' in the north-west. Prentice's dissatisfaction with the club prevented him from paying it much attention after 1826. His coverage of the 1827 annual meeting was very brief. Richard Potter had planned to address it, but for some reason failed to do so. Prentice advised him about suitable content for a speech in a letter of 3 October 1827, so we have some indication of what Potter might have said. In Prentice's view the following points had to be stressed. The premierships of Canning and Goderich needed to be put into perspective, for even though the 'Old' Tories had apparently been overcome it was unlikely that their successors would be willing or able to effect true improvements. As for the Whigs, they had to act with energy, cast off 'mere mouthing and lip service', and identify themselves more closely with the people. Prentice suspected that such a speech would not be warmly received in the club, but he told Potter that this would not matter. The whole idea was to show the

[45] *Gazette*, 3, 17, 24 June, 1, 8 July 1826.
[46] See letters in Shuttleworth Scrapbook, loose leaves, and 'John Shuttleworth', *Biographical References*, especially Wood to Shuttleworth, 31 May, 5, 6 June 1826.

public that the Whigs had to do much more to deserve the name of 'reformers'.[47]

Taylor's *Guardian* regretted the departure of the earl of Liverpool following the prime minister's stroke in February 1827, but was to be a staunch supporter of the Canning-Whig coalition and was sure that the new government would encourage the continued march of progress. Prentice was glad that the marquess of Lansdowne gained office, and wanted Earl Grey to be included in the government too. But he doubted that ministers, even if they wanted reforms, could do much in a parliament that did not represent the people. The *Courier* found the Canning ministry 'monstrous', and with the *Chronicle* expressed fears about the safety of Church and constitution. The Pitt Club was reinvigorated by the appointment of the Canning government. The more uncompromising of Manchester's conservatives sensed that a time of trial was approaching. Speakers at the Pitt Club dinner of May 1827 dwelt on the need for the defence of sound principles.[48]

The fate of the test and corporation acts seemed to Manchester liberals to suggest that fundamental reforms *were* possible despite the apparent strength of the obstructionists. These acts were of special concern to them, of course, for most of them were Dissenters (and proud of it) and they were also interested in progressive principles and civil liberties in the abstract. The *Gazette* and *Guardian* gave full support and extensive coverage to the repeal movement in Manchester, and Prentice in particular was insistent in his call for Manchester's nonconformist congregations to campaign decisively. An early lead in the agitation was taken by the Cross Street Unitarians. The liberal-Dissenting spokesmen in Manchester disliked church establishments and wanted a change in Church-state relations. When the bishop of Peterborough argued that repeal would be the first step in a chain of developments leading to the disestablishment of the Church, Richard Potter commented without remorse: 'I believe the Bishop is quite correct'. Most Manchester Tories were dissatisfied with repeal, though some were more concerned about the Church's reputation for

---

[47] *Gazette*, 14 Oct. 1826, 13 Oct. 1827; *Guardian*, 14 Oct. 1826, 13 Oct. 1827; *Courier*, 21 Oct. 1826; Potter Collection, xii, pp. 119–21.

[48] *Guardian*, 24 Feb., 31 March, 1, 21, 28 April 1827; *Gazette*, 24 Feb., 14, 21, 28 April, 5, 12 May 1827; Prentice, *Sketches*, p. 300; *Courier*, 24 Feb., 3 March, 7, 14, 21, 28 April, 19 May 1827; *Chronicle*, 21, 28 April, 5, 12 May, 11 Aug. 1827; Pitt Club, ii, entry for annual dinner, 28 May 1827; Hay Scrapbooks, xiv, pp. 291–2 (and xiv, xvA and xvB generally for alarm on the Catholic issue).

tolerance than others, and some were mollified by the new declaration which Dissenters would have to make on accepting public offices. No proof was needed, but this issue did show that religious and party affiliations tended to go hand in hand in Manchester. Catholic emancipation was also to demonstrate the power of sectarianism and the role of sect as one of the main factors dividing the respectable Manchester business community.[49]

2. MANCHESTER'S ATTEMPT TO GAIN THE PENRYN SEATS, 1827–28

Manchester's campaign to secure the parliamentary representation of the corrupt Cornish borough Penryn involved respectable men of both conservative and liberals leanings. For a short time it looked as if party differences would be put aside, at least partially, so that the campaigners could present a united front. The majority of townspeople agreed that Manchester deserved to return M.P.s, and believed that this was the most effective way of having local concerns expressed and local interests (especially commercial) defended and advanced. For the reformers this was also a question of right and of principle. Cooperation seemed to be possible. Moderate reformers and moderate Tories shared some common ground and had similar social and economic concerns. But for friction to be kept to a minimum there would have to be a readiness to compromise and perhaps to avoid discussion of difficult questions for as long as possible. The franchise qualification needed to be settled, however, and differences of opinion were bound to be expressed sooner or later. In the event the campaign floundered for lack of agreement in Manchester and lack of a sympathetic hearing from the legislature. Yet for the band this was a crucial episode. Its members were deeply involved in the campaign to gain the Penryn seats and they thereby gained enormously in experience, influence and standing. In some ways this was a trial run for 1830–32.

---

[49] *Gazette*, 31 March, 7 April 1827, 19 Jan., 1, 22 March, 26 April, 3 May 1828; *Guardian*, 13 Jan., 28 April 1827, 9 Feb., 1, 22 March, 5 April, 3 May 1828; Potter Collection, xi, p. 47, xiiiA, pp. 171–2; *Chronicle*, 9 Feb., 1, 22 March 1828; *Courier*, 1 March, 26 April 1828. G. I. T. Machin, 'Resistance to the Repeal of the Test and Corporation Acts', *H.J.*, 22 (1979), pp. 115–39, points out (among other things) that much of the anti-repeal propaganda stressed the influence of the Unitarians.

Lord John Russell's statement, on 3 April 1827, that if the Commons agreed to disfranchise Penryn he would move that the seats be given to Manchester, was apparently made without any prompting. Mancunians had no prior expectation of it and, as with the test and corporation acts, the local reformers had to respond quickly to a stimulus given them from elsewhere. The county M.P. Lord Stanley wrote at once to the boroughreeve and constables informing them of Russell's undertaking, and the local papers quickly took the matter up. Prentice was keen for enfranchisement, recommended immediate agitation in its favour, and argued that the two main requirements would be proper electoral regulations and a franchise based on 'the broadest recognised principle of suffrage'. It is not clear if he meant universal suffrage or something close to it, or the Preston potwalloper suffrage. Later he spoke of a taxpaying suffrage. But he did recognise that Manchester's demands would have to be shaped according to a consideration of what parliament was likely to grant. The *Guardian* looked forward to the better representation of local commercial interests, wanted proper electoral regulations to prevent delay and disturbances, and stated the desirability of a wide franchise. Yet Taylor did not go as far as Prentice, for quality was to be preferred to numbers. There could be no influence for 'that class which, from want of education and from penury, is least likely to use it with honesty and independence'. Prentice later accused Taylor of wanting too exclusive a suffrage. He made the same remarks about the Tory papers. The *Chronicle* thought that Peel's jury qualification of £20 would be acceptable, but added that Manchester might not even get the chance to stake a claim for Penryn's seats. The *Courier* was not enthusiastic about the prospect of enfranchisement, agreed that the evidence against Penryn was not conclusive, and made much of the fact that local opinion was divided on the franchise issue. Towards the end of April Prentice stated that a £20 franchise would be acceptable if this was the very lowest that could be secured.[50]

---

[50] Archives Dept. M.C.L., Manchester Representation Committee (M.R.C.), Minutes and Proceedings 1827–28, p. 3 and press cuttings; *Gazette*, 7, 14, 21 April 1827; *Guardian*, 7, 14, 21 April 1827; *Chronicle*, 7, 21 April 1827; *Courier*, 7 April, 12 May 1827; J. M. Main, 'The Parliamentary Reform Movement in Manchester 1825–32' (unpublished B. Litt thesis, University of Oxford, 1951), pp. 90–94. Peel's £20 jury qualification was prescribed in the 1825 juries regulation act.

A town meeting was called for 23 May 1827. The Potters, Harvey, Prentice and Taylor were among the requisitionists, who included prominent Tories and members of the ruling party as well as moderate and advanced reformers. Emphasis was placed on the need for unanimity and cooperation, though Prentice and his friends must have wondered how long such illusory unity could last. The *Guardian* was less sceptical and was sure that cooperation was possible. Two points are significant: Taylor agreed with those who wanted to shelve awkward questions, and he continued to talk about enfranchisement as if it was an issue that only affected and interested Manchester's cotton businessmen. Prentice later recalled that moderate Whigs and moderate Tories had wanted Penryn's seats so that local commerce could gain clear representation, whereas the decided reformers wanted the seats so as to secure some beginning for the amendment of the whole system of representation. They let the moderates take the lead because potentially the latter could command wider support. The town meeting approved a petition to the Commons and appointed the Manchester Representation Committee (M.R.C.) to conduct the campaign for parliamentary representation. The original list of members was altered because Prentice and others pointed out that it contained too many conservatives, Pitt Club members, present and former town and parish officers and friends of the establishment. Hence it did not fairly represent all the groups taking an interest in the question. After some discussion Shuttleworth, Atkinson, Prentice, Baxter, Taylor and Richard Potter were added to the M.R.C. This was some breakthrough, but the balance of power within the M.R.C. would still be with the moderates and conservatives, and no less than 15 of the 31 men on the M.R.C. belonged to the Pitt Club. The petition approved on 23 May stressed the usefulness and expediency of the representation of commercial interests. It said nothing about natural or citizenship rights, liberal theory, the constitution or justice and freedom. The advanced reformers were certainly leaving the moderates and conservatives to take the lead.[51]

---

[51] M.R.C., pp. 1, 5, 7, 8–9, 10–15 and press cuttings; *Gazette*, 19, 26 May 1827; Main, 'Reform Movement', pp. 95–8; Hay Scrapbooks, xiv, pp. 292, 296; *Guardian*, 19, 26 May 1827; Prentice, *Sketches*, pp. 305–8; Boroughreeve's Papers, i, pp. 217–40; Pitt Club, iii, membership and accounts book; *Chronicle*, 26 May 1827.

The boroughreeve, George Neden, a member of the Pitt Club and chairman of the M.R.C., kept up communications with Russell and the county M.P.s Stanley and Blackburne through May and June 1827, while members of the band were corresponding on their own account. Prentice wrote to Russell and Shuttleworth to John Wood (M.P. for Preston from 1826 to 1832), asking for advice and an assessment of parliamentary opinion, and discussing such matters as the franchise and the regulation of elections. In these weeks there seems to have been a general expectation that Manchester would receive Penryn's seats. J. M. Main is probably right when he says that the reformers saw they were in a minority on the M.R.C., knew they would be outvoted on important matters, and tried to make up for this by cultivating their contacts with sympathetic M.P.s. Hence the letters of Shuttleworth and Prentice.[52] Prentice soon warned that other unrepresented places were making claims on Penryn's seats, notably Glasgow, St Pancras and Marylebone. The *Chronicle* expressed fears too, but Prentice's concern was for the cause of thorough reform:

> We fear the effect of this competition will be a sacrifice of the principles on which every reform in the representative system ought to be founded. It is well-known that parliament is averse to any very broad extension of the elective right, and we fear this may induce some one of the competing places to accommodate itself to this aversion, and to express its readiness to accept the privilege on the terms most likely to be acceptable to those who have it to confer.

Before long parliament's attention was drawn to Birmingham's request to be given the representation of another corrupt borough, East Retford. The moderate Whig merchant G. W. Wood, later joined by the Tory H. H. Birley, went to London on behalf of the M.R.C. to urge that Manchester should get priority. When the *Guardian* reported that Russell had decided to postpone his motion for the transfer of Penryn's seats to Manchester, Taylor assured his readers that this was nothing to worry about. He trusted in the liberalism of the Canning government, its strength in the Commons and its willingness to support Russell's plan. Taylor was assuming

[52] M.R.C., pp. 7, 10–15; Shuttleworth Scrapbook, p. 49; Main, 'Reform Movement', pp. 99–100.

too much, and even he admitted that resistance in the Lords could prove a problem. Russell wrote to Neden on 14 June 1827 recommending that the M.R.C. draw up a draft bill for the representation of Manchester, 'suited to their own opinions which may or may not coincide with mine'. Russell added that he had not yet made up his mind about a voting qualification.[53] A few weeks later Prentice was arguing that a wide suffrage for Manchester would be perfectly safe if the ballot was introduced, but he recognised that parliament would probably not agree.[54]

On 15 October 1827 the M.R.C. appointed a subcommittee to prepare a draft Manchester representation bill. Its members were H. H. Birley, G. W. Wood, Gilbert Winter, R. H. Greg and William Cririe. Wood and Greg were moderate Whigs, Birley and Winter leading members of the Pitt Club and the local ruling oligarchy. Cririe, an attorney, was also in the Pitt Club, but does not appear to have been very active in local politics. A draft was ready by mid-November. This delimited the parliamentary borough, outlined basic qualifications for voters and laid down rules for the organisation of elections. The question of the appropriate property qualification for voters was not decided upon. At the eleventh meeting of the M.R.C., on 14 December 1827, members of the band decided to try and have more of a say in the conduct of the Manchester campaign and pressed for concessions from the M.R.C. majority. Atkinson and Shuttleworth argued that the boroughreeve and constables should not be named as returning officers in the draft (presumably because these town officials had too often been party men in the past), and proposed the county sheriff instead. Their motion was lost by nine votes. Further arguments occurred at the next meeting, on 20 December. Taylor and Shuttleworth pressed for a £15 assessment as the qualification for voters, but lost by seven votes. By the same margin it was resolved that a £20 qualification would be best and that Gilbert Winter and G. W. Wood should go to discuss this with Russell. The band was having no success in the M.R.C. Winter and Wood saw Russell for two hours at Woburn Abbey on 14 January 1828. He approved of the draft but said he wanted to consult Althorp and other colleagues before making a final decision. Regarding the £20 qualification, Russell accepted this

---

[53] M.R.C., pp. 14–28 and press cuttings; *Gazette*, 2, 9 June 1827; Main, 'Reform Movement', pp. 101–4; *Chronicle*, 2 June 1827; Boroughreeve's Papers, i, pp. 217–40; *Guardian*, 7 July 1827.
[54] *Gazette*, 30 June 1827.

while expressing concern about discrepancies between rentals and assessments. He suggested that householders should be entitled to have their assessments raised to the level of their rents. He also suggested that counsel be employed to bring the draft into its proper form, and Wood later secured the services of a Mr Wellbeloved of the Temple. The various proposals of Russell and the M.R.C. were combined in a final draft, approved by the M.R.C. in February 1828.[55]

The divisions within the M.R.C. at this time were matched by disputes over local government, for great controversy was being created by the attempt to reconstitute the police commission. As the 'high' party and the reformers struggled for control of police affairs, representatives of both groups were also arguing over the Penryn affair in the M.R.C. Of course the 'high' party was normally able to control the M.R.C.'s proceedings, the balance of power being decidedly in its favour. Meetings were mostly chaired by the boroughreeve and attended also by the constables and churchwardens. There was no obvious reformer on the subcommittee which drafted a Manchester representation bill, and though there were reformers in the main M.R.C. their proposals were normally rejected. Members of the band must have felt highly frustrated. Tension increased in November 1827 when Charles Cross, the new boroughreeve, began to chair M.R.C. meetings. Cross was a leader of the 'high' party and unpopular with reformers for his role in preventing a town meeting on the slavery issue in 1826. Certainly Prentice was dissatisfied with the way things were going in the M.R.C. There were nineteen meetings between May 1827 and March 1828. He attended eight of the first nine meetings, then did not attend again at all until the very last meeting. Baxter and Richard Potter were more consistent in their attendance but Shuttleworth, like Prentice, appears to have decided that attendance was not likely to achieve very much. He was present at only seven of the first fourteen meetings, and did not attend any thereafter.[56]

In April 1827 Prentice had accepted a £20 qualification as a fair compromise between reformers and conservatives. At some point before the end of the year he changed his mind, deciding that £20 was too high and that liberals should not give up too much in the interests of conciliation. He was probably affected by the policy of the M.R.C.

[55] M.R.C., pp. 28–57; Boroughreeve's Papers, i, pp. 253–75; Main, 'Reform Movement', pp. 105–7.
[56] The attendances at each meeting are recorded in M.R.C., pp. 10, 12, 13, 15, 26, 30, 31, 38, 39, 41, 42, 44, 46, 48, 52, 56, 58, 62, 69.

and by the police dispute. He may also have discovered that the Manchester electorate under a £20 franchise would in fact be much smaller than he had originally thought. In February 1828, as Russell prepared to bring in the bill giving Manchester the elective right, Prentice openly protested against the £20 franchise. His main point was that the whole rate assessment system in Manchester was full of irregularities. Many assessments were inaccurate. This meant that a high number of townsmen who deserved the vote, and strictly speaking did qualify for it, would be excluded. (It is not clear whether Prentice would have regarded the £20 qualification as less objectionable had there been less discrepancy in Manchester between assessments to the rates, the basis of the voting qualification, and the rents paid for occupied property.) Meanwhile the *Courier* emphasised the need for a high voting qualification and the likelihood that Penryn's seats would go to the neighbouring hundreds. Taylor welcomed the £20 franchise as a fitting compromise between all interested parties, and argued that continuing disputes would harm Manchester's campaign. Everyone should accept the qualification, he declared, and be silent. Richard Potter wrote to a friend in Birmingham and expressed his own preference for the enfranchisement of all ratepayers, as provided for in the bill proposing to give Birmingham the Retford seats (framed by Charles Tennyson, M.P. for Bletchingley). As Potter said of the £20 franchise, the apparent *sine qua non* for the enfranchisement of Manchester, 'if it can only be got at such a sacrifice I for one would much prefer us not having the privilege'. Prentice went on claiming that Russell had been misled as to Manchester's readiness to accept a £20 qualification, while Taylor condemned the plan being mooted in parliament for the transfer of Penryn's seats to the neighbouring hundreds rather than to Manchester.[57]

By the end of March 1828 it seemed that Manchester's chances of success were fading. The Manchester representation bill had been substantially modified in the Commons,[58] and it was not clear how

[57] *Gazette*, 9, 23 Feb., 29 March 1828; *Guardian*, 23 Feb., 15, 29 March 1828; *Courier*, 9, 23 Feb. 1828; Hay Scrapbooks, xiv, p. 296; Potter Collection, xiiiA, pp. 179–80.
[58] All the regulations relating to elections had been removed on the grounds that they were unnecessary or else already provided for in existing statutes. Russell said he would introduce a special measure to control Manchester elections, if the town desired it, at some future date. Most of the band were angry that good clauses had been removed and the £20 franchise retained.

the Lords would treat the measure. There was also the problem of what the Wellington government wanted. Peel was speaking of some destination other than Manchester for Penryn's seats, and Russell appears to have lost confidence. Wellbeloved of the Temple saw Russell on 16 and 24 March and informed the M.R.C. that he 'does not seem inclined to opposed Mr Peel's wish, if it should appear to be of a decided nature'. Gilbert Winter and G. W. Wood were deputed to go to London and press Manchester's claims. Prentice and Richard Potter argued at the M.R.C. meeting of 26 March that Baxter should be added to this deputation, so that the reformers would be represented, but this motion was defeated by eight votes to three.[59] Discussion continued in Manchester, with Prentice the most outspoken critic of the £20 franchise. At a town meeting on 24 April 1828, held to consider the latest constables' accounts, Prentice objected to the sums claimed as expenses by the deputation which had gone to confer with Russell and other M.P.s about the enfranchisement of Manchester. He argued that the deputation had assumed a power not delegated to it when it 'bargained for an exclusive suffrage'. After much disputation Prentice's motion was carried and the expenses disallowed (but this was not the end of the matter). Baxter agreed with Prentice that Russell had somehow been misled about the propriety and acceptability of a £20 franchise. Baxter was in London in April 1828 to take part in the canvassing of M.P.s on the Manchester police bill, but the Penryn affair was also on his mind. He told Richard Potter that he hoped to see Russell so that the mystery surrounding Russell's conversation with Manchester's 'parliamentary delegation' could be cleared up.[60]

By early May there was not even the pretence of unity in Manchester on the Penryn affair. In fact the Lords received two petitions from the town, one praying for Penryn's seats and the other opposing enfranchisement on the grounds that the Manchester representation bill as it stood would not prevent electoral tumults. The bill had been lost in the Lords by the end of May. Prentice had never liked the measure, but was still angry about the way the affair turned out. He denounced the conduct of Peel, who had previously stated that the Penryn and Retford questions should be settled so that one

---

[59] M.R.C., pp. 58–70; Boroughreeve's Papers, i, pp. 290–2, 297–8, 302–24, 330–7.
[60] Gazette, 16 Feb., 5, 19, 26 April 1828; M.R.C., press cuttings; Guardian, 5 April 1828; Prentice, Sketches, pp. 308–9; Chronicle, 26 April 1828; Wheeler, History, p. 127; Baxter to Potter, 25 April 1828, Potter Collection, xii, pp. 141–2.

representation went to a commercial town and the other to the neighbouring hundreds, but who now seemed to favour a solution arranging for Penryn to retain its seats and for Retford's to go to the hundreds. Taylor also found Peel's conduct open to censure. Of course the Wellington government was seriously divided on the issue, eventually losing its more liberal-minded members because of these disagreements and related misunderstandings. The final result was that Penryn was not disfranchised and Manchester did not gain representation. At the time Prentice argued that this outcome only served to prove the absurdity of the representative system and the necessity for thorough parliamentary reform. Later he wrote that he was glad Manchester had not gained Penryn's seats. This kind of piecemeal reform could have put off real reform for decades: 'the gradual process would have been much the same as standing still'. The Tory government might have spread over years the changes effected at once by the 1832 Reform Act.[61]

After the defeat of this campaign the recriminations began in earnest. Prentice was determined that the town should not pay the expenses of the M.R.C. deputation which had, in his view, misled Russell about the acceptability of the £20 franchise. This was also an issue on which the advanced reformers could make a stand and try to enforce their own views of what shape parliamentary reform should take over those of the moderates and conservatives who had dominated the M.R.C. and the recent enfranchisement campaign. Prentice had enough support among both respectable and middling sort reformers to make an impressive showing at the leypayers' meeting of 24 July 1828. As before it was argued that the deputation had been appointed by the M.R.C., that the M.R.C. had been appointed by an official town's meeting, and that it was therefore proper for the town to pay the expenses which the deputation had incurred. It was also said that if the expenses were disallowed, public-spirited men would be reluctant to act in the future if they knew they could not claim back sums they expended on the town's behalf. Even Baxter was in some sympathy with this view, but Prentice would not be swayed and his motion that the expenses be disallowed was easily passed. Some called for the votes to be taken

---

under the vestry act but this caused such uproar, and the opinion of the meeting was so abundantly clear, that the act was not invoked. The arguments were not silenced, however, and in January 1829 it was revealed that the deputation's expenses would be discussed at yet another town meeting. These sums had been included in the latest constables' accounts to ensure another vote. The Tory *Courier* approved. Prentice pointed out that town meetings had twice rejected the expenses and that a third attempt to make the town pay would be extraordinary and indecent. He urged townsmen to register their disgust by attending in numbers and rejecting the charges once more. But his opponents had made superior preparations. A large gathering in the town hall on 23 January 1829 heard Taylor argue that opposition to the expenses had been rooted in the belief that the £20 qualification was too high, yet it had been necessary to fix some figure and this one had represented a compromise acceptable to most interested parties. Baxter thought that the M.R.C. had been justified in sending the deputation, but that it would not be right to pass the expenses after the town had rejected them twice. Taylor was undeterred. He proposed their acceptance and the meeting approved. Prentice's next editorial scorned Taylor's conduct, complained about the 'high' party victory won 'in consequence of an extraordinary muster of their friends', and made it absolutely clear that Russell *had* been misled about the £20 qualification. This was the ace up his sleeve: 'How was it that Lord John Russell after writing to the Editor of this paper, "you have convinced me that the qualification ought not to exceed fifteen pounds", afterwards fixed it at twenty?' In the next *Guardian* Taylor defended both his own conduct and the majority decision of the meeting.[62]

Tennyson's proposal to transfer East Retford's seats to Birmingham was finally lost in February 1830. Prentice was neither surprised nor regretful. Such a minor and marginal change was not enough, he commented, for the greatest happiness of the greatest number could only be secured by 'the actual representation of ALL'. The Retford seats went to the hundred of Bassetlaw in Nottinghamshire. Taylor opined that the failure of Tennyson's bill would not prove significant in the long run, for every chief town would soon have M.P.s, such

---

[62] *Gazette* and *Chronicle*, 26 July 1828; M.R.C., pp. 75–6; *Times*, 17, 24 Jan. 1829; *Courier*, 17 Jan. 1829; *Guardian*, 24 Jan. 1829.

was the rapid spread of opinion in favour of substantial parliamentary reform.[63]

3. THE PASSING OF THE FIRST REFORM ACT

Catholic emancipation was a triumph for the cause of reform, and like the repeal of the test and corporation acts it demonstrated that fundamental amendments of the exclusive, oligarchic, Anglican constitution were not impossible. As Prentice never tired of pointing out, one change could easily lead to another. He and Taylor welcomed emancipation in their newspapers, though Prentice detested the 'base bargain' by which concession was secured in return for the disfranchisement of Ireland's 40s. freeholders. Most Manchester Tories were against emancipation.[64] For the band and its allies parliamentary reform retained its position as the central remedy on which all else seemed to depend. Prentice continued to discharge what he saw as his patriotic and journalistic duty, and set about organising and directing opinion on the reform question. His many articles on parliamentary reform in the late 1820s discussed matters such as the borough and county representations, Bentham's views on reform, the spread of enlightened opinions, and the faults and burdens of aristocratic government. In some of these pieces he was prepared to advocate universal suffrage and annual elections (nor did he rule out votes for women). In 1829 and 1830 he also commented on large meetings at which mainly plebeian radical leaders pointed to the links between rising economic distress and an unrepresentative political system.[65] The *Guardian* also kept interest in reform alive during these months, though Taylor was more discriminating than Prentice about the kind of reform he wanted. Taylor used liberal language and spoke of a wide franchise and the proper recognition of individual rights, but he continued to regard reform as something which

---

[63] *Times*, 20 Feb. 1830; *Guardian*, 13 March, 24 July 1830. The amended East Retford bill finally received the royal assent on 23 July 1830.

[64] *Times*, 2 May, 27 June 1829; Prentice, *Sketches*, pp. 253–62, 334–9; *Guardian*, 14 March 1829; *Chronicle*, 11 April 1829; *Courier*, 14, 21 March, 4, 18 April, 9 May 1829, 2 Jan. 1830.

[65] *Gazette*, 5 July 1828; *Times*, 4 July, 19 Sept., 10 Oct., 12 Dec. 1829, 13 March, 22 May 1830.

ought only to interest and apply to the respectable commercial ranks. He opposed universal suffrage.[66]

In October 1829 the Cheshire Whig Club decided to dissolve itself, apparently because of declining attendances and the view that major reforms (such as Catholic emancipation) had been secured and the work of the club substantially done. Prentice reported the dissolution as 'a release from false friends'. By now Taylor had decided that old party distinctions of 'Whig' and 'Tory' were losing their significance, for what mattered now was whether or not a man was a 'political economist'. Taylor found the dissolution of the Whig Club understandable. The *Chronicle*, more stridently partisan after Catholic emancipation, was glad about the club's demise and expressed surprise that it had lasted so long.[67] In January 1830 Prentice welcomed the establishment of the Birmingham Political Union, viewing it as a useful body that would set a valuable example to reformers all over the country. He gave its early activity extensive coverage and continued to write about it in following months. The Tory press condemned such bodies.[68] Prentice stepped up his coverage of parliamentary proceedings early in 1830. Parliamentary news took up a third of all space in his *Times* of 20 February 1830, and one column was written by 'our Private Correspondent'. It had been sent north on Thursday evening ready for insertion before Saturday's publication. Prentice reported the meetings of various reform associations and began to think about the establishment of a political union in Manchester.[69]

The 1830 general election saw members of the band immerse themselves in campaigning and comment. Once again they gained the kind of experience that would help them greatly in their future political endeavours. As usual there was no contest in Lancashire county. Lord Stanley retained his seat and John Wilson Patten,[70] a Tory, took over from the retired John Blackburne, who had been a county M.P. since 1784. The *Times* complained about the lack of a

---

[66] e.g. *Guardian*, 22 Dec. 1827, 6 June 1829.
[67] *Times*, 14 Nov. 1829; *Guardian* and *Chronicle*, 17 Oct. 1829.
[68] *Times*, 30 Jan., 15 May, 9 Oct. 1830; *Chronicle*, 30 Jan., 16 Oct. 1830; *Courier*, 30 Jan. 1830.
[69] *Times*, 20, 27 Feb., 22 May, 26 June 1830.
[70] Patten was a considerable landowner in Warrington and partner in a Manchester firm of patent roller manufacturers. He served as M.P. for North Lancashire after 1832, and was later created first Baron Winmarleigh. See *Chronicle*, 6 Oct. 1832; 'John Wilson Patten', *Biographical References*.

challenger. The *Guardian* had hoped that a sound commercial representative would be returned for Lancashire and was not impressed by Patten, unlike the *Courier* and *Chronicle*. It seems that a challenger was in fact sought in 1830, possibly Edward Strutt, the Derbyshire textile magnate. Shuttleworth was the Strutts' Manchester agent and passed on an invitation to Edward Strutt asking him to stand for Lancashire. Strutt declined in favour of the borough of Derby, where he was successful. There was a contest at Preston, which Prentice covered in detail. Henry Hunt came at the bottom of the poll, and Edward Stanley and John Wood (one of the band's parliamentary contacts) retained their seats. The Cheshire county election was also contested, and Prentice took up the cause of the reformer E. D. Davenport who had a reputation for being a 'poor man's friend'. Prentice attended the hustings at Stockport and spoke on Davenport's behalf, but the entrenched county interests were too strong. As expected the Tory William Egerton of Tatton Park and the 'aristocratical' Whig Viscount Belgrave were returned. Prentice also covered the Yorkshire election in detail, throwing his weight behind the campaigns of viscount Morpeth and Henry Brougham. Both were returned and at the end of September Prentice addressed a Yorkshire freeholders' meeting at Saddleworth in their honour. The *Chronicle* complained that the election results as a whole were not very favourable to the Wellington government. The *Courier* still could not forgive the government for Catholic emancipation, and asserted that its limited success at the polls was a fitting reward.[71]

Prentice's main concentration during the 1830 election was on the contest for Wigan and the connected campaign to have the Wigan franchise restored to its historic character. In recent decades it had been exclusively controlled by the corporation, and the seats had been shared by corporation nominees and members of the Lindsay family (earls of Balcarres and Crawford). The only men who could cast valid votes were the so-called 'elect' or 'jury' burgesses. This contravened the Wigan charter granted by Henry III, which stated that all inhabitants bearing scot and lot should enjoy the full rights of burgesses. Some of the band became involved in the campaign to change this situation, particularly Richard Potter. Potter became Wigan's chief advocate in July 1830 when the inhabitants asked him

---

[71] *Times*, 10, 17, 31 July, 7 Aug., 2 Oct. 1830; *Guardian*, 5, 12 Dec. 1829, 24 July 1830; Shuttleworth Scrapbook, p. 78; *Chronicle*, 14 Nov., 5 Dec. 1829, 31 July, 14 Aug. 1830; *Courier*, 28 Nov. 1829, 16 July 1830.

to stand as a parliamentary candidate along with another respectable reformer, the bleacher Thomas Hardcastle of Bolton. Potter, his brother Thomas, Prentice and other allies were in Wigan for the contested election. Potter's programme included the restoration of the Wigan franchise, corn law repeal, the abolition of the East India Company monopoly and the removal of all other restrictions on commerce. The poll took place on Saturday 31 July. Potter and Hardcastle gained the most votes, but not corporation votes, and they were declared unsuccessful. Potter promised to stand by the people of Wigan and to campaign for justice. Prentice also addressed the crowd. In September there were calls in Manchester for financial contributions to aid the Wigan effort, but in February 1831 a parliamentary committee of inquiry narrowly decided that the right of election did belong solely to the 'jury' or 'elect' burgesses. The *Times* urged Wigan people not to give up, emphasising that the committee had been almost equally divided. The *Guardian's* coverage of the affair was far less extensive. Taylor did not strongly approve or disapprove of Potter's candidature and the Wigan franchise agitation.[72]

Reform excitement in Manchester was also created or increased in the summer of 1830 by the July Revolution in France, which the band welcomed with great enthusiasm,[73] and by Hunt's presence in the town in August for the anniversary of Peterloo. After Hunt addressed a meeting on St Peter's Field he attended a dinner at which an argument broke out over the radical lecturer Rowland Detrosier's toast to 'the rights of man and Thomas Paine'. Prentice spoke for most of those in attendance when he said that he could drink to Paine's politics but not Paine's theological opinions. The controversy created by the toast lasted for several weeks. Another toast at the dinner was to the Manchester Political Union. The draper P. T. Candelet, one of Prentice's political allies, read out the resolutions

---

[72] *Times*, 31 July, 7 Aug., 4 Sept. 1830, 26 Feb. 1831; *Guardian*, 31 July 1830; Hadfield, Personal Narrative, p. 103.

[73] *Times*, 7, 14, 21, 28 Aug., 13 Nov. 1830; *Guardian*, 31 July, 7, 14, 21, 28 Aug., 11 Sept., 9 Oct. 1830; Smith, Reminiscences, pp. 35–6; Prentice, *Sketches*, pp. 364–5; *Report of the Proceedings in Paris on the delivery of the Resolutions passed in Manchester . . . congratulating the Parisians and the French Nation on the Recovery of their Freedom* (1830). Local Tories were more equivocal: *Chronicle*, 31 July, 7, 14, 28 Aug., 13 Nov. 1830; *Courier*, 21, 28 Aug. 1830.

passed at a recent inaugural meeting in the *Times* office, and said that
200 members had so far joined the union.[74]

The fall of Wellington and the appointment of a Whig government
committed to some measure of parliamentary reform was the breakthrough that the band and its allies had been waiting for. But now it
had come, what was the best course for them to pursue? On 13
December some prominent respectable reformers met in the York
Hotel, King Street, to consider the calling of a public meeting on
reform. Baxter, Watkin and Richard Potter were among those present, as were such allies as the attorney George Hadfield, the manufacturer Thomas Harbottle and the merchant Mark Philips. It was
decided that a reform meeting would be held in the near future but
not immediately. This would give time for the preparation of resolutions. Another reason for delay, and a problem that was to plague
the respectable liberals all through the campaign in favour of the
Whig government's Reform Bill, was recorded by Watkin: 'It was
quite evident from what was said that there were serious apprehen-
sions entertained as to the disposition of the working classes, and a
fear of their interference provoked an evident disinclination to a
meeting *at present*'.[75]

The weeks before the introduction of the Reform Bill saw much
discussion and campaigning in Manchester. Members of the band
were prominent and acted throughout as a reasonably cohesive unit.
Some may have been more moderate than others, and indeed Prentice
was the only one who had any regular contact with reformers from
humbler social ranks. None of his respectable friends joined the
political union he helped to form and direct, though this may not
have been because they doubted the usefulness and propriety of such
a body, but rather because they wanted to concentrate on other
aspects of the reform campaign and felt it was best to leave such
activity to one of their number who was best suited to deal with it.
The only friction within the band was that initially produced four

---

[74] *Times*, 14, 21 Aug., 4 Sept., 2, 9, 23 Oct., 13 Nov., 18 Dec. 1830; on the
Hunt dinner see also *Courier* and *Guardian*, 21 Aug. 1830; J. Belchem, *Orator
Hunt. Henry Hunt and English Working Class Radicalism* (1985), ch. 7;
Kirby and Musson, *The Voice of the People*, ch. 11.
[75] Watkin, *Journal*, p. 148. See also J. M. Main, 'Working Class Politics in
Manchester from Peterloo to the Reform Bill', *H.S.A.N.Z.*, 6 (1955), pp. 447–
58, on respectable reformers' fear of arousing a plebeian involvement that
could not be controlled.

or five years earlier over the direction taken by the *Guardian*. It is true, however, that Prentice tended to be more impatient than some of his friends, and had less faith in the readiness to compromise which marked Manchester's attempt to gain some degree of cross-party cooperation on behalf of reform. Moderates on all sides wanted an early show of civic opinion in favour of the idea of reform, and seemed to think that cooperation was possible. At times Prentice was sceptical. In particular, he did not want the advanced reformers to give way on important matters.

As arrangements were made for a public meeting Prentice hoped that the resolutions adopted would be 'such as decided reformers may support without any abatement of principle'. The meeting took place on 20 January 1831 and was chaired by Baxter. This was not an official town meeting because the boroughreeve and constables refused to comply with a requisition to call one, and local conservatives did not attend in any great number. Watkin composed resolutions and a petition before the meeting and these were approved by the rest of the band, including Prentice. Some of the statements were framed in general and cautious terms, but at least reformers of all shades could accept them. They stressed the necessity for reform, expressed gratitude to the government for its promise to introduce a measure, and asserted that reform would not be satisfactory unless it rendered the House of Commons a forum for 'the real representatives of the people', shortened the duration of parliaments and provided for the vote by ballot. A committee of 22 was appointed to further the purposes of the meeting. It was dominated by the band's circle and included Baxter, the Potters, Shuttleworth, Atkinson, Smith, Watkin and Prentice. Members of the band, especially Baxter, Prentice and Richard Potter, also delivered the key speeches at the meeting. The *Guardian* praised the unanimity and peaceful demeanour of this event and stated that credit was due to the labouring ranks. Taylor did predict, though, that a commitment to the ballot would prove divisive in the future. The Tory *Chronicle* wanted only gradual and moderate reform, and complained that some of the speeches and resolutions went too far. The *Courier* dismissed the ballot as an absurdity and the meeting as 'far from respectable'.[76]

[76] *Times*, 18 Dec. 1830, 22 Jan. 1831; Watkin, *Journal*, p. 149; Prentice, *Sketches*, pp. 369–71; Shuttleworth Scrapbook, p. 86; Brotherton Scrapbooks, x, p. 50; *Guardian*, 22 Jan., 5 Feb. 1831; *Chronicle*, 15, 22 Jan. 1831; *Courier*, 22 Jan. 1831.

Though the *Courier* remained strident and uncompromising, Manchester's anti-reform Tories were by now declining in strength and influence. There were no signs as yet of an energetic movement in opposition to the government's reform intentions, and the Pitt Club was rapidly heading towards its demise. The number of its active members had been falling for a while, meetings were adjourned because of poor attendances, and May 1828 had seen the last annual dinner. In 1830 the constitution of the club was changed so that new members could be admitted on the vote of 12 rather than 24 existing members. There was no election of officers in 1831, and indeed no more Pitt Club meetings after May 1831.[77]

Tension rose in Manchester during the winter of 1830–31 not only because of the reform agitation but because of continuing local government disputes (over the salary of deputy constable Lavender, for instance) and a bitter spinners' strike covering much of south Lancashire. The strike was most menacing in the area just to the east of Manchester (around Ashton, Hyde and Stalybridge). The murder of the Hyde manufacturer, Thomas Ashton, increased fears about public order. Manchester's ruling party raised the spectre of disturbance and was accused by the band of trying to dissuade the Whig government from parliamentary reform. Prentice continued to cover reform meetings all over the country. Brotherton and Smith figured prominently in the Salford meeting of 24 January 1831. This was part of Salford's campaign to be enfranchised. Smith and Brotherton were appointed to the town's reform committee, and Brotherton was one of four men deputed to go to London and press Salford's claims. Prentice used his *Times* to keep local reformers constantly supplied with advice and information, and promised the best possible coverage of the latest parliamentary session and the debates on reform.[78]

The band welcomed the Reform Bill. Prentice and Smith recorded their pleasure that it was much broader than had been anticipated. Of course it did not go as far as convinced reformers wanted, but Prentice was prepared to accept it as a valuable first instalment. His *Times* stated that the bill 'though far short of what we demand, and of what we shall ultimately have, sweeps away some of the most odious parts of the old rotten system and opens the way to a

[77] Pitt Club, ii, entries for 2 April, 7, 13 May 1829, 1 April 1830, 7 April, 5 May 1831; also Prentice, *Sketches*, pp. 430–32.
[78] Prentice, *Sketches*, p. 372; Smith, Reminiscences, p. 38; *Times*, 25 Dec. 1830, 8, 22, 29 Jan., 12, 19 Feb., 19 March, 2 April 1830.

reformation of all other abuses, and we accept it with gratitude'. Many reformers regretted that there would be no ballot and no greater extension of the suffrage, but the band spoke for the majority by approving the government proposals as far as they went. Manchester's dominant public men decided that any future pro-reform meeting should be an official civic affair, which meant securing the town officers' sanction. This would give a chance for cooperation between moderates of all parties. On the bill Taylor was more free with his praise than Prentice. He found it a bold plan certain to make the House of Commons a popular representative assembly. He regarded the voting qualifications as admirable: occupation of £10 premises in boroughs, and £10 copyholds, £50 leaseholds and 40s. freeholds in counties. These would give a proper outlet to men of property, knowledge and moral respectability, and best of all there could now be no convincing arguments for universal suffrage. Taylor certainly preferred moderate to radical reform. His closest friends were of a similar outlook, and his stance on reform was a main reason for his growing estrangement from others in the band. The *Chronicle* was not opposed to all reform but argued that the Whig bill went too far, and the *Courier* was totally against this 'revolutionary' measure. The radical *Voice*, edited by John Doherty, accepted the Reform Bill as better than nothing and continued to stress the need for universal suffrage, the ballot and shorter parliaments.[79]

The strength of the Manchester campaign in favour of the Reform Bill owed much to the Manchester Political Union (M.P.U.). Prentice considered political unions to be useful tools for the organisation of reformers, the expression of complaints and needs, and the influencing of public opinion and the legislature. He was also impressed by the class unity aspect of Birmingham's union, the way in which reformers of wealth and respectability could join in a single body with reformers from the labouring ranks, shopkeepers and *menu peuple*. He would have liked to have fostered such unity in Manchester, and on the face of it he was the right man to attempt this. His

---

[79] Prentice, *Sketches*, pp. 373–4; Smith, Reminiscences, p. 38; *Times* and *Guardian*, 5 March 1831; Scott, *Family Biography*, p. 241; *Chronicle* and *Courier*, 5, 19 March 1831; *Voice*, 5, 26 March, 2 April 1831. Asa Briggs is mistaken when he says that Doherty opposed the Reform Bill. Briggs, 'The Background of the Parliamentary Reform Movement in Three English Cities', *Collected Essays*, i, p. 192; on Doherty see also Kirby and Musson, *The Voice of the People*, pp. 423–34.

closest political allies were men of standing in the business community, and he himself had been a muslin merchant. But perhaps his greatest appeal was to the middling sort reformers, men of small means who were interested in personal advancement and the causes of economy and 'improvement', and who wanted to gain for themselves political rights and a secure social status. Prentice was also interested in working-class issues and sympathetic towards workers' problems and desires. He was certainly more favourable than some of his allies towards a wide franchise encompassing the majority of working people.[80] Many impulses operated in Prentice's heart and mind: Benthamite radicalism, Christian egalitarianism, sensible and respectable liberalism and a charitable, humanitarian commitment to the little man who needed a helping hand to take his place in society. Prentice drew on all these impulses during his political campaigning, but he was unable to appeal to all classes of reformers simultaneously or consistently during 1830–32. The prospects for a united reform movement in Manchester were not good. Asa Briggs has shown that the social and economic organisation of Manchester did not favour such cooperation.[81] The often strained nature of Manchester's social and economic relationships was to affect the history of the M.P.U., and behind the calls for unity was the undoubted fact that men like Prentice, if they wanted to bring workers' leaders into partnership, believed that this could not be a partnership of equals. One side should provide numbers, the other leadership and guidance. Prentice and his friends also probably did not appreciate how pedagogic and patronising they often appeared to men of humbler social ranks.

Interesting comments on the failure of Mancunian reformers to stage a united campaign in 1830–32 have been made by N. C. Edsall

---

[80] Prentice supported universal suffrage as an ultimate goal and a sound principle, but recognised that it might be difficult to proceed to it all in one go. He was very much in favour of a franchise linked to education, for as educational opportunities were improved and extended so more people would qualify for the vote. By the later 1830s he had decided that the vote should go to all who could *read* about the conduct of their representatives and *write* their names in the exercise of their constitutional right of petitioning. Bentham had favoured a simple reading test in his *Radical Reform Bill* of 1820. For Prentice's views see his preface to the 3rd edition (1832) of *Remarks*, his *Sketches*, pp. 341–2, and *Organic Changes*, pp. 11–17. See also Read, introduction to the *Sketches*, p. xiii, and Somerville, *Free Trade and the League*, ii, pp. 394–5.

[81] Briggs, 'Reform Movement in Three English Cities', pp. 188–93.

and R. A. Sykes. Edsall emphasises the caution of the moderates, the failure of the 'shopocracy' to advance and bridge the divide between respectable liberals and plebeian radicals, and the limited support for the M.P.U. He concludes that Manchester had no 'central reform tradition' before Cobden.[82] Perhaps he underestimates Manchester's contribution to the extraparliamentary campaign in favour of the Reform Bill. Even though Manchester's reformers were divided for much of the time this did not prevent the town from having a significant influence on the events of 1830–32, and though it is also true that the shopkeepers did not play the dominant role, the contribution of this body and agitators of similar standing was important. The M.P.U. had special appeal for such people, and the shopkeepers' input both in 1830–32 and later during the campaign for incorporation was indispensable to the success of the reform cause.

R. A. Sykes has highlighted the problem of the advanced respectable liberals (that is, members of the band and their circle): while rising to predominance they had to ensure that they did not alienate the less publicly-active but far more numerous moderates. They were also conscious of the strained social relations in Manchester and did not want the workers to become violently agitated. As for the plebeian radical leaders, many of them disliked the M.P.U. because they found it too moderate and exclusive, but they also faced the problem of internal divisions because some workers were ready to accept the Reform Bill as a first step, while others rejected it as insufficient. This prevented a united and consistent plebeian response to what the government was offering and what the M.P.U. and respectable Reform Committee (established in September 1831) were advocating.[83] All this is true enough, but some of Sykes's underlying opinions are questionable. He portrays Prentice as a moderate and cautious reformer who was anxious to make his activities palatable to the Manchester middle classes. This ignores the evidence of his convinced and thorough radicalism, and also underestimates the radicalism of the M.P.U. Its leaders always said they wanted *more* than the Reform Bill. Their activity in 1830–32 was a realistic adaptation of ultimate goals and preferred methods to suit the prevailing conditions. The M.P.U. had to deal in practicalities and it is wrong

[82] Edsall, *Richard Cobden*, p. 30.
[83] Sykes, 'Popular Politics', ch. 8.

to call it 'moderate' without qualifying this description. Sykes is also uncharitable when he says that the M.P.U. was 'completely ignored'. His view that the M.P.U. ceded the leadership of the Manchester reform campaign to the more prestigious Reform Committee and then dwindled into insignificance assumes that the M.P.U. had actually aspired to overall leadership, which is by no means clear. In the circumstances of the time it was inevitable that pro-reform bodies would conduct their own efforts as they saw fit, and the activity of one might or might not correspond with the activity of the others. Since both the M.P.U. and the Reform Committee were working on behalf of the Reform Bill the question of 'leadership' need not have been significant or important. They could easily help each other while making their own useful and separate contributions to the common cause. Sykes also underestimates Prentice's potential role as a bridge between different groups of reformers. Though it may have been disappointing that Manchester's reform campaign was divided, realists knew that this was likely, and the fact of division did not prevent Manchester from making a suitably important contribution in the securing of the Reform Bill. There was no way that the plebeian leaders could have been allowed to be genuine partners anyway, and it seems that many of them did not even want this.

The M.P.U. was controlled almost exclusively by Prentice and his middling sort allies. This probably came about for three main reasons: the existence of a deliberate plan, the failure to interest many wealthy and respectable reformers, and the belief that it might be a mistake to trust or try to control large numbers of workers. The overriding concern was to keep the M.P.U. cohesive, constitutional, and as respectable as possible. The M.P.U. had been mentioned at the Hunt dinner in August 1830 and was next heard of late in October when the *Times* advertised a meeting of its provisional committee. Membership of the union was not automatically open to all. Prospective members had to provide a 'recommendation from some respectable neighbour'. Soon it was announced that members should apply for a card which would gain them admittance to meetings. Prentice and his allies obviously felt it necessary to have as many checks as possible on the character of the membership.[84]

---

[84] *Times*, 21 Aug., 23 Oct. 1830. Prentice's *Times* is the main source for the M.P.U. No substantial collection of M.P.U. papers or records seems to have survived, and the other Manchester newspapers took little notice of the body except to criticise it.

The first properly-documented meeting of the M.P.U. took place in the Mechanics' Institute on 24 November 1830.[85] It was chaired by the manufacturer Robert Bunting, who explained that the meeting was called in accordance with the provisional committee's resolution that an executive political council would be elected as soon as the M.P.U.'s general membership reached 500. The meeting was not a completely harmonious affair. Prentice was the dominant speaker, but was occasionally heckled by plebeian radicals who had attended in force and were led by an Irish-born weaver named Nathan Broadhurst. The meeting approved Prentice's call for an energetic petitioning campaign and resolved to send a reform address to parliament. Then the objects of the M.P.U. were outlined. It would use 'all just and legal means' to influence parliamentary elections, and would campaign for parliamentary reform alongside corn law repeal, lower taxes, the abolition of the East India and other commercial monopolies, the end of slavery and local reforms including the admittance of all Manchester ratepayers to the decision-making process (especially in matters involving local expenditure). This was an extensive programme, though the emphasis was on the need for changes in the parliamentary system. Specific demands were a wide taxpaying franchise, the ballot and the right to replace M.P.s after one year if constituents found their conduct unsatisfactory. The management of the M.P.U. was to be entrusted to a political council. M.P.U. members would pay whatever subscriptions they could afford, but at least a shilling per quarter. A candidate for membership had to be proposed by a member of the council or by a collector of subscriptions; it was then up to the council to elect him as a member. The council had the power to expel any member, and illegal conduct would automatically mean expulsion. The M.P.U. disowned and rejected all such conduct.

In nominating men for appointment to the political council, Prentice emphasised that they should be known to each other and prepared to act collectively. He hoped that no names would be proposed

[85] On what follows see *Times*, 27 Nov., 4 Dec. 1830; also Main, 'Reform Movement', appendix p. 213; Prentice, *Sketches*, pp. 368–9. Prentice described the M.P.U. as the organ of those reformers who did not have full faith in the Whig ministers. They formed the association because they wanted to be ready to support the government if it was sincere, or (more likely) urge it forward if it was not. Though the M.P.U. was dismissed by some as lacking in influence (e.g. Wheeler, *History*, p. 129), Prentice pointed out that the ministers did not think so when they needed its services, and anti-reformers did not think so when they saw that it had an effect in preventing violent disturbances.

in addition to those on his list, for influential men might prefer not to act with individuals with whom they were not acquainted. Prentice was on the list and the others were 'gentlemen' Henry Day and Edmund Grundy; manufacturers John and Thomas Fielden, Robert Bunting and Robert Froggatt; druggists Eli Atkin and G. H. Winder; drapers J. Barrow, P. T. Candelet, John Dracup, James Jones and Roger Rayner; corn dealers G. Greenhough and W. T. Hesketh; woolsorters J. Hulme and W. Pickering; bookseller George Bentham; ironfounder James Cox; shopkeeper Elijah Dixon; commercial agent and lecturer Rowland Detrosier; joiner P. Gendel; grocer James Hampson; weaver John Massey; clerk Thomas Merry; shuttle-maker William Parr; tea dealer Ralph Shaw; spinner D. McWilliams; hosier John Whyatt. Prentice was right when he said that there were 'persons of every rank' on his list, but it is clear that the bulk of the M.P.U. political council was to be provided by middling sort shopkeepers, small traders and craftsmen. As soon as Prentice had finished talking Broadhurst protested that there should be more workers on the list. Prentice reminded the meeting that the addition of other names might prompt some in the council to withdraw. Arguments ensued, during which Prentice was denounced as a 'saucy Scotsman', but the meeting approved his list. The meeting was reported in the *Times*, and also unfavourably in the *Chronicle*. While the latter approved of the M.P.U.'s emphasis on legality, it found the body's aims excessive and stated that political unions in general were unlikely to serve the public interest.[86] The M.P.U. never received any substantial or sympathetic newspaper coverage except from Prentice's *Times*. Not only was Prentice the founder of and dominant figure in the M.P.U., therefore, but he was also its chief propagandist and publicist.

Soon the M.P.U. began to encourage the establishment of branches in various parts of Manchester, and by April 1831 there were groups in Newtown, Hulme and St John's which professed adherence to the main body. A fourth branch was established in Ancoats in November 1831. Prentice took part in and publicised these efforts to gain recruits, and help was also rendered by Candelet, Detrosier and others in the council. It is not clear whether the stringent admission procedures for the main M.P.U. were used in these working-class districts. Possibly the intention was to foster the establishment of

[86] *Chronicle*, 4 Dec. 1830.

small plebeian clubs and to use the M.P.U. to guide and coordinate them, but not to bring the operatives into full and equal membership. There is an interesting parallel here with the activities of Thomas Walker and the respectable Constitutional Society of the 1790s, which acted as patron of the workers' reform associations of that time (the Patriotic and Reformation Societies), even on occasion providing them with rooms in which to meet.[87]

The dissatisfaction of Broadhurst's group with the M.P.U. was one reason for the establishment of a rival political association in Manchester, which clearly put an end to any prospect (if there had ever been one) of class unity in the Manchester reform campaign. The new body was the Political Union of the Working Classes (P.U.W.C.), dominated by the Huntites and consisting mainly of weavers, shoemakers and other skilled workers. Among the leaders were the weavers Curran, Broadhurst and Ashmore, a shoemaker named Gilchrist and a locksmith named Brooks. The P.U.W.C. was formed during the spring of 1831, and organised a meeting and dinner to mark the visit of Hunt on 6 April. Prentice was a speaker at the dinner and proposed a toast to the victims of Peterloo; his participation would suggest that he was not on bad terms with at least some of the leaders of the P.U.W.C. Perhaps he was glad that the workers had their own organisation and hoped to be able to offer advice. But when Hunt declared against the Reform Bill soon after his visit to Manchester, so did the P.U.W.C., while Prentice was prepared to accept it as a first instalment. Nevertheless, on 6 April 1831 he was willing to associate with Hunt and rekindle thoughts of Peterloo in aid of the reform cause.[88] In June 1831 the Tory *Chronicle* noticed that there were now two political unions in Manchester. It considered both of them to be thoroughly radical, but noted that the P.U.W.C. was more prone to wildness and folly and seemed to be trying to recreate the atmosphere of 1817.[89]

According to J. M. Main the foundation of the M.P.U. indicates that reformist shopkeepers and traders were no longer willing to be guided by respectable middle-class leaders, the ones who had been directing them for some time in local government battles.[90] This

---

[87] On the Constitutional Society, see above chapter I section (2). On the M.P.U. branches, see *Times*, 12 Feb., 16, 23 April, 12 Nov. 1831.
[88] *Times*, 9 April 1831.
[89] *Chronicle*, 18 June 1831.
[90] Main, 'Reform Movement', p. 167.

seems to be a misinterpretation, since Prentice was just one such leader and of course it was he who had proposed the members of the political council. It is also likely that the shopkeepers and middling sort reformers were men who, because they were eager for social and political self-improvement, were not as easily offended by Prentice's pedagogic manner as were some workers.[91] A letter of Bentham to Francis Place, written after Prentice's visit to the former in April 1831, suggests that the M.P.U. was entirely Prentice's creation. In fact Bentham referred to both of the political unions in Manchester, 'one a mixed one, aristocratico-democratical of which it appears he (Prentice) was the organiser; the other a purely democratical one, of which it appears he is the influential director, having preserved them from breaking out into fits of mischievous violence'.[92] This reveals that Prentice was indeed involved with the P.U.W.C. in some way, even if the body does appear to have been established as a protest against the exclusiveness of the M.P.U.'s political council. It is also true that the enmity between the two bodies only really became apparent when the P.U.W.C. decided not to support the Reform Bill. Perhaps some kind of cooperation, with Prentice as the link, had initially been possible. But whatever the nature of Prentice's early connection with the P.U.W.C .(if there was one), and whatever the true reason for the P.U.W.C.'s appearance, the two organisations quickly fell out because of a disagreement over aims and methods.

The political council was extremely active in 1831 on behalf of the Reform Bill. The council repeatedly held meetings and organised addresses and petitions for reform, accepting the government's measure as a first instalment while emphasising the need for something more. December 1830 saw a declaration in favour of parliamentary reform and Grey's ministry, and when the Tory Liverpool M.P. General Gascoyne successfully moved (20 April 1831) that the number of members for England and Wales should not be reduced the M.P.U. was one of the first bodies to petition for the Reform Bill in its entirety. The M.P.U. pressed again for 'the whole Bill', without major amendments, in June and July 1831. At this time there was consternation because of a new restriction on the borough franchise: no vote would go to those whose rent was payable more frequently than half-yearly. This would exclude thousands who had been

[91] Read, introduction to Prentice's *Sketches*, p. x–xii.
[92] B.L., Add. MS. 35149, f. 74, cited in Main, 'Reform Movement', p. 168.

promised the vote in the original bill. The council approved a petition to the Commons on this matter on 29 June. After some uncertainty Prentice's *Times* of 20 August 1831 was glad to report Althorp's assurance that all *bona fide* payers of £10 rent would receive the vote.[93]

As tension mounted in July and August 1831 because of the slow progress of the Reform Bill, the council drew up a petition urging the Commons to end the delay. The council warned of the prospect of disturbances if delay continued, and argued that if the Reform Bill was going to be altered it should be extended, not diluted, with provision for the ballot and a wider suffrage. Similar points were made in an address to Grey in September 1831, by which time the council had come to favour a creation of peers. The M.P.U.'s canvassing for members and organisation of meetings went on, as did its censure of the P.U.W.C. In this criticism Prentice and the M.P.U. were joined by the Edinburgh Political Union, of which Prentice's elder brother John seems to have been a leading member. The Lords' rejection of the Reform Bill on 8 October 1831 made it likely that the government would water the measure down to overcome some of the peers' objections. The council of the M.P.U. could not countenance such a step, and on 9 November resolved that what was really required was a scot and lot franchise for all boroughs (which would get rid of the 'invidious distinction between the man who pays a ten pound rent and his neighbour who happens to pay a pound or a shilling or a penny less'), an opportunity given annually for each constituency to replace its M.P. if he had not discharged his duties satisfactorily (which would overcome anti-reformers' claims that popular electorates would mean 'noisy and unprincipled' instead of 'able and virtuous' representatives), and the protection of the ballot (which would remove the danger that 'in large towns the respectable inhabitants will be deterred from the free exercise of their choice by the fear of personal violence'). The council urged all reformers to throw aside their differences and unite in the common cause. Though its members wanted more than the Reform Bill they would still accept it provided its essential character was not changed. 'Their principle is to advance – to the extreme point as speedily as possible – but at all events, to ADVANCE'. If the council really expected that the government's bill would be amended in the desired fashion it was

[93] *Times*, 1 Jan., 23 April, 2 July, 20 Aug. 1831.

being more hopeful than realistic. Even so, Prentice was bitter about the Whigs' response to the approval and support they received in 1830–32. Commenting on the above resolutions in his *Sketches*, he wrote:

> Such was the generous waiving of present demands, considered just and reasonable, which the reformers conceded to the Whig administration, believing that when a beginning had been made, and made safely, they would acknowledge the principle of progression; and if they did not themselves urge on other reforms, would at least leave the shortening the duration of parliaments, the adoption of the ballot, and the extension of the suffrage as open questions. It was an ungenerous return to declare the doctrine of finality.[94]

The P.U.W.C. continued its agitation while the *Guardian* continued to condemn political unions as 'mock parliaments' that were irresponsible, divisive and probably of no help in maintaining order, despite their claims to the contrary.[95] The M.P.U. went on with its activities through the winter of 1831–32 and kept up the pressure in favour of the Reform Bill. A royal proclamation of 1831 banned political associations composed of separate bodies and subdivisions, with a hierarchy of ranks subjected to the general control of a central committee. This was aimed against the Birmingham plan for sectional organisation, which was abandoned. The council members of the M.P.U. met on 23 November to declare that their organisation did not come under the ban and that there was no reason for it to cease its activity. Prentice followed this up by printing a summary of the laws relating to political societies. This was designed to boost the confidence of members of the M.P.U. and other such bodies, to show them that they were acting constitutionally, and to advise them of the methods they should not employ. Taylor, for his part, approved of the proclamation and argued that political unions did not advance the cause of reform but created a prejudice against it.[96]

At the same time as Prentice was devoting much energy to the M.P.U., he and the others in the band were involving themselves fully in the 'official' town campaign in favour of the Reform Bill.

[94] *Times*, 6, 13 Aug., 17 Sept., 1, 15, 29 Oct., 5, 12 Nov. 1831; Prentice, *Sketches*, pp. 403–4.
[95] *Guardian*, 5 Nov. 1831.
[96] *Times*, 26 Nov., 3 Dec. 1831; *Guardian*, 26 Nov. 1831.

The respectable reformers dominated the public meeting of 9 March 1831, held in the town hall and chaired by the boroughreeve James Burt, a merchant and member of the declining Pitt Club. Richard Potter, Baxter, Watkin and Shuttleworth were among the requisitionists, and Watkin was the author of a petition to the king in favour of the government's bill, which the meeting approved. The *Times* gave the meeting a full seven columns of space and Richard Potter, Baxter, Prentice, Shuttleworth and Watkin were all speakers. They dealt with the need for parliamentary reform and the other improvements it would make possible. The *Guardian* praised the meeting, emphasising (as usual) that reform should primarily serve the interests of local commerce and the middle classes. The *Chronicle* pointed out that local Tories had stayed away from the meeting, which did not say much for cross-party cordiality, and complained about the wearing of white hats by some members of the audience.[97] Before long a knot of committed Tories organised a petition against the Reform Bill. Prentice's remarks about them and their petition led to his trial for libel in July 1831. He was really on trial for his political opinions.[98] Victory vindicated him, was a great source of personal celebration, and helped to advance the causes espoused by Prentice and his circle. It strengthened their confidence and their sense of duty and mission.

The success of Gascoyne's motion on 20 April was followed by a dissolution and a general election. The band was pleased that the principle of reform was not going to be abandoned by the government, and looked forward to a contest for Lancashire county. J. W. Patten's vote in favour of Gascoyne's motion provided an opportunity for local reformers to insert a new candidate who would be committed to the Reform Bill. The *Courier* defended Patten while a committee combining moderate and advanced reformers from Manchester's respectable business classes discussed a suitable candidate to run against him. The body included Atkinson, Baxter, the Potters, Smith and Shuttleworth. Lord John Russell was the first choice, but he preferred to stand for Devon county. The respectable reformers therefore selected one of their own number, the wealthy Unitarian

---

[97] *Times* and *Guardian*, 12, 19 March 1831; *Chronicle*, 12 March 1831; Watkin, *Journal*, pp. 149–50; Brotherton Scrapbooks, ix, p. 67; Shuttleworth Scrapbook, p. 86–7; Boroughreeve's Papers, ii, pp. 27–9; Prentice, *Sketches*, pp. 375–6.
[98] See above, chapter II section (3).

banker Benjamin Heywood. As the band and its allies wrote, spoke and canvassed for Heywood, it became clear that local opinion was very much behind him and the Reform Bill, and Patten withdrew. Heywood's success was warmly welcomed in the *Times* and *Guardian*. Richard Potter stood for Wigan again, after declining invitations to stand for Preston and Blackburn. Hardcastle stood with him in Wigan, but as before the exclusive voting system prevented their return even though they gained the most votes from the burgesses at large. Despite this disappointment the general election did produce a large majority favourable to the Whig government and the Reform Bill, and members of the band had helped to ensure that Lancashire returned two supporters of the bill, one of whom was of their own circle.[99]

Discussion soon turned to what would happen when the Reform Bill went up to the Lords, and there was also much debate about the continuing reappearance in the town and neighbourhood of Henry Hunt. He was having a disturbing influence. For the band's circle, of course, Hunt's stance on the Reform Bill and the willingness of many plebeian radicals to follow him were bound to cause friction in Manchester and embarrass the town's 'official' campaign in favour of the government's measure. Prentice wrote articles in May and June on 'The Proper Business of a Reformed Parliament', stressing that the Reform Bill should be viewed and used as a means to further ends. The *Guardian* also considered this subject on occasion, though Taylor was more temperate in his comments than Prentice. Taylor was less impatient and wanted proper time and deliberation to be given to all reform proposals. Late in May the band's party marked King William IV's birthday with a special reform dinner. The Potters, Baxter, Atkinson and Watkin were among the organisers. Prentice was involved with a second dinner, organised by the St Andrew's Society. Soon his *Times* was commenting unfavourably on the delegate schemes and excessive language of some plebeian radicals. Prentice explained that the reform of parliament would be nothing without the reform of persons. The workers were often let down by the individuals they followed,

---

[99] Potter Collection, xi, p. 168; Smith, Reminiscences, pp. 40–42; Prentice, *Recollections of Bentham*, p. 6, and *Sketches*, pp. 377–8, 394; *Courier*, 23 April, 28 May 1831; *Guardian*, 23, 30 April, 7, 14 May 1831; *Times*, 23, 30 April, 7, 28 May 1831; *Chronicle*, 7 May 1831, 6 Oct. 1832; Brotherton Scrapbooks, x, p. 53.

unreliable, loud and unruly men such as Nathan Broadhurst, who discredited the workers' cause and robbed it of any chance of success. The workers would get nowhere unless they learned to follow the right men, the inference being that Prentice and his allies were the right men.[100]

In the summer of 1831 Manchester fell prey to a wave of controversy and indignation on account of the provision in the amended Reform Bill that, in boroughs, a man would be denied the vote if his rent was payable more frequently than once every six months. The band organised a meeting for 30 June in the manor court room. It was chaired by Richard Potter. Some P.U.W.C. members attended and became disruptive, demanding the approval of universal suffrage and trying to force Potter to leave the chair. The radical leader, John Doherty, also recommended a delegate scheme. But the band retained control and the meeting approved a petition to the Commons asking that the vote be given to all payers of £10 rents. Prentice's speech emphasised that the workers had many friends in the middle classes, and that he, Baxter, Potter and others were keen to help and advise and did not deserve to be accused of self-interest, for nobody was forcing them to fight against restrictions on the franchise nor lend a sympathetic ear to the workers' views. The *Times* attacked those who had disturbed the meeting, criticised the timid Whig government and stressed that it was no reflection on a man's character if he was required to pay his rent monthly or even weekly. Prentice also accused M.P.s who had been returned at the last election because of their commitment to 'the whole Bill' of a breach of faith. The *Guardian* was glad that the plebeians had not been able to hijack the Manchester meeting, and argued that the best portions of the labouring classes were not hostile to the Reform Bill. In August the *Times* reported that all payers of £10 rents would be enfranchised. The *Chronicle* did not approve of this settlement, found it inconsistent with the principles embodied in other parts of the bill, and warned that the franchise would lead to 'pure democracy' in large towns.[101]

---

[100] *Times*, 7, 28 May, 4, 11, 25 June 1831; Prentice, *Sketches*, pp. 416–17; *Guardian*, 4, 25 June, 9 July 1831, 7 Jan. 1832; *Chronicle*, 28 May, 11 June 1831.

[101] *Times*, 2 July, 20 Aug. 1831; *Guardian*, 2 July 1831; *Chronicle*, 2 July, 3 Sept. 1831.

By mid-September it was clear that the Reform Bill would soon complete its passage through the Commons. A requisition was presented to the town officers on 15 September asking them to call a public meeting to consider petitioning the Lords to pass the bill without delay. There were hundreds of signatures, of moderates as well as advanced reformers, *menu peuple* as well as prominent figures in the business community. The Potters, Shuttleworth, Harvey, Taylor, Baxter and Prentice all signed the requisition, as did most of their regular allies. Watkin had written the requisition on 13 September, along with some tentative resolutions and a draft petition to the Lords. The meeting was chaired by the borough-reeve, James Burt, and took place in the manor court room on 22 September, the day the Commons finally passed the bill. It was dominated by the respectable reformers, though the band did have to put up with interruptions from some popular radical leaders. The most telling speeches came from Richard Potter, Shuttleworth, Baxter and Prentice. The petition was approved and a committee of 28 men (the Manchester Reform Committee) was appointed to further the purposes of the meeting and supervise the town's campaign until the Lords passed the Reform Bill. The committee included the town officers and some moderates, but the advanced reformers were also well-represented. There were five of the band (the Potters, Shuttleworth, Baxter and Watkin), several of their closest allies (including Mark Philips, J. C. Dyer and Thomas Harbottle), and four members of the M.P.U.'s political council (Candelet, Hampson, Winder and Bunting). Prentice was not a member but did attend some of the committee's later meetings. His *Times* gave full publicity and backing, and he was the close friend of some of its members. In various ways, therefore, he was involved in the Manchester reform campaign on three levels: with the respectable Reform Committee, with the predominantly middling sort M.P.U., and with the workers' P.U.W.C. (at least in its formative period, before its leaders adopted an anti-Reform Bill policy) and the plebeian branches attached to the M.P.U. After its approval by the manor court room meeting, the Manchester petition received over 33,000 signatures in only five days and was entrusted to Richard Potter and Baxter, who left for London on 29 September. The *Guardian* found the meeting 'important and satisfactory' and was delighted that the Huntites had not been able to take it over, while the *Chronicle* welcomed it as a triumph for the cause of sensible reform. At this time the *Courier* was expecting and hoping that the peers would considerably modify the Reform Bill and make it less harmful.[102]

The committee established at the meeting of 22 September 1831 was to meet sixteen times between that date and the end of December. The attendance record shows how influential members of the band and their allies were, in contrast to what had happened with the Manchester Representation Committee during the Penryn campaign of 1827–28. Then the moderates and conservatives had dominated, much to the band's frustration. But in 1831–32 the respectable reformers were strong and influential. The Reform Committee spoke for the town and, more often than not, members of the band dominated the committee's deliberations. Thomas Potter attended seven of the sixteen meetings, four of which he chaired. Richard Potter attended three meetings, chairing all of them. Shuttleworth attended nine and chaired three, while Baxter attended three and Watkin nine meetings. It is significant that the boroughreeve and constables were not regular attenders; nor were the moderates and conservatives who did not belong to the band's party. Hence the situation in 1831–32 was almost the reverse of that in 1827–28. The respectable reformers were determined and able to have more of a say this time. Between September and December 1831 at least one of the band was always present at committee meetings, and usually there were three or four. Members of the band also chaired ten of the sixteen meetings. Close allies J. C. Dyer and Mark Philips chaired another five between them, which means that all meetings except one were presided over by men who were prominent in Manchester's liberal circles. In May 1832 the committee met a further four times, with Shuttleworth chairing three meetings and Thomas Potter one. Smith, Brotherton and Prentice joined their friends at these meetings, underlining once again the opening for and extent of the band's influence.[103]

Through September Prentice reported reform meetings held in counties and towns all over the kingdom, including that in Salford addressed by Brotherton and Harvey. Opinion seemed to be

[102] *Times*, 17, 24 Sept. 1831; Boroughreeve's Papers, ii, pp. 98–104; Potter Collection, xi, p. 176; Prentice, *Sketches*, pp. 395–6; Watkin, *Journal*, p. 152 (also Archives Dept. M.C.L., Watkin Papers M219/1/1–6 for the resolutions of September 1831); Shuttleworth Scrapbook, pp. 88–9; *Guardian*, 24 Sept., 1 Oct. 1831; *Chronicle*, 24 Sept. 1831; *Courier*, 17, 24 Sept., 1 Oct. 1831.

[103] For attendance lists and details of meetings, Boroughreeve's Papers, ii, pp. 104–19, 158–62.

spreading in favour of a creation of peers, though Taylor preferred to think (almost until the last moment) that the Lords would pass the Reform Bill. Prentice called for a petitioning campaign in favour of a creation, and the establishment of local associations for the protection of persons and property (in case a rejection by the peers endangered the public peace). The Lords did reject the bill, on 8 October. The *Guardian* found the margin of 41 votes surprisingly large, but Taylor later said that a creation of peers should still be regarded as positively the last resort. The *Courier* asserted that the Lords had taken the most appropriate and statesmanlike course.[104]

Members of the band reacted quickly when news of the peers' rejection reached Manchester, posting placards, framing resolutions and organising a requisition for a public meeting. This was arranged for 12 October in the Lower Mosley Street riding school, but it did not go as planned. The P.U.W.C. leaders promoted a large attendance of their own supporters, succeeded in having the meeting moved to the open air on Camp Field, and then amended the respectable reformers' address for a creation of peers. The amended version called for annual parliaments, universal suffrage, the ballot and the sending of writs to populous towns so that a reform including these features could be quickly secured. The band was embarrassed and annoyed by what occurred, and Thomas Potter was placed in the difficult position of being expected by the P.U.W.C. leaders publicly to approve of the amended address in his capacity as chairman of the Camp Field meeting. He had agreed to chair the huge assembly when the boroughreeve refused to participate in a meeting that would not be held in the riding school as arranged. Prentice was also disappointed at the way the meeting had gone, but was able to use it to demonstrate that if the Lords did not reconsider their position on reform they would eventually have a far more radical measure forced upon them. The Reform Committee did not allow the Camp Field fiasco to interrupt Manchester's 'official' campaign in favour of the Reform Bill. Thomas Potter wrote to Grey to explain what had happened, the committee refused to pay any of the expenses relating to the meeting claimed by the P.U.W.C. leaders, and when the latter demanded that Potter sign the amended address they met with another refusal. The committee decided to send the

original unamended address to the king. By early November it had
received over 23,400 signatures. Some of the plebeian radicals threatened violence and the committee decided that no more public meetings should be held until they became absolutely necessary. Watkin
noted 'an evident dread of commotion in the Committee', and
concluded that no further expression of local opinion on the Reform
Bill would be attempted 'for fear of the Radicals'. R. A. Sykes might
be right when he sees in Camp Field 'a decisive working class
rejection of middle class political leadership'. Certainly the meeting
provided the clearest possible expression of the split between some
popular radicals and the respectable liberals in Manchester. The
P.U.W.C. was never again to achieve such a mobilisation and would
soon decline, but from Watkin's evidence it is clear that in October
and November 1831 the band's circle was greatly alarmed by plebeian radical activity and possible threats to order.[105]

On 14 October 1831 Smith chaired a reform meeting in Salford.
There was no attempt by popular radicals to hijack this affair and no
repeat of what had occurred in Manchester. The Salford meeting
approved an address to the king urging the adoption of decisive
measures to overcome the peers' resistance. Prentice's *Times* was
enthusiastic, and jubilantly confirmed that the Manchester address
for the creation of peers which had been amended at Camp Field
would be sent in its original form. The Camp Field controversy was
not over, though, because the P.U.W.C. leaders attended a leypayers'
meeting on 26 October to argue that the town ought to pay the
expenses relating to Camp Field since the costs incurred by previous
town meetings on reform had been covered by the constables' accounts. This argument was rejected. The boroughreeve had expressly
stated that he would not chair an open air meeting, and the change
of location from the riding school made the claim for expenses
unacceptable. The boroughreeve's absence from the Camp Field
meeting deprived it of official status. Like the *Times* the *Guardian*
approved of this resistance to the designs of the P.U.W.C. leaders,

---

[105] Prentice, *Sketches*, pp. 398–400; *Times*, 15 Oct. 1831; Watkin, *Journal*, pp.
152–6; Shuttleworth Scrapbook, pp. 88–9; Wheeler, *History*, pp. 129–30;
Smith, Reminiscences, p. 44; Boroughreeve's Papers, ii, pp. 111–19; Potter
Collection, xi, p. 177; Sykes, 'Popular Politics', p. 369. The original draft
resolutions for the meeting of 12 October are in Watkin Papers, M219/1/1–6
(handwritten 'Resolutions for the public meeting on the rejection of the
Reform Bill Oct. 12 1831, meeting upset by the Radicals').

and was disappointed by what happened at Camp Field. Taylor called the P.U.W.C. 'a most dangerous conspiracy' and welcomed Thomas Potter's refusal to let his name be used by the victors of Camp Field. Prentice went on advocating a creation of peers, Taylor was more reticent, but both men pointed to the vote of the bishops on the Reform Bill as a sign of the improper role and position of the clergy in the state. The *Courier* defended the bishops.[106]

Discussion was kept up as Prentice argued for something more than the Reform Bill (he was now focusing on household suffrage as a suitable objective), as the Bristol riots gave both reformers and conservatives useful propaganda material, and as the P.U.W.C. advocated a declaration of rights and a National Convention. The third Reform Bill was introduced on 12 December. Prentice was pleased that the 'clogs' surrounding the £10 borough qualification had been removed while Manchester conservatives evinced mixed feelings. There was also the problem outlined by Shuttleworth in a letter to Grey in January 1832. By giving the vote to tenants and occupiers of houses and business premises, whether they were resident or not, the Reform Bill would create in Manchester up to two thousand electors who had only a limited connection with the town. Grey referred the matter to Russell and an amendment was soon introduced to the effect that those qualifying for the vote in Manchester on the grounds of occupancy had to reside within seven miles of the borough limits. The Reform Bill passed the Commons on 22 March and discussion again turned to the peers' attitude. Prentice still pressed for a creation, not just to pass the bill but 'to neutralise on other questions the Tory creations of the preceding kings'. Taylor hoped that the peers would see sense and give way, the *Chronicle* suspected that a creation would be necessary and the *Courier* predictably opposed such a step. Meanwhile Richard Potter was in touch with the radical Middlesex M.P. Joseph Hume. Hume told him that Grey, Althorp, Durham and the Whig leaders lacked confidence and strength, and that there were grounds for pessimism regarding the prospects for true reform.[107]

[106] *Times* and *Guardian*, 15, 22, 29 Oct. 1831; *Courier*, 29 Oct. 1831. The Salford address is in Brotherton Scrapbooks, ix, p. 70.
[107] *Times*, 29 Oct., 5, 12, 19, 26 Nov., 3, 17, 24, 31 Dec. 1831, 14, 21 Jan., 11, 18 Feb., 3, 10, 17, 31 March, 7, 21 April 1832; *Guardian*, 5 Nov., 17, 24 Dec. 1831, 7, 28 Jan., 11, 25 Feb., 10, 31 March, 14, 21 April 1832; *Courier*, 5 Nov., 17 Dec. 1831, 7, 28 Jan., 31 March 1832; *Chronicle*, 17 Dec. 1831, 31 March 1832; Shuttleworth Scrapbook, p. 92; Potter Collection, xii, pp. 253–5.

On 7 May the government was defeated on Lord Lyndhurst's motion to postpone the disfranchisement clauses until the enfranchisement clauses had been considered. The ministers resigned. There was much agitation in Manchester. When news of the resignation came through on Thursday morning, 10 May, crowds gathered in the streets, business was suspended and hundreds rushed to the town hall where the Reform Committee was sitting. Shuttleworth chaired a hastily convened public meeting which approved a petition composed by Watkin. This called for the Commons to refuse to vote any supplies until 'a measure essential to the safety and happiness of the people, and the safety of the throne, shall be carried into a law'. By 6 p.m. that evening 24,000 signatures had been gained. Richard Potter, Shuttleworth and the radical manufacturer, John Fielden (a member of the M.P.U. council), carried the petition to London, spreading the news of Manchester's decisive response at each stopping point. They arrived late on Friday morning, 11 May, contacted the Preston M.P. John Wood, and the petition was presented that evening. It was the first formal expression of public opinion following the government's defeat. Back in Manchester Thomas Potter, Smith, Watkin and Baxter helped to organise a public meeting, which was called for 14 May. Smith noted the 'frantic enthusiasm' which had gripped Manchester and was impressed by the local determination to pay no taxes until the Reform Bill was passed. He wrote to Shuttleworth in London on 12 May with information about what was happening. Shuttleworth replied on 14 May that he had passed the information on to some London papers, and that all the signs were that the king would soon have to recall the Whigs to office. Meanwhile Watkin recorded that the plebeian leaders were again threatening to disrupt Manchester's 'official' campaign by promoting a movement against a creation of peers. The Tory *Courier* welcomed Grey's resignation and dismissed the Manchester petition as a dishonest and desperate measure.[108]

The St Peter's Field meeting of 14 May saw a good deal of unanimity between reformers of all ranks and opinions. Thomas Potter, Prentice and Harvey were among the speakers, and an address to the king calling for the reappointment of Grey was

---

[108] *Times*, 12, 19 May 1832; Prentice, *Sketches*, pp. 407–10; Watkin, *Fragment No. 1*, p. 19, and Journal, pp. 158–60; Smith, Reminiscences, pp. 46–9, and Parliamentary Elections, p. 10; Shuttleworth Scrapbook, pp. 96–7; Hadfield, Personal Narrative, pp. 109–10; *Courier*, 12, 19, 26 May 1832.

approved.[109] But behind the apparent cordiality there was continuing friction. The plebeian leaders tried to exact concessions in return for their goodwill while members of the band were trying to keep the plebeians in line. At the popular leaders' suggestion the address proposed at St Peter's Field was more radical in tone than the one originally envisaged. Some promise of cooperation was also embodied in the plebeians' scheme for a new Association to Promote Reform, which would unite moderates and radicals, masters and workers, in a movement for the Reform Bill *and* something more. The body would, for example, formally endorse the principle of universal manhood suffrage. On 15 May Baxter, Shuttleworth, Watkin, Richard Potter and their occasional ally, R. H. Greg, accepted the plan in theory, but said they wanted time to work out suitable rules for the proposed association. Days passed and the plebeian leaders grew impatient. Finally on 21 May there was a meeting at Hayward's Hotel. To the anger of the popular radicals and their spokesman John Fielden, Shuttleworth, Baxter and Greg said that the association had been rendered unnecessary. The Whigs were coming back and the Reform Bill would be passed. The respectable reformers were accused of inconsistency and desertion by the bulk of the meeting and there was bitter argument, but they had successfully extricated themselves from an embarrassing and troublesome undertaking. Most of them felt, as Watkin did, that no cooperation with the plebeian leaders could work for long because the latter 'seek for confusion and want only the countenance of the wealthy to enable them to produce it'. It would seem that the plebeian complaint about a betrayal was not without foundation. The respectable reformers had only spoken of compromise so that the 'official' Manchester campaign in favour of the Reform Bill could continue undisturbed, and now the need for concession had passed. The Reform Bill seemed and was secure.[110]

---

[109] *Times*, 19, 26 May 1832; Prentice, *Sketches*, pp. 410–14; Boroughreeve's Papers, ii, pp. 158–62; Wheeler, *History*, p. 131. For original resolutions see Watkin Papers, M219/1/1–6 ('Resolutions for the public meeting to be held in St Peter's Field May 14 1832'). See Brotherton Scrapbooks, ix, p. 77 for the Salford meeting of 16 May, addressed by Smith and Brotherton, adjourned because news came through that the Whigs had returned to office.

[110] Watkin, *Journal*, pp. 160–63; Dinwiddy, *Luddism to Reform Bill*, p. 67.

VII *Conclusion*

The 'small but determined band' included Manchester's most assertive, ambitious and public-spirited reformers of the early nineteenth century. Their dynamism and persistence were facilitated by earned status, growing wealth, and individual talents (literary, oratorical and organisational). Their public endeavours were squarely based on an impatience with the present and a confidence that they knew what was wrong with society, the economy and the political system. The ideas they advanced concerning solutions to the problems of their day owed much to theological and moral premises, for the spiritual impulse was one of the main driving forces behind their political careers. Members of the band also gained encouragement from the examples set by their predecessors. Progressive middle-class reformers had been active in Manchester before 1815 despite the lack of widespread support, disapproval from the ruling party, coercive legislation and wartime persecution. The band appreciated the bravery and persistence of this earlier generation of reformers and paid tribute to their patriotism, determination and heroic struggle against a range of obstacles. There was, in addition, indignation about the treatment received by such men as Thomas Walker and Joseph Hanson, and this was another powerful spur to action after 1815. Prentice, the Potters, Shuttleworth and their friends also saw that they could use their knowledge of what had happened to previous Manchester reformers to make sure that their own campaigns were more impressive and successful. Hence they took Walker's stance on the link between reformist activity and educational provisions a stage further (and it is interesting that Walker made the connection long before philosophic radicals such as John Arthur Roebuck popularised their ideas about the relationship between education and political rights).[1] Members of the band also paid more attention than had their predecessors to social and

---

[1] The educational and other ideas of Roebuck and the philosophic radicals are discussed in W. E. S. Thomas, *The Philosophic Radicals* (1979).

economic questions, and to the needs and desires of humbler social groups. According to the band, these groups contained individuals who deserved to be treated as free-born, dignified human beings as well as potential supporters for the reform cause.

Members of the band participated in the development of the provincial newspaper press. The *Guardian* in particular set new standards in newspaper business management, organisation and presentation, and was also an organ of opinion. Prentice's papers were more avowedly political organs, designed to create and direct opinion on the salient issues of the time. The *Gazette* and *Times* were the band's representative mouthpieces and media of communication. They played a crucial role in the discussions and mobilisations of this period, and indeed the band's contribution to the development of nineteenth-century political journalism was not insubstantial. As writers for and proprietors, editors and financial backers of newspapers, Prentice, Taylor, Shuttleworth, Baxter, the Potters, Smith, Watkin and the others helped to extend political agitation, propaganda and debate, and this was not only important for the viability of Manchester liberalism. Since many newspapers became political weapons in some degree, wielded by conservatives as well as reformers, the use of the press became a dominant factor in contests for control of local affairs and in the course of provincial urban politics generally. The band made it clear that if local politicians wanted influence they had to have a newspaper. This was as true of Sheffield, Bristol, Liverpool, Birmingham or any other large town of turbulent politics as it was of Manchester.

Among the band's main preoccupations was the movement against Tory and then 'high' party control of Manchester affairs. What is striking is the respectable reformers' readiness and ability to make the challenge. This activity, however, opened up new rifts between Taylor and some of the others. Disagreements about the editorial line followed by the *Guardian* were strengthened as Taylor decided that he could not go as far as some of his colleagues in the attempt to open up the local government system. He believed that rank and property had to be protected against numbers. Prentice and the others initiated and engaged in local government disputes because they desired a proper balance between opposing political interests, a more genuine respect for the rights of townspeople, and clearer rules for the conduct of local officials. The most progressive band members appealed to groups of lower social status and displayed great talent for agitation and organisation. What is more they made important advances, for the ruling party was often in difficulty. In pursuing more influence for themselves the reformers spoke and acted for those who felt excluded or improperly treated. They emphasised the need for change and improvement, all the time conscious of their own rising local status and public profile.

The 1820s represent a transitional decade in Manchester politics. The polarisation of parties became starker and more deeply pronounced. Basically Tory-Anglican and liberal-Dissenting amalgams within the large business community collided on a range of issues connected with the questions of who was to possess local authority and how that authority should best be exercised. Ideas which had been difficult to express in the war years were increasingly articulated as the challenge to the ruling party gathered strength. Peterloo was important in this development because it encouraged Manchester's 'outs' to assert themselves. The ruling party no longer seemed so unassailable. The band rose to prominence and influence in the 1820s, preparing the way for parliamentary enfranchisement (1832), incorporation (1838) and the establishment of the League (1839), and forging links with reform-minded shopkeepers and others of the middling sort in an on-going campaign for justice and reform in local arenas. All this required great effort and persistence, and at first liberal victories were slow in coming. The crucial change was the increase in public interest and involvement in local affairs. Disputes intensified as attention was drawn to local expenditure, officers' conduct, accountability, salaries, rates and problems related to street improvements. Bitterness only increased with the infusion of sectarian feeling, as in the arguments over new churches, church rates and tithes. The gas dispute encompassed several important questions. What, for example, was the best way to pay for local improvements? Manchester's inadequate and archaic system of local government, along with the social and administrative problems posed by rapid urban and industrial expansion, certainly cried out for a large and permanent fund that could be devoted to remedial measures. Yet this issue was far from straightforward. Should there be a general improvement fund or an employment of the rising profits made by the municipally-owned gas establishment? Which should prevail, the interests of the gas consumers or the welfare of the town as a whole, and was there a way of reconciling the two? Once the appropriation of the gas profits was a *fait accompli*, members of the band sought some form of reconciliation through gas price reductions, and these were gradually secured. But the gas dispute had put Manchester's rulers on their guard: the respectable reformers and (perhaps more dangerously) their humbler allies were becoming too assertive. The police body was remodelled in 1828, though the liberals were at least able to amend the police bill into a less objectionable measure than the one originally devised. This gave them an important taste of success and encouraged them to mount new and more ambitious campaigns in the future.

Members of the band were deeply involved in educational, welfare and relief efforts, and engaged in the social debates of the era with growing alacrity. They helped to identify problems and to find solutions. They were concerned about the improvement of the lower ranks, about living and working conditions, health, morality and social conduct. They also studied industrial relations and the rights, status and behaviour of the labouring classes. What are we to make of the picture of segregation and heartlessness in Manchester presented by Friedrich Engels in the 1840s? Did the middle classes move out to the suburbs and wash their hands of the problems experienced in the more central working-class districts? Engels described the charity that was given as worthless and hypocritical, for the 'bourgeoisie' was giving back only a fraction of what it took from the workers, and the motivation was not true philanthropic concern but pure self-interest. Charity was meant to buy the workers' obedience.[2] Engels overstated his case. It would be going too far to say that all Mancunians of affluence and respectability were as unconcerned as he claims, just as it would be untrue to say that they all took a close interest in the conditions of the lower ranks. There was residential segregation in Manchester and this became increasingly clear from the 1820s to the 1840s,[3] but it did not mean the complete removal of the town's natural leaders. Removal was not available or desirable for all, and even the middle-class Mancunians who left the central areas returned each day for business and for social and cultural activities. There was no complete detachment. Local government issues and the questions of education, social welfare, poverty and living standards continued to attract attention. A strong sense of duty and responsibility was manifested in a wide range of improving ventures. One corollary of such activity was an undoubted desire for

---

[2] Engels, *Condition of the Working Class*, pp. 314–15.
[3] K. Chorley, *Manchester Made Them* (1950), pp. 137–9; Reach, *Manchester and the Textile Districts*, pp. 2–3; c. f. Engels, *Condition of the Working Class*, pp. 64–6, 84–111.

social prominence and the recognised rewards it could bring. Altruism was mixed with self-interest. There was also a concern for and pride in urban society, a desire for 'culture' as well as status and authority, a belief in and eagerness to act upon the voluntary ideal, and a desire to provide restraints, controls and alternatives as a means of dealing with social problems and objectionable conduct. Nor can we ignore the religious and moral imperatives behind the activity of the band and other reform-minded public men.[4]

The most progressive members of the band were truly interested in the lives and views of the lower ranks. In political campaigns they cooperated with humbler allies. Like many middle-class well-wishers, though, they sometimes proved unable to communicate their genuine concern. To some workers the respectable reformers seemed patronising and self-interested, the agents of restraint and control. As the spinner Jonathan Hodgins, a plebeian ally of Prentice and the band, told a Manchester meeting in May 1825: 'I know there are gentlemen present of great eloquence, and much better qualified than I am to discuss the question; but then their eloquence is not always convincing to the working man's mind because it is frequently above comprehension; it is a dish of fish that he does not understand'.[5] This illustrates the failure or inability of Manchester's middle-class philanthropists and reformers to hit the right note for workers, and possibly also the workers' lack of proper facilities for understanding and appreciating what was being done and said on their behalf. The reformers' statements and activities confirm their authentic commitment to improving ventures and their interest in corrective remedies affecting social welfare, poverty, education, plebeian home life, wages and working conditions. They were also keen for workers to be accorded appropriate political and social

[4] On these points see Kidd, 'Middle class in nineteenth-century Manchester' and M. E. Rose, 'Culture, philanthropy and the Manchester middle classes', both in Kidd and Roberts, *City, Class and Culture*, pp. 1–25, 103–17; Garrard, 'The middle classes and 19th-century national and local politics', in Garrard *et al.*, *Middle Class in Politics*, p. 54; Hindle, *Provision for Relief*, pp. 3–6; Kay, *Moral and Physical Condition*, pp. 99, 112; Morris, 'Voluntary societies and British urban elites', pp. 95–118; Dobbs, *Education and Social Movements*, p. 92; R. J. Morris, 'The Middle Class and British Towns and Cities of the Industrial Revolution, 1780–1870', in Fraser and Sutcliffe, *Pursuit of Urban History*, p. 303; Frangopulo, 'Municipal Achievement', p. 55; Pollard, *Modern Management*, p. 195.

[5] Prentice, *Sketches*, p. 257.

recognition. Some workers did not want what was being offered. Their rejection of what they could not understand was only natural, as was their opposition to what appeared to be too overtly sponsored, designed to control or aimed at moulding the worker in the middle-class image. Some workers quickly recognised the truth of the point made by U. R. Q. Henriques: 'Rescue meant conversion to the moral and social imperatives of the rescuers'.[6] Within the band, though, philanthropic concern was at least as important as any ideas about social conditioning. The band believed in the worth of the individual and in the need for and value of good works. To engage in such works was part of one's duty to God, self, neighbours and municipality.

The fact and extent of paternalist sentiment and activity in Manchester weakens V. A. C. Gatrell's thesis about the dominance of *laissez-faire*.[7] Most of the band do not fit neatly into the mainstream Manchester School, which was a heterogeneous body in any case. Although Taylor was a doctrinaire and notable populariser of *laissez-faire* political economy before the rise of Cobden and Bright, most of the band represent another important section of Manchester opinion, perhaps best described as its liberal-paternalist wing. These men were not rigidly tied to doctrines. Prentice was not consistently Benthamite, as may be seen by his preferences regarding the 'best' educational system, his religiosity and his views on such moral and social issues as birth control. Nor was Prentice a true 'political economist', as shown by his views on wages, factory regulation, poor laws and other questions. Most of the band resembled Prentice in that they took what they wanted from the ideologies and value systems on offer, and mixed these borrowings with their own radical opinions and moral creed. Prentice's views on Ireland, especially his advocacy of productive public works and poor laws, had little to do with orthodox political economy. As in so many fields, of course, the band's interest in and discussion of the Irish question saw its members contributing to a much wider debate, outlining principles and suggesting solutions that were later taken up by more famous figures. The success of the *Guardian* suggests that Taylor was most in tune with the views of the majority of liberal-minded Mancunians who took an interest in public affairs. He often spoke for the

---

[6] Henriques, *Before the Welfare State*, p. 202.
[7] Expressed most clearly in Gatrell, 'Manchester Parable', pp. 28–36.

moderates who were far more numerous but normally less active than Prentice and the reformist vanguard.

At times Taylor was obsessively enthusiastic about political economy. An avid reader of Smith, Ricardo, Mill and others, he imbibed all the main principles and then regurgitated them each week in the *Guardian* in simplistic and straightforward form. This type of instruction and information appealed greatly to his readers among the Manchester business classes. In Donald Read's words:

> The influence achieved among the generally untheoretical Northern businessmen by the theoretical principles of 'laissez-faire' was remarkable. Social psychologists would explain the development as an example of 'rationalisation'. Laissez-faire political economy, understood in its crudest and most unqualified form, rationalised the self-interest of the industrial employers into an apparently God-given system. Employers found their profit-making impeded by legislative restrictions and by vested privileges – Political Economy taught that such impositions and privileges were unnatural. The employers were readily converted and by the 1820s we find the hard-headed businessmen of Manchester hailing the new era in political science.[8]

Like Gatrell, Hertz and Marshall, Read has exaggerated the intellectual and practical control that a particular body of doctrines could achieve in Manchester. Even respectable liberals believed that *laissez-faire* could not be applied to each and every aspect of economic and social organisation. Nevertheless, the influence that *laissez-faire* did achieve owed much to Taylor and the *Guardian*. Prentice's newspapers were less dominated by doctrine. Prentice could not accept absolute *laissez-faire* because of, among other things, his strong Scots-Presbyterian morality and his paternalistic concern for the condition of the operative classes. He believed in the value of some protective legislation to improve the workers' lot, for example, supporting the legal right to combine and rejecting the notion of a totally free and unfettered labour market on the grounds that it encouraged continual wage reductions. On most political subjects there could be broad agreement between Taylor and others in the

[8] Read, 'Reform newspapers and Northern opinion', p. 307; see also Read's *Press and People*, pp. 31–2 and ch. 4.

band because their basic ideas and approach were the same. They may only have differed on the methods to be employed, or on the speed at which desired reforms could and should be implemented. Perhaps their disagreements on social and economic questions were more important. Taylor was the most doctrine-bound of the band and it seems that the break between him and the others had more to do with the use and application of political economy than with disagreements on such matters as parliamentary reform. It is also clear that conflicts of personality played an important part in the rupture, as did disagreements about the direction taken by the *Guardian*. Since the *Guardian* dealt with all issues at the same time, social, economic and political, it might be inaccurate to say that one particular subject was a greater cause of disagreement than another.

As men who were or had been engaged in trade and manufacturing, these respectable reformers were keenly interested in commercial questions and aware of the needs of local business. Their role was to assist in the articulation of grievances and in the campaign for more enlightened and appropriate government policies. Members of the band were successful in mobilising townsmen and in enhancing their own local standing as businessmen, reformers and economic commentators, but for much of the time Manchester's commercial campaigns faced obstructions even when there was a degree of cross-party cooperation. Some of the most important obstacles stemmed from the government's concern to protect its revenues and to preside over a steady and sure-footed movement towards economic security after twenty years of war (1793–1801, 1803–15).

If we consider the politics of commerce in Manchester we find that campaigns were cautious and non-partisan in many cases, and that the approach was an intensely practical one rooted in the need to present particular local grievances and the desire to solicit favoured solutions. Interest and activity were largely limited to those matters of most concern to Manchester businessmen specifically. There could be tension, though, between moderates who were sometimes represented by Taylor, and more active and radical campaigners led by Prentice and some of the others in the band. Taylor differed from them in his views on such subjects as the national debt, minor currency and taxation questions, Huskisson's commercial reforms and to some extent the corn laws. As on other matters disagreement could be related to theory and also to the nature, extent and speed of desired changes. All of the band were free traders. This was a matter of ideological commitment, moral rectitude and sound commercial sense. But this approach to free trade was not that of the majority of interested Mancunians, for they were concerned more with the practice and expected benefits of freer trade than with its morality or intellectual soundness. The growing commitment to free trade was insular and parochial in character, even cynical, and certainly inconsistent. If free trade looked like increasing his profits the typical Manchester businessman was for it. Otherwise he was not interested.

The corn laws became a central preoccupation of the band, whose members helped to keep debate and concern about the corn question alive in the years from 1815 to 1832. During this period they presented a view of the corn laws which differed from that of the majority, but they gradually converted enough townspeople to make a campaign for full repeal a viable proposition. It is clear that the Anti-Corn Law League began with self-interested local and sectional motives, yet the participation of the band meant that this was not the whole story. Of course from 1815 to 1832 the meetings on the corn question in Manchester were characterised by self-interest, the main concerns being wage levels and the town's export trade. The dominant (Ricardian) notion was that food prices and wage rates were directly linked. The most important contribution of Prentice, Shuttleworth and their closest allies was to deny this and to argue that repeal would benefit everyone. They were saying this more than twenty years before the establishment of the League. They also made the corn issue a Manchester issue. Local reformers regarded corn law repeal as very much a Manchester question, one on which it was urgently necessary for Mancunians to act. The band constantly engaged in efforts to stir Manchester up on the matter and repeatedly managed to do this during the 1820s and 1830s. But these efforts only really came to fruition in the time of the League, which also saw Manchester unmistakably at the forefront of the repeal campaign. The Manchester free traders' agitation and propaganda had a cumulative effect until large numbers of townspeople were moved. The situation was different in London, and Cobden was to be concerned about this because historically the provinces had always tended to follow the capital. But the Manchester reformers were happy to take the lead. To them repeal was a local issue and the League's policy was and should be a Manchester policy. This was why Cobden could tell the town council in 1841:

The question of the corn and provision laws is as much a local question in Manchester as that of poor rates, police rates or any other local matter; inasmuch as I believe that a vast amount of your local expenses arise out of the operation of these laws. I may, I believe, further congratulate you and the town generally, that we are now arrived at that point in which there is no-one to be found in Manchester who is in favour of the corn law as it now stands.

In 1846 the town council passed a vote of thanks to the League's leaders. This idea that the corn issue was a Manchester issue survived. In 1946 there was a celebration to mark the centenary of repeal. The commemoration included a grand exhibition of letters, books, prints and other items describing the League's campaign and emphasising Manchester's role as the League's birthplace and headquarters. Mancunians were still proud of the fact that the anti-corn law movement had gained its spirit and direction from Manchester men.[9]

Within Manchester's liberal circles there was no uniform, indiscriminatory acceptance of free trade and *laissez-faire* ideas. In fact some of the respectable reformers focused as much on the exceptions to theoretical patterns and rules as on those areas where doctrine was deemed applicable. It is notable that most of the band made a distinction between freedom for trade, a matter of moral, political and commercial propriety, and a *laissez-faire* approach to social and economic affairs, which they did not accept as a general or universally suitable rule. Prentice and his fellows on the liberal-paternalist wing of Manchester politics believed in and advocated economic liberalism except when its dictates seemed adversely to compromise their superior attachments to humanitarianism and welfare, social justice and individual rights. A policy or principle was judged according to its morality and usefulness. It was not followed for fashion's sake or for its apparent reasonableness and intellectual persuasiveness. The Mancunian liberal-paternalist belief in free trade was fairly constant, especially with regard to international commercial relations, tax and tariff policies and the regulation of production, carriage and exchange. But the commitment to *laissez-faire* in social and economic policy was far more changeable and selective, and

---

[9] Hughes, 'Cobden's economic doctrines', pp. 407–8; 'Corn Law Repeal Centenary', *M.R.*, 4 (1946), 223–4.

depended on the issue being addressed. Liberating and managerial approaches were considered to be equally valid in their own separate spheres.

Throughout this period parliamentary reform retained its central position as the remedy of remedies and the means to further ends. The band engaged wholeheartedly in the reform movement. Peterloo was followed by a remarkable increase in the band's activity and influence, though at the time there was probably more cause for frustration than self-congratulation. For all their effort, honest indignation and effective marshalling of opinion, the band and its allies had few victories in the immediate aftermath of Peterloo. The affair was more important in the long term, because of what it enabled the respectable reformers to achieve later on, than in the shorter term, when the forces of reaction were too strong for the reformers to secure major concessions. Peterloo did provide a valuable foundation to build on, though this was a cumulative process and the reformers needed time to arrive at aims, methods and principles suited to prevailing circumstances. But an advance had been made. The Twenty Six of February 1818, for example, became the 4,800 and more who signed the *Declaration and Protest* after Peterloo. Not all of these signatories would follow the band on each and every issue, but at least a potential reservoir of approval now existed. This potential was fully exploited in the local government disputes of the 1820s, and also in the parliamentary reform campaign of 1830–32. In the latter movement, though, account had to be taken of the equivocation and disagreement in Manchester regarding the Reform Bill. Manchester's social and economic organisation was such, moreover, that it was difficult to construct a united cross-class reform movement in the town. This continued to be the case. It is significant that on the same day, 24 September 1838, Manchester was to see a mass Chartist meeting on Kersal Moor, at which Feargus O'Connor and J. R. Stephens led a demand for the 'six points', and the first meeting of the Anti-Corn Law Association in the York Hotel, King Street.

After March 1831 Manchester conservatives were divided in their responses to the Whig government's Reform Bill. Some accepted it, others quietly acquiesced, there were some who viewed reform agitation with a degree of tolerance, while the most convinced Tories opposed both the bill and its supporters. Many plebeian radicals followed the Hunt line and condemned the bill, even if they had initially welcomed it, but others (notably John Doherty) believed it would be a useful first step. With Manchester Toryism divided and with popular radicalism also divided, it was perhaps inevitable that members of the band should have come to the fore as they did. There was some talk of unity and compromise, and a hope that all parties could join in support of a measure that was apparently designed to promote the national good, but as usual such cooperation was not achieved in any substantial or lasting sense. If anyone was going to speak and act effectively in favour of the Reform Bill it was going to be the band and its circle, with some middling sort allies in support. The band truly came of age as a political force in the early 1830s. The activity in which its members engaged, and their consciousness that they had helped to secure the passing of the Reform Bill, increased their confidence and prestige and strengthened their ability and willingness to campaign for further reforms, particularly incorporation.

If the passing of the Reform Bill was a great victory for the band, another success came with Manchester's first parliamentary election late in 1832. This saw the return of two reformist free trade candidates, local Unitarian merchant Mark Philips and Charles Poulett Thomson, the Whig vice-president of the Board of Trade.[10] In 1832 the band also celebrated the return of Brotherton in Salford and Richard Potter in Wigan. Just as members of the band had played the key role in Manchester's campaign for the Reform Bill, so the return of these four candidates also owed most to their efforts. The 1832 election provided them with possibly their greatest triumph of this pre-incorporation and pre-League era, represented a fitting end to twenty years of activity in the cause of progress and reform, and showed conclusively that the band had truly arrived. From a position of weakness at the end of the French wars, these respectable reformers had risen to have a decisive influence on the course of public affairs. The band's *Times* was the only local paper to support both successful candidates in Manchester. Prentice and Smith were particularly active propagandists for Philips and Thomson as well as for Brotherton and Potter. The others in the band dominated the

---

[10] Philips came from a wealthy local commercial family and had been acting with members of the band in Manchester politics for several years. Thomson had been in the Commons since 1826, was promoted to the cabinet as president of the Board of Trade in June 1834, later served as governor-general of Canada and was created Baron Sydenham in 1840 (the year before his death). He was a leading parliamentary exponent of the new political economy.

election committees of all four candidates, canvassing, writing and speaking on their behalf.[11] The bitterly contested Manchester election of 1832 showed how powerful the band had become and also emphasised the connection between respectable liberals and their supporters from humbler social strata. A prominent reason for the liberal victory in Manchester in 1832 was the successful appeal to voters among the operatives, artisans, petty traders and shopkeepers (especially the latter, for shopkeepers represented 22 per cent of the Manchester electorate in 1832). It could be that the campaign for incorporation in 1837–38 was based partly on the reformers' desire to cultivate and confirm their ties with the middling sort. The band and its allies could not ignore the fact that Manchester Toryism remained dangerously resilient despite the 1832 result, and the 'high' party still dominated the organs of local government. The Tory vote in Manchester's parliamentary elections, in fact, averaged well over 35 per cent between 1832–80 (and in 1868 and 1874 was over 50 per cent).[12]

The idea that Manchester was a liberal town by about 1820 has been advanced most notably by L. S. Marshall and G. B. Hertz.[13] It is untenable: neither commercially nor politically does the Manchester of 1820 fit this description. It is true that free trade and *laissez-faire* principles were becoming more and more widely accepted, but this had everything to do with practical self-interest. The ideological commitment was far from complete and in any case there remained a strong body of hostile opinion, for many townsmen opposed certain forms of commercial liberalisation. Politically Manchester was in the hands of an entrenched conservative oligarchy. This was

[11] The local newspapers are an excellent source for the 1832 elections, especially the *Times*, *Guardian*, *Courier* and *Chronicle* from June to December 1832, but see also Prentice, *League*, i, chs. 1–2; Smith, Parliamentary Elections, pp. 1, 11–26, 29–30, 34–7, 40, 43–4, 48–50, 55, and Reminiscences, pp. 50–64; Shuttleworth Scrapbook, pp. 96–8, 105–6, 108–10, 112, 116; Atkinson Papers, M177/7/9 (political tracts); Hadfield, Personal Narrative, pp. 114–24; Brotherton Scrapbooks, xi, pp. 3–11, 14, 16–18, 20, 25–6, 36–9, 71, xii, pp. 30, 45, 49, 59; Main, 'Reform Movement', ch. 8; L. S. Marshall, 'The first parliamentary election in Manchester', *American Historical Review*, 47 (1941–2), 518–38; Gatrell, 'Incorporation and liberal hegemony', pp. 38–44.
[12] See statistics in Marshall, 'First parliamentary election', pp. 534–7; Gatrell, 'Incorporation and liberal hegemony', pp. 38–41; Fraser, *Urban Politics*, ch. 9.
[13] See especially Marshall, *Public Opinion*, chs. 8, 10; Hertz, *Manchester Politician*, chs. 3, 4.

increasingly challenged by the respectable reformers and their middling sort allies (and sometimes by the popular radicals too), but these 'friends of progress' faced an uphill struggle throughout the period before 1832. There were more reverses than successes. Gradually the 'high' party expanded to take in moderates and Whigs who were as keen as the Tories to defend exclusivity and the interests of rank, wealth and property. The police act of 1828 did not weaken the ruling party's control and it was another ten years before the reformers could capture a commanding position in the local power structure. They secured this through incorporation in 1838 and took on new responsibilities and prerogatives in the following years.[14]

What did it mean to be a liberal reformer in early nineteenth-century Manchester? The brand of liberalism represented by the band evinced several prominent features. Using the band as our guide we can say that, essentially, a liberal believed in progress, reform, freedom and inquiry, upheld the worth of the individual and wanted to protect and extend the dignity, rights and opportunities of all regardless of birth, rank, occupation, party or theological persuasion. An important part of the band's liberalism was the attempt to make its political creed attractive and relevant to other social groups. This was not just a manipulative manoeuvre; the reformers were honestly trying to do something for these groups. The liberal reserved a central place in politics for devotion and morality, believing that public activity was and should be based on spiritual commitment, moral impulse and personal integrity. This was the feature that most impressed the aged Bentham about Prentice when the two met in April 1831.[15] The liberal was also animated and characterised by generosity, humanity, enlightenment, candidness and rationality. He was against unmerited privileges, unreasonable restrictions, obscurantism, exclusivity, corruption and inefficiency. The liberal was greatly dissatisfied with the present, and this was often the most obvious motive behind his public efforts. All of this had much to do with the situation, priorities and ambitions of those who were attracted to liberalism, for no set of principles has an existence

---

[14] On the early history of the incorporated borough see A. G. Rose, 'The Churchwardens and the Borough: a struggle for power, 1838–41', *M.R.*, 10 (1963–5), pp. 74–90.

[15] Bentham recorded that his visitor was 'juggical, Calvinistic; is descended from two parsonical grandfathers of considerable notoriety'. Bentham to Francis Place, 24 April 1831, cited in Wallas, *Life of Place*, pp. 81–2.

independent of the people who ratify, embody and advocate it. Liberalism as a programme of means and ends could also be modified and expanded over time, in keeping with prevalent circumstances. The ideas that were used and the ways they were used could be changed in the very process of employment. Respectable liberalism in Manchester encompassed such a wide field of concerns that cohesion and homogeneity were never guaranteed. The friction within the band can be seen as indicative of a certain amorphism within Manchester liberalism generally. Indeed, this also applies to the whole contemporary provincial reform agenda. Liberalism was still developing and lacked a distinct, settled form. It was an adaptable process of thought and action. As suggested above, if one of the most fashionable and persuasive liberal tenets of the age was *laissez-faire*, there could nevertheless be many disagreements about its applicability and relevance. This was most obvious in debates concerning commercial policy, factory reform, public health and poverty relief. But there were also general disagreements about the speed at which changes should be introduced and about the means used to secure these changes. Such friction would lead to the breaking up of the liberal bloc in Manchester after corn law repeal (1846), but it was already evident in earlier decades when the band rose to prominence.

On the whole the band worked as a unit. There was enough common ground on many public issues to make this possible, yet internal arguments were nevertheless a part of the band's existence. There were differences on matters of ideology, priorities, methods and conduct, and discord on the nature and extent of necessary reforms. Although Prentice and Taylor viewed some issues and problems in a similar way, they represented the two poles of opinion within the band (and most of the others were closer to Prentice than to Taylor). Taylor conducted the *Guardian* as a business venture as well as an organ of opinion. His eagerness for reforms was clear and vigorous. But it existed alongside an enthusiasm for orthodox political economy and a certainty that some men, locally and nationally, were more deserving of influence and power than most other men. He thought that reformers had to take account of prevalent circumstances. They should not aim too highly and should accept gradual changes if these were all that could be secured. Prentice was more impatient and more concerned about the unprotected and unrepresented groups in society. His liberalism included a paternalistic and humanitarian outlook that was not usually found in Taylor's words and actions. Prentice favoured poor laws, combinations, a wide franchise for local and parliamentary elections, and energetic interventionist policies to deal with the moral and social problems of the lower classes. He rejected Taylor's political economy in favour of what he called a '*generous*' political economy. His stance was probably more radical than that of some of his friends, but an agitator such as Prentice was needed to make things happen, to prompt others into action and to provide men more moderate than himself with the information and encouragement they needed to make their contributions as reformers, citizens and Christians. His journalistic and political career has significance and meaning because it pointed the way forward.

What the band said and did in the years before 1832 is important in itself and also for what followed. These respectable reformers laid the foundations for incorporation, the League and Manchester's rise to prominence as the most important provincial town in Victorian England, with its active politicians, influential newspaper press, wealth-creating commercial affairs and pioneering role in cultural discussions and social programmes. The band helped to bring all this about but has been relatively neglected.[16] Even Prentice, the most active and radical of these reformers, has not been credited with the importance that his ceaseless exertions as writer, speaker and agitator deserves. If he is mentioned at all by historians who have studied nineteenth-century Manchester he is normally brushed aside as virtually insignificant. N. C. Edsall has written: 'Essentially Prentice was a political busybody, intervening in print and in person in every aspect of local affairs; but he was no great agitator nor, for that matter, an especially skilled newspaperman'. Yet a much earlier commentator, Alexander Somerville in 1853, gave a totally different and far more favourable verdict. This radical reformer, free trade lecturer and acquaintance of members of the band was convinced that: 'To bring [Manchester] men to their senses on public affairs, to direct them in the study of political science, to save the intellectual waste and out of it to form and give to Manchester a political mind, no single man has done so much as Archibald Prentice'. The leading modern historian of the League, Norman McCord, seems to lean towards the Edsall verdict. While admitting that Prentice 'was far from being a negligible quantity', McCord believes that his role as

---

[16] Only three of the band have entries in the *D.N.B.*: Prentice, Brotherton and Taylor.

the first historian of the League 'has tended to exaggerate the part he played'.[17] The statements of Edsall and Somerville display much bias. Somerville is presenting a series of laudatory biographical sketches of free traders involved in the campaign against the corn laws. Edsall is trying to show that Prentice was not too important a figure in Cobden's early political career, that Prentice needed Cobden far more than Cobden needed him. Edsall fails to appreciate the valid point made by Donald Read, that Cobden's acceptance as a 'coming man' in Manchester owed 'something' to Prentice.[18] It was Prentice who recognised Cobden's promise, encouraged his writing and platform speaking and publicised his activities in the mid-1830s. Cobden's career would not have been all that it was without the earlier preparatory work of Prentice and the band. The Manchester reformers of the years before 1832 were precursors and prophets. They created the climate of opinion that was necessary for the League to be established and for a Mancunian liberal party to be effective. This is the fact that has often been ignored: the real history of the League and incorporation, of the Manchester School and of politics in Victorian Manchester begins with the ideas and activities of the 'small but determined band' in the 1810s and 1820s.

[17] Edsall, *Richard Cobden*, p. 34; Somerville, *Free Trade and the League*, ii, p. 381; McCord, *Anti-Corn Law League*, pp. 34–5, 42, 166–7.
[18] Read, *Cobden and Bright*, pp. 15–16.

Select Bibliography

I. UNPUBLISHED SOURCES

Chetham's Library, Manchester

Association for the Preservation of Constitutional Order against Levellers and Republicans, constitution and minutes of committee, 1792–99.

Hay, Revd W. R., Commonplace Book, and Hay Scrapbooks (uncatalogued).

Pitt Club, Manchester, papers 1812–31

Wray, Revd C. D., Wray Pamphlets

London School of Economics

Richard Potter Collection:

    Vol. 1 Memorandum Book, 1793–99

    Vol. 2 French diary, 1800–1

    Vol. 3 Diary, 1801–23

    Vol. 4 Diary, 1824–28

    Vol. 5 Account Book, 1798–1812

    Vol. 11 Book of press cuttings and comments on political and social affairs.

    Vol. 12 Miscellaneous correspondence

    Vol. 13A Letter Book, 1798–1833

Manchester Central Library

Atkinson, F. R., Family and Personal Papers (M177): letters, sale catalogue of library, collection of political tracts and printed sheets.

Atkinson, F. R., Scrapbook

Baxter, Edward, A Catalogue of the extensive and valuable collection of Pictures, the genuine property of Edward Baxter Esq., of Manchester (Sept. 1829).

Biographical References: obituaries, press cuttings, letters, pamphlets, card-indexed, Local History Dept.

Boroughreve's Papers. Proceedings of Public Meetings in Manchester appointed by the Boroughreve and Constables, 2 vols. and loose papers.

Braidley, Benjamin, Diary 1815–23, 2 vols.

Chamber of Commerce. Annual Reports of the Board of Directors.

Hadfield, George, The Personal Narrative of George Hadfield M.P., 1882.

Harland, John, Harland's Annals 1806–68; Harland Ms., 3 vols.; Manchester and Lancashire Collection (f. 492. 72 L230); Scrapbook (f. 942. 73 H15).

Leary, Frederick, History of the Manchester Periodical Press, 1889.

Manchester Mechanics' Institute, Letter Books

Manchester Representation Committee, minutes and proceedings, 1827–28.

Royal Manchester Institution, Ledgers and Letter Books of the Council.

Shuttleworth, John, Shuttleworth's Scrapbook

Smith, J. B., Papers:

> Memoranda and Letters on public and private affairs, with Biographical Sketches.
>
> Newspaper Cuttings on Speeches and Letters by J. B. Smith, and articles referring to him.
>
> Papers and Letters relating to Parliamentary Elections in Manchester and Salford, 1832.
>
> Reminiscences

Watkin Family Papers, M219/1 on Manchester Reform Committee, 1831–32.

Salford Local History Library

Brotherton, Joseph:

> Commonplace Book, 1809–16.
>
> Scrapbooks c. 1824–57.
>
> To the Electors of the Borough of Salford, annual addresses 1832–57, incomplete.

University of Manchester John Rylands Library

English Ms. 1196, Letters and papers of the Revd W. R. Hay.

English Ms. 1197, Peterloo. Letters, papers, notices, assembled by Revd W. R. Hay and deposited by A. P. Wadsworth.

Fielden Papers, seven boxes, temporary labels, not indexed.

2. PUBLISHED SOURCES: NEWSPAPERS

Aston's Exchange Herald
Manchester and Salford Advertiser
Manchester Courier

Manchester Examiner and Times
Manchester Gazette
Manchester Guardian
Manchester Mercury
Manchester Observer
Manchester Political Register, or Reformers' Repository
Manchester Times
United Trades' Cooperative Journal
Voice of the People
Wheeler's Manchester Chronicle

3. PUBLISHED SOURCES: BOOKS AND PAMPHLETS

(Published in Manchester unless otherwise stated)

Aitkin, J., *A Description of the Country from thirty to forty miles around Manchester* (1795)

Aston, J., *The Manchester Guide* (1804)

——, *A Picture of Manchester* (1826)

Bamford, S., *Autobiography*, ed. W. H. Chaloner (London, 1967): *Early Days* (1849), *Passages in the Life of a Radical* (1844)

Battye, T., *A Disclosure of Parochial Abuse in the Town of Manchester* (1796)

Brotherton, J., *Mr Brotherton and the New Poor Law* (Salford, 1841)

——, *Mr Brotherton's Religious Opinions* (undated)

——, *Mr Brotherton's Speech on the Corn Laws, delivered at the Town Hall, Salford, Wednesday 23 June 1841* (1841)

——, *On Abstinence from Intoxicating Liquor*, ed. W. E. A. Axon (1890)

——, *Speech of Mr Joseph Brotherton, M.P., at the Vegetarian Banquet, held at Hayward's Hotel, Manchester, 28 July 1848* (London, 1848)

——, *Speech on the Ten Hours Factory Bill, in the House of Commons, 3 March 1847* (1857)

Earwaker, J. P. (ed.), *Records of the Manchester Court Leet* (12 vols., 1884–90)

Engels, F., *The Condition of the Working Class in England in 1845* (London, 1973)

Faucher, L., *Manchester in 1844. Its present condition and future prospects* (London, 1969)

Gaskell, P., *The Manufacturing Population of England* (London, 1833)

Hanson, J., *Address of Joseph Hanson to his Friends and Country; with many particulars from the contested election at Preston, till his return from the King's Bench. Including his Address to 39,600 Subscribers to the Gold Cup and Salver* (1809)

———, *Brief Remarks on the Present Volunteer Establishment* (Salford, 1805)

———, *A Defence of the Petitions for Peace presented to the Legislature. Addressed to the Merchants, Manufacturers and others, of the Counties of Lancaster, York and Chester* (London, 1808)

———, *A Short Sketch or Memoir of the late Joseph Hanson Esq., of Strangeways Hall near Manchester* (Salford, 1811)

———, *The Whole Proceedings on the Trial of Joseph Hanson . . . for conspiring to aid the Weavers of Manchester in raising their wages* (1809)

Kay, J. P., *The Moral and Physical Condition of the Working Classes employed in the Cotton Manufacture in Manchester* (1969)

Love, B., *Manchester As It Is* (1839)

The Manchester Socinian Controversy (London, 1825)

Ogden, J., *A Description of Manchester by a Native of the Town*, ed. W. E. A. Axon (reprint, 1983)

Philips, F., *An Exposure of the Calumnies circulated by the enemies of social order, and reiterated by their abettors, against the Magistrates and Yeomanry Cavalry of Manchester and Salford* (London, 1819)

Philips, G., *The Necessity of a Speedy and Effectual Reform in Parliament* (1792)

Pigot and Dean's Manchester and Salford Commercial Directories (from 1813)

Potter, T., *A Prayer and Sermon delivered in Cross Street Chapel Manchester, on the Sunday after the interment of Sir Thomas Potter: The Value of Energy in Union with Benevolence* (1845)

———, *Sir Thomas Potter, first Mayor of Manchester* (undated)

———, *Sir Thomas Potter, Knight, Magistrate for the County Palatine of Lancaster, and first Mayor for the Borough of Manchester* (1840)

Prentice, A., *Historical Sketches and Personal Recollections of Manchester. Intended to Illustrate the Progress of Public Opinion from 1792 to 1832* (London, 1970)

———, *History of the Anti-Corn Law League* (London, 1969)

———, *Lecture on the Wages of Labour as affected by Temperance* (1851)

———, *Letters from Scotland by an English Commercial Traveller* (London, 1817)

———, *The Life of Alexander Reid, a Scottish Covenanter, Written by Himself and edited by Archibald Prentice, his Great-grandson* (1822)

———, *One Day's Rest in Seven. The Right of the Working Classes* (1855)

———, *Organic Changes necessary to complete the System of Representation partially amended by the Reform Bill* (London, 1839)

———, *The Pitt-Peel Income Tax and the Necessity of Complete Suffrage* (1842)

———, *Remarks on Instruction in Schools for Infants* (1830)

———, *Report of the Trial of Archibald Prentice for an alleged libel on Captain Grimshaw, at Salford Quarter Sessions, 14 July 1831* (1831)

———, *Sanitary and Political Improvement promoted by Temperance* (1849)

———, *Some Recollections of Jeremy Bentham* (1837)

———, *A Tour in the United States. With two Lectures on Emigration* (1849)

Reach, A. B., *Manchester and the Textile Districts in 1849*, ed. C. Aspin (1972)

Rules and Orders of the Manchester Constitutional Society (1791)

Scholes's Manchester and Salford Directories (1794, 1797)

Scott, I. & C., *A Family Biography 1662–1908. Drawn Chiefly from Old Letters* (London, 1908, 75 copies printed for private circulation)

Shuttleworth, J., *Memoir of the Late Rowland Detrosier* (1834)

———, *A Sketch of the Life of Rowland Detrosier* (1860)

———, *Some Account of the Manchester Gas Works* (1861)

Taylor, J. E., *A Sermon preached in Cross Street Chapel Manchester, 14 January 1844, on the occasion of the death of Mr John Edward Taylor: The Importance of Conscientiousness in the Use of Influence* (1844)

———, *A Full and Accurate Report of the Trial of Mr John Edward Taylor of Manchester, for an alleged libel on Mr John Greenwood, of the same place, at Lancaster, on Monday 29 March 1819* (1819)

———, *Notes and Observations, Critical and Explanatory, On the Papers relative to the Internal State of the Country, recently presented to Parliament: To which is appended a Reply to Mr Francis Philips's Exposure of the Calumnies* (London, 1820)

Taylor, W. Cooke, *Notes of a Tour in the Manufacturing Districts of Lancashire* (London, 1968)

Walker, T., *Biographical Memoirs of Thomas Walker Esq. of Manchester* (London, 1820)

———, *A Review of some of the Political Events which have occurred in Manchester during the last five years* (London, 1794)

———, *The Whole Proceedings on the Trial of an Indictment against Thomas Walker of Manchester (and others) for a conspiracy to overthrow* the Constitution and Government, and to aid and assist the French (being the King's Enemies) in case they should invade this Kingdom (1794)

Watkin, A., *Extracts from his Journal*, ed. A. E. Watkin (1920)

———, *Fragment No. 1*, ed. E. W. Watkin (1874)

———, *Fragment No. 2*, ed. E. W. Watkin (1878)

Wheeler, J., *Manchester: its political, social and commercial history, ancient and modern* (London, 1836)

Index

Manchester Representation Committee (1827–8) 144, 281–4, 286–8, 310
Manchester Savings Bank 28, 176, 227
'Manchester School' 1–2, 4, 213, 237, 322, 333
Manchester Statistical Society 19, 153, 156, 168, 186
Manchester Temperance Society 173–4
Manchester Thinking Club 47
Manchester Times 3, 7, 9, 11, 77–84, 86–8, 90–2, 94–100, 118, 123, 125, 127, 142, 146, 158, 165, 175, 184, 202, 220, 226, 230, 246, 271, 290, 292–3, 295, 299, 301, 304, 306–9, 312, 318, 328
Manchester Typographical Society 69, 76
manorial administration 105–9, 120–5, 129–31, 134, 136, 141
market regulation 124
Market Street improvement commission 68, 133–4
Marylebone (London) 282
Mechanics' Hall of Science 158–9
mechanics' institutes 152, 157, 159
Middlesex Justices Bill (1792) 106
Middleton (nr Manchester) 130
'middling sort' 5, 56, 77, 83, 86, 105, 110–12, 116–19, 129, 131–3, 140, 145–6, 159, 248–9, 287, 296–9, 301–3, 319, 328–30
military barracks 130–1, 269
Mill, James 199, 323
Milton, Viscount, (succeeded as 5th Earl Fitzwilliam 1833) 247
Moral and Physical Condition (1832) 165
Mosley, Sir Oswald (lord of manor of Manchester) 124
Morning Chronicle (London) 26, 173

Morpeth, Viscount, (succeeded as 7th earl of Carlisle 1848) 291
Mosley Street Unitarian chapel 22, 32, 41, 152

Nadin, Joseph 120–2, 129
Napoleonic decrees 52
National Association for the Protection of Labour (N.A.P.L.) 97, 199
National Education Society 161
National Public School Society 161
'National Regeneration' 177
National Schools 53, 154
Necessity of a Speedy and Effectual Reform in Parliament (1792) 41
Neden, George 282–3
New Cross (Manchester) 83, 166
New Lanark 177
New Mechanics' Institute 158–9, 178
Newark 223
Newton (Manchester) 108, 155
Newtown (Manchester) 301
Nightingale, James 123
Nolan, J. W. 116
Norfolk 12th duke of 259
Norris, James 122
Northenden 30
Notes and Observations (1820) 17, 64, 264–5, 268
Notes and Queries 22
Nottingham 270

Oakden, Benjamin 17
O'Connell, Daniel 195
O'Connor, Feargus 327
Ogden, Robert 109
Oldham inquest (after Peterloo) 267
On Abstinence from Intoxicating Liquor (1821) 174
Orders in Council (1808, 1812) 47, 52
Otley 69